mtg.

Pericles:
22 Sept 94
LFC + the
Mexico Lindo
Restaurant

Barbarian Asia and the Greek Experience

Ancient Society and History

Barbarian Asia and the Greek Experience

PERICLES GEORGES

*From the Archaic Period
to the Age of Xenophon*

The Johns Hopkins University Press
Baltimore and London

©1994 The Johns Hopkins University Press
All rights reserved
Printed in the United States of America on acid-free paper

The Johns Hopkins University Press
2715 North Charles Street
Baltimore, Maryland 21218-4319
The Johns Hopkins Press Ltd., London

Library of Congress Cataloging-in-Publication Data

Georges, Pericles.
    Barbarian Asia and the Greek experience : from the archaic period
to the age of Xenophon / Pericles Georges.
       p.   cm. — (Ancient society and history)
    Includes bibliographical references and index.
    ISBN 0-8018-4734-6 (acid free paper)
    1. Iran—Foreign public opinion, Greek. 2. Aliens—Greece—
Public opinion.   3. Public opinion—Greece. 4. Iran—
Relations—Greece. 5. Greece—Relations—Iran. 6. Greece—
Civilization—To 146 B.C.
I. Title. II. Series.
DS274.2I7G46   1994
935—dc20   93-36319

A catalog record for this book is available from the British Library.

Για·τον·Καραβασιλι·και·την·Λουλα
·ρωμαοι·

✚ Αιωνια·των·η·μνημη ✚

Contents

Contents

Contents

Preface

This book examines certain critical episodes in the formation of the Greeks' ideas and attitudes concerning those foreign peoples of Asia with whom they came into the closest historical relations—and against whom they defined themselves. Therefore it is also a study of the Greeks' intramural debate about their own identity or, more properly, identities as a group of peoples with a shared language, common deities, and a way of life that set them apart from others in their world, but who as Greeks were nonetheless polemically divided among themselves over issues of origin, custom, and culture.

As such, this book stands on the shoulders of much previous work on images of the Other in the Greek mind. I have not, however, tried to deal with this endlessly ramifying subject encyclopedically. I have left aside some important questions of intellectual exchange, in particular the question of Iranian influence on various of the pre-Socratic thinkers, debated between Martin West (1971) and his critics. At best, I hope that the issues I have dealt with shed light on those I have neglected.

I have, nevertheless, included some familiar material to function as connective tissue, chiefly narrative, in order to give some historical continuity to a necessarily episodic exposition. Also, I wished to provide enough background to make this book accessible to scholars in other fields who might wish to read it for comparative purposes. For this reason, too, I have translated the Greek citations wherever their meaning is not clear from the surrounding discussion. (The translations are my own unless otherwise noted.)

A few words about theory, method, and approach: I am uncomfortable in the presence of the programs and ideologies of theoretically driven scholarship. Generally speaking, the widely different character of the evidence relevant to this book has led me to employ various approaches as they seemed suitable. My single genuflection to Continental styles of thinking concerns Herodotus. Here I have been much influenced by François Hartog and other structuralist critics, as readers will recognize. But Herodotus is the most protean and least explicit of Greek authors; Seth Benardete (1969) understood this when he declared, at the outset of a book that shows just how difficult an author Herodotus can be to read with accuracy, that "the *Inquiries* present the evidence for an argument that is in the evidence and not imposed on it. The universal *logos* which Herodotus tries to uncover lies completely embedded in the particulars that he narrates." I have taken what Hartog and company have provided less as a method than as an aid to intuition, or even as a *façon de parler*, to describe things found hidden in Herodotus. But elsewhere I have taken other points of view: Xenophon, who is as direct and simple as Herodotus is implicit and cryptic, I have treated on his own terms and, inevitably, by means of a biographical essay: for he himself is his only witness.

My training is as a historian, and I have worked in the historian's way, across the course of time. I have chosen to do so not simply from an artisanal bent: I have seen too little work on when and how Greek beliefs and attitudes concerning barbarism and barbarians arose, grew, and changed over time, especially concerning those barbarians of Asia—Lydians and Persians—with whom the Greeks were most engaged. So I thought it best to make the arrow of time the spine of this book.

I begin with a short and simple chapter on myth, written with
Paul Veyne's recent work (1983) in mind. Since the Greeks placed
the non-Greek peoples whom they encountered by means of myth,
I felt that I had to address the question of the everyday, conscious,
and unanalyzed *functions* of myth and mythical genealogy for the
Greeks themselves before I could take up the issues occupying
the second and third chapters, which concern those early images
of the Asiatic foreigner that grew out of the actual history of the
Greeks' encounters with the Lydians and Persians successively,
from their beginnings in archaic Ionia to the Persian wars. Succeeding chapters then take the story —in the contexts of Aeschylus'
Persae, of the Histories of Herodotus, and of Xenophon's life and
works (especially his *Cyropaedia*)—chronologically to the eve of
Philip of Macedon's accession and the dawn of a new stage of
Greek civilization.

This book's purpose, however, does not include any new description of the Asiatic "barbarian stereotype" in these authors or in
the Greek mind generally. The content and operation of this stereotype has been examined many times since the path-breaking work
of Julius Jüthner (1923), most recently and admirably by Edith
Hall's monograph on barbarians on the tragic stage (1989). Among
the questions I do examine in this book are those concerning how
this stereotype arose, especially as it appears in Aeschylus' *Persae*,
which crystallized Athenian popular beliefs about Persia and the
Persians into a picture so compelling that the Athenians—and
perforce the Greeks as a people—never deviated from its essentials
in their imagination. Edward Said (1978) was altogether correct
to place the *Persae* at the beginning of his account of the West's
vision of the Asiatic as sensual, irrational, effeminate, cruel, and
weak—in short, servile by nature.

In the way of a historian, I have tried to better define the original
impact of the *Persae* by considering its context and its audience.
Although everyone recognizes that the *Persae* was presented in the
midst of the very war that forms its subject, and that it portrays
Persia as a slave society, I have found little exploitation of these facts
in its interpretation. This seems a notable omission to me, since the
play must have resonated with its audience's anticipation of the new

fighting season as well as with the Athenians' everyday experience of slave management and slave psychology.

The Greeks were among the most exclusive and agonistic peoples who have left their mark on the historical record; among them this "Aeschylean" stereotype was too powerful a conception to remain projected against barbarian Asia alone. Inevitably, it was manipulated against Greeks by other Greeks, especially since it bore features in common with the already existing opinion that the Greeks of Asia—especially Ionians—tended toward that unmanly softness deemed characteristic of the Asiatic barbarian type.

Herodotus was deeply preoccupied by measuring the varying distances that Greek peoples put between Asiatic barbarism and themselves. As he observes his own world in particular, dominated by imperial Athens in the early years of the Peloponnesian War, he sees the Athenians through the lens of his experience of Asiatic barbarism. I believe that he did so, at bottom, for reasons having to do with his own Asian birth and his mixed blood. Bringing the reader to see through that lens is one of my goals in the two central chapters on Herodotus.

A maxim of Heraclitus declares that "the eyes and ears are bad witnesses for men with barbarian souls" (22 B 107 DK). Since Heraclitus was addressing his fellow Ephesians, he must have had some of them in mind—perhaps all of them save himself. The solipsism of Heraclitus and that of Xenophon answer to one another across the span of the principal creative age of the Greeks.

If there is any general theme or tendency informing this book, it is what I call the varieties of solipsism deployed by the Greeks—who, after all, were a small people until Alexander made them great—in defining themselves against the rest of an immense world that threatened to dissolve them into itself. For Asia, in its ultimate meaning to the Greeks, was the continent into which they would be absorbed and disappear—or not. This fear kept them Greek until they could suffer absorption on their own terms. But that is another history in itself, a history that began with Alexander and ended, if it may be said to have ended, with the death of Emperor Constantine XI Paleologus at the breached walls of Constantinople on 29 May 1453.

I have incurred many debts in the course of writing this book. Anne Michelini was kind enough to read my views on the *Persae*, and I have incorporated numerous of her suggestions and heeded her cautions. I am grateful to the many colleagues with whom I discussed this book's issues. Among these is Ernst Badian, whose insights were always of help to me. The usual disclaimer applies, of course: whereas these friends and colleagues helped to improve this book, they are not responsible for its contents, and most especially not for its errors and puerilities.

I began work on this book with the help of a fellowship awarded by the American Council of Learned Societies and continued it with generous grants from the Departments of History in Harvard University and Lake Forest College.

I dedicate this book to my late parents and to the traditions that formed them. I would also like to associate with their memory the memory of Ellen Mary Herman, the person most directly responsible for this book's existence; she helped support me through graduate school while seeing into production many fine books as Assistant Production Manager for the University of California Press.

After her I owe most to my professors, especially Ronald Legon, Raphael Sealey, Ronald Stroud, Kendrick Pritchett, Peter Brown, and most especially, Erich Gruen.

My wife, Professor Margaret Sinclair, is also my editor. For far too long she and our children, Andrew and Anna, and my sister, Helen, have had to put up with my manuscript, my moods, and my absences in spirit. They are all glad to see the end of this book at last, especially Margaret. My debt to her is inexpressible.

Abbreviations

AR	*Archaeological Reports.* The Society for the Promotion of Hellenic Studies and the British School of Archaeology at Athens
ARFP[2]	J. Beazley, *Attic Red-Figured Vase Painters*, 2d ed., 3 vols. (1963)
AthMitt	*Mitteilungen des deutschen Archäologische Institut. Athenische Abteilung*
CAH[2]	*Cambridge Ancient History*, 2d ed. (1970–)
CHI ii	*Cambridge History of Iran*, vol. 2 (1985)
Dittenberger Syll.[3]	W. Dittenberger, ed., *Sylloge Inscriptionum Graecarum*, 3d ed., 4 vols. (1915–24)
FGrH	F. Jacoby, ed., *Die Fragmente der Griechischen Historiker* (1923–)
FHG	C. Müller, T. Müller, and V. Langlois, eds., *Fragmenta Historicorum Graecorum*, vols. 1–4 (1848–70)
IG	*Inscriptiones Graecae* (1873–)

LSJ^9 H. Liddell, R. Scott, and R. McKenzie, *A Greek-English Lexicon, with Supplement*, 9th ed. (1968)

OCD^2 *The Oxford Classical Dictionary*, 2d ed. (1970)

PMG   D. page, ed., *Poetae Melici Graeci* (1962)

Powell   *J. Powell, A Lexicon to Herodotus*, 2d ed. (1938)
  Lexicon

Pritchard   J. Pritchard, ed., *Ancient Near Eastern Texts*
  ANET   *Relating to the Old Testament* (1969)

RE   A Pauly, G. Wissowa, and W. Kroll, eds., *Paulys Real-encyclopädie der classischen Altertumswissenschaft* (1893–)

SEG   *Supplementum Epigraphicum Graecum* (1923–)

SGHI   R. Meiggs and D. Lewis, eds., *A Selection of Greek Historical Inscriptions to the End of the Fifth Century B.C. (1969)*

Tod, i^2 M. Tod, *Greek Historical Inscriptions*, 2d ed., vol. 1 (1946)

Barbarian Asia and the Greek Experience

One

Mythology and Representation: The Greek Appropriation of the World

> These mythes or current stories, the spontaneous and
> earliest growth of the Grecian mind. . . furnished
> aliment to the curiosity, and solution to the vague
> doubts and aspirations of the age; they explained the
> origin of those customs and standing peculiarities with
> which men were familiar; they impressed moral lessons,
> awakened patriotic sympathies, and exhibited in detail
> the shadowy, but anxious, presentiments of the vulgar
> as to the agency of the gods.
> —George Grote (1849)

> The Greeks believe and do not believe in their myths. They
> believe in them, but they use them and cease believing at
> the point where their interest in believing ends.
> —Paul Veyne (1988)

> There are still signs left in my country that Pelops and
> Tantalus once dwelled in it.
> —Pausanias 5.13.7

What Was Myth For?

The post-Mycenean Greeks accurately remembered their earliest history as a series of migrations and colonizations by small and threatened groups which grew mainly by assimilating other populations, both Hellenic and foreign.[1] Many times their movements took them into absolutely unfamiliar human and geographical terrain, in which the greatest dangers were less physical than spiritual: disorientation, despair, deracination.

Alexander's desperately homesick troops once found ivy growing on a mountainside in the Hindu Kush and were overjoyed to discover this proof that the god Dionysus had passed there before them (Arrian *Anab.* 5.2). They were no longer alone in this stark natural immensity far beyond their known world. Their identification of new places with familiar mythological landscapes was not only the Greeks' way of claiming those places for their own;[2] it was at the same time a healing fantasy evoked to allay the terror and soothe the *pothos*, the longing for home, of uprooted peoples making new lives in a cultural or natural wilderness. The psychological drama of the first Greek diaspora gave birth to the compulsion ever after to exorcise the fear of the unknown by populating it with familiar images from inherited traditions, heavily weighted with religious associations, of ancestors, gods, and heroes.[3]

Mythopoeisis thus grew from the bones of the Greeks' early experiences and continued as long as Greeks found themselves threatened by outlandish environments and peoples. Their poets in particular became tamers of places.[4] Not long after Greeks began to explore and settle the coasts of the Pontus in the late seventh century, the poet Stesichorus domesticated this forbidding sea, which was the furthest outback of the Greek world in his day and afterward. Stesichorus once insulted Helen in a poem and afterward went blind. A story was told in his home town of Himera in Sicily about what happened to him and to the first man to voyage to *Leukê*, to the White Island at the mouth of the Danube. This man was a certain Leonymus, who sailed there in obedience to a Delphian response. There Leonymus entered a timeless and still existing venue of heroes. He encountered Achilles and Patroclus, together with Antilochus, the two Ajaxes, and Helen, who was living with Achilles. Helen commanded Leonymus to tell Stesichorus that he had been blinded by her curse, and with Stesichorus' composition of his *Palinode*—his apology to Helen—*Leukê* became a colonial outpost of the Elysian Field.[5]

The steppe itself and the unknown outback of the Ionian colonies on the northern Black Sea coasts became a haunt of Apollo himself (Hom. *Hymn* 7.28-29; Pindar *Pyth.* 10.30; Hdt. 4.32), while the visit to Apollo's island of Delos of two Hyperborean maidens who were said to have died there was commemorated in Herodotus' day by a children's cult at their tomb on the island (4.33-35). In such ways was the Pontus mythographically "discovered" and put safely "on the map."

It was Heracles, however, who became the great explorer of the early Greeks' new world.[6] The legends that arose of this wandering hero's loves in regions of archaic Greek colonization give us our best examples of the mythmakers' accommodation of the exotic places of the world at their extremes of attraction and inhospitality. In Lydia, which had been a part of that Mycenean world whose memory the Ionian emigrants brought with their poetry,[7] the ancestry of the chieftains on whose coasts they settled came to be traced from the union of the native Queen Omphale with Heracles. These Asiatic chieftains, with whom the Greeks had to deal, were thereby awarded honorable kinship with Greeks at an early date, for the so-called Heraclid dynasty of kings at Sardis ended early in the seventh century.[8]

A far cry from the royal and presumably beautiful Omphale in the climate of Lydia, so congenial to the Greeks' way of life (Hdt. 1.142.1-2), was Heracles' bedmate in forbidding Scythia. The Greeks of Pontus categorized the origins and nature of the steppe nomads by coupling the hero with a cave-dwelling Echidna, virgin above and viper below, who forced herself on him by holding his chariot mares for ransom. Afterward she conceived the eponymous ancestors of three native peoples of the region, Agathyrsus, Gelonus, and Scyths (4.8ff). This unnatural female expresses what the Pontic settlers thought about the inhospitable steppe and its savage inhabitants (4.8.3, 13, 28, 32, 64f, 103, 106).[9]

Natives had lived with Greeks in the Pontic settlements from an early time, however, and by the later sixth century some natives and Greeks of the northern Pontus had formed Greco-Scythian communities in the hinterland for which Heracles furnished a validating precedent; meanwhile, close political relations were forged between the Greeks of Olbia on the Bug-Dnieper estuary and the Scythian chieftains on the steppe.[10] Yet no part of the

Greeks' area of colonial settlement was more inhospitable to the Greek way of life than Scythia (4.76ff). The poets found a way to express the character of their relations with the Scyths that preserved the Greeks' abiding sense of their otherness in a way similar, but opposite, to the union of Heracles and Omphale in salubrious Lydia.[11]

The exploits of Heracles marked the limits of the known world and expressed the relationships of Greeks with other peoples; they were, so to speak, snapshots of those relationships taken at the time of their formation. In Egypt Heracles overthrew the barbaric pharaoh Busiris, when his servants were preparing the hero as a human sacrifice. The Busiris tale, which attributes to the highly civilized Egyptians one of the most primitive characteristics of the barbarian stereotype,[12] appears to reflect on the one hand Greek ignorance of Egyptian religion and culture, and on the other a lively consciousness of the Egyptians' dislike of foreigners, especially Greeks, whom Egyptians shunned as ritually unclean.[13] Moreover, the Saïte pharaohs, who ruled until late in the sixth century, allowed Greeks into the country only as segregated groups of mercenaries and traders under close supervision at Memphis and Naucratis.[14]

In Phrygia Greeks had been unable to settle in numbers before the overthrow in the early seventh century of the Phrygian kingdom and its king, titled "Mita of Musku" in the Assyrian annals (717-709).[15] Later traditions associate him anachronistically with Delphi and with the Greeks of the Aeolid. Some contact with Greeks existed, since the Phrygians borrowed their alphabet at an early date.[16] This monarch, who kept Greeks out of his wealthy realm, was nevertheless represented by the Greeks in the character of Midas (of the asses' ears and the golden touch); the Midas genre even included a Heracles story in which the hero slew Midas' son.[17] Predictably, no good comes to the hubristic Phrygians in myth, as witnessed by the stories of Phrygian Niobe, Marsyas, and Tantalus. Legends such as these preserved early Greek attitudes of frustration and resentment concerning their segregation in or exclusion from these lands, where Heracles left no progeny behind him, just as Heracles' loves marked out areas of early and successful

Greek penetration. Eventually this hero of fecundity appeared even in Italy, where the Romans adapted him to their political purposes as they entered the Hellenistic world. By the late second century, when the Romans needed to hold their Greek allies against Hannibal in southern Italy, the Fabii were claiming Heraclid descent.[18]

It is in the Hellenistic period, in fact, that we can see in greatest detail this continuing process. The conquests of Alexander naturally produced a new spate of mythopoeisis that appropriated the new world into the categories of the Greeks' familiar old one. The period of the Diadochi saw an efflorescence of conscious mythographical invention, which redefined the whole world once again in terms of the hero tales and epic poetry that remained the ordinary Greek's gazetteer of Asia imagined. Even the Amazons continued to be reinvented after Alexander by writers catering to universal taste, even though the progress of exploration had proved to critical minds that they no longer existed, if indeed they ever had. Nevertheless, Cleitarchus' fable that the conqueror had slept with the Amazon queen Thalestris in Hyrcania remained in circulation.[19] If Theseus had done it, why not Alexander?

The *Argonautica* of the third-century poet Apollonius of Rhodes is the only surviving example of a large genre of Hellenistic epic devoted to these purposes.[20] The poem unites the new Greek world from Italy to Persia by a single web of blood kinship among the characters of the poem. The father of Medea, Aëetes king of Colchis on the Black Sea, is the brother of the sorceress Circe, whose haunt in turn is the Adriatic (3.304ff); these were the opposite poles of the old nautical world of the Greeks. Circe and her niece Medea accordingly confer in the Colchian language (4.731; cf. 4.559ff). The Colchians themselves are descended from the union of Perse the daughter of Helios with Oceanus (3.304ff), and Perseis is the patronymic epithet of the goddess Hecate, whose priestess is none other than the Colchian Medea (3.467, etc.); the poet thus implies that Medea is the ancestress of the Medes and, through her offspring, the Persians as well.

Minyas, the hero-founder of Boeotian Orchomenus, also becomes a Colchian in Apollodorus' hands, and the dragon's teeth from which the Boeotian Spartoi spring came from the dragon that Cadmus the Phoenician slew at Thebes. Athena had given them to Cadmus and also to Aëetes; Cadmus sowed his at Thebes to found "an earthborn people," whereas Aëetes carried his away to Colchis (3.1093ff from Pherecydes: *FGrH* 3 F 22a). In sum, Apollonius creates a genealogical relationship between the Colchians and their kindred Medo-Persian peoples on the one hand, and on the other between the Colchians and the Minyan and Cadmeian peoples of Boeotia.[21]

Existing syncretisms between Greek and native religions, where lay the deepest connections between Greeks and other peoples, were also consciously rationalized and promoted at this time. The *Argonautica* Hellenizes, or rather re-Hellenizes, the Asiatic Mother Dindyme with her cymbals, drum, and dance of the native rite, for which the poet provides a Hellenic etiology. In the poem Orpheus leads the Argonauts in a sword-clashing dance in armor to drown out the wails of the Cyzicenes mourning the deaths of their divine lord and his consort the goddess (1.1117ff). Apollonius' younger contemporary Neanthes, a native of Cyzicus, wrote that the Argonauts themselves had founded the shrine of Cybele (= Dindyme: Diod. 3.52.1) at Cyzicus (*FGrH* 84 F 39; cf. T 2).[22] For more than a dozen years after 260 B.C., Apollonius himself was *Prostates* or Director of the Museum at Alexandria,[23] where the cult of Egyptian Isis and Osiris, already long naturalized at Greek Cyrene and known at Athens before the death of Alexander,[24] was reinvented in Hellenized form by Greek scholars and propagated by a subsidized professional priesthood under the first Ptolemies.[25] It is not accidental that Apollonius' poem also celebrates that other great native goddess, Dindyme-Cybele, adapted to Greek worship and native to the Ptolemies' possessions and interests in Cyprus and the Levant.

The geographer Strabo, whose work is filled with notices of such bonds between the old and new Greek worlds, knew the *Argonautica* (14.2.13 C655). Strabo's own account of the kinship (*epiplokê*) thought to exist between the Armenians and Medes on the one hand and the Thessalians on the other shows how naturalization myths were created even as Alexander was carrying out his conquests.

It is said that during his voyage to the Colchians Jason with Armenus the Thessalian pressed on as far as the Caspian Sea and entered not only Iberia and Albania [in the Caucasus] but also many places in Armenia and Media. . . . Armenus came from Armenium, one of the cities on Lake Boebeïs between Pherae and Larisa; he and his followers settled Acisilene and Syspiritis as far as Calachene and Adiabene; Armenia he even left named for himself. (Strabo 11.4.8 C503)

Cyrsilus the Pharsalian and Medus the Larisaean, who marched with the army of Alexander, say that Armenia is named for Armenus and that his followers settled Acisilene and and Syspiritis. They say too that the native dress of the Armenians is Thessalian as well as their style of horsemanship, as is the Medes'. To this the [traditions about the] expedition of Jason bear witness as do the Jasonia, some of which the native kings built just as the shrine to Jason at Abdera was erected by [Alexander's marshal] Parmenion. (11.14.12 C530-31)

Some say that Medea introduced the feminine robes worn in Media when she and Jason together ruled in these regions, even veiling her face when she appeared before the people in the king's place. The memorials of Jason in Media are the heroöns called Jasonia, which are greatly revered by the barbarians; there is also a high peak called the Jasonium above the Caspian Gates. . . . The natives' dress and the name of the country are memorials of Medea. But it is also said that her son Medus succeeded to the kingship and left it his name. (11.13.10 C526)

From all of this it is reckoned that both the Medes and Armenians are in a way kinsmen (*syngeneis pôs*) of the Thessalians and the descendants of Jason and Medea.

This is the account of ancient times (*palaios logos houtos*); the story of the more recent period from the Persians down to our time (*neôteros kai kata Persas . . . mekhri eis êmas*) may be summarized as follows. . . . (11.14.14-15 C531)

In such ways, then, the history of Greek invention concerning foreign peoples continued after Alexander, with similar causes producing similar results. Mythography was nothing less than the anthropogony of the Greeks, and for this reason it became all the more important in this new age, when bloodlines once again, as in the Greeks' original diaspora, would become entangled among

Greeks and natives. Useful legends would go on being created, in this case by two Thessalian savants in Alexander's train out of earlier notions about the Medes,[26] to give new places their familiar heroes and to people a conquered land with men who are "kinsmen of the Thessalians and descendants of Jason and Medea." Strabo does not impeach the truth of these mythograpical inventions. Unlike Herodotus, who places them in the empirically inaccessible hero-time before the present "generation of humans,"[27] Strabo treats them as empirically verifiable and adduces empirical confirmations. For Strabo the only distinction that remains between "fact" and "legend" is the chronological distinction between remote antiquity and the present age. Plutarch, who was almost Strabo's contemporary, in works such as his *Life of Theseus* also blurred the line between these categories of testimony, which Herodotus had labored so long ago to firmly distinguish.[28]

Strabo was a Stoic;[29] he believed, therefore, in the universal kinship of humanity.[30] But he did not adduce Jason and Medea simply to bring forward proof-texts for Stoic beliefs about human nature. He was from Amaseia, deep in the native hinterland of the Greco-Iranian kingdom of Pontus, and his conspicuously noted proofs of kinship between the Armenian natives of his homeland and the Greeks through Jason—a relationship that he also mentions prominently twice in the introductory book of his work (1.2.39 C45f, 3.2 C47)—take on meaning from the fact that his family, which was prominent in the service of the Mithridatic kings of Pontus, had closely intermarried with the native aristocracy.[31]

In the fourth century A.D., the Neoplatonist Synesius of Cyrene, who belonged to a city whose aristocracy was already of mixed blood in the archaic period,[32] traced his own ancestry back to the first kings of the Dorian Peloponnese, descendants of Heracles.[33] This was Synesius' patent of nobility, as had been almost a millennium before the logographer Hecataeus' boast of descent "from a god in the sixteenth generation."[34] Hecataeus had been born in Miletus, a mestizo community where tradition held with great plausibility that the Ionian conquerors had forcibly taken the Carian women of the place as wives (Hdt. 1.146.2-3) and whose aristocracy (not to speak of the peasants) in Hecataeus' own time had intermarried with important Carian and Lydian families.[35]

Thus mythographical genealogy had necessary social uses in the Hellenistic age, by endowing the barbarian kin of mixed-blood Greeks with an ancestral Hellenic *cachet*, just as we shall see in the next chapter how it had served a similar purpose much earlier in Ionia after the Dark Age migrations to Asia. From the foundation legends of the Ionian cities and Homer onward, mythology furnished the most natural and direct means of accepting not only new lands but new peoples. By endowing natives with Greek— or Trojan—origins, Greeks freed themselves to assimilate native men of power, native women, and native cults while protecting their own cultural identity.

The Power of the Canon

In a book titled *Did the Greeks Believe in Their Myths?* Paul Veyne replies—not at all perversely—that they both believed and did not believe.[36] That is, myths had their indispensable cultural uses but also could come under reductionist scrutiny by critical minds. It is plain that all ancient writers did not accept every story about their gods and heroes; skepticism concerning details and intellectual playfulness abounded. But these are symptoms of a mandarin culture regarding its innocent beginnings: Veyne is at his best in showing that the critics were motivated by the aim of salvaging the true or "factual" kernel of myths from their carapaces of implausibilities in order to verify the whole received system, because it was literally unthinkable to do without it.[37]

The evidence is overwhelming for the real mental functions of myth and mythical genealogy throughout antiquity. They provided a coherent and infinitely flexible structure that was psychologically and epistemologically needed to define and bind together the human world and its divine origins. To scrutinize the stories about the gods and heroes too closely was to rudely examine their passports into this world, and this not even the most elevated philosophical souls ever thought of doing. From the perspective of the whole of antiquity, Xenophanes and Plato were voices in the wilderness.

9

Homer was never to be cast out of the games even by the Christians, who accepted in their turn the myths as an order of reality.[38]

The power of the canon over rational minds was first demonstrated by the tough-minded empiricist Thucydides, who wrote in reaction to Herodotus and authors of the stripe of Hellanicus.[39] Thucydides (whose family traced its descent from the hero Aeacus)[40] accepted the received myths as valuable, if raw, testimonies to early antiquity, and he based his own view of primeval Greece on them.[41] The secular and pragmatic historian Polybius likewise regarded legendary material as a given.[42] In the Roman period Pausanias testifies to the undiminished strength of popular belief (2.23.6; trans. Levi):

> I have already accounted for Priam's son Helenos, who went to Epiros with Achilles' son Pyrros and was guardian to Pyrros' sons. He lived with Andromache, and Kestrine is named after their son Kestrinos. And even the Argive guides have noticed something wrong with their story, though they still tell it; to reverse a majority opinion takes some doing.[43]

In the beginning Hesiod and his interpolators in the *Theogony* had derived all divinity and humankind from the only universally valid creative and ordering principles that archaic society knew: procreation, family politics, and war. The universe of the *Theogony* mirrored human society; the poem thus corresponds to mythical systems among primitives, except for its characteristically Greek coherence in applying ordering principles to nature.[44] This ongoing cultural ritual remained the pattern for all Greek mythopoeisis, and the world continued to be recreated and populated in this way during the Persian Wars and beyond. In the fifth century, not only poets and tragedians, but didactic authors in prose, such as Acusilaus of Argos (*FGrH* 2), Pherecydes of Athens (*FGrH* 3). and Hellanicus of Lesbos (*FGrH* 4), established this category of knowledge as an *epistêmê*, and produced compendious Theogonies and Genealogies. The character of their works demands an audience of believers, including those aristocrats whose family trees went back, quite literally, "to a god in the sixteenth generation."

Inconsistencies among these mythographers, and later inventions and variations, inspired scholarly confusion among the commentators and scholiasts of later antiquity. Conviction might be suspended where competing traditions could not be reconciled, though doubt and speculation existed only on the penumbrous borders of the immense system. Pausanias could wonder, for example, whether the shrine of Artemis Lycaea at Argos, which was said to have been founded by Hippolytus, might rather be the cult of an Amazonian avatar of the goddess imported by Hippolytus; but he did not doubt the fact that the shrine itself had been founded by him (2.31.4).

Even so, variations of myth in themselves were less mutual refutations than multipliers in the net of human relationships; inconsistencies were tolerated precisely because they strengthened the assertion of human unity that motivated these successive acts of mythopoeisis, which after all were items of a *religious* ideology. It is a measure of the pale Galilean's victory over paganism that Veyne can remark (following the weighty authority of Nilsson and Nock) that myth was "basically nothing but a very popular literary genre . . . whose connections with religion were very loose": a hard saying which depends on a narrow definition of Greek religion.[45] I would prefer to say that myth was *continuous* with religion and flourished by nourishment from a constant and uncontrollable "seepage" of religious emotion and belief out of their main channels. An example of this "seepage" is contained in the Neoplatonist Porphyry's account of his master Plotinus' encounter with his own guardian spirit during a séance in a temple of Isis. The magician who called Plotinus' spirit declared that it was no ordinary numen, but a genuine divinity—a divinity, that is, invented for the occasion and belonging only to Plotinus himself. Moreover, no one present suspected any fakery at all when the magician's boy, who was holding the birds intended to be the medium of communication with the philosopher's guardian god, strangled them before the spirit could speak through them.[46] In such a climate of belief, criticism could only be a mere business of tidying up after the innumerable such inventions going back to their dim beginnings before Homer. Fantastic elements would be rationalized,[47] allegorized,[48] even discarded[49] by critics from Hecataeus (*FGrH* 1 F 1)

11

onward. But the real existence of the characters of myth was never doubted; they were the ancestors of the human race.[50]

Finally and most decisively, there was simply nothing to replace myth; even the Christian Fathers had to accept it.[51] Thus the corpus as a whole could never for a moment be collectively disbelieved or discarded except by those ultimate outsiders who did have something to put in its place and rejected the armature of Hellenism itself for their own cultural myths, the Jews. Josephus made the very persistence of the Greeks' belief in their canon a weapon of his polemic against the pagan enemies of his God: "It would be superfluous for me to point out . . . what discrepancies there are between Hellanicus and Acusilaus on the genealogies, how often Acusilaus corrects Hesiod, how the mendacity of Hellanicus . . . is exposed by Ephorus, that of Ephorus by Timaeus, that of Timaeus by later writers, and that of Herodotus by everybody" (*Against Apion* 1.3). The Greeks' religious opponents themselves therefore bore witness to their faith in the necessity and authenticity of the mythographers' world picture.

Two

Asia and the Image of Tyranny

> It was no accident that the Greeks—in particular
> the Greeks of Anatolia's coasts—called the man
> who put himself over his aristocratic peers and
> ruled over his own people as a monarch precisely
> by a word, *tyrannos*, born from an Asiatic tongue.
> So powerfully did they perceive its likeness to
> foreign despotism.
> —Helmut Berve (1967)

The Greeks in Asia

The Greeks' mythopoeitic appropriation and representation of the foreign helps explain how the first miracle of the Ionian civilization occurred, the miracle by which the Greeks of Asia remained Greek.

They remained Greek because their poets and storytellers held them to their identity under very unpromising conditions. For much mixing of blood and culture accompanied the building of Ionian society. Among aristocracies and peasants alike, no line of separate blood or unacceptable custom firmly divided the Greek and native peoples; family bonds between Greeks and natives had been formed, in some cases, as far back as the age of migration. Yet these relationships did not result in the disappearance of the Greeks, though vastly outnumbered, into the native environment of an immense continent. Historically it was the native peoples, the Carians and Lydians, who Hellenized and not the other way about.

13

Their isolation amid the natives' hostility in itself must have encouraged the Greek invaders to maintain their identity intact from the beginning.[1] The *Iliad* testifies directly to a strong and immediate resistance to deracination in the cultural ego of the Ionians' warrior-leaders, which was based in the old Greece preserved in the memory of lays ancestral to the epics. Whatever misfortunes they had endured, these hard-bitten survivors of the Mycenean destructions arrived in Asia with their culture sufficiently intact and immune to native influence to assure the development of epic from Mycenean heroic traditions.[2] The epos itself is proof of the solidarity of identity and cultural independence of the landholding and military classes of primitive Ionia from the first migrations onward.[3] And, if they sensed that their cultural identity was proof against threat, they would be all the more ready to cultivate alliances with the natives on equal terms and with a minimum of distinctions, just as the *Iliad* itself, as has been often remarked, does not distinguish between Asiatic Trojans and the invaders' Achaean ancestors.[4]

Yet the *Iliad* is also our earliest source for Ionian attitudes to the peoples around them, especially Carians and Lydians. We have seen how the Greeks' early hostility to the Phrygian kingdom appears to be reflected in the Midas legends and other stories outside Homer. But the Phrygian kingdom had passed away by the age of the formation of the mature *Iliad*, broken up by invading nomad peoples from the Eurasian steppe and then absorbed by Lydia in the early seventh century. The poem merely recalls the Phrygians' ancient power in the mind's eye of the aged Priam (3.184–90).

The *Iliad*'s treatment of the Carians, whom the Ionian immigrants met, fought, and married to secure their footholds in Asia, is broader and reflects a surviving ambivalence between hostility and accommodation among peoples in close contact.[5] A suggestion of the later stereotype of the Asiatic as a luxurious and effeminate weakling—which is unique in the poem—marks one of the leaders of the Carians, named Nastes, who "came like a girl to the fighting, in golden raiment" (2.872), only to be killed by Achilles. *Nastês* simply means "inhabitant," "native,"[6] and the Carians themselves, who in the poem still hold Miletus, Homer calls *barbarophônoi*.

This word, however, is a *hapax* which looks like a late formation and for which exists the common metrical equivalent *karterothumoi.*[7] Moreover, Nastes' brother bears a good Greek hero's name, Amphimachos, which also belongs to a warrior from Elis (13.185). Although we ought not press the argument too far, it does appear that the ambivalence in these contrasting portraits of Nastes and his brother corresponds to an ambivalence in the Ionian view of their Carian neighbors in the age of the formation of the *Iliad* and even later.[8]

The Ionians remembered how they took Carian Miletus from the natives by violence, and relations between the invading Greeks and the surviving Carians evidently remained bitter in the early period. Herodotus tells how the invading Greeks killed all the Carian men in Miletus and took their women into their own beds (1.146.2–3). The context of this passage implies that other immigrants did likewise, and this is not improbable, especially in light of the prominence given to raiding in the *Iliad*. Pausanias (7.2.7) mentions similar violent conflicts at the foundation of the other Greek cities in the rich plain of the lower Maeander, Myus and Priene.[9]

Herodotus also attaches a significant *aitia* to the crime of the Milesians: this is why, he explains (1.146.2–3), the Milesians' wives refuse to eat with their husbands or call them by name. This may not be the true explanation of the Milesians' domestic regime. Greeks, and Herodotus in particular, were especially prone to find historical motivations in ancient crimes. But as an index to the tenacity of the influence of this tradition in Miletus, where bloods had mixed from the beginning, it is nevertheless significant that the Milesians themselves put even their conjugal customs down to blood hatreds between Greek and native that may have divided the community for generations. For at Miletus in the sixth century a civil war filled with atrocities marked the rise of a Hellenized peasantry of native—almost certainly Carian—origin, the Gergithes, to membership in the *polis*. This event in itself must have revived tales of the original conquest of Greeks over Carians at Miletus.[10]

In the end, then, the long antagonism between Ionians and

Carians did conclude in the formation of a single polity at Miletus, while similar accommodations are attested elsewhere in Asiatic Greece.[11] Ionian attitudes to Carians, though complex, tended toward assimilation as time wore on. Carians did not speak Greek, but they were formidable warriors who employed the same armor as the Greeks and like them gravitated naturally to the trade of the mercenary.[12] Homer's Nastes does not fit in very well here, but Amphimachus does. These two aspects of the poem's portrayal of the Carians, then, may well mirror successive stages in the Greeks' relationship with them: at first hostility and contempt perhaps combined with envy of their princes' greater wealth (viz. Nastes' raiment), followed by a warmer attitude when their aristocracies had established common interests and a common way of life, including intermarriage.[13]

We do find that the aristocracies of Ionia—in particular those of Ephesus, Colophon, and probably the Colophonian foundations of Smyrna and Clazomenae—maintained dynastic connections from very early times with leading native families.[14] Strong inscriptional evidence associates the Lydian royal Heraclids with the aristocracy of Colophon and the cult of Apollo at Colophonian Claros.[15] Ephesus was the most Asianic in culture of the Ionian cities.[16] The Ephesian royal clan, the Basilids, intermarried both with the Lydian Heraclids and with their Mermnad successors.[17] The Milesian aristocracy also established family ties with Lydian and Carian princes.[18]

Mixtures of blood and custom came from below as well, at least in the known cases of the Gergithes of Miletus and also those of the Milesian foundation of Lampsacus in the Troad. Herodotus says the Gergithes in the Troad—native peasantry like those of the Milesiad—were descendants of the ancient Teucrians of Troy (5.122.2, 7.43.2). Attributing Trojan descent to natives was the common way for Ionian mythographers to Hellenize them when necessary; and, though the evidence is too late to be strictly useful for the early period, the Lampsacene Gergithes were regarded as Greeks at least by the time they came under the rule of the Attalids of Pergamum, and probably well before then.[19]

The archaeological history of early Miletus reflects a mixture of cultures from the Dark Age onward. The earliest post-Mycenean buildings and pottery confirm the literary tradition of a cohabitation of Carians and Greeks.[20] The Gergithes at Miletus evidently succeeded in forcing their way into the community before the end of the sixth century by attracting the championship of a Milesian tyrant. Therefore, part of the landholding aristocracy, among whom must have been some of mixed ancestry, considered the Gergithes sufficiently Hellenized to weld them together with the older citizens.[21] Finally, the tradition that Apollo of Didyma favored the cause of the Gergithes attests their acceptance—most likely when their victory had already become an accomplished fact—among the immensely prestigious and noble priestly clan of the Branchidae who controlled Didyma.[22]

More evidence for similar events at Miletus and elsewhere are the foreign tribal names attested in a number of Ionian communities. At Ephesus the names of three of the five tribes suggest foreign or mixed origins.[23] At Miletus and some of its colonies, two other tribes besides the four Ionian tribes proper (Geleontes, Argadeis, Hoplêtes, Aigikoreis) are attested—a fact which indicates that here assimilation largely preceded the age of Milesian colonization. The non-Ionian tribes were named Oenôpes, possibly pejorative in origin, if the meaning is "Redskins" or "Darkies,"[24] and Boreis, or "Northerners."[25] From Teos an inscription lists the names of the city's twenty-six original temenos-holders; eleven bear Iliadic or Mycenean names, but at least another six names are non-Greek, and it is suggested that these were natives who assisted the Greek settlement.[26]

This relatively secure evidence lends weight to those reflections of early accommodation with native populations found in our least secure category of evidence, the Ionian and Aeolian foundation myths. Thus, according to the Teian legend, the Greek founders mingled here, as elsewhere, with native Carians (Pausanias 7.3.3). Other legends commonly recount associations between natives and the incoming Greeks, notably at Ephesus and Colophon, the two cities whose ruling families were closest to the Lydian Heraclids.[27] Ephesus and Colophon alone did not observe the Apaturia, a festival common to the rest of the Ionian Dodecapolis

17

and regarded as a distinguishing mark of Ionian nationality.[28] Pherecydes' fifth-century account of the Ephesian legend relates that Androclus the Neleid, founder of Ephesus and ancestor of the Ephesian Basilids, came to terms with the Lelegian, Carian, and mostly Lydian natives around the already existing precinct of the Anatolian goddess who entered the Greek pantheon as Artemis.[29] The early Ephesian kings were said to have claimed the leadership of the Ionians.[30] This could well be propaganda dating from the latest period of Lydian hegemony over the Ionians, when Alyattes and Croesus based their Greek policy in part on a conspicuous patronage of Ephesian Artemis. But even if this were to have been the case, the Lydian kings' interest in Ephesus and Artemis goes back to Heraclid times, and the city's highest families probably traced their blood to the mixture of peoples who shared the city's chief cult. Intermarriage of the royal Ephesian clan with Lydian royalty was continuous in Ephesian tradition from the establishment of the city itself.[31]

Native religion appears to have mediated associations between natives and Greeks in Miletus again. The Lydian god Bakillis[32] also migrated into Greek worship at Bakchos (= Dionysus) in Ionia; the *Iliad* (6.132–33) associates Dionysus with a locality sacred to him, Nysa, which Strabo locates on the upper Maeander about midway between Miletus and Sardis.[33] Bacchic worship in early Miletus may explain the otherwise mysterious presence of a noble Bacchiad clan here, which could not have been associated originally with the Bacchiads of Dorian Corinth, who were not Ionian but claimed pre-Dorian, Heraclid descent.[34] If the Milesian Bacchiads had originated as the native clan that brought the cult of Bakillis into the city and then required a suitable Hellenic origin, their need would explain why the pre-Dorian Corinthian hero Bellerophontes appears in the *Iliad* as the grandfather of Lycian Glaucus.

The birth and adventures of Bellerophontes form a self-contained episode in the *Iliad*, reflecting the story of an originally independent lay worked into the poem (*Il.* 6.152–202).[35] The poets' invention of such a genealogy would naturalize important native "Bacchiads" at Miletus who could thereby claim a royal status; for Herodotus (1.146–47) comments that the Ionians set up as kings not only Athenian Neleids but others descended from Lycian Glaucus, especially at Miletus. The Milesian legend was later glossed by Ephorus (*FGrH* 70 F 127), who says that Sarpedon, the Lycian kinsman of Glaucus (*Il.* 2.876), founded Miletus together with Cretans before the Neleids arrived.[36] This is to say that Sarpedon represents the native aristocratic element in Miletus' mixed population.

The Colophonians' legend of the foundation of their own oracular shrine of Apollo at Claros also preserves memories of early mixture with natives in the context of an Ionian appropriation of a native holy place, recounted in the categories provided by the Trojan epic. In common with the Milesian story the Colophonian legend names the first Greeks at the site as Cretans, who joined the native Carians there before the Trojan War. The Cretan leader is said to have married Manto, the daughter of the Theban seer Teiresias, who arrived from Delphi. Later, Ionians under Codrid (that is, Neleid) kings arrived and settled with the earlier population, according to Pausanias (7.3.1).

Since Ionians probably did not patronize Delphi in large numbers before the destruction of the hugely influential oracle of Apollo at Didyma in 494, the anachronistic inclusion of Delphi dates this version to no earlier than the sixth century.[37] But another version of the myth, repeated by Strabo, contains elements going as far back as the early seventh-century elegist Callinus of Ephesus and to an imitator of Hesiod. In this version the seer Calchas goes from Troy to Claros,[38] where he dies upon his defeat at the hands of the native seer Mopsus in a mantic contest at the site of the already-existing shrine.[39] This and other legends are obviously contaminated with Homerizations on the one hand, and fifth century Athenian propaganda emphasizing the foundation of the Ionian cities from Athens on the other.[40] But the phenomenon of Greeks settling down with natives around existing holy precincts— in what were the spiritual hearths of the *poleis*—is common to the foundation myths of the Ionian cults.

The belief that Greeks were at Colophon before the Trojan War is supported by archaeology. A Mycenean tholos tomb has been found here, indicating that it was a place of some importance.[41]

19

The myth provides a native origin for the Colophonian cult, which like Didyma, where the eponymous prophetic ancestor of the priestly Branchidae, Branchus, bore a Carian name, was already an oracle according to tradition when the Ionians arrived. Oracles apparently were native to the Luwian peoples of Asia Minor, notably the famous oracle of Telmessus (Hdt. 1.78.2; Arrian *Anab.* 2.3.3), which like Claros and Didyma also became a home to the Greeks' oracular Apollo.[42] The early reflection in Callinus of important native elements at Claros casts light on associations found in later authors. In a passage based on the fifth-century *Lydiaka* of Xanthus, Nicolaus of Damascus calls Mopsus a Lydian, and associates him with the Heraclid king Meles of Lydia.[43] The ancient Lydian association with the sanctuary at Claros was celebrated; it survived even into the Roman imperial period, when inscriptions from Claros honor hereditary temple officials who traced their descent from the Lydian Heraclid Ardys.[44]

Poetic Homerization of some native Asiatics served at first to bring the real natives of original memory into the environment of Greek epic and there Hellenize them. Other native peoples besides Herodotus' Gergithes also came to be identified with Homeric Teucrians, and with the Pelasgians, Leleges, and Caucones who existed on both sides of the Homeric Aegean.[45] Later they were barbarized by their association with the Trojans, when Troy came to stand for the Asiatic barbarian power of Persia, especially in tragedy.[46] As allies, the Pelasgians, Leleges, and Caucones had been brigaded together in the camp of the Trojans (*Il.* 10.429) and were therefore considered kindred by the poem's Nestorian rule of the battle order (*Il.* 2.362ff), as Strabo (13.3.1 C619f) and other ancient readers of the poem would conclude from the former passage.

The Ionian singers not only worked out a mythical taxonomy that brought Greek and native peoples into wholesale conjunction, they accommodated native aristocrats directly by Hellenizing them. The story that Homer composed *The Capture of Oechalia* for his host Creophylus of Samos is evidence for complimentary invention by singers indulging their hosts' pride during individual performances for wealthy landholders.[47] Bardic invention of this kind could provide respectability and a heroic pedigree to Hellenized native houses such as the Aeneidae of Scepsis in the Troad, who traced their ancestry to Trojan Aeneas and to his mother Aphrodite (Strabo 13.1 52 C607). The *Iliad* (6.21), for example, tells how the nymph Abarbareê ("Not-barbarian") bore to Boukolion ("Cowherd"), a son of the Trojan king Laomedon, the heroes Aesepus and Pedasus. The former is the eponym of a river in the Troad and the latter of the Carian town adjacent to Halicarnassus. Abarbareê shows how native lords claiming descent from Trojan heroes and their people would wish to be seen.

We have noticed how the *Iliad* links the "Lycian" kings of Miletus with Corinth through Bellerophontes and Glaucus. Besides Glaucus, a few other heroes possess usefully bivalent ancestries or identities in the *Iliad*, notably the Heraclid Tlepolemus, whose people live anachronistically in Rhodes and the other islands of the Dorian settlements of Asia Minor despite the facts, well-established in mythical chronography, that the war was fought in the generation after Heracles' sojourn at Troy and therefore in the fourth generation *before* the Dorians' arrival in the Peloponnese under the descendants of Heracles (Hdt. 7.204). This anachronism was avoided by making Tlepolemus a son of Heracles and the Trojan princess Astyocheia, whom he captured from Ephyra on the river Seleëis (*Il.* 2.657ff).[48]

It is plausible that Tlepolemus, or his ancestry, was imported into the poem by singers to give their hosts in the Dorian Hexapolis a place in a poem that arose in Ionia, entirely outside the Dorian diaspora. If so, his death at the hands of the Lycian hero Sarpedon, kinsman of that Glaucus from whom some Ionian royalty claimed descent (Hdt.1.147.1), may be the first trace in literature of the hostility between Dorians and Ionians.

Similarly, the character of Teucrus, a son of Telamon of Salamis from a nameless mother (*Il.* 8.266ff), would give Hellenized natives in the Troad a claim to Achaean identity on the left hand, although his genealogy may well owe its actual origin to Athens' quarrel with Mitylene over Sigeum in the Troad.[49] Though he fights on the Achaean side, Teucrus' very name means "Trojan."[50] Figures such as Teucrus and Tlepolemus assume a kinship between natives and Greeks, Achaeans and Trojans characteristic of the *Iliad* as a

whole. The poem preserves the nonexclusive ethnocultural attitudes of the Ionians before their own cultural progress brought
them to that parting of the ways in the sixth century signposted
by Heraclitus' dictum: *kakoi martyres anthrôpoisin ophthalmoi kai
ôta barbarous psukhas echontôn*, "Eyes and ears are bad witnesses
for those who have barbarian souls" (22 B 107 DK).

Ionians and Lydians

The Lydians in the *Iliad*, called Mêiones[51] and located around the
lake of Gyge (2.864-65), are citied folk settled in a lovely land,
artisans and warriors who, like the individual heroes of the poem,
fight from chariots (3.401, 4.141ff, 10.431, 18.291). They are
presented with some warmth, and *palmys*, a Lydian word meaning
king or lord, appears in the *Iliad* (13.792) as the name of a Trojan
warrior.[52]

This felt closeness of Greeks to Lydians does not otherwise
occur in Homer; but it is nevertheless contemporary with the very
beginnings of the Ionians' historical memory. They synchronized
the foundation of the first historical Lydian dynasty, the Heraclids,
with their own migration to Asia, giving the Heraclids 505 years
in power before the twenty-second king, Candaules, was displaced
by Gyges, founder of the Mermnad dynasty and the ancestor of
Croesus (Hdt. 1.7.4). This chronology placed the first Heraclid in
the generation after Herodotus' own implied date of the Trojan
War (*c.* 1250).[53]

The elaborated Heraclid myth awards Hellenic descent to the
dynasty from the decisive, paternal side by the union of Heracles
with Lydian Omphale—a name, incidentally, that appears to reflect
the archaic Ionians' own view of Lydian Sardis as the navel of
their own world, as well as the Lydian kings' famous relationship
with the *omphalos* itself, the navel of the world at Delphi, in the
period of Lydian greatness. In this way the myth incorporates the
racial memory of those post-Mycenean refugee communities which
began life by appropriating the native women as well as the native
cults, and survived the Persian conquest to be celebrated by Herodotus' elder kinsman Panyassis in his epic *Heraclea* in the early fifth

century.[54] It reflects an early state of relations with the lords of the Lydian countryside and of Sardis that almost from the beginning must have included hospitality and family alliances cemented by intermarriage. For Heraclid descent for the kings of Lydia must necessarily have been invented before the dynasty's fall in the early seventh century, and is therefore the Ionians' earliest known attempt outside the lays of the Ur-*Iliad* to bring the peoples and kingly houses of Asia into relation with their own Neleid and Glaucid hero-founders.

In this early and almost undocumented context, genealogical legend, reinforced by the portrait of the civilized and princely Mêiones from the *Iliad*, allows us to be present at the creation of a long and profound relationship. Lydia was to remain a part of the Greek world as no other foreign kingdom or people ever did.[55] Sardis later presented material and political attractions to the Ionians in its imperial age under the Mermnad dynasty. Its founder Gyges (*reg. c.* 680-644) was remembered by the mercenary soldier Archilochus, who knew the job market in his day, as a Homerically wealthy paymaster, "rich in gold."[56]

Sardis itself had been a part of the Mycenean world, and maintained strong and continuous links of material culture with the Aegean Greek world through the destructions that marked the Mediterranean Bronze Age.[57] But Sardis was not a truly great place until the reign of Alyattes (*reg.* 612-561), father of its last representative Croesus (*reg.* 561-546?), when the lower town was enclosed by a huge circuit wall, and the old Heraclid palace probably rebuilt; in the earlier archaic age the city was no further advanced than the Greek towns themselves.[58] Equality would admit familiarity, so that the small kings of Sardis, boasting a Heraclid ancestry conferred by the Ionians, could stand with the heroically descended royal clans of Ionia, while the lords of the Lydian countryside, whose demesnes neighbored those of the Greek aristocracies in the lower Hermus and Maeander valleys,[59] could share a way of life in the hunt and feasts, in the giving of gifts and brides, and in feuds and raids, which in Homer are the stuff of aristocratic friendship and rivalry in this age and place.

Thus the weight of the Lydian Heraclids' ancestry is precisely

equivalent to that of the hero Tlepolemus of Rhodes, son of Heracles and the Trojan princess Astyocheia. It tells us that in the
imagination of the early Ionians the Lydian Heraclids were no
more distant from themselves than were the Dorians of the Hexapolis, who are present in the poem anachronistically as allies of
the Achaeans, just as the Mêionian charioteers are Priam's Lydian
allies (*Il.* 2.864-66).

What historical imperatives might lie behind the closeness between
Ionians and Lydians reflected in early tradition? The Lydian homeland lay inland of the Carians, where Homer puts it. The Carians
possessed the fertile and well-watered lower reaches of the Caüstrus, Maeander, and Hermus valleys. It is natural to suppose that
the Lydians of the uplands wanted these lands too. If so, these
were grounds for alliances between the arriving Greeks and the
early Lydians against the Carians, who occupied valleys coveted
by both peoples. At any rate, we can infer from the later history
of Lydian aggression against the Greek cities under the Mermnads,
which was aimed more at political control than territorial conquest,
that the Lydians and Greeks reached a *modus vivendi* on the land
early on, and necessarily at Carian expense.[60]
    It is in the light of this common history of Greeks and natives in
Asia that we should follow the outlook of our most knowledgeable
observer, Herodotus. He noted the rise of tyranny among the
Greeks of Asia and their mainland imitators; and it was the Lydian
Mermnads above all who taught the Greeks what it meant to be
a tyrant.

Mermnad History, Tyranny, and Delphi

The Mermnads overthrew the Lydian Heraclids late in the seventh
century, and with the Mermnads begins the historical age of Lydia
and Ionia alike. The dynasty's founder, Gyges son of Dascylus,
was the first flesh-and-blood Asiatic monarch named by a Greek
contemporary, the soldier-poet Archilochus (fr. 25.1 Bergk, 22 D;
cf. Arist. *Rhet.* 1418b):

I pay no mind to the wealth of gold-rich Gyges:
   envy's never taken hold of me.
I've no longing for the works of gods,
   I don't ask for a great tyranny.
All of this is simply beyond my horizons.

Gyges laid the foundations for Lydia's age of magnificence, already visible in the fragments of Alcaeus and Sappho at the end of the seventh century, when palatial Sardis was first rising as the Versailles of archaic Ionia.[61] The Mermnads also abandoned the old and easy coexistence of their predecessors to open a long era of aggrandizement against the Ionians, and the last Mermnads, Alyattes and Croesus, finally succeeded in incorporating some of them into their kingdom.

The geopolitical case for the hostilities of the Mermnads at inland Sardis against the port cities of the Greeks in their kingdom is obvious, but it does not explain the course of Lydian policy toward the Ionians from Gyges onward.[62] The Lydians were not a seafaring people and never tried to organize the Ionians' sea power in their interest, as the Persians were to do. The ports of the valleys descending from Sardis were Smyrna and Phocaea near the outlet of the Hermus, Ephesus at the head of the Caüstrus, and Miletus together with Priene at the head of the Maeander.[63] The Mermnads remained at peace with the Phocaeans and cultivated a close, if ambivalent, relationship with Ephesus. They did make war against Priene and Miletus, but the Lydians' relatively immense resources of precious metals were a magnet for trade with Sardis, a trade that Milesians and other Ionians must have carried on whatever their city's political relations with the Mermnads.[64]

A stronger and more complete picture of relations between the Greeks and the Lydians emerges out of the cultural and religious evidence for Mermnad history. The Mermnads became conspicuous patrons of distant and non-Ionian Delphi. Delphi was an oracle of Apollo like those of Claros and Didyma in Ionia, but of only local importance in the Peloponnese at the time of Gyges' accession. Yet by the reigns of Alyattes and Croesus it was the leading oracular shrine in the Greek world. In light of these facts, why did hostilities arise between the Mermnads and some—by no means all—Ionian cities, and what role did Delphi play in the Mermnads' policies toward the Ionians and the Greek world as a whole in the era from Gyges to Croesus, which is dominated in Herodotus' account by tyrants in Greece and the power of Lydia in Asia?

The answers to these questions are highly relevant to the rest of this chapter. Accordingly, I state them at the outset: the Mermnads, I conclude, made war not so much against the Ionians but against the surviving influence of the deposed Heraclids in Ionia, and appealed to Delphi's influence against them because Delphi's business included the support of tyrants, who paid for that support. These conclusions help explain the rise of Delphi to its leading position in the Greek world, in which the Mermnads' patronage played a very prominent role. Moreover, the Mermnads' example deeply influenced the style of Greek tyranny, when the Lydian monarchy became the envy of Ionia's aristocracies and a model for tyrants throughout archaic Greece.

These conclusions reflect the main outlines of Herodotus' Lydian history, in particular the dynasty's relationship with the Oracle, which is supported by the very tendentiousness of the oracular history of Gyges' usurpation and Croesus' fall that we read in Herodotus. The point has often been made that it obviously embarrassed the Oracle when Croesus' devotion to Apollo of Delphi did not save him from the Persians, so there arose at Delphi an apologetic story explaining how from the very beginning the dynasty was fated to fall with Croesus, but how the god nevertheless saved Croesus himself when he was about to be burned alive on a pyre.[65]

However, in Gyges' day faraway Delphi was a local shrine of little or no influence among Ionians.[66] Claros and Didyma in Ionia, and Ammon in Egypt, were the important oracles within the sphere of East Greek commerce, travel, and tradition.[67] Although votives of archaic East Greek or native Asiatic provenance have been found at Delphi,[68] responses to East Greek petitioners, genuine or invented, are virtually absent in the traditions about Delphi.[69] None of the many, genuine or fictional, colonizing oracles attributed to Delphi sanction colonies sent out by Greeks of Asia,[70] and only one of the Greek tyrants of Ionia, as contrasted with the Mermnads of Lydia, is said to have patronized Delphi.[71]

All of the evidence together strongly indicates that the Ionians in general did not consult Delphi before the eclipse of Milesian Didyma in the Ionian Revolt at the end of the sixth century. In mainland Greece itself the earliest event that attests to Delphi's growing reputation was the First Sacred War (*c.* 595–591/0), after which the Pythian festival and the recently instituted games were organized, traditionally in 582, when the mares of Clisthenes, tyrant of Sicyon, won the chariot race. It is significant that the first securely attested victors were all from central Greece.[72] Before the sixth century Delphi's sphere of influence did not extend much beyond the states of the Amphictyony and of Sparta's sphere of influence. Corinth and Sparta enjoyed intimate relationships with Delphi since well before the First Sacred War, and it is no accident that the oracle's influence in peninsular Greece grew at the same time as the rise of the Cypselids and the advance of Sparta after her conquest of Messenia and victory over Tegea, in *c.* 650–590.

It is probable, then, that before the sixth century the Oracle had gained only a modest reputation across the Aegean, as we see it reflected briefly in poetry.[73] It is possible, even probable, that the tradition of Gyges' relations with Delphi is anachronistic. For, in addition to the facts about Delphi just cited, no evidence of significant cult activity before the beginning of the eighth century has been found there, and there is no secure evidence for a temple building at the sanctuary before the mid-seventh century at the earliest, shortly after the earliest habitation level.[74]

However, soon after Gyges seized power he was faced with an invasion of nomads, against whom he sought relations successively with the Assyrian warlord Ashurbanipal and Psammetichus (Psamtik) I, founder of the Saïte dynasty (664–610) and the first large-scale employer of Greek mercenaries of whom we know.[75] If Gyges had sought to cultivate a distant shrine in central Greece it would have been to advertise for mercenaries, not for oracular responses.[76]

The Mermnads' patronage of Delphi was undoubtedly historical; but their purchase of Delphi's oracular prestige must be located in the period, not much earlier than the beginning of the sixth century, when it had achieved a pan-Hellenic reputation. It was not the Lydians, moreover, who would be swayed by a response from an oracle far away in the mountains of Phocis, where surely few or none of them had been, but the Ionians whose relations with the overthrown dynasty had been close. At some point, surely not before the rise of Cypselus at Corinth in the 650s, and probably a generation or more later, a successor of Gyges advertised Delphic sanction for Mermnad rule to Greeks whose enmities the dynasty was still concerned to allay, and whose loyalties Gyges' descendants would try to attract, especially at Ephesus, in the Colophonian group of Ionian cities, and finally at Miletus.

At this point it is necessary to sketch in some detail the Mermnads' relations with these cities. The main source for Mermnad history is the Lydian logos of Herodotus, supplemented with caution from Nicolaus of Damascus, who wrote in the Augustan age but drew upon the Lydian history of Herodotus' contemporary, Xanthus of Sardis, through a Hellenistic intermediary.[77] Together they form a chronicle, on the one hand, of the Lydian kings' relations with Delphian Apollo and with the most powerful Greek tyrants on both sides of the Aegean. On the other hand, they define Lydian attitudes to the Ionian possessors of the three most important shrines in Lydia devoted to Artemis and her brother, the oracular god Apollo, who were the deities central to Ionian religion. These were the oracle at Claros belonging to the Colophonians, the Artemisium of Ephesus, and the oracle at Didyma in the Milesiad.[78] Gyges and his successors appear to have deliberately shunned the oracles of Claros and Didyma, but cultivated Ephesian Artemis and, later, Delphi. Claros and Didyma, together with the Artemisium, all belonged to cities where relationships with the deposed Heraclids are attested in the Mermnad period; they must have contained groups that continued to view the usurpers as illegitimate, at the very least.[79]

In the Ionian traditions examined in the first section of this chapter, it is these very shrines that serve as focuses of early Greek coexistence with the Lydians and their Heraclid kings. In the light of these traditions, along with other evidence linking the Heraclids with Colophon, Ephesus, and Miletus, the stories about Gyges and his successors can be shown to contain the elements of a coherent Mermnad course of action in Ionia spanning the whole history of the dynasty. Remarkably enough, moreover, the pattern of the Mermnad dynasty's policy toward Colophon, Ephesus, and Miletus allows us to conclude that its first and apparently least credible element, the story of Gyges' petition to Delphi to secure a response legitimating his usurpation, had its first foundation not in Delphian apologetic but in Mermnad propaganda. This story is connected in turn with the Cypselid tyrants of Corinth at Delphi, who also enjoyed close relations with Mermnad Lydia.

EPHESUS

Ephesus was the natural port of Sardis (Hdt. 5.54, 100),[80] and was to a greater extent than the other Ionian cities culturally and politically appended to Sardis, as the ancient home in Ionia of the Lydian goddess Artimu.[81] The city's Codrid kings, the Basilids, had been connected with the Heraclids since very early times through the worship of Artemis.[82] Gyges wed his daughter to a Basilid named Melas I in order to inherit this relationship. The usurper's material inducement to the Basilids to accept him and discard the Heraclids was territory belonging to the neighboring Magnesians, which Gyges took and attached to Ephesus.[83] The significance of the legitimizing effect of this dynastic connection with old Ionian royalty, and with a cult shared by Greeks and Lydians alike as far back as the Ionian migration, is measured by the fact that it was maintained through thick and thin by every succeeding Mermnad king down to Croesus, who could finally afford to discard it. For the Mermnads' connection with the Basilids came to be marked by occasions of violence and estrangement that would appear to reflect ongoing struggles involving the Basilids for influence within the court at Sardis.

Gyges' son Ardys (*reg. c.* 644–624) gave his daughter to an Ephesian noble, descended from Ardys' uncle-by-marriage Melas I, named Miletus (*Milêtos*: his name was identical with that of the city Miletus). Ardys also sought alliance with the Assyrian king Ashurbanipal against the chief threat to the kingdoms of Asia in this epoch, invasions by nomads from inner Asia, the Cimmerians,

29

as well as a tribe from Thrace, the Treres. These were dangerous times. The Cimmerians reached the walls of Sardis and destroyed the lower city.[84] Gyges himself died fighting them.[85] Ardys could afford to alienate no one until the nomad threat had passed. But afterward he took Priene and launched the first of many Mermnad attempts at Miletus (Hdt. 1.15–22).[86]

Ardys' son Sadyattes (*reg.* 624–612), whose reign was secure from invasion, continued the Milesian war (Hdt. 1.17.1) and repudiated the Basilids. He hounded Miletus, husband of Ardys' daughter, out of Lydia and married her himself (she was his own sister: Nic. Dam. 90 F 63.1 and 3). It is likely that Sadyattes' motives were altogether dynastic and concerned with ending the harem influence of the Basilids by transferring his sister from them to himself. He would have in this way eliminated the risk of a Basilid capture of the dynasty by inheritance, as seems to have been a possibility once again at the accession of Croesus, who secured his position by putting to death a half-brother whose mother was Ionian (Hdt. 1.92.2–3).[87]

The successive refuges of Sadyattes' Basilid brother-in-law Miletus, first to Lydian Dascyleium and then to Milesian Proconnesus, may identify friends of the Basilids and enemies of Sadyattes. Dascyleium had been the birthplace of Gyges and remained the ancestral seat of the dynasty (Nic. Dam. 90 F 47.1–4), and Proconnesus was founded in the period when, by tradition, Gyges offered the Milesians permission to found Abydos on the Hellespont (Strabo 13.22 C590 *fin.*). Thus the fugitive's itinerary implies an alliance of Ephesian Basilids and members of Sadyattes' own family against him, assisted by the Milesians for whose city this Basilid had been named—a practice that among the Greeks normally celebrated a hereditary alliance. In essentials, then, Nicolaus testifies to discord between the Basilids and Sadyattes in the context of a *rapprochement* between Ephesus and the Milesians, who were at war with Sadyattes, and who would not be reconciled with the Mermnads before the reign of Sadyattes' son and successor Alyattes (Hdt. 1.17–22).

Sadyattes' son by his sister, Alyattes (*reg. c.* 612–561), inherited this state of affairs. He renewed the dynasty's persecution of the

Heraclids by destroying Smyrna, but he abandoned his father's
unsuccessful hostility to the Milesians and the Basilids. Alyattes
ended the war against Miletus and gave a daughter in his turn to
a Basilid, Melas II, tyrant of Ephesus.[88] Alyattes had an obvious
motive for this conciliation of his father's Greek enemies. Like his
ancestors Gyges and Ardys, who had been on friendly terms with
the Basilids, Alyattes too faced an enemy from the interior in the
rising power of the Medes and needed his hands free of Ionian
entanglements.

Yet the first object of his son Croesus was once again Ephesus,
which he besieged. A famous story told how the Ephesians dedicated their walls to Artemis by stretching a rope to the shrine
from the fortifications after Croesus had arrived beneath them;
whereupon Croesus lifted his siege in homage to the goddess
revered by the Mermnads.[89] But since the Artemisium was below
the city's fortified heights, the Ephesians obviously could not have
linked their walls to it without Croesus' acquiescence. What surely
must have taken place, then, was something on the order of a
procession bearing the rope to the shrine under a sacred truce
granted by Croesus, a ceremony meant by both sides to be the
occasion for a parley.

The story of this sacred dedication, with its singular details
unlikely to have been fabricated, proves that Croesus had no
intention of conquering Ephesus by force. His aim was the one
ancestral to the Mermnads regarding Ephesus, of controlling the
influence of the Basilids. Croesus therefore confined his actions
to the exile of the Ephesians' Basilid tyrant, Pindarus, who had
inherited his position from his father Melas II. The Ephesians
elected another Basilid who ruled, however, as *aisymnêtês*.[90]

An aesymnetes held, in Aristotle's words, an "elective tyranny"
(*Pol.* 1285b25), which implies that at Ephesus Croesus intervened
during a stasis provoked by a feud within the Basilid clan and
that he was invited to intervene by the stronger faction. Afterward,
the Ephesians lived under Croesus' protection and that of Artemis.
He brought them down from their fortified acropolis and established them around the precinct of the great temple,[91] which
was then completed under his patronage.[92] As for the Basilid

aesymnetes, who was later assassinated,[93] he was succeeded during Croesus' reign by an aesymnetes from Athens who put an end to the Basilids' power at Ephesus forever.[94]

Croesus' decisive interference at Ephesus is best explained from the Lydian side by harem politics; for the rival candidate to his accession had been a half-brother named Pantaleon, whose mother was Ionian. The Mermnads' conspicuous connection with the Basilids from Gyges onward encourages the identification of Pantaleon's mother as a Basilid whose family had backed her son against Croesus.[95] This identification is made more attractive by Croesus' dedication of the wealth of his half-brother's chief ally to Ephesian Artemis—returning it to its rightful owner, so to speak.[96]

We may conclude that Alyattes' reconciliation with Ephesus had led to a resurgence of Basilid influence at court, which threatened Croesus' accession.[97] Accordingly, he disestablished the Basilids while benefiting the Ephesians and Artemis himself; thus he discarded the Basilids themselves while making safe the larger connection with the goddess and her servants which had long been an integral element in the Mermnads' relationship with Ionia.

COLOPHON AND ITS COLONIES OF SMYRNA
AND CLAZOMENAE

The Heraclids had attachments to the noble hippotrophoi of Colophon, which possessed the oracle at Claros.[98] The enmity between Colophon and the Mermnads ended only when the last Mermnad king but one, Alyattes, inveigled the hippotrophoi into a false friendship and then murdered them at a feast.[99] Thereafter Colophon became a political appendage of the Mermnads.[100]

Alyattes then destroyed Colophonian Smyrna, which was associated in Heraclid tradition as the city from which the Lydians who founded Etruria had sailed to Italy (Hdt. 1.94.6).[101] Next he tried but failed to take Clazomenae, the other Ionian city founded from Colophon.[102]

Alyattes ended his father's war with the Milesians, however, and was otherwise occupied against the remnant of the Cimmerians, who had invaded Asia Minor a generation before, and against the new power of Media. Therefore his unremitting hostility against the Colophonian cities is best explained by the hereditary Mermnad enmity to the Heraclids, who may have fled to Smyrna after Alyattes' slaughter of the Colophonian nobility, and whose final refuge after the fall of Smyrna was the island city of Clazomenae.

MILETUS

Miletus was the third city of Ionia that possessed a great shrine, to the oracular Apollo of Didyma, as well as a strong Heraclid connection.[103] The Mermnads turned against Miletus when both they and the Milesians began to grow great toward the close of the seventh century. No testimonies comparable to the rich evidence for Lydian relations with Ephesus exists to illuminate the relations between the early Lydian kings and Miletus, a fact that in itself indicates a long and wary aloofness following Gyges' attempt on the city (Hdt. 1.14.4).

Extant traditions suggest an ambivalent relationship from the beginning. On the one hand, Gyges attacked the Milesians; but on the other, Gyges and his successors encouraged Greek—and particularly Milesian—settlement in their new territories, where the Phrygians had kept them out.[104] Gyges is said to have sponsored the Milesian colony at Abydos, which controlled the mouth of the Hellespont and was near the site of valuable electrum deposits.[105] Cyzicus, one of the few sites in Phrygia to yield evidence of an early Greek presence, may also have been augmented by Milesian settlers at about this time, when a circuit wall appeared.[106]

Gyges' sponsorship of Milesian colonization of newly won Lydian lands may best be explained by his need for Greek help against the Cimmerians. When this threat passed, however, Gyges must have fallen out with Miletus, where Heraclid refugees would presumably have sought refuge with members of a kindred Milesian phratry, the Tylonids.[107] Sinope, another Milesian colony in formerly Phrygian territory controlled by Lydia, was founded—or refounded—by Milesian exiles long after the period of the Phrygian Kingdom's dissolution about the time of Alyattes (*c.* 600 or slightly later),[108] who was in alliance with the Milesians after the first years of his long reign.

It is plain that the Branchid priests of Milesian Apollo had refused to recognize Gyges: the god's attitude to the usurper is revealed not only in Gyges' hostility (Hdt. 1.14.4) but, more signally, in the fact that Milesian Apollo would receive no rich offerings from the Mermnads until Croesus, at the end of the dynasty, who is said to have consulted the oracle (1.46.2) and duplicated at Didyma his dazzling gifts to Delphi (1.92.2). These gifts to Apollo had been anticipated by his father Alyattes' dedication of a twin shrine to Athena at Milesian Assesus, which memorialized a permanent peace between Miletus and Sardis (1.21.4). A dynastic alliance between the Lydian monarchy and the Milesian nobility appeared at this time as well. The marriage of a Milesian heiress to a son of Alyattes—she may have been a daughter or kinswoman of the contemporary Milesian tyrant Thrasybulus—inaugurated the new relationship.[109]

The needs and therefore the policy of the Mermnads had changed with the emergence of a new threat from the East. Alyattes, and Croesus in his turn, needed a firm grip on the Ionians' loyalties the better to face the Medes and Persians. With the governor and the goddess of Ephesus within his orbit, and reconciled to the Milesians with their powerful and ancient priestly clan of Branchids, Croesus then proceeded to bring the rest of the Greeks of his kingdom under his sway.

The central theme of Mermnad history in Herodotus lies in the tradition that the Mermnads turned first to the foreign and distant shrine of Delphi to secure the mandate of heaven. We have now seen that this recourse, imposed by necessity, works through the pattern of their historical relationship with Ionia, and we should conclude that in this case the programmatic concerns of our sources correspond to a historical reality. The Delphian solipsism of Herodotus' presentation of Lydian history as controlled by the ordinances of Pythian Apollo, and Nicolaus'-*cum*-Xanthus' preoccupation with the Mermnads' relationship with Artemis and the Ephesian Basilids, reflect real and conspicuous elements in the historical association between Ionians and Lydians.

The Mermnads' need for legitimation by a deity against the members and allies of the former dynasty, who remained in Ionia to vaunt the ancient prerogatives of their lineage, and against the early hostility of Didyma as well as Claros, forced a religious policy upon the new dynasty that, *faute de mieux*, favored Delphi over the native oracles of Ionia. The Ionian oracles remained loyal to their associations with the Heraclids and, within Ionia, sought to continue the ancient Lydian patronage at Ephesus of their own goddess, Artimu.

Herodotus heard a version of Gyges' relations with the Delphic Oracle from Delphian sources in reference to the rich dedications there called "Gygean" after their supposed donor. Possibly the tradition of their donation indicates that they were dedicated by a descendant of Gyges in his ancestor's name, to lend *cachet* to the house's relationship with the Oracle. These gifts lay in the treasury of the first Corinthian tyrant, Cypselus (Hdt 1.14.1–3). This is a fact of great significance in the light of the exceptionally close relationship between the Cypselids and Delphi, and in light of Corinth's early commercial relations with Delphi, attested archaeologically as far back as the ninth century, even before the earliest securely datable votive objects appear.[110]

The oracle supported Cypselus' rule and in return he became a great patron of the god. His was the earliest treasury at Delphi, erected at the end of the seventh century,[111] and he built a magnificent temple to Apollo at Corinth as well.[112] The tyrant dynasty could advertise that the god had addressed Cypselus and his son Periander as "king of famous Corinth" (Hdt. 5.92ε2). In Herodotus' narrative, this response and others are prominent elements in the story of Cypselus' rise. In their original form they must have been procured or invented with the connivance of Delphi to legitimize the dynasty's position.[113] In this sense, these responses must be genuine, since their invention after the fall of the tyranny would have been otiose.

What drew tyrants toward Delphi was just this need for legitimation. The sacred authority of the Spartan kings themselves, after all, rested on the voice of the Oracle (Hdt. 6.52; Plut. *Lyc.* 6 = "Great Rhetra" from the Aristotelian *Lac. Pol.*), who once addressed one of them as "the seed of the demigod son of Zeus." Pheidon of Argos, named by tradition as the first tyrant among the Greeks, had himself been a Heraclid king like those at Sparta, whose scepter was from Zeus. But elsewhere in Dorian Greece, good claim to royal descent was harder to come by for the outsiders who overthrew the ancient families' power. So the tyrant's primacy would require the gods' assent because his giving of justice, his exercise of command and supervision of cult, and even his safety, depended on the gods.[114] Legitimation by acclamation of a god— who alone could bestow it—was accordingly a sovereign requirement of usurpers such as Cypselus, who was a Heraclid and royal Bacchiad only through his lame and imperfect mother.[115] Clisthenes of Sicyon also secured Delphic approval. The surviving response calls him a "stone-thrower," the very opposite of the warrior-hero who battles it out with his foe hand to hand. But this is an anti-Orthagorid invention; it very likely supplanted Delphic propaganda favorable to the dynasty after its fall.[116]

The Cynic Oenomaus, writing a work on oracles with the full literature at his disposal in the second century A.D., astutely observed that Apollo praised both tyrannicides and tyrants.[117] The Oracle not only was apolitical in serving the needs of its petitioners; neither could it exercise any *police des vaticinations* concerning what was attributed to the god by others. Thus a would-be tyrant like Cylon of Athens, for example, himself could have advertised to his comrades and the rest of the Athenians the "response" that bade him seize the Acropolis on the greatest festival of Zeus. Cylon's failure did not in the least detract from the repute of the Oracle, whether the response was genuine or, as most likely, invented (Thuc. 1.126.4 = Q64 Fontenrose 1978).[118]

In Corinth Cypselus probably achieved power as early as 657 and certainly no later than about 635.[119] In Lydia it was Gyges who had arisen by murdering the legitimate ruler while lacking good royal ancestry; he belonged only to an impure junior line of the Lydian Heraclids.[120] As noted earlier, Gyges ruled *c.* 680– 644; thus either he or his successor Ardys (*reg. c.* 644–624) were contemporaries of Cypselus for a time during this period, when Corinthian workmen using Corinthian materials were raising the first stone buildings at Delphi,[121] and Corinthian pottery had achieved prominence in Ionian trade. Much has been found in

Sardis, and if some items were carried there by Corinthian traders drawn inland by the fame of the city, the need for a proxeny-relationship between the Cypselids and Mermnads would have have arisen.[122] But pottery does not tell us who carried it, and it is better to depend in this case on the literary tradition, which informs us that Cypselus' son and successor Periander was remembered at Miletus not only for his influence at Delphi (Hdt. 1.20) but for his friendship with Sardis.[123]

If Periander had inherited these relationships from his father, then Cypselus stands as the earliest identifiable link between Delphi and the Mermnads. And in Delphi's profitable legitimation of tyrants in old Greece in the age which began with the rise of Cypselus and ended with the fall of Croesus, we may have discovered the truest reason why Delphi attained pan-Hellenic importance in the course of the sixth century—not as an oracle of colonization,[124] but as a purveyor of the gods' approval of the new men of power in a Greek world that included Mermnad Lydia.

Tyranny and Barbarism

Although the kings of Lydia did not impose tyrannies on the Greeks within their orbit, nevertheless tyranny as a style of rule, if not the word itself,[125] passed to the Greeks from Lydia, while Delphi mediated the naturalization of the Mermnads to the Greek category of tyrant. The later Mermnads almost surely supported political movements in Asia Minor conducive to popular power and the rise of tyrants.[126] Additionally, they were full participants in the network of mutually supportive relations among the archaic Greek tyrannies, not only in the leading Ionian cities of Ephesus and Miletus but in old Greece too. Through the Cypselids of Corinth, they became close to the Pisistratids of Athens, whose illegitimate scion Hegesistratus ruled at Sigeum in Lydian territory (Hdt. 5.94.1).

Alyattes and Croesus also cultivated the other most distinguished and ambitious Athenian families of this period, the Alcmaeonids and Philaids. Through the Alcmaeonids, who married into the family of the tyrant of Sicyon (6.131), who competed for the tyranny at Athens, and who exercised great influence at Delphi (cf. 5.62.2–63.1), the dynasty had another link to the Oracle. Alcmaeon, the father of Megacles and grandfather of Clisthenes, gained immense wealth for his great services to Alyattes at Delphi.[127] Croesus also protected Miltiades II the Philaid (whose uncle Miltiades I was the son of another Cypselus, attesting a dynastic relationship between the Philaids and Cypselids: 6.34.1) from his Lampsacene enemies in the Thracian Chersonese (6.37.1).[128]

Thus when Myson of Athens painted Croesus on the pyre late in the sixth century, he visualized him as a Greek monarch, in reflection of the view of late archaic Greeks.[129] Herodotus thought of the Lydian kings and of their own great tyrants as members of a single species, not only because they formed a single "club" of autocrats, but for deeper reasons of imitation. Not only did the Lydian monarchs Hellenize; the Ionian Greeks Lydianized. The Lydian kings themselves, in their magnificent self-projection within the close historical relations between Ionians and Lydians, which had developed from Heraclid times onward within a shared aristocratic style and shared material values of display,[130] and in mainland Greece through Delphi, would define tyranny and tyrannical display as a powerful cultural ideal.

When tyranny arrived among the Ionians they located its roots in the Asianic way of life exemplified by the Lydians. The Ionian poet Xenophanes understood tyranny as the final expression of the competitive ostentation of an Orientalized aristocracy. He condemned his fellow Colophonians, who "learned useless luxuries from the Lydians, while still they were not subject to hateful tyranny. They would come to their meeting place in purple cloaks—a full thousand of them as a rule, not less—flaunting their comely locks and drenched in scented unguents."[131] The Ionian medical writers understood tyranny as a consequence of the Asianic *physis* shared by Asiatic barbarians and Asiatic Greeks alike.[132]

Our best witness is Herodotus, who is the *locus classicus* for both aspects of this association. His Ionians possess the Hippocratic *physis* of indolent and servile Asiatics;[133] but tyranny itself he correctly understood to arise as the outcome of aristocratic rivalries (cf. esp. 3. 82.3-4). Herodotus assimilated Greek and foreign tyranny not only by the word itself, since he refers unselfconsciously and indiscriminately to Greek and foreign autocrats alike as tyrants,[134] but also according to its fundamental character, which he identifies without distinction in barbarian and Hellenic societies.[135]

Tyranny was viewed by the Greeks as the antithesis of political freedom of speech and action—the Greeks' *idiên eleutheriên*, belonging to them alone of all the peoples of the world (Hdt. 7.147.1). Tyranny was thus a principal cultural marker of barbarism. Herodotus begins his profoundly instructive story of the rise of Deioces, the first king of the Medes, who were the imperial forerunners of the Persians, by contrasting autonomy and tyranny. "Though all the peoples of the continent were autonomous" after the fall of the Assyrian kingdom, "they came round again to tyrannies in the following way." He then goes on to relate how Deioces aimed to achieve a tyranny by arbitrating justly among those who came to him in those lawless times, so that he became indispensable to a people themselves incapable of self-government. Lacking another choice, the Medes accordingly gathered in assembly and chose him monarch (1.96.1ff).[136] Elsewhere Herodotus makes Darius say, with irony unconscious to a Persian, that depotism is the Persians' *patrios nomos*, by which they achieved their "freedom" (3.82.5).

Even more significant for Herodotus' own views, however, is his treatment of tyranny among Greek peoples, as when a Samian in assembly rashly spurns the tyrant Maeandrius' offer to step down and establish the Samians' liberty. Herodotus contemptuously concludes that "indeed, it looks as if they didn't want to be free" (3.143.2). The Samians, and all the Ionians, in Herodotus' belief, were barbarian in origin (1.56.2) and therefore naturally congenial to tyranny—*andrapoda philodespota*, "slaves who cling to their master," in the epithet of Herodotus' Scythians (4.142). At Ionian Athens, too, there had been many who assisted Pisistratus to gain his tyranny, "for whom," Herodotus remarks, "tyranny was more welcome than liberty" (1.62.1).

We shall see that, in this sense, race is a paramount element in Herodotus' thinking. We may anticipate a little further by noting that the Dorians—who are originally Hellenic and are exemplified by the Spartans—are by contrast naturally indisposed to tyranny. It is striking that all of the tyrants over Dorian peoples mentioned by Herodotus were themselves, according to the traditions about them that Herodotus chose to relate, non-Dorian in origin. Pheidon began as a king of Argos and was therefore a non-Dorian Heraclid (6.127; cf. Arist. *Pol.* 1310b6). The Cypselids of Corinth were pre-Dorian Lapiths (Hdt. 5.92β1). Herodotus treats Clisthenes of Sicyon as a non-Dorian upstart against the Dorian tribes hitherto dominant at Sicyon (5.67-69) and as the model for the Athenian Clisthenes, whom he regards as a would-be tyrant who uses the demos against his aristocratic rivals.[137] LIkewise, the savage Battiad tyranny at Dorian Cyrene was Minyan (4.150.2), and the Hecatomnid tyranny of his own Dorian Halicarnassus, from which he was in exile for much of his life, was not Greek at all but Carian in origin.[138]

The second characteristic of tyranny is *megaloprepeiê*, "magnificence," expressed by a courtly style that combined lavish patronage of public shrines and festivals, a generous personal magnanimity to petitioners and the poor (cf. Arist. *AP* 16.16.6–7; Hdt. 3.42.1–3), and an open welcome to artists and intellects.[139] The tradition of Solon's meeting with Croesus may be *non vero*,[140] but it is nonetheless *ben' trovato*: the tale of their encounter could not have been imagined unless it were true that the splendid Croesus drew to his court such men from the whole Greek world (Hdt. 1.29.1). Periander too had drawn Arion (1.24.1) to sing his praises, and Polycrates his Anacreon (3.121.1), as Croesus expected Solon—who after all had praised Philocyprus the ruler of Soli "above all tyrants" (5.113.2)—to celebrate his grandeur in like terms.

The vivid court life of the Mermnad kings and the wealthy tyrants of Greece, with their great public monuments, their festivals, and their offerings, reflected a common court style shared by aristocratic cultures of similar customs and material tastes for Asianic modes and Asianic luxuries. The storied magnificence of Polycrates was surpassed only by the Gelonids among Greek tyrants (3.125.2). Polycrates not only kept the Teian poet Anacreon (3.121.1) to embellish his own splendor. His wealth was also a river to his people. To serve the Samians he drew the physician

Democedes from Pisistratid Athens with a nobleman's income.[141] The engineer Eupalinus came from Megara to drive the city's great tunnel and acqueduct and, presumably, to supervise the building of the great mole in the harbor of Samos (3.60).[142] At the Mermnad court across the water the wandering luminaries of Greek art and wisdom enjoyed an open welcome, and Greek musicians were naturalizing the Lydian mode in Ionia already in the age of Sappho and Alcaeus.[143] The Lydian kings traded brides with Ionians, setting fashions doubtless emulated by the lesser Lydian nobility. Sappho's friends circulated in polite Lydian society and brought home Lydian *haute couture*, while their husbands served in the royal army, celebrated for its show even by Sappho.[144]

Display is power. Splendor and munificence were a tyrant's political weapons. Opulence and an open-handed style set the tyrant high above his defeated rivals. Some tyrants pretended to the legitimacy of ancient *basileia* as it was celebrated in the poems of Homer,[145] while all of them took care to avoid any definition of the position that might set limits to their power. The Gelonids were pleased to be styled *basileis* of Syracuse, but no evidence exists to show that either Gelon or Hieron had any constitutional position.[146] In another age Caius Octavius of Velitrae, like Pisistratus just a jumped-up *domi nobilis*,[147] would claim the honorific style of *augustus* and *princeps*, epithets without constitutional definition that served to acknowledge, as he himself acknowledged in the *Res gestae* (34.2), his all-powerful position and sacred person.

The Pisistratids stood to one side of the existing apparatus, managed it (Thuc. 6.54.5–6), and let the power of their house manifest itself by drawing under their patronage the greatest social and political prerogatives of their class. They monopolized the great civic liturgies with unprecedented magnificence and thereby bought the approval of the gods and the mass of Athenians with meat and wine, while occupying the center of public attention as the impresarios of Athens' festival life.[148] The tyrant's purpose, like the purpose of Augustus, was to clothe his usurpatory victory in a contest of factions with a sacral and traditional protocol, administered with a universal generosity and majesty that eclipsed the prestige of rivals and captured the loyalty and the awe of the humble.[149]

Everybody knew that this was what tyranny was all about. Miltiades I, a descendant of the hero Aeacus who also boasted a close dynastic connection with Cypselids,[150] left Attica to found his own principality—it was yet another tyranny sanctioned by Delphi—because Pisistratus at home would give his own ambition for primacy no scope (Hdt. 6.34–35); his nephew Cimon I secured his return from exile only by surrendering his own prestige to Pisistratus, when he announced the third and greatest of his chariot victories at Olympia in the name of the tyrant. Even so Cimon's achievement remained too conspicuous to survive the succession: he was assassinated, it was said, by Pisistratus' sons.[151]

All of this is implied in Herodotus' verbal association of Greek tyranny with oriental monarchy, and is further reason why the Greeks thought of these quite different institutions as being essentially similar. The visible similarities worked to accommodate the structural differences. The Herodotean story of the Mede Deioces spans the gap effortlessly. Deioces began as a Greek would, by distinguishing himself for probity in order to gain the trust of all factions in a period of anarchy; he was freely elected to power, like Solon or any Greek aesymnetes. But then Deioces established an oriental protocol of hieratic inaccessibility behind the seven walls of Ecbatana so that, as Herodotus shrewdly thought, his contemporaries—"men who had grown up with him and were of no lesser family and courage"—could no longer look upon him enviously and plot to take his place, but would consider him other than what he had been (1.99.2).

This transformation in the eyes of his rivals was the impossible goal of the Greek tyrant—impossible but nevertheless many times attempted.[152] The style and pretensions of Greek tyrants emulated the Asianic magnificence of the Mermnads. But the result was determined by the nature and needs of Greek—not Asiatic—society. Like oriental monarchy, the essence of the tyrannical style lay in its monopoly of power, both sacred and profane. Among Greeks, however, the result was not monarchy but a devaluation of aristocratic privilege that helped open the way for more egalitarian government by a process of civic leveling. Although the tyrant did not so much raise the humble (the *kakoi*, on whom he based his appeal) closer to the level of the noble, the *kaloi k' agathoi*, he did bleed the distinction between the humble and the noble of its ancient force by making it impossible for his rivals to carry out their traditional lordly functions, so they could no longer be *seen* so easily to be the *kaloi k' agathoi*, "the beauteous and nobly virtuous."

The tale of Deioces, in contrast, provides an essential clue to the institutional stability of oriental monarchy in the elevation of the king to a godlike role in exercising an *imperium absconditum*. But in the polis the tyrant could not disappear; he had to strive continually to maintain a trembling gap between himself and his fellow nobles, "men of no lesser family and manly worth," not by hired guardsmen alone, necessary as these were,[153] but by a *megaloprepeiê* of incontestable scale. So even at Syracuse, whose fourth-century tyrants possessed a little Ecbatana in their island refuge of Ortygia, the monarchy was not continuous, because no Greek could stand a permanently inferior status.

Among the strongest factors in the Greek makeup, and therefore in Greek politics, was *phthonos*, the furious envy that kept a man on guard against his rivals and eager to step over them. Consider Thucydides' analysis of the psychology of the insecure leaders of the Four Hundred at Athens in 411 (8.89.3, my emphasis). According to Thucydides, their profession that the franchise of the Five Thousand should be established in fact, and not merely in name, and so establish the government on a footing of practical equality

> was merely a propagandistic political tactic, and in their private ambition most of them pursued that course whereby an oligarchy formed out of a democracy is most surely ruined: for all of them forthwith sought, not how they should maintain equality among themselves, but how each himself could become by far the foremost; whereas in a democracy, it is easier to bear the outcome of popular elections, *for then it is not as if one is defeated by one's peers.*

Tyrants sought a monopoly of prestige and unchallengeable power by purchase, which began with mercenaries but ended necessarily with shrines and festivals to the gods. To gain the gods as allies, great temples rose everywhere in this age of tyrants: Basilid and Mermnad Ephesus, Gelonid Sicily, the Samos of Polycrates and his predecessors, the precinct of Apollo Didymaeus at Miletus, the Athenian Acropolis and Eleusis under Pisistratus, and Delos too.[154]

The tyrant about whom we know most is Pisistratus. At Athens, he had started from nothing, his claim to the Neleid blood of Athens' ancient kings notwithstanding (Hdt. 5.65.3). Isolated from Athens and central Attica in his home at Brauron, in the east Attic *hyperakria* beyond Hymettus and without a known family connection to an important community cult at Athens, he created from scratch a position at the center of the public religion. When he grasped at power again after an initial period of rule from his seat of government on the Acropolis (1.59.4), he devised a solemn gesture to encourage his reception by all parties to the faction struggle at Athens. He came in procession to the city in the chariot of Athena accompanied by a stand-in for the goddess herself, as heralds preceded them crying, "Athenians, receive Pisistratus with open hearts, whom Athena herself has honored above all men and is leading back to her own acropolis" (Hdt. 1.60.3ff).

A sumptuous liturgical procession to his former seat in or near Athena's precinct probably lies behind this story. Although Pisistratus' patronage of the city's goddess did not in itself lay the basis of his eventual domination, which he secured by armed force, yet his sacred advent on this occasion shows that, although a Greek might win power in the ordinary, human way, he could keep it only by divine ratification. Unlike Cylon, Pisistratus took successful possession of the Acropolis in the only possible way— by serving its deities. His place in Athena's chariot prefigured his association with the cult of Athena Polias, for whom he erected a new temple in stone and whose festival he splendidly augmented. The Panathenaea was founded in 566, when Pisistratus already had achieved a leading position in public life (he was polemarch for the Megarian war *c.* 565), and only five years before his first attempt at the tyranny. It was named "pan-Athenaea," the festival inclusive of *all* the goddess's cults in the various demes, perhaps by Pisistratus himself in the spirit of the regime's aim of conciliation and in celebration of Salamis, the new land he had helped secure for Athena's portion.[155]

Pisistratus appropriated the Panathenaea as the centerpiece of his public role because it memorialized the definitive synoecism of Attica. Under the patronage of his house the festival ratified the intrusion and domination of an east Attic family in the politics of the city. Here, in his seat upon the Acropolis he could overlook the demesnes of the Eupatridae in the central plain and gaze across the water to his prize of Salamis. Athena and her lord in Attica were hand in glove.

Thus for tyrants in Lydia and in Greece alike the divine apparatus conferred not merely personal authority but the very means by which the ruler created and expressed a national identity that incorporated his own person at its center. The Mermnads who flaunted their relations with Artemis of Ephesus, and who sent treasure to Didyma and Delphi, were also taking measures necessary to incorporate the Ionians, in soul as well as body, into Lydia, while clothing their own power with a sacred aura.

But of course the tyrant was something more than the impresario of his city's festival life. In order to deprive his defeated fellow aristocrats of any honors that did not flow from him, and to protect those who looked to him for aid and safety, he needed to gather into his competence all of the community's public responsibilities. Thereby some of these tyrants became the first comprehensive state authorities in the post-Mycenean history of the Greeks. They supervised justice, war, and the public treasury, whether in their own persons or by manipulating the existing organs of public authority.[156] The tyrants monopolized the prestige of public action and strove consciously to concentrate and express the whole life of their cities through their own personalities and works.

Thus the historical traditions of archaic Miletus, Ephesus, Samos, Corinth, and Athens, and of Sicily into the fourth century, are largely the traditions of their tyrants, just as those Asiatic monarchs depicted by Herodotus personify the histories of their realms. The merger of tyranny and barbarism in the classical Greek stereotype of the Other bears a genuine correspondence to the history of the Greeks in Asia and the Asianic influences that inevitably flowed into archaic Greek culture. Prominent among these in the Greeks' own eyes was the Asianic style of their tyrants.

Three

Tabula Rasa: The Invention of the Persians

> Thus saith the LORD to his anointed, to Cyrus,
> whose right hand I have holden, to subdue nations
> before him; and I will loose the loins of kings, to
> open before him the two leaved gates; and the
> gates shall not be shut;
> I will go before thee, and make the crooked places
> straight: I will break in pieces the gates of brass,
> and cut in sunder the bars of iron;
> And I will give thee the treasures of darkness, and
> hidden riches of secret places, that thou mayest
> know that I, the LORD, which call *thee* by thy name,
> *am* the God of Israel.
> —Isaiah 45:1–2

The familiar splendor of the Lydian monarchy vanished with the conquest of Cyrus (*reg.* 559–529). The invader from unknown inner Asia who had come before, only to lap round the walls of the citadels, disperse into pockets of the countryside, and ultimately recede into the Anatolian hinterland, now was here to stay. The aim of this chapter is to explain how the Greeks, first in Asia and then in Europe, developed their ideas of the Persians in the era from the Persian conquest to Xerxes' invasion of Greece, and to identify the real and the imaginary elements contained in these ideas.

From the beginning of Persian rule in Ionia, the Greeks noted the public facts—things that could be seen and talked about, and which became common report. But for the most part the Persians remained a tabula rasa upon which the Greeks drew a portrait in their own idiom, a portrait that answered to their own imaginative purposes. Indeed, the Persians projected themselves to the Greeks largely in Greek terms. As they conquered the various peoples of their empire, the Persians uniformly defined themselves and their motives in the language and imagery of their subjects. Just as the priests of Babylon hailed Cyrus as the Chosen of Marduk, and the Jews called him the Anointed of the Lord, Xerxes would cross to Europe bearing the ancestry of Laomedon and Priam, and the vengeance of Troy against the Achaeans. This Trojan aspect of the Persian identity, which outlived the invasion of Xerxes and transformed Homer's Trojans into Asiatic barbarians in the Greek mind, arose spontaneously among the Greeks of Asia. But its major feature—the association of Xerxes' armada with the Trojan War— was the work of the Achaemenids' Greek clients, who guided their propaganda in the age of the Persian advance to Europe.

Memnonian Susa

The Persians were caught up in the Greeks' universal dragnet of mythographical assimilation as soon as they came into contact with them in the mid-sixth century. Inevitably the Greeks once again used Homer, their gazetteer of Asia, to imagine the Persians' place in the world in descent from the heroic age. They identified the Great King with the dynasty of Memnon, son of the goddess Dawn and the Trojan Tithonos, a son of King Laomedon. Memnon had ruled the Homeric Aethiopians; he was mythical personification of the furthest East.[1] To the Greeks of Herodotus' day, Achaemenid Susa remained the *Memnoneion asty* (Hdt. 5.54.2); the palace complex was known as the *basilêia ta Memnonia* (5.53), and the royal road from Sardis to Susa the *Memnoneia hodos*.[2] Thus even the marriage alliance between the royal house of Macedon and the Achaemenids in the 490s (5.21.2; cf. 7.22.1; 8.136.1), which brought Macedon into the Persian sphere as a vassal kingdom, was defined in terms of Memnonian genealogy by Pherecydes, who gave Memnon a brother Emathion, "from whom Macedonia [is called] Emathia" (*FGrH* 3 F 73).[3]

Together with the Greeks' initial confusion of Persians and Medes, which persisted in their habit of calling the Persians, "the Mede,"[4] their nonspecific association of the Persians with the generic Eastern figure of Memnon reflects the great distance between Persians and Greeks, cultural as well as geographical. The Persians' association with Troy in particular remained even when some few Greeks did come to know Persians well, because Xerxes' war propaganda in 480 exploited this link.[5] At that time the Persians had themselves appeared to ratify the Greeks belief that the Kings of Persia were descendants of Trojan Memnon.

Persians were very thin on the ground in Asia Minor until the campaigns of Cambyses and Darius in the West and the Persians' appropriation of Ionian territory after the Ionian Revolt (Hdt. 6.20 *fin.*). But even then Persians were not seen in the market squares of the Greek towns (1.153.2); they kept aloof even from those Greeks whom they received, as they remained aloof from their other subjects, by the gorgeous and impermeable carapace of formal protocol.

Because the typical Greek encounter with Persians was in a formal audience, what the Greeks knew best about the Persians, from Herodotus onward through Ctesias and the *Cyropaedia*, was their court protocol.[6] The Achaemenids themselves testify, in the formulaic chancellery style of their inscriptions and in the Persepolis reliefs depicting every gesture, insignia of rank, and detail of costume in the palace style of the Achaemenids with otherworldly and silent grace, how the Great King and his satrapal imitators wished their power to be regarded: universal, immutable, and unapproachable.[7] Especially in the early period of Persian domination in Ionia, before Cambyses and then Darius enlisted many Greeks directly into pursuit of their mutual—and eventually conflicting—ambitions, it is hard to imagine that any but a few Greeks had occasion to approach Persians, and when they did so the audience was ritually hieratic and buffered by courtiers and interpreters. The long persistence of Greeks in calling Persians "Medes," then, was not mere carelessness.[8] For the Greeks could and did make careful distinctions among the Asiatic peoples closer and more familiar to them.

Medes and Persians were tribal folk, at home far from the Greek world behind the Zagros rampart in the Iranian highlands which lay far beyond Babylon, the terminus of the Eastern world to all but a handful of Greeks before Alexander. On his own showing Herodotus himself never went beyond Babylon,[9] and Greek envoys to Persia always came to court under Persian escort; very likely nobody without a Persian *laisser-passer* freely traveled the royal road for many stages, especially beyond Babylon toward the Persian Gates.[10]

Cyrus' first capital, at Pasargadae in Fars, was far to the east of his conquests in Mesopotamia and Anatolia. Strikingly unlike other capitals and royal seats of the ancient East, Pasargadae was not a densely inhabited palatial agglomeration, but was laid out in sparsely settled country on the field where Cyrus is said to have defeated the Medes (Strabo 15.3.8 C730), in an open pattern recalling a military encampment.[11] In itself Pasargadae testifies to the degree of the Persians' cultural distance from the urban civilizations of the lowlands in the era of Cyrus (cf. Hdt. 9.122).

Darius was the first to build city palaces at Elamite Susa and at Babylon in Mesopotamian style.[12] But the Persians who were drawn into the western provinces by Darius' reconquest of the empire and the multifarious duties of administration remained isolated in rural fortified estates[13] or around the satrapal palace centers away from the coast.[14] They looked back to the homeland with such nostalgia that the highest of them brought their own environment with them, in the form of the palatial *apadana* and the *paradeisos*, the "paradise" that was the Iranian horseman's walled hunting-park.[15]

The Persepolis Fortification Tablets provide a detailed picture of the other side of the Persians' oriental *imperium absconditum*, in the bureaucratic distance between the ruler and his subjects.[16] Communications went up and down the line *via* ration chits and messengers. However, the bureaucracies of oriental empires were empowered and exalted only by the binding sacral authority of the invisible Great King.[17] Herodotus' picture of the Persian guard of the satrap Oroetes doing homage to the Great King's commands written over his seal, as if the King himself were present (3.128.2–5), is an accurate one, glossed by Xenophon's admiring reflection upon the *mana* of the emperor: "Who else but the King has ever had the power to punish enemies at many months' distance?" (*Cyrop.* 8.2.7). It was natural that Ionians should typically see the Medes and Persians in vanishing perspective. Once again we may cite Herodotus' tale of Deioces, this time in order to watch Deioces recede ever farther from the open bench of justice in a crowded Iranian village, to disappear forever behind the walls, tapestries, guards, and eunuchs of Ecbatana (Hdt.1.96ff).

Even for Greeks in Persian service, opportunities to learn about Persians at first hand were limited by protocol. The fragments of Ctesias testify that the closer one came to the center of the Achaemenid system the more obscure it became. We think badly of Ctesias not only because he set out to contradict and supersede Herodotus out of his own head, but also because we imagine that he had opportunities for observation, discovery, and report that he signally failed to use. Yet even as physician to the consort of Artaxerxes II, and as the King's envoy to Conon and Evagoras, he was after all only a foreign servant in a great oriental palace. His place on the backstairs of the royal ménage is undoubtedly a chief reason why much of what we have of him reads like harem gossip.[18]

Acquaintance

The distance between Persians and Greeks began to narrow perceptibly among a few individuals at the top in the context of intensifying diplomacy and intrigue from the Persian war onward, at the latest.[19] Even so, Herodotus—our witness for this period—shows how little Greeks on the outside knew or could discover in his own day. Through the years there has been much speculation on Herodotus' sources for his Persian material, beginning with the suggestion that he knew the Persian exile Zopyrus at Athens.[20] However, it is not demonstrable from any of his Persian material that he was acquainted with Persians, much less that he had interrogated any Persians with profit. On the contrary, on closer examination his information bears all the marks of observation of the foreigner at a remove, and hearsay collected from other Greeks, as when he cites the *logioi tôn Perseôn*, "the Persians familiar with the stories," to tell Greek tales (1.1–4).

Herodotus' attribution of these stories to Persians leads us to opposing conclusions. Either some Persians had Hellenized sufficiently by Herodotus' day that his Persian purveyors of Ionian burlesque were not grossly improbably figures, or the cultural relationship between Asiatic Greeks and Persians was still so distant that gross improbabilities could be imputed to the Persians due to Greek ignorance. We know almost nothing for certain about how Persians and Greeks got on together in Ionia during the age of Athens' empire, but for three reasons I strongly prefer the latter assumption. First of all, it is likely that there was less rather than more opportunity for contact in the period 479–413, between Mycale, when Persian forces abandoned the coastal towns and countryside, and the Ionian War.[21] Second, it was surely Xerxes' Greek agents who invented the motif of Asia's historical mission of revenge against Europe; and it is just this motif that lies behind the burlesque *aitiai* of women-thefts in Hdt. 1.1–4, culminating in the abduction of Helen.[22] Third, the number of loan words from Persian to Greek in this period is very slender, as it is indeed for the whole of the classical period.[23]

Xenophon, the only surviving Greek author who came into intimate contact with Persians, belongs to the fourth century. He was a member of that large but singular category of Greek mercenary warriors and commanders whose skills and ethos appealed to the Persians. Warrior Greeks, notably Spartans like Agesilaus and the diplomat Antalcidas, and gentlemen soldiers like Xenophon, had most in common with Persians of rank. It was in the fourth century, the age of Greek mercenaries in Persian service and of continuous personal diplomacy between Greeks and Persians, that some Greeks finally gained a fuller appreciation of the Persians.

Once admitted to intimacy with a Persian noble, a useful petitioner could find himself treated to a direct and disarming relationship. The Spartan navarch Lysander, for example, had evidently been charmed by the younger Cyrus as he strolled with the prince through an orchard, while Cyrus proudly described how he had ordered its plan himself and planted the trees with his own hands.[24] Above all, life together in the field and on the march weakened protocol and gave both Greeks and Persians opportunities to observe one another and to form personal alliances. In Xenophon especially, Persians are presented vividly as individuals by one who knew them. In Xenophon an air of mutual direct address between Persians and Greeks is always present, notably in the scene of Agesilaus' encounter with Pharnabazus.[25]

In Herodotus a similar air marks only the intimate, despairing outburst of a nameless Persian noble to his Boeotian couch-companion during a feast on the eve of the battle of Plataea, who later recollected it directly to Herodotus (9.15.4–16), and the colloquies between the Spartan exile Demaratus and Xerxes—all the more strikingly because Demaratus plays the role of a wise advisor disbelieved by Xerxes.[26] The vignettes of Xerxes in Herodotus featuring Demaratus (7.101–4, 209, 234–37) portray his attractive side, displaying the Great King's magnanimity and ease of royal manner. And, more than any others in Herodotus, they are likely to reflect direct personal recollection of Xerxes by one who had known him.[27]

Herodotus himself had no such *entrée* and he lived, besides, during the Athenian imperial era of the fifth century. His discussion of Persian customs (1.131ff) must reflect the normal distance between Greeks and Persians in Asia Minor at that time. Herodotus thought he knew something about Persian names, that all of them end in sigma (1.139; cf. 6.6.98.3).[28] But Old Persian *sh* was retained only after terminal *i* and *u*;[29] Herodotus' ignorant generalization holds good only for the Greek forms of Persian names, from which arose also his misconceptions about their meaning. In fact Greek names of Persians and Medes in Herodotus and other Greek authors appear often to be pseudonomastics based on real or fanciful resemblance to the Persian pronunciation and sometimes they are altogether Greek.[30]

53

On the Persians' feasting customs, he avers that they are addicted to wine and accustomed to deliberate together about the gravest matters when drunk, and then to review their decisions next day when sober, or if sober to decide again when drunk (1.133.3–4). Possibly, but overindulgence is an prominent element in the barbarian stereotype.[31] Herodotus or his informant may have misunderstood what they had heard about the Zoroastrian *haoma* ritual, in which the intoxicating juice of a sacred plant was ritually imbibed as a central act in the Zoroastrian liturgy of the Yasna.[32] Perhaps he interpreted his information according to the stereotype of the barbarian seeking occasions for hard drinking. Herodotus includes a miscellany of Persian life in the provinces, the glimpses the Greeks obtained from outside, such as the Persian birthday feast which an occasional Greek *xenos* might attend or vice versa, since Herodotus has the Persians impolitely complain about the plain tables set by Greeks (1.133.2). Of course, this could be another example of projection, something that Greeks imagined Persians would say about them.

It is striking that, whereas Herodotus' most committed curiosity lay in the realm of religion,[33] nothing in his account of Persian religion reflects direct inquiry among accessible Persians. He could report upon the Persian manner of animal sacrifice because it happened out of doors. He knows that the Persians did not use fire to roast the parts in the Greek way (1.132.2), "for," as he remarks in another context, "the Persians think that fire is a god" and they do not give dead things to a god (3.16.2), a misinterpretation of Zoroastrian ritual and belief, in which fire was sacred to the god Mithra, and of the Zoroastrian prohibition against the pollution of fire and water.[34] He states correctly the observable fact (for Persian Asia Minor in the later fifth century at any rate) that Persians did not erect temples or statues of the gods as did the Greeks, but he betrays his distance from the Persians, and his programmatic determination to contrast Persian religious practices in all ways with Greek, when he asserts incorrectly that they used no altars, fires, or libations (1.132.1). In fact the Persians in Iran, and presumably within their satrapal palaces in the provinces, built shrines and fire altars, and depicted the presence of Ahura Mazda as a twin of the Great King in the winged cartouche above Darius in the Bisitun Frieze.

Herodotus also knew that the Persians abjured lying as the foulest of all offenses (1.138.1; cf. 153.2); but he reflects no independent awareness of the central place of honesty, of enmity to the Lie, in Persian worship and doctrine: he even confounded Mithra, the Persian lord of fire and of the sun who was the witness and guardian of oaths, with the Persians' worship of the Celestial Aphrodite (1.131.3).[35] It is only in this mistaken way that he notices the Persians' appropriation in Ionia of the Greco-Lydian cult of Aphrodite-Kubaba, with whom the Persians equated their goddess Anahita,[36] and whose temple at Ephesus they had provided with an administrator-priest (*neôkoros*) titled by the Achaemenid proper name Megabyxus or Megabyzus.[37] By virtue of his position the Megabyxus surely was one person knowledgeable about Persian religion whom Greeks could freely approach (cf. Xen. *Anab.* 5.3.6–7: 395; this man was either a Greek or a Hellenized Persian). But it does not seem that Herodotus ever searched him out or spoke with him.

By Herodotus' day the Greeks of Asia had been under Persian overlords for more than a century, and syncretisms were noticeable. Yet he had no knowledge of Zoroaster (as did his contemporary Xanthus: Diog. Laert. *proem.* 2), and no knowledge of Zoroastrianism beyond some of the observable externals of sacrificial ritual and the incorrect inference from the absence in public spaces of Persian images of their gods that the Persians regarded them simply as the elements of nature—a misconception that has important consequences for the character of Persians in his work.[38] He does report another, evidently notorious, fact shocking to Greek sentiment, namely, the Magian custom of exposing corpses to carrion beasts (a Zoroastrian practice), as well as their zeal to kill all living things except dogs and humans, especially insects and snakes. Herodotus concludes his account of Persian customs with the comment that for the most part their burial practices are not easily known: *tade mentoi hôs kruptomena legetai kai ou saphêneôs peri tou apothanontos* (1.140.1).

The fault lay not altogether with Herodotus, however; we can take his reportage for the best one could do in his place.[39] Moreover, the Persians themselves misleadingly addressed those Greeks with whom they dealt in their own terms, through Greek agents who gave familiar, readily comprehensible—and altogether mis-leading—answers to some of the principal questions that Greeks asked about the Persians. These answers abetted the Greeks' own tendency, already seen in their evidently spontaneous association of the Achaemenids with Memnon, to assimilate the Persians to themselves and their own categories of identity, belief, and action.

The Persian practice of burning the abodes of enemy gods is a cardinal example. Since Herodotus and, *a fortiori*, other Greeks believed that fire was a god for the Persians, one Persian practice above others that might have led Greeks to inquire more closely about the religious doctrines of the Persians was their burning of some Greek shrines, not only by Xerxes' army at Eretria, in Phocis, and at Athens, but earlier at the conclusion of the Ionian Revolt—which stood in contrast to their veneration of yet other Greek holy places. Indeed, Darius had advertised his homage to oracular Apollo and put the god's precincts under royal protection. An inscription records his ancestors' remembrance of Apollo, who "always spoke truth to the Persian," and orders his satrap to desist from imposing a *corvée* and taxes upon the gardeners sacred to the god.[40] And at Rhodes, Datis, the Persian general who received the Lindians' guarantees of loyalty and service, dedicated gifts of the highest honor to Lindian Athena: the jewelry, robes, and scimitar of the Great King himself.[41]

When the Ionians revolted from Persia and thereby went over to the Lie, the Persians did not explain that the temples they threatened to burn if the Ionians did not return to their loyalty had, by their peoples' defection, become shrines of false demons, *daivas*, who misguided their votaries to embrace the Lie, as Cyrus had burned the shrines of Nanna at Babylon.[42] Instead, the Persians' Greek agents took a line that made sense to the compatriots they were addressing.[43] The threats to fire the temples of Ionia were included in an ultimatum meant to terrorize the Ionians into submission (Hdt. 6.9.2–4), and the destructions of the Eritreans' and Athenians' acropoleis were represented as vengeance for their destruction of the temple of Cybebe at Sardis.[44]

Terror and vengeance were surely among the Persians' motives in these and other instances. But no Greek—certainly not Herodotus—ever appears to have discovered the religious significance of the Persians' cleansing fire.[45] When Xerxes burned the temple of Athena at Athens and then sent the Pisistratids up to the smoking ruin to offer sacrifice after their own manner, Herodotus wonders whether Xerxes had seen some vision in his sleep, or had even repented of destroying the shrine (8.54). Surely in his own mind Xerxes was destroying a place where *daivas* had been worshipped. He was establishing true worship pleasing to Ahura Mazda and Arta ("Justice") through the Pisistratids;[46] for all the Athenians only the Pisistratids and their companions in exile had not been followers of the Lie.[47]

In 490 the Persians punitively destroyed the shrines of the Naxians, who had staved off a Persian armada ten years before. But at Delos the Persian commander Datis made proclamation in which he addressed the Delians as *andres hiroi*, "sanctified men," and bade them return to their homes, assuring them that "I myself in any case so far intend—and it has been commanded of me from the King [Darius]—to spoil nothing of the land where the two gods [Apollo and Artemis] were born, neither the land nor the dwellers in it." Datis then censed the altar with a bloodless burning sacrifice of 300 talents of frankincense (Hdt. 6.97.2–3). The Delians, like the Delphians, never appear in Greek history in arms; their sacred immunity from the interstate warfare that possessed the other Greeks must be part of the meaning of *andres hiroi*; the Persians had no cause to make war against them or their gods. So Datis was able take Delos under his protection and give conspicuous homage to its deities. Moreover, these were *Greek* gestures of hegemony over Ionia and the sea, as Pisistratus (Hdt. 5.94.1, 1.64; Thuc. 3.104.1; Polyaen. 1.23), Polycrates (Thuc. 1.14, 3.104), and imperial Athens (Thuc. 1.96.2, 8.1; 3.104; 5.1) all demonstrated before and after Datis.

Although Herodotus reports instances that make clear for us the Persians' consistency in making war only on the gods of their enemies, and giving cult status to those of their loyal friends, he himself does not notice it. Such a distinction was foreign to Greeks. Gods were gods, and they took sides in war for reasons of their own, from the *Iliad* onward. Thus in the *Oresteia* Agamemnon's fate is anticipated when the audience learns he has destroyed the shrines of enemy Troy (Aesch. *Ag*. 339–47; 525–29); Aeschylus' Agamemnon recalled to the audience Xerxes, who was damned as a hubrist without distinction in the eyes of the Hellenes for burning the temples of Phocis and Attica (e.g., Hdt. 8.109.3).

Further, the idea of honoring or contemning deities according to their propensity for the truth, though not in principle incomprehensible to Greeks, was not intrinsic to their common conception of the gods. No Greek honored his gods in particular because they told the truth, least of all Apollo, who played a riddling game of wits with his oracular petitioners. Truth would emerge only in retrospect.[48] Hermes in particular is the Loki of the Greek pantheon, *polytropon, haimylomêtên, lêistêr', elatêra boôn* (Hom. *Hymn* 4.13–14); and it is Odysseus, most brilliant of mortals in ruses and deception, whom Athena admires and honors above all men (*Od*. 13.291–99).

What we see in the Greeks, therefore, is the absence of any imaginative or ethical basis upon which to understand either the Persians' ethical ideal of divinity, or their indigenous motives for making war upon the false gods of their enemies. Upon this blank slate of the Persians' religious conscience, Herodotus and the Greeks to whom he spoke would write their own solipsistic messages concerning the nature of these Asiatic barbarians.[49]

Troy and the Myth of Persian Origins

When Cyrus took Babylon he projected himself as a savior in the native idiom through the Babylonian priesthood, proclaiming that he had come as the Chosen of Marduk to restore the old religion. The Cyrus Cylinder implies that Cyrus himself escorted the holy image of Marduk in procession on the Babylonian high holiday:

> The lord of all the gods became terribly angry. . . . He scanned and looked through all the countries, searching for a righteous ruler willing

to lead him (in the annual procession). (Then) he pronounced the name of Ku-ra-ash, king of Anshan, pronounced his name to become the ruler of the black-headed, whom he (Marduk) has made him conquer. Marduk, the great lord, a protector of his people/worshippers, beheld with pleasure his (Cyrus') good deeds and upright heart (and therefore) ordered him to march against his city Babylon . . . going at his side, like a real friend.[50]

To the Babylonian Jews Cyrus said, "The Lord, the God of Heaven, has given me all the kingdoms of the earth and he has charged me to build him a house at Jerusalem, which is in Judah. Whoever is among you of all his people, may his God be with him, and let him go up to Jerusalem, and rebuild the house of the Lord, the God of Israel."[51] And in conquered Egypt, Cyrus' son Cambyses likewise venerated the Apis-bull. A tradition even arose—doubtless fostered by the Achaemenids' Egyptian collaborators—that made Cambyses' mother the daughter of the former pharaoh Aprias and thereby connected the line of Cyrus with the Saïte pharaohs.[52]

In Ionia, finally, under the reign of Darius at the latest, the Persians adopted Ephesian Artemis and Apollo, who were also worshipped by Lydians and other native peoples in contact with Ionian culture, as deities of special veneration.[53] Both before and after the Greek war of Xerxes the Persians not only patronized these cults of the highest political importance, but worshipped avatars of their own deities in these Greek gods. In making their diplomatic address to the Greeks in the language of their sacred traditions, however, the Persians were necessarily the pupils of their Greek adherents, men such as Histiaeus, the *syssitos* and *symboulos* of Darius at Susa (Hdt. 5.24.3), Demaratus of Sparta, and Praxilaus of Halicarnassus (9.107.2ff).[54] The Pisistratids too were among the exiles and petitioners who had reached Susa by the 480s,[55] and with them came the chresmologue Onomacritus (7.6.5):

Onomacritus went up [to Susa] at that time with the Pisistratids, who spoke in solemn terms about Onomacritus whenever he came into the presence of the King, and he would recite the prophecies; if there were some that portended failure for the barbarian, he would say nothing of these, but choose out the most fortunate and say how it was fated for the Hellespont to be yoked by a Persian, and describe the march. Thus would Xerxes be set upon by him with his prophesying.

In such ways the Persians learned an appropriate vocabulary of propaganda toward the Greeks and found agents to manipulate it on their behalf. The Persians' Greek servants invented important contributions to the Greek image of the Persians on critical occasions, as propaganda directed to other Greeks, which survived to deeply influence the popular mind. It was undoubtedly from the mouth of one of Xerxes' Greeks, for example, that the Hellenic world at large learned that Xerxes claimed hereditary possession of the Peloponnese through Pelops, who for this purpose was styled a Phrygian slave of Xerxes' forefathers (7.11.4). So too, on the eve of his crossing into Europe, Xerxes went up to Troy and rendered conspicuous homage to Trojan Athena (7.43): "When Xerxes arrived at the Scamander he went up to Priam's Tower because he wished to behold it. When he had seen it, and informed himself about each of the monuments there, he sacrificed a thousand oxen to Athenia Iliadis, and the magi poured libations to the heroes."

These hecatombs could not have appealed to the Persians themselves and the other Iranian contingents from inner Asia, to whom the Greek rites and their meaning were not only foreign but entailed the sacriligious pollution of fire by flesh. Surely it was Greeks of his retinue who taught Xerxes the historical significance of Ilium and bade him advertise the crusade with hecatombs to Athena at Troy. Very possibly he was encouraged by the Pisistratids themselves, since Xerxes' gesture is easily understood as diplomatic signal to Athens; in the *Iliad* Athena receives worship at Troy only once (6.271ff) and in the conspicuously Athenian form of an elaborately embroidered robe, which has led some scholars to associate this episode with the Panathenaea and the Pisistratids, who had a base near Ilium at Sigeum.[56]

Athens had been singled out by Persian propaganda as the object of the war for the burning of the temple of Cybebe at Sardis.

If this signal implied an offer of clemency and the preservation of the city, with its Pisistratid temples, in the event of the Athenians' timely surrender and a Pisistratid restoration, it would have accorded with Xerxes' attested efforts to bring the Greeks to submit without fighting (Hdt. 7.146-47). The Persians, moreover, had made an identical offer to the Ionians before Lade in fear of their naval power (6.9). Finally, Harpagus' conspicuous homage to Delian Apollo before the battle of Marathon could well have carried a similar message to Athens. For the temple at Delos had been rebuilt in the sixth century by Athenian craftsmen, almost certainly under Pisistratid patronage.[57]

But whatever its implications from the Pisistratid and Persian viewpoints, Xerxes' immediate audience at Troy consisted of Greeks and the Hellenized native peoples in his armada, who were also the participants in his feast of a thousand oxen. This sacred festival surely was intended to inspire and rally the Ionians, Aeolians, and the native peoples who had learned of their own Teucrian descent from them. Many Greeks of Asia associated themselves racially with Trojans and their native allies, including the Milesians and those other Ionians who founded their royal lines from Lycian Glaucus,[58] the royal Hectorids and Aeneads of Scepsis,[59] and the Aeolian peoples of Cyme, Lesbos, and Lampsacus.[60] From the mid-sixth century at the latest the tower of Priam was pointed out as a monument of the Trojan War itself,[61] and the cult of Athena was believed (on the evidence of Homer) to go back to the age before the fall of the city. On the occasion of Xerxes' presence, Athena's priests would have presided over the immense sacrificial slaughter and shared out the meat to their feasting coreligionists encamped by the thousands around the precinct of the goddess, a hallowed place that was a part of their homeland, as European Greece was not.

Xerxes' homage to the deities and shades of Troy spoke directly and a with grand meaning to the Ionians in Xerxes' armada. In Greek eyes Xerxes was the descendant of Memnon the grandson of Laomedon, whose barrow his Magi would have honored with libations.[62] At the tower of Priam, Xerxes put himself forward as the avenger of Troy in the eyes of his Asiatic Greeks, and thereby provided the seed from which grew the mythological *aitia* of the Persian Wars, which Herodotus attributes to the Persians at the outset of the Histories (1.1–4).

Xerxes and his Greek advisors thus appealed to the Greeks of Asia themselves to take historical vengeance on the Greeks of Europe. The recent disasters of the Ionian Revolt gave this appeal sharp relevance. Barely more than a dozen years had passed since the acropoleis of the Ionians' cities had gone up in flames at the hands of the Persians. Many of the Greeks in Xerxes' armada must have experienced the cruelties of the suppression of their revolt. But they all remembered that the revolt had been inflamed by the reckless destruction of Sardis by a fleet from Europe. Violent as the Persians had been against some Ionians, it had been the ships of the Athenians and Eretrians, summoned by the Milesians, that had been the beginning of their evils (5.97.3).

Herodotus would not have been the first Greek to recall this verse of Homer's appositely (*Il.* 5.62, 11.604; cf. Thuc. 2.12.3). The Persians' war propaganda since the Marathon campaign, that the war was being fought to take vengeance on Eretria—burned in 490—and now on Athens, directed the Ionians' animus away from them and toward Athens, the metropolis of the Ionians, which had betrayed its children by leaving them to finish a disastrous war they had not begun. Seen in this light the revolt easily evoked parallels with the destruction wrought by the fell host of Agamemnon. At Troy, therefore, Xerxes acted out a gesture consistent with a genuine climate of enmity against Athens among the Greeks of Asia, a gesture that defined and justified the Ionians' historical role in the present war.

This war, moreover, carried the Ionians' hopes of rehabilitation, not only through the King's rewards for good service, but even more by the exploitation of new Persian provinces. Victory also would restore to Ionia the commercial primacy and naval power that had since passed to Aegina, Corinth, and Athens. Thus the Ionians had good reasons to fight hard for Xerxes and Themistocles' appeals to the Ionians to revolt as brethren, or at least to hang back in the fighting (Hdt. 8.22), went conspicuously unheeded. Most of the Ionians fought well at Salamis (8.85.1, cf. 90. 1–3), and did not openly turn against the Persians until their power in Ionia was decisively broken by the slaughter at Mycale. The Athenians in turn justified their rule over the subject cities in part on the ground that they had fought with the Persians (Thuc. 6.82.4).[63]

After Xerxes' defeat, the victors would play Xerxes' game against him and thereby reinforce the Homeric interpretation of the conflict. At Elaeus on the Hellespont the Athenian admiral Xanthippus ignored the opportunity to win an immense ransom in order to take public vengeance on a Persian grandee who had profaned the sanctuary of Protesilaus, the first Achaean who died on the soil of Asia. The local Greeks said that the Persian had treated Protesilaus as a hereditary enemy of his King (Hdt. 7.33; 9.116, 120.4).

This vocabulary of epic was swiftly employed to give a Homeric dimension to the war, which at the same time put it at a Trojan distance. Two years after Xanthippus took vengeance for Protesilaus, the Athenian commander Cimon dedicated herms inscribed with epigrams for the capture of Eion in Thrace from the Persians. One of these remembered how the Athenians had gone to Troy (Plut. *Cimon* 7.5):

> From this city Menestheus with the Atreids
>   once led his men to Troy's holy plain:
> Among the close-armored Danaans Homer called him
>   Orderer of the Fight: The Best of Those Who Came.
> There is no unseemliness thus in naming
>   Athens' men now too Adorners of Battle and of Manhood.

The fit between Xerxes' gesture and the Greeks' own need for a heroic archetype had been a compellingly perfect one, and the association between Troy and Persia, which had been made by Asiatic Greeks for Persians, was turned against them by the Athenians. It was to be exploited with great power, especially in the vivid medium of tragedy,[64] in order to treat the themes of Hellenism and barbarism through the old stories.

In this way the epic of Troy took on independent life as the historical vocabulary of the enmity between Europe and Asia, which would ever after express the irreconcilable conflict of Hellene and barbarian, of Europe against Asia. It is relevant to the theme of this book, therefore, to digress briefly beyond the period treated here to observe the future of this mythologem.

On the eve of his invasion of Asia in 396 the Spartan king Agesilaus began to perform sacrifice before his assembled army at Boeotian Aulis, on the very spot enshrined as the place of Agamemnon's sacrifice of Iphigeneia for a fair wind to Troy. His act was interrupted by the Thebans, notorious as Medizers since the war of Xerxes (Xen. *Hell.* 3.4.3; cf. 7.5.35). Both his sacrifice and his campaign were inconclusive. But afterward Alexander would sail from Aulis to Troy, and his arrival in Asia would soon be hailed as the Millennium of the Trojan War.[65] It was an age when even the Persians themselves had recognized their association with Troy in Greek eyes, for the statue of a Persian satrap stood at Ilium.[66]

At Elaeus, Alexander sacrificed at the tomb of Protesilaus. At Ilium he sacrificed to Athena and offered libations upon the barrows of the heroes (Arrian *Anab.* 1.11.5–8; Plut. *Alex.* 15.8–9). The Macedonian king thus solemnly overlaid the image of Xerxes' identical homage with his own and, furthermore, assimilated himself personally to the image of his ancestor Achilles as did his great friend Hephaestion to Patroclus, each laying a wreath symbolizing victory upon the tomb of his epic counterpart.

Alexander also sacrificed to the shade of Priam to avert his anger; but this act he carried out at the altar of Zeus Herkeios, guarantor of the bond between guest and host,[67] in order to recall at the same time that the cause of the war had been Helen's abduction by another Alexander. He was not embarrassed by the fact of his name; he exploited it by suggesting that in his person the crime of his namesake was once more to be expiated. Alexander thus played upon the *Doppelgänger* effect that his act and his name projected not merely to imply that Hellas was on the march once again against Troy; his meaning was altogether more subtle and more consonant with his combined descent from Hellenic Achilles and Andromache, the wife of Trojan Hector and the ancestress of the royalty of Epirot Molossia.[68] At Troy, therefore, Alexander advertised the coming end of the millennial conflict between Asia and Greece in his own person, in a reconciliation and assimilation between Hellas and Troy that was remembered in the next century by Lycophron in his *Alexandra* (line 1440), in which Alexander is "the lion of the race of Aeacus and Dardanus" who ends the struggle between East and West. Alexander's Homeric propaganda was consistent with his aims and his future intentions toward the Persian aristocracy.

So closely had Alexander assimilated the heroic past to the historical present in his person and achievements that, after his death, this symbolic language could be made to express, with astonishing irony, opposition to his house and his memory. When Cassander son of Antipater, the enemy of the heirs of Alexander, restored Thebes he reconsecrated the city destroyed by Alexander to the protection of a most powerful relic. Reverently reinterred in the new city were the bones of Trojan Hector.[69]

Finally, Antiochus III, on crossing to Greece in 192 B.C. to "liberate" the Greeks from the Roman descendants of Trojan Aeneas, stopped at Troy *ut Minervae sacrificaret* (Livy 35.43.3). Antiochus thus offered the concluding chapter in this assimilation to the Romans who, as the conquerors of Asia in their turn, could not fail to add their gesture. When they marched against Antiochus, Lucius Scipio and the praetor Livius Salinator sacrificed to Athena at Ilium (Livy 37.37.2–3).

Throughout later antiquity this language lived on in the imagination of the Greeks as the vocabulary of the most sublime victories of the race, so that with time and repetition it finally tended to efface, like a slow rain of silt upon some submerged landscape, the historical distinction in the popular memory between the Trojan and Persian Wars. When the traveler Pausanias visited the Hellenium at Sparta in the reign of the emperor Hadrian he wrote: "The story about the place called Hellenion is that when Xerxes crossed into Europe and they were getting ready to fight for Greece, this was where they planned their method of defence. The other story is that the men who fought the Trojan War for Menelaos made their plan here to sail to Troy and punish Paris for the rape of Helen" (3.12.6, trans. Levi). After seven centuries the reality and the mythologem had united to refract in one another the whole remembered glory of the Greek civilization, which even then had become ancient.

Xerxes the Argive

We return to the year 480 to note that among those Greeks whose names would not be inscribed upon the Serpent Column at Delphi, which memorialized those who had fought Xerxes, were the Argives.[70] In 480 they collaborated with the Persians as far as their safety and their own impotence allowed. The Argives' Medism would not be forgotten (Hdt. 9.12), and it was recalled when the Argives sent an embassy to Susa shortly after the accession of Artaxerxes I (*reg.* 465–425) to renew their status of Friend of the Great King, which had been given by his predecessor Xerxes. Their mission was apparently a much-discussed diplomatic scandal (7.151). It recalled to many Greeks the context of the Argives' decision to remain aloof from the war against Xerxes. According to Herodotus (7.150.2–3),

> Xerxes sent a herald to Argos before he set out to march against Greece. It is said that on his arrival the herald declared, "Men of Argos, King Xerxes says this to you: 'We Persians believe that Perses is he from whom we are descended, who was the son of Danaë's son Perseus and who was borne by Andromeda the daughter of Cepheus. Thus we must be your descendants. It is accordingly fitting that we should not make war on our forefathers nor that you should oppose us by helping others, but remain at home in peace. For if I succeed according to my intentions I shall honor no one more highly than you.' " It is said that when the Argives heard these words they gave them great weight and, though they made no immediate solicitation, when the Hellenes invited them the Argives asked the Spartans to share the command, knowing full well that they would never give it up in order to gain a pretext for remaining at peace.

The Persian envoy's offer to the Argives of a paramount position in the Peloponnese gives this story its credibility. It is very similar to the offer, which has every claim to belief, that the Persians made to the Athenians in the winter after Salamis (cf. 8.140ff).

Xerxes' diplomatic claim to kinship with the Argives was itself contemporary with the war. It was known to the European Greeks at the time in association with the Argives' sympathy to Persia, and is proved by the language of the oracular response adduced by the Spartans shortly after Thermopylae,[71] which refers to *andrasi Perseïdêisi*, "Perseid warriors" (Hdt. 7.220.4), that is, by descendants of the Argive hero Perseus. The same is implied of Xerxes' descent by Aeschylus in the *Persae* of 472 when the chorus refers to his *khrysogonou geneas*, Xerxes' "line conceived in gold" from Danaë, who bore Perseus after Zeus had come to her as a shower of gold.[72] Elsewhere in the play, in the dream of the Queen, appear two maidens of *kasignêta genous*, sisters allotted from their paternal estate the lands of Hellas and the barbarians respectively (lines 185–87). These must be genuine reflections of Persian diplomatic propaganda that presented the Persians to the Greeks of Europe as a kindred people.

In style and intention these Persian addresses to the Greeks of Europe were identical to the aims of Xerxes' gesture at Troy. By inserting the Achaemenids directly into the line of descent of Greek peoples, Persian propagandists intended to neutralize their foreignness. This course certainly had already been employed by Greeks in the service of the Persian commander Datis at the time of the battle of Marathon, when we saw him in the temples at Lindos and Delos. In a section of his work based on Ephorus, Diodorus recounts the following exchange between Datis and Miltiades on the eve of Marathon:

> Datis the Mede had received from his ancestors the tradition that the Athenians were descended from Medus, who had founded the kingdom of Media. He sent to the Athenians demanding they return the ancestral sovereignty which had belonged to his ancestors. For before he had gone to Asia to found Media his progenitor Medus had been deprived by the Athenians of his kingship over them. If they returned it he would forgive them this crime and also their expedition against Sardis. Miltiades replied that according to his envoys' statement it was fitter for the Athenians to rule the empire of the Medes than for Datis to lord it over Athens. For an Athenian had founded the Median monarchy, whereas no Mede had ever held power over Athens. (10.27, condensed)

67

This version of Median origins had already appeared in Hecataeus' *Asia* (*FGrH* 1 F 286). It is a product of an age that still thought of Trojans and Achaeans as kindred peoples, and explains how Xerxes' Greek agents could represent him as descended from Memnon and Laomedon for one purpose, and from Perseus for another.

The mythological genealogies which drew the ancestors of all peoples into a network of kinship would simply go on existing after Xerxes' invasion by the side of the new idea that the Trojan War had been a chapter in the eternal conflict between the Greek and Asiatic barbarian. In the fifth century some Athenian tragedians were making Medus out to be the son of Medea and Aegeus, the king of Athens who was also the father of Theseus (Diod. 4.56.1). Hence Medus the eponym of the Medes and Theseus, the king of Athens who synoecized all Attica, were half-brothers. Medus' paternity by Aegeus is not absurd to the mythopoeic mind, but a necessary inference from the canonical element in the traditional tale, that Medea had fled to Athens having slain her children by Jason. If the Isocratean *mot* of Miltiades is discarded from the Ephoran account of Diodorus, what is left is a straightforward Persian diplomatic approach to Athens very like that made to the Argives in 481. It was based on a mythological genealogy already current in Ionia at the time of Marathon, which Herodotus reproduced in his catalogue of the peoples who followed Xerxes against Greece (7.62.1): "Everyone formerly called the Medes Arioi, but when Medea of Colchis came to the Arioi from Athens, they too changed their name. This is what the Medes themselves say about themselves." Herodotus assumed that the Medes themselves took their eponym from Medea because this is what their Greek spokesmen had claimed on their behalf, or what Greek mythographers who professed to be knowledgeable concerning the Medes and Persians said about them: they belonged to the same genus as the Persians familiar with the stories (1.1.1) who invented a Persian motive for making war on the European Greece out of the traditions of Greek myth.

As for the Persians themselves, Herodotus says (7.61.2–3) that "in antiquity were called by the Greeks Cephenes (i.e., 'people of Cepheus,' father of Andromeda], but Artaioi by themselves and their neighbors. But when Perseus the son of Danaë and Zeus came to Cepheus the son of Belus and took his daughter Andromeda a son was born to him whom he named Perses and left there; for it so happened that Cepheus had no male issue. It was from this Perseus that the Persians took their eponym." Like Memnon, Cepheus was not localized to a specific Asian vicinity and could therefore be planted in Persia at need. There the two founding monarchs coexisted; Greeks continued to refer to Susa as the City of Memnon even after the Persians became the people of Cepheus. Finally the stories merged and Cepheus himself became a king of the Aethiopians (Apollodorus 2.24ff).

Hellanicus calls the Persians Artaioi and the people of Cepheus Chaldaeans, that is, Mesopotamians, the same people of Babylon whom Herodotus calls Assyrians. Elsewhere (6.64) Herodotus reports a version, akin to that of Hellanicus,[73] alleging that the Persians themselves regarded their ancestor Perseus as an Assyrian who became Greek:

> I write according to the common account of the Greeks, who record these kings of the Dorians [i.e., the Heraclids] correctly as far back as Perseus the son of Danaë, and I shall show that they were Greeks: for by that time they had come to be counted as Greeks. I said "as far back as Perseus" and no farther for the reason that no human father of Perseus is named; but if the origins of the Dorians' leaders are followed father by father backward from Danaë daughter of Acrisius they will be found to be of direct Egyptian descent.
>
> But the version current among the Persians holds that Perseus was an Assyrian who became Greek. The ancestors of Acrisius they say are not related to Perseus but were, as the Greeks also say, Egyptians.

Hellanicus related that the Chaldaeans under Cepheus had invaded the land of Artaia, which was "the Persian land, which Perses, son of Perseus and Andromeda, colonized," and in his *Arkadika* even made this Cepheus out to be Arcadian (F 37).

This is to say that the Greeks identified the Medes and Persians in terms of their own mythical universe of human origins *even though* they knew that these Iranian folk identified themselves on the contrary as Arioi and Artaioi (from Old Persian *aryâ*). The

69

Lycians are a parallel case: they were formerly known as Termilae, and are still called Termilae by their neighbors, says Herodotus; but the Greeks call them Lycians from Lycus son of Pandion of Athens (1.173.2–3).[74] Nothing indicates more clearly how little weight the Greeks gave other peoples' accounts of themselves.

The ancestry of the Medes and the Persians explained from myth—that is, from the materials of early human history—is the Ionian Greek answer to the question of Iranian origins. The Ionian envoy of Xerxes to Argos did not invent Argive ancestry for his master on the occasion of his mission. He resorted to a received view, probably shared throughout Asiatic and European Greece by this time. As has just been noted, the parallel mythologem naming Medus the son of Medea as the founder of the Median empire goes back at least to Hecataeus. It appears in Europe by 472 in the *Persae* (765) of Aeschylus, who knew Hecataeus.[75]

The Argives could seriously entertain the view that their own Perseus had founded the line of Persian kings, and not merely because it flattered them to believe that an Argive hero was ancestral to the world monarchy on their horizon. The Ionian envoy of Xerxes knew his audience. At this time Argos had given to the world the mythographer Acusilaus, who is the only Argive author known to us before the Hellenistic period; his work, accordingly, must represent the character of high culture in late archaic Argos, which obviously harbored a strong self-interest in its own and other peoples' origins and descent.[76] Acusilaus taught that the Argive Phoroneus was the first human being; his daughter Niobe (in other authors, daughter of Phrygian Tantalus) was the first of Zeus' conquests, and she bore Argos and Pelasgus, the eponyms of the Argives and the Pelasgians of the Peloponnese, who in turn became ancestors of Perseus. Phoroneus' own son was Sparton, eponym of the Spartans (*FGrH* 2 T 17a; 2 TT 2, 3, 6, 7, FF 23a–28).

The remaining fragments of Acusilaus are testimony that the Argives in the assembly addressed by Xerxes' envoy believed, quite simply, that their own ancestors had given birth to humankind, as did the Greeks generally in their individual versions of antiquity. The Heraclid kings of Sparta, for example, contained in their ancestries representatives of the whole aboriginal Peloponnese, and their legends located the foundation of culture in the Eurotas valley.[77] Hellanicus could derive the Etruscans from a group of Pelasgians who had separated themselves from the Ur-Hellenes under their king Nanas (a great-great grandson of Pelasgus and Menippe daughter of Peneus), had taken Croton in Italy, and thence had settled in Tyrsenia (*FGrH* 4 F 4). Inexhaustibly at work was the Greeks' ethnocentric compulsion to populate the world with familiar images from their own traditions.

Xerxes' envoy to the Argives also addressed their belief that another of their heroes, Danaus, had been sired in Egypt in the line established there by Zeus and Io, before arriving in Argos to establish the line of Acrisius, who fathered Perseus' mother Danaë. We have seen that Herodotus defends this as the common Greek view, which calls the kings descended from Io Egyptians. Pherecydes, for his part, had made the Egyptian Agenor the father of Phoenician Cadmus and Aegyptus alike (*FGrH* 3 F 21). Herodotus' contemporary Euripides (*ap.* Apollodorus 2.1.4) followed a genealogy that made brothers of Aegyptus, Danaus the ancestor of Perseus, and Cepheus the first ancestor of the Persians. Egyptians, Argives, and Persians were thus united in a single ancestral nexus.[78] Together with the Phrygian Tantalus, a son of Zeus by the nymph Plutô who, with his son Pelops, first possessed the Peloponnese and sired the house of Atreus and Agamemnon, and the Phoenician Cadmus, who had founded Boeotian Thebes, they united Hellenes and barbarians into a single human world.

"Fire and Sharp Ares"

If, on the eve of the war, Xerxes' agents in European Greece were able to exploit these unities of myth successfully to present their distant master as a kind of Greek to some Greek audiences, the contrary reality held sway among other Greeks, especially the Athenians, who lay in the path of Persian advance.[79] Dread of the Persians in the aftermath of the burning of Ionia had cost the tragedian Phrynichus a silver mina for reminding the Athenians of their *oikêia kaka* (Hdt. 6.21.2), "their own troubles," by staging a bathetic *Fall of Miletus* for an audience who knew they were the Persians' next target.[80]

The victory at Marathon saved Athens and showed the immense superiority of the Greek infantry over the Persian levies. The passage of Aeschylus' *Persae* recalling Marathon (lines 235–48) focuses on the Persian Queen's apprehensions about that superiority and may reflect former Athenian assumptions for a few years after Marathon that Darius now respected that superiority. We shall see that Aeschylus also was to present the spirit of Darius ambivalently, by recalling him vengefully from the blessed ignorance of death to witness the ruin of his life's work, but nevertheless casting him as the moral genius of the *Persae*.[81] The years of *rapprochement* between Clisthenian Athens and Persia (*c.* 508–500), and the hiatus between Marathon and Xerxes' preparation for conquest (490–484), appear to be reflected in Aeschylus' "good" Darius. He was in life a ruthless conqueror but, defeated at Marathon, he could learn from defeat, or so the Athenians might think. Darius died in 486, before he could disabuse them.

Two years after his father's death, however, it became evident that Darius' son would resume the advance westward. Although the Persians advertised a veneration of Ionian Apollo and Artemis, these aloof warriors, who had emerged out of the continent of mountains beyond Babylon to appropriate the world's kingdoms, had wreaked unheard-of destruction upon the holy places of the Greek divinities. At the time of the resistance to Xerxes, these Greeks saw the Persians neither as a cultural question mark nor as a people of common descent, but as a profoundly menacing foe, who did not scruple even to make war on the gods of their enemies and to castrate their enemies' sons (cf. Hdt. 6.19.3, 32).

This fear was deliberately fostered by another category of Persian propaganda. The Persians' posture of invincibility in 480, as it is reflected in Herodotus and in the parodos of the *Persae*, is undoubtedly historical. This posture was designed to conceal real weaknesses of the Persians' warmaking capacities, especially at sea. But it was nonetheless obviously appropriate to an empire that had ingested all of the older powers of the East, and it had been deployed effectively against the Ionians. When the Persian generals feared that they would be unable to overcome the Ionians' 353 triremes at Lade, they resorted to psychological warfare by threatening condign punishments and mass enslavements, and declaring that Darius would send another fleet five times as great even if the present armada were defeated.[82]

These threats, according to Herodotus, divided the Ionians and emasculated their resistance; the technique was used again and again in Greece by Xerxes, whose best hope of victory lay once again, as at Lade, balanced on the fulcrum of his navy, and within that navy on the Phoenicians, to whom the Ionians had proven superior during the Ionian Revolt at the Keys of Cyprus in 499 or 498 (Hdt. 5.108). At Lade again, the Phoenicians had barely emerged victorious over the rump of the Ionian fleet that stayed to fight, consisting mainly of 80 Milesian and 100 Chian vessels and perhaps not many more than 200 in all (6.8, 14–15). At Artemisium the Persian navy would face an enemy fleet of 271 ships (8.1), reinforced by 53 more on the last day of fighting (8.14). At Salamis the Greeks mustered 366 triremes (8.43–47).[83] When Xerxes had ordered preparations for the war in 484, Athens' fleet—the core of the Hellenic navy—had not yet been built.[84] The war had turned out to be a much dicier proposition for the Persians, depending on the vital element of the sea.[85]

Herodotus tells the story that, when Xerxes was at Sardis overseeing the muster of his army, he was informed of the capture and impending execution of three spies sent by the enemy (7.145.2). The Great King ordered them spared and showed them the whole army, horse and foot; then he had them released. Xerxes explained that otherwise the Greeks would have no forewarning of his resources, which surpassed description. "But if they were to return to Greece," Xerxes thought, "then the Greeks would give up that liberty in which they were exceptional, and there would be no need to make the march against them" (7.146–47). In a similar vein, Xerxes allowed cargoes of grain to pass out of the Hellespont to Aegina and the Peloponnese, as if they were merely increasing his own stocks of food (7.147.2–3).

These strokes against the Hellenes' nerve followed naturally upon the ominous and unceasing ostentation of the Persian progress toward Greece, which had been in train for more than three years, since 484 (7.7). The canal across Athos was wide enough for two triremes (7.22.1), so that the Greeks would have no salvation this time from stormwreck (cf. 6.44.2–3); the Persians had established great bridges (7.33ff), roads, stores of provisions, and garrisons across the breadth of Thrace; their universal levy of fighting men was said to number in the millions; and finally, there was the Persian rape of Phocis, whose men had indulged the folly of resistance. The Boeotians did not make the same blunder (8.31–34).

It was later said that Xerxes could not believe that the Greeks at Thermopylae would abide his coming (7.209–10). Even after Salamis, when the Persians were reduced to Mardonius' forlorn hope, Alexander I of Macedon arrived in Athens to insist that Xerxes was invulnerable and to offer handsome terms of settlement (8.140α1-β3). From Lade onward this and other aspects of the Persian monarchy's "Middle Kingdom" ideology of invincibility and universal domination, attested in the Persian inscriptions,[86] are visible in the Greeks' observation of Persia.

The Greeks of the resistance faced the necessity, therefore, of inventing another identity, vulnerable to the righteousness of their own cause, for this ruthless and exotic foe of incomprehensibly great wealth and power: an identity that would exalt their own warriors and rebut the Persians' own propaganda of invincibility.

This propaganda in any case had already been vitiated for acute Greek observers, first by the difficulty the Persians had met in achieving their naval victory over the Ionians, and afterward at Marathon. It rang false and played into the hands of the Greeks of the resistance. What emerged from their imagination was a conception of the universal meaning of the war, perfectly in accord with their needs and beliefs, that seized upon the Persians' hollow boast of invincibility to portray the Great King hubristically appropriating to himself the power of divinity and themselves as the agents of his nemesis.

This conception lies at the core of the Greeks' memories of the war as they come down to us. Herodotus tells us that, on the eve of Thermopylae, when the Greeks broke up their parley at the

Isthmus to face the invader, they declared the manifesto of their cause. On the march to the pass, Leonidas, king of Sparta and supreme commander of the Hellenes, sent ahead to the Greeks living around the pass the exhortation that "the invader of Hellas was no god but a man; and there is no mortal nor will there ever be who is not allotted evil at birth, and to the greatest man the worst of evils (Hdt. 7.203.2; cf. *Il.* 24.525ff; Pindar *Pyth.* 3.81). This leitmotif of the Hellenes' propaganda was reinforced by the oracular responses attributed to Delphi that circulated at the time and other manifestations indicating the gods' alliance, recorded by Herodotus with assiduous piety. This crusaders' vision of the war exerted a commanding influence on the Greeks' memories and beliefs, and through them on the shape and purpose of the two greatest literary monuments of the war, the *Persae* of Aeschylus and the Histories of Herodotus. It is to these that we turn in the next chapters.

Four

Aeschylus: The Human Fabric of the *Persae*

> What are you but mere tools, which I can break at
> will; who exist only insofar as you can obey; who
> are in the world only to live under my laws, or to
> die as soon as I command it; who breathe only as
> long as my happiness, my love, or even my
> jealousy, require your degraded selves; and who,
> finally, can have no other destiny but submission,
> whose soul can only be my will, whose only hope
> is that I should be happy?
> —Usbek to the First White Eunuch: Montesquieu,
> *The Persian Letters* (1721)

> Russian policy has melted the Church into the State
> and confounded heaven and earth: a man who sees
> a god in his master scarcely hopes for paradise,
> except through the favors of the Emperor.
> —the Marquis de Custine (1839)

The Genre: History and Tragedy

The development of tragedy toward its first maturity in Aeschylus must be considered in the light of the tremendous events and dangers that defined the national ideology of Athens in the generation between the fall of the tyranny and the Persians' ongoing attempts to reimpose the Pisistratids in 500, in 490 and again in 480.

Aeschylus was present at the birth of the free Athenian state. When the Pisistratids fled Athens, he was about fifteen years old.[1] In the next years, as he neared manhood and full warrior status, Aeschylus witnessed the creation of Athens' new government and military power, victorious in one day over the strongest states of central Greece:

> The Boeotian peoples and Chalcidians
>   The sons of Athens broke by deed of war,
> Quenching dark in iron bonds their vile pride:
>   From the Athenians these horses, a tenth to Pallas.

This dedication of a bronze chariot-and-four commemorates the famous victories of 506.[2] This group and the cult statues consecrated to the Tyrannicides are the earliest known public monuments of the free demos,[3] who had now overturned the whole power balance of Greece and confined the Spartans' influence largely to their own peninsula.

The Pisistratids had taken refuge within the Persian empire at Sigeum, an Athenian possession in the Troad, while the Spartan king Cleomenes worked to restore them in preference to the revolutionary government in Athens, whose military power reduced the primacy of Sparta in Greece. In the face of this threat the Athenians necessarily ignored the fact that in Asia tyrants were everywhere favored by the energetic and rationalizing new regime of Darius; they made a formal submission to the Great King's brother Artaphrenes (Hdt. 5.73: c. 508 B.C.). The Athenians made this tie, which they must have thought committed them to nothing, to counter the Pisistratids' solicitation of Persian support.

The Persians were not yet prepared to move against Athens; but when they were ready Artaphrenes would demand that they take back their tyrant (5.96: 500 B.C.).[4] By this time, however, the Spartans and Cleomenes had acquiesced to the emergence of a powerful Athens as an ally against the Persians' advance. It was not simply the resistance of Corinth and other allies of Sparta to the return of the Pisistratids (5.75–76) that persuaded him to tolerate the new state of affairs. The daunting spectacle in the summer of 500 of the Milesian and Persian armada that sailed

against Naxos, the island that controlled the Cyclades and direct
naval communications between Asia and Greece, must certainly
have been the principal factor that changed the mind of Cleomenes.

The European direction of the Persians' expansion had been
evident already for more than a decade, with their occupation of
the Thracian littoral and the marriage of a Macedonian princess
into the Achaemenid clan (5.21.2, 8.136.1). Now, in Aeschylus'
twenty-fifth year, came a Persian-sponsored fleet into the Aegean
and with it the Persians' ultimatum to Athens to restore the Pisistratids. The Naxian expedition, which aimed to open the Aegean to
Milesian and Persian penetration (5.31), was undertaken after the
Pisistratids had won the Persians' favor and induced Artaphrenes
to unequivocally demand their restoration (5.96–97).

It is likely that amid these events, long before the invasion of
Xerxes and the production of the *Persae*, beginning with the mur-
ders that Hippias carried out after his brother's assassination, and
followed by his flight to Persia, a more sinister connection arose
between tyranny and barbarism than had existed in the previous
era, when Cyrus and Cambyses had avoided interfering with the
governments of Ionia,[5] and Pisistratus had lorded it magnanimously at Athens.

Aeschylus and Sophocles (b. 497/6) are the two surviving tragedians whose minds were formed in Athens' era of liberation from
tyranny and the threatened absorption into the world monarchy
of Persia. The fight against tyranny, at home and abroad, was the
great theme of their times. In what remains of their work, they
concentrated upon the catastrophes of tyrannical monarchs,
whereas under Pisistratus the character and fate of rulers—for
example Croesus—may have been nobly represented.[6]

Even if we were to grant this much, we are otherwise almost
uninformed on the subject matter and tendencies of the earliest
tragedies, composed by Thespis, and first performed at the Greater
Dionysia no earlier than 536/5, in Pisistratus' tenth year. Four
titles survive: *Phorbas* or *Games for Pelias*, *Priests*, *Ghosts of the
Unwed*, and *Pentheus*.[7] Only the last title suggests the possibility
of a political tragedy. However, we also have the title of a single

tragedy of Thespis' later contemporary Choerilus, the *Alopê*,[8] which shows the direction tragedy would take after Clisthenes in celebrating the new state. Alope, in Athenian legend, conceives by Poseidon the hero Hippothöon, eponym of one of the ten new Clisthenic tribes.[9]

The themes of tragedy surely must have reflected the atmosphere of the overthrow of the Pisistratid tyranny and the foundation of the cult of the Tyrannicides, at a time of increasing danger from Persia culminating in the brutal suppression of the Ionians. It would have been natural for Attic tragedians to celebrate the meaning of the city's liberation by depicting the self-willed fall of other monarchical houses. Indeed, the fall of Hipparchus and Hippias itself was treated by Athenian tradition in some respects as an erotic tragedy.[10]

Later tragedies such as the *Oresteia* and the *Antigone* are set in cities that are ruled tyrannically. In these plays, the political atmosphere is projected dramaturgically by the ethos of the chorus. In one-actor tragedy before Aeschylus it is thought that the chorus took a protagonistic part; but in extant political tragedies choruses are frequently portrayed as fearful, confused, and even servile before their rulers,[11] as for example in the *Agamemnon*, the *Seven*, the *Antigone*, and most extremely in the *Persae*.

The contrast between tyranny and the free polis, as exploited by the political tragedies of Aeschylus and Sophocles, celebrates the fragile achievement of *nomos* by the Athenians in their own day, and nowhere more explicitly than in the *Oresteia* of 458 B.C. The progress—dramatic and historical—within the *Oresteia* is built upon an antithesis between ancient Mycenae and modern Athens.[12] Aeschylus' audience travels imaginatively forward from the one city to the other, both in time and in the solution to the problem of public justice, in the course of the healing of the ancient curse and crimes of the Atreid dynasty—and those also of an earlier Athens. For the sanctuary promised by Athena to the Erinyes in the *Eumenides* (804ff) had in fact been founded, according to later tradition, in connection with the purification of the city in the late seventh century by the Cretan seer Epimenides, following the Alcmaeonids' impious murder of suppliants of Athena. The victims were the companions of Cylon, who had seized the Acropolis in an attempt to found a tyranny,[13] some of whose followers were killed "at the altars of the dread goddesses" (Thuc. 1.126.10), that is, within the then-existing precinct of the Erinyes themselves.

In the background of the drama, therefore, is the "curse of the Alcmaeonids" inherited by Aeschylus' younger contemporary Pericles (an Alcmaeonid on his mother's side: Hdt. 6.131.2; cf. Thuc. 1.127.1). Pericles had recently supported a limitation on the powers of the aristocratic Areopagus engineered by a senior popular leader, Ephialtes, an event thought to provide the political context of the *Oresteia*.[14] Ephialtes himself had been assassinated not long before the *Oresteia* was produced, but the killer's suborners were never identified.[15] In this respect the trilogy celebrates the resolution of the vendetta, under the laws of the city, between the Alcmaeonids and the descendants of their victims, while reinforcing ancient and terrifying religious sanctions against bloodshed before an audience that would certainly have included those men, powerful and unpunished aristocrats unreconciled to the democracy, who were behind Ephialtes' murder.

From Mycenae to Athens is a journey from barbarism to Hellenism.[16] The redress that is achieved in the citizens' court of the free city could not have been possible in the Mycenean tyranny, where the old justice that blood must answer for blood drives catastrophe onward from generation to generation. It is just this ancient conception of justice, a "barbarian" justice antithetical to the justice of the polis, which the chorus of Asiatic barbarian bondwomen celebrate in the *Choephori*.[17] No advance upon this conception of justice and no cure for the curse of the Atreids can occur so long as the action remains within the ancient venue of Mycenae.

In a similar way no moral progress can occur in the *Persae*, which is altogether Persian in the way that the *Agamemnon* and the *Choephori* are altogether Mycenean. The purpose of this chapter is to understand the *Persae* dramaturgically from the point of view of its original audience and to set it in its historical context. These purposes, as we shall see, cannot be separated. Aeschylus' depiction of Persia as a total and hermetic slave society, from which even mental escape is impossible, influences the nature of the choices that face the Persians in the ongoing war with Athens and her empire. This is especially true in the way that Aeschylus imagines these choices will be made by Xerxes, who is at the same time the protagonist of the drama and the real ruler of a real Persian Empire.

Aeschylus had presented his first tragedy during the anxious Olympiad of 499/496,[18] in the immediate aftermath of the fateful siege of Naxos and the insurrection of the Ionians under Persian rule. Not long after Aeschylus' debut, Phrynichus' *Fall of Miletus* was suppressed by the Athenians, who not only sorrowed for Miletus but feared for themselves: at the time of the play's production news may already have arrived of the Persian fleet and army which was gathering in the ports of Ionia in the spring of 492 (Hdt. 6.43.4ff).

But in the changed world after Salamis the Athenians could forgive Phrynichus everything. At the Dionysia of 476 the prize fell on his oriental drama, the *Phoenissae*, which—as we can infer from the *Hypothesis* of its successor the *Persae*—was scored for musical lamentations by a chorus of Sidonian women mourning the slaughter of their men in the great seafight.[19] His choregus was Themistocles.[20] The *Phoenissae* was a tour de force whose subject and choral performances must have forcibly recalled to the audience the author's long-forbidden play on the Milesians' catastrophe because, like his new play, the unhappy *Fall* must also have contained lamentations in the Asianic mode.[21] Thus the *Phoenissae* was a dramaturgical *déja vu* that defined the whole historical peripety of the Persians from the Ionian Revolt onward by evoking the catastrophe at Salamis in the action of the play and, in its choral recollection of the *Fall*, both the Persians' destruction of the queen city of Ionia and her recent liberation, with all the rest of Ionia, into alliance with Athens.

Reading the Persae

Aeschylus surpassed his older rival when, alluding pointedly to Phrynichus' *Phoenissae*, he presented his own spectacle of an oriental chorus chanting the dirges of Asia.[22] This play is the earliest tragedy to come down to us as well as the unique survivor of an experimental genre of tragedy as contemporary theater. Although its historical context is still dimly available to us we are ignorant of its context within the development of the form. However, the critical attention this play has received has come not from historians, but from philologists, who regard it as a tragedy that observes the intentions as well as the laws of tragedy and, beyond that, one that is remarkably sympathetic under the circumstances to the defeated enemy.[23] In this canonical view, the *Persae* is a tragedy whose victims are the imperial Persian nation and in particular its royal house. The sympathies of the audience are focused less on Xerxes—who after all had destroyed the homes and shrines of the Athenians—and more on the noble and morally sane Queen and the Ghost of Darius, a tremendous presence who expounds the transcendental meaning of Persia's catastrophe.

This view is far from doing justice to Aeschylus' full intention. Consider the character of the Ghost. Since Aeschylus set the *Persae* in Persia and moves wholly within the Persian viewpoint, to whom could he have provided the part of moral exemplar if not to a Persian? Euripides might have brought down a god at the end, but his was another kind of tragedy. Aeschylus brought on a ghost in the second act, with better logic and (I would say) better art. For the underworld, unlike Asia, belongs to no one nation but is the habitation of all men alike. By virtue of his passage to the underworld Darius has been universalized for Aeschylus' purposes, and by virtue of his brief liberation from death he is rendered more than human, though less than divine. The Ghost is not the ruthless conqueror of Greeks, but a "laundered" Darius who imparts the moral paedia of the *Persae*.[24]

Yet this is not the whole content of Darius' figure upon the stage. Aeschylus' audience would have included many of those Athenians who, it was later said, had approvingly witnessed the living sacrifice of three children of Xerxes' sister to Dionysus Eater of Raw Flesh after Salamis (Plut. *Them.* 13.2, *Arist.* 9.1–2), and then the crucifixion of the Persian governor of Sestus after his son was stoned to death before his eyes (Hdt. 7.33, 9.120.4). This pitiless audience also knew who Darius had been in life, and would demand to recognize their Darius in Aeschylus' Ghost. We shall see that Aeschylus never allows his audience to lose sight of the Darius whom *they* had feared and hated—the despot whose troops burned Ionia, the islands, and Eretria, and who had brought Hippias to Marathon.[25]

This audience, who had mourned many war dead in these years, would have seen in the Queen something other than what her virtues alone suggest to the modern reader. In her single-minded concentration on the welfare of her son she suffers in comparison to the polis-ideal of the warrior's mother, seen on so many Attic vases arming her son for the salvation of the community.[26] So the Queen has her dark side also. The mother of Xerxes, for whom nothing was really lost as long as her boy came home to her, was neither privileged to participate in the polis-ideal nor, as a Persian, was she even equipped to understand it. There is, therefore, more than one perspective to bring on the Persians in this play than the sympathy so admired by modern critics. To be sure, the Ghost and the Queen, if not the chorus and Xerxes, do exist as dignified, distant, and universal figures: it is this dignity and the distance of tragic universalization that many critics mistake for sympathy.

There are three reasons why Aeschylus was able to present Persians on the stage with dignity and distance, eight years after Salamis. First, from Homer onward Greeks considered warfare and its rewards, together with all of its atrocious consequences for the defeated, natural to humankind.[27] We live in an age of hate-mongering attitudes against which the *Persae* is measured consciously or unconsciously. Thus some critics seem almost surprised that the play is not Hun-bashing propaganda.[28] Greeks hated well and warmly, but they did not descend to the hypocrisy of damning the Persians as monsters *simply* because they wanted to conquer them, either in the *Persae* or in any other literature which we have concerning Greek opinions of Persians. The Greek attitude was above all agonistic, and vis-à-vis the Persians is perhaps best seen at the popular level in the obscene Eurymedon vase.[29]

Second, granting martial virtue to the defeated enemy enhances the quality of own's own victory. There is no glory in a walkover,

as Aeschylus knew. He emphasized Persian vigor in his battle
descriptions—while describing the slaughter of the enemy with
unquenchable gusto,[30] including a phrase, *kreokopousi dystênôn
melê*, in which the playwright takes poetic vengeance for his brother
Cynegirus, killed at Marathon by a Persian who hacked off his
arm with an ax (463; Hdt. 6.114; cf. Justin 2.9). Since the outcome
at Psyttaleia was of hardly any significance beside Salamis, Aeschylus' gory emphasis on the killing-ground on this islet in the straits
of Salamis has disturbed critics who do not perceive the force of
his emphasis from the audience's viewpoint.[31] At Psyttaleia, as at
Salamis, Aeschylus kills off the *best* of the Persians, *psychên t' aristoi
keugeneian ekprepeis / autôi t' anakti pistin en protois aei* (lines 443–
44). He has no time for the drowned subject peoples, slaves of
slaves, upon whom not incidentally the Phoenician widows of his
rival and predecessor Phrynichus must have spent much time and
effort lamenting. In the play, Psyttaleia is important because it
yielded the richest and most concentrated slaughter of the real
enemy, Persian "heroes," as opposed to the wallowing, anonymous
billows of sailors' corpses (lines 419ff). In this respect it is the
only Athenian action of the war that stands comparison with the
achievements of the Spartans, first against the Persian Immortals
and the royal kin at Thermopylae, and afterward against Mardonius' picked force at Plataea. Aeschylus was no sailor, but a warrior
proud of his courage against the Mede, and at this date so was
the mass of his audience.[32]

Third, in themselves the Persians would remain almost as unfamiliar to the Greeks of Europe in the aftermath of the war as they
had been before it. This abiding distance is immediately reflected
in the literature of the time, as in the epigram translated in an
earlier chapter and its companions.[33] Notably absent in the Greek
attitude to the Persians—they are presented contemptuously from
the Persian Wars onward, especially in comedy[34]—is the degree
of intimate detestation which, for example, informs the Simonidean
epigram (cited earlier) of Athens' victory over the Boeotians and
Chalcidians, a victory over men who were free warriors and as good
as the Athenians. The vivid emotion of this epigram celebrating a
victory over fellow Greeks is nowhere matched in the literature

of the victories over Persians, who came to Greece and were gone again after two battles by land and two by sea, and who were remembered as faceless strangers in procession.

The epigrammatic reflections on the Great War are uniformly transcendent and bloodless in mood; in language restrained, distant, and contemplative they celebrate the deliverance of Hellas from the fearsome enormity of the Persian mass, against which the individual warriors had fallen as imperishably glorious sacrifices to Greek liberty. The epitaph that Simonides composed for a friend who fell at Thermopylae, the seer Megistias, thus depersonalizes the Persians who killed him (7.228.3):

> Here is the tomb of splendid Megistias.
>   The Medes killed him when they crossed the Spercheus.
> He was a seer who clearly saw Death coming.
>   He chose to stand with Sparta's king.

In order to heighten the impact of Megistias' sacrifice—to make of him all the more an individually realized hero in contrast to the faceless horde—Simonides made the Persians an abstract quantity, to allow the reader to visualize, for a moment within the poem, Megistias' death from a Persian viewpoint as simply another anonymous Greek casually bowled over in the course of their march. The *Persae* is of a piece with this perception of the Persians at the time of the war, with this view from beneath the juggernaut, as it were, of an enemy surpassing human scale. But it also exploits the Greeks' reaction after the victory to regard the Persians as beings not altogether human, occupants of that limbo between humanity and livestock which slaves inhabited.[35]

It is this contrast, too, that stands at the head of Herodotus' Histories, when Solon recommends the pattern of life of the Athenian citizen-warrior Tellus to the barbarian monarch Croesus (1.30.3–5). Herodotus had memorized the names of every Spartan who fell at Thermopylae (7.224.1; cf. Paus. 3.14.1), but on the enemy side he gives only the names of the highest commanders (7.61ff, 99.1). Slaves of a despot possess no individuality; of the many famous Persians slain at Thermopylae he names only two sons of Darius (7.224.2).

The Problems

If the *Persae* is usually discussed as if it were a tragedy of the normal Aeschylean type draped in the externals of a Persian *mise en scène*, it is principally because, as the story of a tyrannical house, it fits naturally into the conventions and intentions of the genre as it developed afterward.[36] Critical attention is thereby diverted, however, from the two unique problems that the *Persae* posed to Aeschylus as a dramatist.

First was the problem of portraying the character and institutions of a wholly foreign people who are real and contemporary by the means of an art acclimated to the stories of Hellenic antiquity. The Persians were not Greeks and in this play they do not behave as if they were Greeks—not even ancient, "barbarian" Greeks. On the contrary, the *Persae* is a tragedy of the purest barbarian ethos, which could take place, in the terms imagined by Aeschylus, only among barbarians.[37] Studied from this point of view, the *Persae* is a *Schadenfreudestück* in which the universe of the Persians in the orchestra operates antithetically to that of the Athenians in the tiers above, and contradicts Hellenic nature at every point with radically pathological human consequences.[38]

The second problem that Aeschylus faced was the relationship of the play to the contemporary reality of the ongoing war, which Plataea and Mycale had by no means ended. It is one of the arguments of this chapter that both its ethos and the reality of the ongoing war define the *Persae* in singular ways beyond the scope of generic categories of analysis.

Aristotle denied tragic significance to the peripety of a morally depraved (*mokhthêros*, etc.) character (*Poetics* 1452b34—53a16). Although the *Poetics* is more relevant to later tragedy, Aristotle's observation casts its shadow back over Aeschylus' Xerxes; it becomes difficult to see how Aristotle, at any rate, could have regarded Xerxes' individual peripety in the *Persae* as tragic in any but the most rudimentary sense. For the usual—but unnecessary—assumption of critics that Xerxes is the tragic victim is embarrassed by the play itself.[39]

Those who know Xerxes best regard his transgressions as gross impieties committed by a violent and puerile character. *Thourios Xerxês*, his mother says, was taunted by malign associates to prove his manhood by augmenting his father's conquests (lines 753ff). The Queen's defense of her son is not altogether off the mark; but it is, after all, also a mother's forgiving view. His father's shade condemns him. Xerxes "ignored my commands," says the Ghost (783), and so he proceeded to violations of the divine prerogative so extreme as to constitute a moral insanity (750; cf. 805ff), which provoked Lord Zeus to smash him and the Persians in condign correction (739ff, 800ff). "When a man hurries the god meets him halfway" (742) is the judgment of Darius upon his son. No tragic significance inheres in the fate of the totally blameworthy. That is why Aeschylus is free at the end to employ satyr-play Grand Guignol in the kommos, when the shade of Darius and his consort have disappeared into the tomb and into the serail, leaving the lamenting Persians and their King as fatally uncompre-hending of the cause of their catastrophe as they were at the beginning.

Winnington-Ingram's view of the play, which has received little critical attention, provides the insight that unravels the entire intention of the drama. In the closing scene,

> Darius has come and gone, having interpreted events upon the highest moral and religious level. His closing instructions to the Chorus are that they should bring Xerxes to a proper understanding by the admoni-tions of reason (*eulogoisi nouthetêmasin* 830) so that he may cease in his overweening rashness (*hyperkompôi thrasei*) to offend the gods. Atossa leaves the stage on an errand concerned rather with his body than with his mind. The Chorus remain to greet their king. Is there any sign whatever that they have taken the words of Darius to heart? When Xerxes enters full of remorse, he is received with lamentations, recriminations. But of "admonitions of reason" there is no trace. For the Chorus, loyal subjects and faithful counsellors though they may be, are but ordinary Persians. Xerxes and his subjects are upon the same moral level, and it is not the level of Darius. The last scene returns to the moral level and the religious ideas of the first half of the play; and it is as though Darius had never spoken.[40]

In the *Persae* there is *pathein ton erxanta*, "the transgressor shall suffer" (Aesch. *Ag.* 1564) aplenty for the Persians, but not a jot of *pathei mathos*, "suffering's lessons" (ibid., 177).[41] This is a direct consequence of the Persians' ethos. They cannot comprehend the meaning of chastisements imposed by god because barbarians are uncomprehending by nature. In the *Persae* the chorus of Elders is incorrigibly mistaken concerning every issue raised in the play; and in the kommos Aeschylus exhibits a master who is no better than his slaves. Critics have been disturbed by the kommos, which veers dangerously toward the grotesque.[42] Aristotle said that tragedy intends to portray beings better, and comedy beings worse, than ourselves (*Poetics* 1448a16–18). The kommos, in which the Athenian audience witness the base Xerxes at the moment of his deepest abasement, is not comedy; but neither is it tragedy: Aeschylus' Xerxes is beneath tragedy.

But the Ghost is not. In the opposed characters of Xerxes and his father, Aeschylus creates superimposed dramas that meet different goals. In the drama of Darius he exquisitely draws the pathos of a great father cursed in his weak and deluded son. This is at once a posthumous revenge on Darius and a fully realized tragic reversal: Darius meets a posthumous fate, which he fully understands in its moral dimensions, which his noblest efforts in life did nothing to avert, and whose future operation in his house he will remain powerless to halt.[43] By contrast, Aeschylus denies to Xerxes and the Persians any moral understanding of their fate.

In this way Aeschylus also solved the play's relationship to reality. In 472 Persia was still at war with the Hellenes: therefore nothing can have changed in the incorrigible moral outlook of Xerxes and the Persians since Salamis. Dramaturgy and reality coalesce at the conclusion of the play. The play's *dénouement* returns the audience to the anticipated fighting season of 472; it is to the audience, therefore, that Aeschylus gives the task of composing a sequel outside the drama, aboard the triremes they will soon board for the summer's warfare.

The immense distance that separates us from the Greater Dionysia of 472 has effaced the centrality of the ongoing war and the Persians' barbarian ethos for the meaning of this play. Another, less obvious but also less excusable, factor contributing to misinterpretations lies in the neglect of two principles of criticism. The first of these is that Greek poets mean what they say.[44] When the Elders speak of Darius as a god (lines 157, 643) it does not constitute progress to comment that this language "is not, of course, to be understood literally."[45] The critic's task is not to dismiss what does not fit his or her conception, but to explain all of the facts given to the audience by the poet. One fact, of the highest importance, is the Elders' inability to distinguish between man and god in conceptualizing their rulers. This fact above all others defines that environment of spiritual delusion in which Xerxes sped to fulfill those *thesphata* which contained the fate ordained by Zeus for Persia in the passage of ages (lines 739–42, 800–802; cf. 762–64).

The other neglected principle is that in an Attic tragedy intended to stand alone as a whole of connected action and consequence— and the *Persae* is a tetralogy in itself[46]—the meaning is completed within the play: it is not left to the audience to imagine future and decisive developments unless these have been specified within the play itself and remain uncontradicted by events within the play.[47] Many critics imagine the Elders' admonitions of reason to Xerxes occurring *exô tês tragôidias*, "outside the play,"[48] because the Ghost has ordered the Elders to do so, and since choral admonitions appropriate to the Ghost's directions do not occur within the play the playwright is therefore referring them to an indefinite future time.

This view, however, ignores the fact that the Elders have their opportunity to instruct Xerxes within the play itself and do not take it—indeed, quite the contrary occurs in the kommos. Moreover the scenario of a future beyond the play's conclusion, in which the Elders will instruct Xerxes, not only contradicts present reality, that is, what the audience knows about the Persians' continuing intransigence; it also assumes that the Elders are reasoning beings who will do their job. This future is impossible in the Persia imagined by Aeschylus because the Elders neither reason nor do they ever do their job. Theirs is the unreasoning incompetence of ultimate slaves. Their incompetence and disobedience govern the play.

I address this point in detail later, in the context of the ethos of the Elders, but first let us proceed to an overview of the occasions of the Elders' incompetence. Their incompetence, together with the initiative of their mistress the Queen, drive the play toward repeated surprises of the expectations of the audience. These reinforce the dramatic definition of Persia as a society antithetical to Athens, a Persia that lacks any capacity for self-correction because it is deaf to the gods and to moral paedia.

The Action

The structure of the *Persae* up to the return of Darius' shade to the tomb forms a compressed trilogy whose parts are segmented by the respective entrances of the Queen, the Messenger, and the Ghost; the kommos completes the tetralogy, as if it were a satyr-play.[49] The action begins with the entrance of the chorus of Elders, alone on stage. In the parodos the Elders ponder the fate of the hitherto invincible army and voice their fears that an incomprehensible deity might nevertheless compass the defeat of their King. The Queen now arrives in her chariot of state and the Elders greet her with the following salutation (lines 150–58):

> Now here approaches radiance
> Like the eyes of the gods.
> Mother of the King
> My Queen. Prostrate in obeisance (*Coryphaeus and Elders kneel*
> We must all salute her. *in prostration*)
>
> Our Lady most exalted of Persia's deep-
>   girdled women
> We hail you. Xerxes' venerable mother and Darius' wife:
> Consort of a Persians' god—and mother of a god
> Unless the army's ancient *daimôn* has departed.

Dawn is at hand in the theater. The Queen voices her own apprehensions and describes the dream from which she has awakened, of Xerxes overthrown in his chariot by an Ionian maiden yoked to it, and the omen she lately witnessed of an eagle put to flight by a hawk. The Elders counsel her to supplicate the gods for the good fortune of the house and to prepare libations and offerings to Earth and the dead, reassuring her that these signs (obvious portents of Xerxes' defeat) are favorable (lines 224–25). She then questions them about the Ionian enemy, the Athenians; the Elders answer that they are numerous and wealthy, fight not with the bow but in close array with spear and shield, are free men who serve no master, and have already once before defeated a Persian host. At this she exclaims that the parents of the departed Persians have dire food for thought (245). Whereupon the Elders espy the Messenger approaching.

With his first words announcing the doom of the Persian host the Elders fall into a lament, which draws in the Messenger as well. He is rescued by the intervention of hitherto silent Queen, who brings him up short with an order to conquer his lamentations and attend to his report (295). She then interrogates him about the facts of the catastrophe. At the end she realizes the true meaning of her dream, and of the omen she had witnessed, and addresses the Elders on their failure to read them (518–20):

> O transparent sleeping vision of the night,
> Evils all too clearly did you show to me.
> But *you*, Elders, judged them all too lightly.

She determines nonetheless to follow their counsel in respect of the gods and retires to the palace to prepare a sacred offering to Earth and the dead, bidding the Elders meanwhile to devise trusty advice concerning the events and to receive Xerxes, should he arrive in her absence, with consolations lest some further evil otherwise befall him.

But despite this preparation for his entrance, Xerxes does not arrive and, in the stasimon following her exit (532ff), the Elders devise no trusty counsel in obedience to their Queen. Instead they fall again into lamentations as they contemplate the ruin of the King's power in Asia. Instead of Xerxes the Queen now reenters, shorn of the chariot and pomp that accompanied her first appearance, and carrying libations and flowers to propitiate the gods below. Then she once more takes the initiative, and instructs the Elders not simply to propitiate Earth and the dead but—in a departure once again from what the audience has been prepared to expect—to invoke the *daimôn* of Darius at the altar (598–622).

They do so with a congeries of appellations for Darius both human and divine (628–80). Their cries summon the apparition of their former King, who impatiently commands the Elders to tell him why they have called him, as he has but little time granted to him above the tomb. They will not do so, however, declaring themselves paralyzed by ancient reverence and dread of him. Again Darius demands that they speak, and again they refuse in fear to impart the news of the catastrophe (681–702). Thereupon he turns to his hitherto silent consort, who does tell him, immediately and without mincing words.

The Ghost now condemns Xerxes' impious venture and specifically forbids the Elders to consider another expedition to Hellas. Nonetheless the Elders—hitherto abject before the apparition of the old King—resist this counsel in a further display of the unreasoning will to empire (787–99) which they had revealed in their previous odes. The Ghost then departs with the direction to the Elders that Winnington-Ingram found to be the key to the play, to "bring Xerxes to a proper understanding by the admonitions of reason so that he may cease in his overweening rashness to offend the gods" (829–31). The Queen he directs to bring new vestments for Xerxes, who has rent his own to tatters in grief, and to console him with soft words (832–38).

The Queen exits upon her task. Xerxes arrives and it is the Elders, not the Queen, whom the shattered monarch encounters. They greet him neither with the admonitions of reason specified to them by the Ghost (830), nor by the soft words which he instructed the Queen to use, but with lamentations and recriminations. In this scene, Xerxes' only orders to his subjects are to accompany him in the violent mourning of the exodos that ends the play (1040 *ad fin.*), a spectacle that recalls the Elders' own fantasy at the beginning of the mourning women of Asia weeping, beating their breasts and rending their garments (120–25).

Aeschylus' "dramaturgical sleight of hand" keeps surprising the expectations of his audience.[50] The Queen's parting direction to the Elders upon her first exit, to receive her son kindly (529–31), raises the expectation that Xerxes will next appear;[51] an experienced playgoer might even anticipate that the ruined King and his mother will soon occupy the orchestra with the Elders for lamentations.[52] Instead the Queen herself reappears and—out of the blue—abruptly changes the announced direction of the action by ordering up the shade of Darius.

The Ghost in his turn commands the Elders to admonish Xerxes by reason and directs the Queen to clothe and comfort him, adding that "I know that he will bear to heed only you" (838), a remark that again miscues the audience. The implication of this line encourages the audience—against the grain of their experience so far—to expect that the Queen will soon be on hand for her son's entrance, while the Elders will respond with lyrics embodying their educated reflections on the disaster, in obedience to Darius' Ghost. This expectation is reinforced by her exit in preparation for his arrival (845ff), which "mimics the form and situation of the first" exit of the Queen,[53] when she had left only to return after the choral ode that occupied the interval of her absence (532–97). But Xerxes enters instead of his mother—just as before his mother had entered instead of her son—and the Elders have their way with him, in which they provide neither comfort nor admonitions of reason.

In sum the *Persae* induces the expectation of one climax but ends by providing quite another. This device gains in effect because it suggest an outcome—the rehabilitation and reformation of Xerxes onstage—that outrages the natural bias of an audience relishing the expectation of a squalid and humiliated Xerxes. The poet thus gratifies his audience all the more deeply for having teased and baffled them in the meanwhile.[54] Broadhead is among those critics who, misled by the ruse of Darius' remark to the Queen at line 838, have forced their interpretation to conform to the scheme announced by Darius by projecting its requirements *exô tês tragôidias*.[55] But just as other expectations are superseded in the previous instances of surprise entrances of the "wrong actor"—including that of Darius himself—events within the play will supersede this scheme. For in the kommos, the Elders have their opportunity to admonish Xerxes according to the directions of Darius within the play itself and before the eyes of the audience. But they do not.

There are strong arguments for accepting at this point Wilamowitz's attractive assignment to Xerxes of the floating line 955, [*oioioi*] *boa kai pant' ekpeuthou*, "cry out and search into everything," thus giving the Elders a positive invitation to enlighten him.[56] Although Wilamowitz did not make the argument for it, his attribution possesses a compelling dramaturgical logic, in that it completes the armature of mirror-correspondences created by the Elders' failures and acts of disobedience: at the end of the play a (vain) demand by Xerxes at his entrance for the Elders to enlighten him would recall both the Ghost's (vain) demand to the Elders to enlighten him upon his entrance, and the Queen's (vain) demand at her first entrance for enlightenment from the Elders about her visions.

Reality

husband's ?

Thus, despite her father's directions and his own to the chorus, Xerxes will not be enlightened at the close of the *Persae*. This outcome is inevitable, if the play is to respect its historical context. For outside the theater the Athenians were actively at war with no call for quarter from Persia. Only five or six years had passed since the Athenians had founded their hegemonic alliance with the King's former Greek subjects for the stated purpose of ravaging his territories (478/7 B.C.: Arist. *AP* 23.5), and they were still campaigning in Thrace and Asia Minor.[57] More than another decade was to pass before the first diplomatic contact can be attested between Athens and Susa in the aftermath of Salamis (Hdt. 7.151; cf. 8.140–44), with Xerxes' successor.[58] At home the Persian menace continued to be represented as immediate and irreconcilable, especially in the persecutions of Pausanias and Themistocles as Medizers (Thuc. 1.96ff, 128ff).

Events themselves, therefore, render absurd any interpretation of the *Persae* that imagines that Aeschylus wanted to bring Xerxes to his senses at the dramatic date of 480 by any agency, let alone by the Elders, whom the playwright draws as perfectly servile, incorrigibly deluded, and psychologically emasculated beings. No Athenian in 472 was ready to be convinced that Xerxes had learned moderation, and no tragedian who took that line could have hoped to win the approval of the judges, much less the liturgical sponsorship of Pericles the son of Xanthippus, whose Alcmaeonid relations had conspicuously advertised their enmity to the Pisistratids and to the Persians as a matter of political necessity ever since the scandal of the shield-signal at Marathon.[59] The Persians tenaciously maintained claim to the territories lost after 480 and would see to the recovery of their Asiatic possessions by the end of the century.[60] At this time the Persians and Xerxes were not ready even to speak to the Athenians until their navy had once more been smashed at the Eurymedon, and a new emperor, the first Artaxerxes, had come to the throne.[61]

These facts explain why, at the dramatic date of 480, Aeschylus' Elders remain stubbornly revanchist at the end of the play. In their opening ode, in which they announce their character, the Elders sing that it is the Persians' divinely ordained mission to conquer others, as if by compulsion (mss. lines 101–6).[62] But in fact this is not Persia's destiny; it is only the Elders' ambition. For the Queen's questions about Athens make it evident that they know—and have ignored—the lesson of Marathon. Their will to conquest remains unquenched even in the face of supernatural authority. The Ghost announces to them the mandate of Lord Zeus, that the Persians' monarchy is given to rule in Asia alone (759ff), and warns them accordingly against future invasions of Greece (790–92). The Elders respond by ignoring both the will of the god and that of their former master: they propose the dispatch of a picked force with a boldness that contradicts the reverential fear in which they met Darius' apparition (693ff).[63]

Autistic belligerence of this kind is a leading element of the Elders' ethos. Before the Ghost's arrival they had voiced a central question (555–56). Why had Darius in his time been (from their point of view) a blameless ruler? His shade arrives to answer them at length.[64] Yet when he retires to the tomb the Elders ignore his transcendental message; instead they dwell upon Darius' conquests and the corresponding magnitude of his son's defeat (852ff), in terms that recall the ambitions of global conquest they had voiced at the beginning. It is indeed, in Winnington-Ingram's observation, "as though Darius had never spoken." The audience most logically expect a chorus of the Elders' character and outlook to nurse, rather than to renounce, ambitions on Greece when Xerxes resumes his sway over the Persians *exô tês tragôidias*.

The Ethos of Aeschylus' Persians

Were the Elders to heed Darius' mandates for Persia and for Xerxes they would not only betray their own character and the audience's perception of Persian revanchism in 472. They would also contradict the play's basis of dramatic consequence, which consists of successive acts of disobedience within a society predicated on obedience. The first cause of the Persian catastrophe lay in Xerxes' disobedience to his father's will (line 783), which involved him simultaneously in disobedience to the ordinances of divinity (807ff).[65] The Elders disobey Darius at the central moment of the drama, when his shade appears (693ff).[66] In their final exchange as he disappears he bids them *khairete*, "rejoice: even in disasters vouchsafe gladness to your spirit, for wealth is nothing to the dead" (840–42). *Êlgêsa* is the Elders' contradictory rejoinder: "I grieve to hear the barbarians' many woes, accomplished and yet to come" (843–44), they reply, as they fall into that soliliquy in which they will ignore the unwelcome wisdom of Darius. Then comes Xerxes' arrival and the concluding kommos, in which the Elders disregard Darius' command and disobey not only the Queen's earlier instruction to comfort Xerxes on his arrival, but (if we accept Wilamowitz's emendation) Xerxes' own despairing call for enlightenment.[67] They deny to Xerxes the tragic paedia of his catastrophe, and confirm to the audience once again and finally that they themselves have learned nothing from Darius' apparition.

The theme of obedience and disobedience is central to the drama because Aeschylus defines Persia as a slave society and represents Persia microcosmically as a household in which the royal family are the masters and the Elders their slaves. The King's subjects did not adore him as their god (line 710, etc.) altogether from delusion: like a god he held their lives and fortunes in his hands (cf. 369–71). Armed by this fact and by the rhetoric that called the Great King's subjects his slaves, the slaveholding Athenians who made up the best part of Aeschylus' audience would interpret the action and the ethos of the *Persae* from a standpoint squarely within their own daily household experience of slave manage-ment.[68] The irony borne in every detail of punctilio in the relations between the Elders and their rulers is most visible from this perspec-tive. Their rulers address the Elders in language of affectionate and familiar trust and dependence. The Queen commonly addresses them as *philoi*, "friends" (163, 206, 231, 445, 598, 619). Darius' shade greets them as *pista pistôn êlikes th'êbês emês* (681; cf. 528), "Trustiest of the Trusty, companions of my youth." "The Trusty," *pista*, is in fact their proud collective title as the most faithful servitors of the Crown, and by this title they introduce themselves to the Athenian audience (2). It is extended also to the defeated dead, in particular to the band of noblest and bravest Persians who perished at Psyttaleia (443) and to the King's Eye himself (979).

There is an obvious, even cheap, irony in Aeschylus' choice of title for a chorus that is anything but worthy of its trust and for the leaders of the annihilated armada. But that was not the whole of his intention. The affection that often did exist between slaves and masters was a key element in the strategy of the relationship. Xenophon was to explain this strategy in a remarkable passage of the *Oeconomica* (14.6–9: trans. Marchant, adapted):

> By applying some of these principles [from the laws of Dracon and Solon] and others from the laws of the Great King I try to make the house-slaves honest in the business that passes through their hands. For the laws of Dracon and Solon only punish the wrongdoer; however, the laws of the Persian king not only punish the guilty but also reward the upright: thus seeing that the honest grow richer than the dishonest, many slaves, although greedy, nevertheless take great care to avoid dishonesty. So should I find any slaves still persisting in dishonesty though well cared-for, I rid myself of them as incorrigibly avaricious. If on the other hand I discover anyone who is honest not simply

because he gains by honesty but also from a desire to win my good opinion, I treat him like a free man (*ôsper eleutheros*), not only by enriching him but by regarding him as a gentleman (*kalos k'agathos*).

Xenophon's admiration for Persian justice is taken up later;[69] what is relevant here is that the author, an Athenian slaveholder and a passionate student of the art of inducing willing obedience from loyal subordinates, argued that the slave who is cherished, reassured, and rewarded for doing his best by a steady and benevolent master is a slave who is likely to do his job with that initiative which is defeated by fear of the master's wrathful and undeserved punishment. Had Xenophon been able to witness the *Persae* he would have been struck by the inconcinnity between Darius' evident regard for the Elders and their old dread of him (*deos palaion*, 703), and conclude that something was very wrong with the slave-handling methods of the Persians, including Darius, in this play.

Here again the *Persae* possessed a resonance for its original audience that is unavailable to the modern reader, for two reasons. First is the nearly universal tendency to interpret the play according to formal ideas of how tragedy conveys meaning, ideas that undervalue the psychological realism of a highly stylized form—what European, or perhaps what modern Japanese, can respond to Nō drama with the intensity of the audiences for which it was originally performed? Second, the modern reader inevitably is far from sharing the outlook of the Athenian slaveholder. The fact that the Elders are unable—or unwilling—to give the Queen the correct interpretation of her dream and the bird omen she had witnessed as obvious portents of disaster, or to convey the news of the disaster to Darius upon his epiphany because they are frightened silly of him, would convey to an audience intimately habituated to the means, objectives, and psychology of slave management the play's fundamental perspective of Persia as a world whose very perfection in altogether destroying the will and initiative of the slave defeats even the masters' own goals. In the *Persae* the masters hear only what their slaves believe is safe to let them hear.

From the *Persae* onward, capricious cruelty toward those in their power becomes a leading element in the Persian stereotype.

When Herodotus' Xerxes consults the exiled Spartan Demaratus on the prospects for battle before Thermopylae, Demaratus asks, "Shall I tell you the truth or what will please you to hear?" To his credit, Herodotus' Xerxes replied that he would prefer the truth— Demaratus must after all be given his opportunity to warn Xerxes— but Xerxes also thought it necessary to reassure Demaratus that he would not thereby fall into danger (Hdt. 7.101.3).[70] For, notwith-standing his forthcoming mood on this occasion, Herodotus' Xerxes is capable of ferocious caprice. In Asia he had ordered the youngest son of a benefactor, who had requested in consequence of an omen that Xerxes spare the eldest alone of his five sons from service with the army, to be cut in half and the halves displayed on each side of the road as the army passed between (7.27–28, 38–39). The enraged Xerxes addressed the father as "my slave," saying, "Impulse dwells in men's ears; when they hear worthy things they fill up the body with pleasure, but when they hear the opposite it swells with anger" (39.1). The theme of servile deceit and perfidy, *apistia*, is the obverse of the theme of despotic cruelty and caprice, and in the hostile Persian stereotype it becomes characteristic of the masters themselves. *Persica fides* is foreshad-owed in Herodotus' Cyrus and is uppermost in his Darius;[71] it is a major theme in Xenophon's *Anabasis*.[72]

The Xerxes of the *Persae* threatened his captains with execution before the battle (cf. lines 369–71) and, according to Herodotus, actually beheaded some defeated Phoenician captains at Salamis (8.90.1–3). The inventive atrocity of Persian punishments was studied by the Greeks with lascivious fascination. Their description becomes a feature of the literature on Persia as a prominent element of their conception of the Persians' nature.[73] In life, Aeschylus' Darius had available to him the methods of his son; that is why his old courtiers dare not give him the ghastly news. They claim indeed that they fear to do the Ghost's pleasure by "uttering what is hard to utter to a beloved" (700–702), but only to pass the burden on to the Queen, who need not fear their master's wrath.[74]

The slave's fear of capricious punishment extends as far as the Elders' theology and, indeed, explains it. To them their former master is actually (643) and functionally in his lifetime (711) a god, and to them gods are beings of incalculable and deceitful will (mss. lines 93–94).[75] The only free persons in the play (besides the victim Xerxes) are the masters, namely, the Queen and the Ghost, and because they are free their theology differs from that of the Elders. As we shall see, the Queen is morally sane in just those ways that the Elders are not, and the Ghost is of course the enunciator of the gods' true and universal justice, of Aeschylus' own theology, as has often been observed.

Sufficient information exists about the ways and attitudes of Athenians toward their own slave population, at any rate from the later fifth century onward, to infer an audience perspective of the slave society in the *Persae*.[76] This society differs concretely from Athens precisely in that the comparandum of the free man and therefore the goal of manumission do not exist. At Athens both sentiment and legal protection against cruelty to slaves existed. The argument for clemency based on the common humanity of slaves at Athens goes back formally to Xenophon and Plato (*Laws* 776cff).[77] Neither private nor public slaves at Athens were altogether at their master's disposal, but enjoyed some protection in law and custom, certainly before the fourth century.[78] Although at Athens too the predicament of the slave and the slave regimen internalized the slave's sense of helplessness, inferiority, and "otherness,"[79] the picture of the slave in Attic comedy and in the complaints of Laconizing conservatives such as the "Old Oligarch" (Ps.-Xen. *Resp. Ath.* 1.10–12), who is offended by the freedom of manners and dress accorded to slaves, suggests the stereotype of a slave full of alacrity, intelligence, and—in New Comedy especially—intrigue. In the later classical period the intriguing slave becomes a stock type in comedy, which was the theater of contemporary home life.[80] This is the type of slave who possesses the clever initiative to manipulate and exploit his relationships within the master's family. In real life he would be on his way to living on his own among the class of *khôris oikountes*, including slaves working to purchase their freedom and join the sprinkling of manumitted metics.[81] Demosthenes commented on the outspokenness granted to slaves as a commonplace in his day, when the category of slaves *khôris oikountes* was reckoned along with the metics for military service (Dem. 9.3, 4.36): even a category of private lawsuit existed against slaves "for maligning a free man" (Arist. *AP* 59.5).

So even in the treatment of slaves Athens was considered outrageously libertarian by the oligarchical mind. Compared to the Persia imagined by Aeschylus, Athens was, if not altogether at the opposite pole, so different a society as to constitute a wholly distinguishable slave regime and which therefore produced a wholly different slave type. A slave regime founded upon encouraging the honest initiative of one's servants by steady fairness and reward can work only in a society in which the humanity of the slave is acknowledged within the psychology of the relationship and expressed socially by institutional means of manumission into a free society. The *anêr Hellên* who in the *Persae* carries the false tale to Xerxes that begins the doom of the fleet (line 355) was a house-slave of Themistocles bearing the foreign name Sicinnus, whom he freed and established as a wealthy citizen of Boeotian Thespiae (Hdt. 8.75.1), as free a man and as honorable as any Greek.

Thus we arrive at the only sense in which the Persian Elders are truly *pista pistôn*, "most faithful of the faithful," as the arising Ghost addresses them (line 680; cf. 2). Their whole being is attuned to servitude as the natural condition of life, whereas the masters regard the perfect devotion of their servants as natural in turn and accept adoration as their due. Government in this society is simply a regime of slave management in which the slave cannot hope or even imagine himself to be anything but a creature at the full disposal of his masters, much less a potentially free man. The slave's only psychological choice in this predicament is to identify his interest totally with the fortunes of his masters' household while avoiding any initiative that carries blame or the risk of offending the masters. Although the Elders enjoy a simulacrum of the free man's *parrhesia* in the kommos when Xerxes has destroyed his patrimony and their common prosperity, *parrhesia* is really a part of their political nightmare when they contemplate the consequences of the disaster to the King's power (591–94).[82] In fact they conform immediately to Xerxes' posture of remorse and self-abasement before them (913–17). Their recriminations in the kommos not only answer their master's lead but remain firmly within the bounds of their interest in the survival and prosperity of their household. Their loyalty is, and should remain, unquestioned. The Elders do not interpret the Queen's dream correctly as portending disaster. In this case they lack the insight. But neither do they have the will to inform the Ghost that the achievements of his reign have been destroyed by his son. Insight and will together are absent from the character of these psychologically emasculated "ultimate slaves."[83]

Gender and Mind in the Persae

Hoi men andres gegonasi moi gynaikes, hai de gynaikes andres: "My men have become women and my women men," is the famous lament placed by Herodotus in the mouth of Xerxes as he witnessed the disaster of Salamis (8.88.3). Herodotus knew the *Persae*, and here possibly his Xerxes speaks a memorial to that drama, familiar as it was to his Athenian audiences in revival.[84] For in the *Persae* the men are women and the Queen is a man. Every recoverable detail of the Persians' ethos shows that the nominally male Elders are dramaturgically female, as well as Xerxes himself; for he takes on the Elders' ethos in the kommos, when he directs them in the lamentations of the exodos.

The Elders' role consists largely of ritual lamentations of a kind mandated by Greek custom to women mourners alone;[85] but these go far beyond what was permitted at Athens even to women.[86] In their first and third odes, the Elders themselves are made to imagine the mourning women of Persia uttering antiphonal cries (lines 121) accompanied by insatiate tears and moans (133–34, 539, 545) as they rend their garments (125, 537–38)—just as Xerxes is visualized in his mother's dream (199) and reported by the Messenger *rhêxas de peplous k'anakôkêsas ligy* (468), where *peplous* carries the taint of effeminacy already visible to the audience in the trailing robes worn by the swaying Elders (1060). At the end they join Xerxes in a striking realization of their own earlier images of the bereaved widows of Asia when they all depart in an orgy of weeping, antiphonal cries, Mariandynian and Mysian laments (938, 1054), beating of breasts, tearing out of beards and hair, and rending of garments (935 *ad fin.*).[87]

I have argued that the direct inspiration of the Elders' female ethos was the *Phoenissae* of Phrynichus. The *mise en scène* of the *Phoenissae* likewise had been Susa, but the chorus had been the mourning widows of the drowned Phoenician sailors, and the prologue had been recited by a palace eunuch—a being who was castrated, foreign, and enslaved. The prologue of the *Persae* echoed its predecessor in its first line, which is sung by the Elders. These correspondences, and the direct testimony of the *Hypothesis*, together compel the conclusion that from its very opening Aeschylus meant his chorus of Elders to recall both the enslaved eunuch and the barbarian women of the *Phoenissae*.

The contrasting figure of the Queen renders the Elders' effeminacy in high relief. She is the foil to the Elders and dominates the first two panels of its triptych structure. Essentially the Queen is male in her dignity, intelligence, moral sanity, and iron self-control—the qualities, in sum, that the Elders altogether lack. Her sanity is uppermost from the beginning, in her entering soliloquy addressed to the Elders in response to their salutation (159–72).[88]

> These very fears bring me from the gold-appointed palace,
> Beyond the bedchamber that we shared, Darius and I.
> Painful care lacerates my heart as well. To you I say
> Dear friends, I am utterly afraid
> That our great wealth in its headlong rush
> May overthrow the prosperity which
> Darius gained—not without some god's aid.
> These very cares, pondered doubly, speak silently in my mind:
> Neither is unmanned wealth revered in honor by the many,
> Nor is the poor man's worth illumined in true light.
> We have ungrudged wealth, yet I fear for my very eyes:
> For the eye of this house, I say, is the presence of its lord.
> So matters stand. Advise me then, Persians,
> Show yourselves in aged, trusty wisdom.
> For all the surety of my thoughts lies in your counsel.

Her words implicitly contradict the entire complex of misconceptions uttered by the Elders in their parodos and salutation, in particular their regard of Darius as a divinity and their vision of Xerxes divinized by victory (158). She is right and they are wrong about fundamental issues. She knows that Darius was human (cf. her lines 709–11 versus the Elders' line 643, *Persân Sousigenê theon*) and she acknowledges the role of genuine deity in hitherto preserving the prosperity of Persia. Moreover, she fears human excess, playing on that very *plêthos* which the Elders have just been celebrating as the surest guarantee of Persian invincibility (21–22 and especially 73–92; cf. 790–94).[89] She is morally sane in just those ways in which the Elders are not: that is why she is vouchsafed in her visions a communication with the divine to which the Elders are altogether blind, and that is why her first waking initiative is a rightly directed attempt to propitiate the gods who ward off evil (202–5).[90]

Wilamowitz long ago saw the aporia created by the Elders' resolve, as they conclude their long and thematically comprehensive entering song, to devote *phrontida kednên kai bathyboulon*, "careful and deeply pondered thought," to the fortunes of Xerxes and the chances of the war in Greece (142ff: the parodos' closing anapests echo 1–64). But their resolve is plainly otiose, since they have evidently been trying to devote careful and deeply pondered thought to these questions through the whole of their soliloquy, with no material result.[91]

In this play about the mental processes of barbarians, references to thought and to the mind recur with insistent frequency. The Elders' *phrontida* would require an article in itself to fully gloss. *Phrên, phrenes, phroneô* and its cognates occur nineteen times in all.[92] The problem of the Elders' aporia, here in the parodos and throughout the play, is insoluble unless we regard it as the product of their ethos. It is in fact the product of their belief that everything lies in the decision of a trickster deity, who with smiling countenance draws his victim into the snares of ineluctable disaster (mss. lines 93–100). The logic of their theology itself—which lacks any conception of divine justice—deprives them of any means of reasoned judgment about the course of events. Should Persia's *daimôn palaios* now desert the army (158), the absent armada's apparently invincible weight and its accomplishment in mastering both elements under its warlike and divinely descended new lord—indeed, Persia's own divinely ordained destiny of incessant conquest (as they would have it)—would count for nothing.

The emotional structure of the Elders' first ode marches in step with their intellectual and theological aporia. At first they salve their forebodings in the absence of news of the host with images of its greatness and its *thourios archôn, isotheos phôs* (73, 80), its "impetuous chieftain," a "mortal equal to a god."[93] On this bubble of optimism they rise to the momentary conviction that the King's armada shall prove invincible by divine ordinance, now as in the past (mss. lines 101–6).

But swift depression comes upon them when they next reflect that no man can escape the *dolomêtin d'apatan theou* (mss. line 93), the wily deceit of the god, who entangles his victim just as he is lulled by the smiling moment (mss. lines 93–100). Their brief buoyancy evaporates into a sudden, anxious fantasy of annihilated Persian manhood and bereaved Persian womanhood (115–39), which anticipates the threnodies of the Messenger scene and the kommos. The Elders' vacillation between emotional extremes is the obverse of their intellectual and theological predicament: since all of their hopes lie in the gift of an unfathomably deceitful deity they are left to swing without moorings from elation to despair.

Facts—which are the concrete material of careful thought about the possibilities in events—arrive only with the Queen, wherein the Elders' aporia becomes all the more evident. The Queen has been vouchsafed true visions (176ff, cf. 518–20), which we "can interpret as we read, as could the Athenian audience."[94] The Queen intuits the fearsome purport of her visions (161, 210, etc.) but she is ignorant of mantic science and defers to the Elders, whose office it is to interpret signs from the divinity (170–75, 215–27). But (quite apart from their servile fear) the Elders' own theology of divine deceitfulness does away with the possibility of reading divine signs, whose plain meaning may well be a trick of the god to lull his victim. They intone comfortably, *eu de pantakhêi soi tônde krinomen peri* (225), assuring the Queen that the portent of her visions is altogether favorable. So much for the Elders' first encounter with facts arriving from the other world. Their *kako-mantis . . . thumos* (10–11) has turned out to be a sinister pun not only on their mood and meditations during their entering ode but also on their imperviousness to communication from the other world.[95]

The Elders are no wiser in recognizing the import of facts of material experience, specifically in the facts about Marathon, facts that they have possessed for a decade and which are of the utmost relevance in considering the outcome of any new contest between Persians and Greeks, between bow and spear, *toxou rhyma* and *dorikranou logkhês iskhys* (147–49)—an opposition that would have recalled to the audience not Plataea, where the Athenians had faced the Thebans, but Marathon. But the facts of Marathon had found no place in the Elders' opening soliloquy, and will be forgotten when they propose to dispatch a picked force once more to Greece (795).

The Queen now elicits these facts and directly concludes *deina toi legeis kiontôn tois tekousi phrontisai* (245), "You say fearsome things for the parents of the departed to consider." Aeschylus presents her as a harem-bred lady, up to now evidently quite uninformed about the war and even of Marathon, who immediately arrives at a true estimation of the enemy from facts which the Elders had possessed but could not appreciate.[96] Hers is the governing intellect in this colloquy, which is not simply a eulogy of Athens pitched to the groundlings but an essential element in the intellectual structure of the play.

An analogy exists in Plato's *Meno*, in which Socrates demonstrates that a slave boy "knows" a geometrical proof by prompting him through its steps (82bff). Like Meno's slave, however, the Elders' "knowledge" is passive and irrelevant to their mental processes.[97] At the end of the *Persae* they will agree with Xerxes that the disaster had been *atekmartotatê*, "utterly without presentiment" (910ff; cf. 921 and especially 1006 and 1027, echoing *pêm' aelpton* at 265), even though the Queen at the beginning had elicited the empirical *tekmêria* by which they (and Xerxes) could have correctly assessed the balance in a new contest between bow and spear, not

106

to speak of a contest on the new element of the sea. Darius' shade as well will imply that his son, by forgetting his father's commands (783), ignored the lessons of Marathon, which he himself had learned and heeded.

Aeschylus reinforces the antithesis of chorus and Queen by visually and emotively contrasting their respective relationships with the second actor, first as the Messenger, then as the shade of Darius, and finally as Xerxes in the kommos. The Messenger's news provokes the Elders into uninhibited lamentations. The Messenger fulfills their recent fantasy of death and mourning, and they cry out in syncopated meters that echo the rhythms of their anticipatory despair in the parodos (lines 256–89; cf. 115–39), while they draw the Messenger antiphonally into their threnody (256ff), which prefigures the hysterical intensity of their final duet with Xerxes.

Meanwhile the Queen stands apart, still and aghast (290–92) within her chariot of rank, in statuesque counterpoint to the tumult boiling up in the zone of the orchestra occupied by the Elders and Messenger. When at length she speaks it is to reassert control of the dramatic action and dramatic progress by recalling the Messenger to emotional and moral balance (290–95):

> Heartsick and stunned to silence am I
> By these disasters; a catastrophe so beyond all bounds
> Its losses bear neither tale nor question.
> Yet man's necessity is to shoulder burdens
> Assigned by the gods. Though you may groan
> Stand to attention and reveal the full measure of our loss.

She demands of herself a similar fortitude in contrast to the Elders' lamentations.[98] Several times she represses the grief that breaks through her circumstantial and intelligently directed interrogation: it is she, and not the Elders, who as before (230ff) elicits the *facts*. She then resumes the initiative of action both religious and practical to meet the crisis, by preparing apotropaic sacrifices to the gods (521ff; cf. 202ff) and directing the Elders to receive Xerxes soothingly, should he arrive in her absence (529ff); for the rest she directs them to devise *pista bouleumata*, "trusty counsels," concerning the events (527–28; cf. 171–72).

But they do not. *Pista bouleumata* are once again undiscoverable in their succeeding ode, in which they renew and deepen their ritual lamentations (531–97). The Elders do invoke the true author of their catastrophe, *O Zeu basileu* (532), although "ignorantly," as Winnington-Ingram accurately remarked.[99] Balance is restored only with the Queen's reentry *aneu t'okhêmatôn / khlidês* (607–8).

She calls upon them to invoke the shade of Darius at his tomb, whereupon they call out a disordered series of appellations: *psykhên* (630), *monos . . . thnêtôn* (632), *daimona megaukhê* (641), *theon* (643), *anêr* (647), *Aidoneus*(649 *bis*), *theomêstôr* (654–55 *bis*), *ballên* (657–58 *bis* = Aramaic *ba'al*?), *pater akaka* (663 and 671: *Akakêta* is a Homeric epithet of Hermes), *despota despota despotou* (666), and finally *thanôn* (674, cf. 632). This farrago ignores any distinction between mortals and immortals as, in sixteen swift lines, the Elders range the entire space between deity and humanity.[100]

Again the Queen stands in silent dignity as the Elders grovel, now fearfully mute, before her husband's risen shade. Only when he turns to her does she speak, hailing him with words of sane recognition of his mortal nature (709–14),[101] words that stand out in forthright contrast to the Elders' confusion of epithets and craven panic:

> You who by fortunate destiny rose above all
>   mortals in prosperity
> Envied of all as long as you beheld the sun
>   you lived a blessed life—a god in Persian eyes.
> Now I envy you dead—gone before beholding
>   an abyss of evils.
> You shall hear everything, Darius, within the moment:
>   in a word all the state of Persia is in ruins.

Once again the Queen returns sense and order to the orchestra: the Elders fall still as she tells Darius all in the rapid stichomythia leading up to his great aria on Persia's destiny and his son's insane hubris (739ff).

But when Xerxes arrives, finally, the Queen is absent, as she

must be: for it is with her very absence that the trammels of order
which she had imposed upon the Elders at the entrances of the
Messenger and the Ghost are now gone as well; and in her absence
the manhood of Persia, such as it is, is free to descend into that
oriental and feminine orgy of grief which ends the play.

Aeschylus' Darius

Aeschylus' fourth-century posterity remembered the greatness of
Darius' tremendous apparition, the *Commendatore* of Greek tragedy, as he appears to us in the *Persae*. For Plato in particular
Darius was the very type of great monarch.[102] Yet this later Greek
view was based not on Aeschylus' portrayal of Darius but on the
recognition of his real accomplishments in an age when Marathon
was faded glory and the Persian King's support was the principal
diplomatic goal of all the leading Greek states. This was an age,
besides, when political theory at Athens had turned to doctrines
of rational and beneficent despotism that regarded most men,
barbarian and Greek alike, to be *andrapodôdês*—human livestock
who, as natural slaves, must be directed for their own and the
common good by their natural superiors.[103]

In 472, however, Marathon was fewer than twenty years past
and Athenians remembered that they and the Eretrians had been
the declared enemies of Darius since the burning of Sardis.[104] In
the first years after Marathon the Athenians may well have hoped
that Darius had had enough of Athens; they were confident enough,
at any rate, to ostracize the younger Hipparchus, leader of those
"friends of the tyrants" who, until then, had remained in Athens
unmolested (Arist. *AP* 22.3–4: 488/7). It is a point of view possibly
reflected in the *Persae* (line 780), as I have suggested, and also in
Herodotus' remark that Themistocles persuaded the Athenians to
build the fleet that defeated the Persians against *Aegina*, not Persia
(7.144.1).[105]

But Xerxes adopted his father's *casus belli* in his own prewar
propaganda by declaring Athens, which alone had escaped his
father's vengeance, to be the aim of his war in Greece.[106] The
Athenians who saw and heard Darius' Ghost had not forgotten or

dismissed Marathon. They had a sharper perspective from which to judge Darius, who for them resembled neither the Darius of Herodotus nor that of the fourth-century theorists of monarchy.

The Ghost of the *Persae* understands that Zeus ordained all Asia to be the limit of his monarchy (762–65). Taught by Marathon he warned his son not to surpass those limits (782–83). Like his predecessors he preserved the prosperity of Persia by his *sôphrosynê* (765–86). This is of course the point: a slave society is directed by a single will, and only the sanity and judgment of that will determines success or disaster. Death, and power among the dead, has cleansed and universalized Darius for the poet's need of a voice of transcendental moral authority. But death has not freed him from his life as monarch of Persia, nor from the slaveholder's dilemma that belongs to the Persian master of the perfectly servile society mandated by Zeus for Asia.

Aeschylus' Darius projects a double image. From beyond the tomb he understands perfectly the transcendental causes of his son's catastrophe. On the other hand, he remains opaque to the human consequences of his own regime, which achieved as its characteristic products not only his courtiers but his son. Darius describes his own and his predecessors' rule in benign, even constitutional, language. Zeus ordained that one man should *tagein*, holding the *skêptron euthyntêrion* (762–64). This is not the language of irresponsible domination. The verb *tageô* implies command by virtue of public election or approbation, and the principle that the holder of the rod of upright rule must also rule himself is immediately affirmed by Darius' catalogue of kings. Medus was the first *hêgemôn* of the army, a term connoting responsible leadership willingly bestowed by the led. Medus' son[107] fulfilled his father's work, *phrenes gar autou thymon ôakostrophoun*, "since his mind steered his impulse" (767)—the very anatomy of *sôphrosynê* and the very antithesis of Herodotus' Xerxes (cf. 7.39.1). Cyrus perfected the *pax Persica* because *theos . . . ouk êkhthyren, hôs euphrôn ephy*; in consequence he won to his rule the Lydians, Phrygians, and Ionians (770–72). Cyrus' son in turn *êuthyne straton* and Artaphrenes ("Ready Mind") who was *esthlos*, put an end to the disgraceful rule of Mardus (776). Darius himself did no such harm to the state as has Xerxes, who *neos nea phronei*, has brought unprecedented ruin upon the Persians.

The Entropy of Tyrannies

We have seen Darius' own view of the responsible Persian monarch in contrast to his son. But his own vocabulary of *sôphrosynê* glosses what the audience knows has been a Persian career of restless and incessant conquest halted, as far as they knew, only for the present. His own subjects' view of him is supplied less by the Elders' adoration than by their fear. Behind Darius' view of his reign lurk the aims of the barbarian conqueror and the methods of the barbarian slaveholder. It is this Darius whom Aeschylus resurrects in order to behold the catastrophe worked by his son and his slaves, a catastrophe which—though even in death he is blind to the fact—is the product of his own methods and his own example in life. Aeschylus had his second actor play the Messenger, the Ghost, and Xerxes in succession, to reinforce all the more his audience's sense of ethical continuity and contingency between Persians and their rulers, and between father and son.[108]

The ruin of Persia was not accomplished because Xerxes happened to turn out badly, as if by an unhappy accident of heredity. It is an inevitable consequence of the very nature of Persia as ordained by Zeus—an empire whose fate was mandated by those divine *thesphata* fulfilled by Aeschylus' Xerxes. The free contention of free citizens in a polis will contain—or ignore—such violent and impetuous natures as Xerxes'. The necessary consequence of absolutism is a universal servility so perfect that the idea of liberty, and therefore of *nomos*, lies outside the ken of ruled and rulers alike.[109] In such a society, godhead accurately defines the monarch's absolute license and absolute claim upon his subjects: everything proceeds from him, everything is accomplished by him, everything is subject to his will, and nothing within the orbit of his will can stand against him. That is why the Elders fear Darius upon his epiphany. However, that is also why they will disobey the absent and deceased Darius when their present master Xerxes appears. They need fear Darius no longer, and in any case his

wisdom lies outside their ken. As slaves they consult their immediate safety. As barbarians they are Heraclitean *affolés*.

At the end of the *Persae*, the playwright returns the audience to
the realities of the year 472 and the incalculable future. Persia has
survived defeat to remain in control of all Asia save the Greek
cities, and Xerxes is still on the throne. Therefore the play cannot
be, and is not, simply a drama of disaster. It is also a drama of
survival and the restoration of order after disaster. The laments of
the Elders serve not only as the vehicle by which the playwright
evokes the emasculated, virtually female nature of the barbarian
slave. They belong to the ritually funereal dramaturgy integral to a
drama of survival and the restoration of order after disaster. Persians
die and they are mourned; the principal dramatic action takes place
around a tomb where a ghost-raising takes place; the ghost then
returns to the tomb, and life—such as it is—goes on in Persia.

Funerary customs—the expression of bereavement in culturally
approved ways—universally function to mediate the passage from
a former state of order, through the period of disorder imposed
by death, to a new state of order.[110] In ancient Greek society, as
in other societies in which the central cultural roles are appropriated by the men, the part belonging to disorder at the obsequies
is given over to the women mourners; the men by their formal
orderliness, their *kosmos*, represent the order that will again super-
vene when the obsequies are consummated.[111] I have argued that
the dramaturgical contrast between the male *kosmos* of the Queen
and the female *akosmia* of the Elders mandates that she must be
absent during the kommos, because her dramaturgical function
is always to return sense and order to a scene threatened by the
Elders' *akosmia*. In the kommos Persia's disorder is consummated
in the *folie à deux* between the Elders and Xerxes. The absent
Queen, however, is said to be preparing his literal rehabilitation
in new vestments, and thereby to represent the recreation of a
future order (843, 849, 920).

Aeschylus brings his audience beyond the play to present reality
exô tês tragôidias by leaving Xerxes between the influences of his
incorrigible courtiers on the one hand and his simple but sane

mother on the other. It is not farfetched to see depicted in this a dramatic representation of the imponderable course of future Persian policy. The essential choices represented by the Elders and Xerxes' mother remained for Xerxes: war or peace, blind revanchism or acceptance of the burdens assigned by the gods.

Nor is it farfetched to see in Xerxes' assimilation to the Elders in the kommos not only a reference to the Persians' continuing resistance after Mycale and Sestus, and the notorious Pausanias affair (Thuc. 1.128ff), but Aeschylus' own informed calculation of the future. By 472 Athens had begun turning on her own allies in order to keep her alliance intact, disciplined, and effective. Aeschylus' audience itself was in no mood for a peace that would destroy the raison d'être of an increasingly profitable hegemony. Persian intransigence and Athenian ambition were to meet again within a few years at the Eurymedon.[112]

The Source of Aeschylus' Conception

For the historian there remains the final question of the source of Aeschylus' central conception, from which all else in the Persian ethos and the Persian tragedy arises: the relationship between the King and his subjects seen as the relationship of slaves to a master whom they are ready to regard as their god.

Our source for European Greek attitudes to Persia and the Great King at the time of the war is Herodotus. He collected his material some decades after the events,[113] but his central testimony on this point can be dated with precision to the aftermath of Thermopylae. The Delphic response that the Spartans alleged or solicited to excuse their failure at the pass cannot have been promulgated later than the winter of 480/79, when the Spartan authorities needed not only to explain the catastrophe to their own citizens, but to keep the Athenians—whom they had alienated by their culpable failure—in the war when proposals of peace and alliance were coming to them from the Persians (Hdt. 8.140ff). The Spartans published this response as soon as they thought to do so in order to portray in Leonidas' death the salvation of Sparta and *a fortiori* the rest of Hellas.[114]

The implied subject of the second verse of this oracle is Xerxes, and he is said to possess the power of Zeus: *Zênos gar ekhei menos* (7.220.4). Since we can accept this one instance of comparison of Xerxes with Zeus as contemporary with the war we are free to notice the reappearance of the theme in the eve-of-battle manifesto that Herodotus attributes to the Hellenic high command, led by the Spartans, just before Thermopylae: *ou gar theon ton epionta epi tên Hellada, all' anthrôpon ktl.* "It is not a god who is invading Greece but a man" (7.203.2). The comparison of Persian power to divinity was an idea belonging to the times. It was naturally complementary to the Persian propaganda of invincibility and also to what the Greeks already knew by this time about the reverential protocol of the satrapal and royal courts, including the notorious requirement to do obeisance (cf. Aesch. *Pers.* 152; Hdt. 7.136.1) which they regarded not only as altogether servile but as a positive sacrilege, reinforced by whatever they themselves had been able to observe of all this while Xerxes was in Greece.

So, in attributing ruler worship to the Persians, Aeschylus proceeded in a way that the conventions of tragedy would in any case have led us to suppose: he invented nothing, but interpreted the whole meaning and consequence of his audience's existing belief about the divinity of the Great King in the eyes of his subjects just as if it were a received element of a traditional myth.[115]

Five

Herodotus' Typology of Hellenism

> Some regard [Herodotus] as a citizen of Thurii, but
> his attachment is actually to the Halicarnassians,
> those Dorians who took their harems with them on
> the expedition against Greece.
> —Plutarch, *On the Malice of Herodotus*
>
> *Les tyrans sont gens entre la Grèce et l'Asie.*
> —François Hartog (1980)

Prologue

In 480 the Greeks of Europe defeated a people who were almost strangers to them, and who remained as distant in their real nature in the aftermath as they had been before the war.[1] The great changes in European Greek images of the Persians occurred not in the realm of knowledge but in that of fantasy and stereotype; at Athens we observe these changes occurring in recognizable stages as Athenian relations with Persia passed from friendship to enmity.

I have already suggested that Darius' Ghost may well be a fossil from the period of Athenian friendship with Persia. It is natural to identify in the magisterial Darius of the *Persae* a bygone visualization of that monarch from this period, when the still-unthreatened Athenians—surely influenced by the descriptions of Persian magnificence brought home by their envoys to the King's brother at Sardis—imagined Darius as a commanding personage, as great as the empire over which he ruled. The Persians soon demanded,

115

however, that Athens take back the Pisistratids. Anxious years of watching and waiting culminated at Marathon. At the time this victory seemed decisive; in an exalted mood of national salvation the Athenians buried the heroized dead where they had fallen on the field beneath a Homeric barrow.[2]

In the years after Darius' death in 486, it must have seemed ever less likely that the Persians would come again. At first the Athenians were unwilling to believe that Xerxes' new activity in Europe was aimed at them, for as late as 483/2, when the first Persian preparations were already under way in Thrace, Themistocles would convince the demos to put the silver of Laurium into a fleet instead of their pockets by pointing not to Persia over the distant horizon, but to Aegina, the enemy visible from the Acropolis.[3]

Then, unexpectedly, the new Great King launched a terrifying new progress to Greece, reported to be of immense scale. The Ionian Revolt and Marathon had taught the Persians to respect the warmaking powers of the Greeks, especially on their own ground. Xerxes' plan was intelligently conceived to overawe the Greeks by displaying all the resources at his command as well as his determination in deploying them, step by inevitable step, ever closer to the Greek peninsula. The Persian preparations against Greece occupied four years and were as much psychological as material—a fact that Herodotus recognizes in opining that it was Xerxes' arrogant pride (*megalophrosynê*) in his power that led him to order the cutting of the Athos canal as a memorial of it (7.24).

This strategy of creeping terror, by which Xerxes hoped would win him the Greeks without major fighting (7.147), nearly worked. The majority of Greeks either Medized actively or took care to stay out of a war against a power that now appeared not only invincible but even demonic. The oracular responses invented at the time likened the approaching enemy to "fire and sharp Ares, driving a Syrian-bred horsecar" (7.140.2) and the power of Xerxes himself to that of Zeus, "which neither the fury of bulls nor of lions shall withstand (7.220.4)."[4]

Fear of Persia survived the victories of 480–479; it dominated the Athenian imagination at least down to the extermination of the revived Persian navy at the Eurymedon and the peace, or *modus vivendi*, between Athens and Persia inaugurated in the late 460s. In the early 460s,[5] the accusers of the Spartan Pausanias had claimed that he not only conspired with Xerxes to enslave Greece but even cast off his Spartanness to ape the barbarian. Thucydides (1.130) relates that when Pausanias received a letter from Xerxes promising ample support for his alleged project to subject Greece to Persia,

> he was far more elated and could no longer bear to live in the customary way, but would go forth from Byzantium [which he held as a private adventurer] in Median apparel and travel through Thrace accompanied by a guard of Medes and Egyptians; he banqueted in the Persian style and all in all could not conceal his motives, but by these small things betrayed the greater designs he was contemplating for the future. He made himself difficult to approach and displayed so violent a temper toward everyone alike that no one could come near him.

Pausanias was done to death at Sparta about 467, and the Spartans then accused the Athenian Themistocles of complicity in Pausanias' grand treason, whereupon the Athenians and Spartans together hounded him out of Greece. He seemed to prove his accusers right when he entered the service of the Persians in Asia, where he was safe. We cannot know whether these accusations of Medism were justified against either man.[6] For our purposes, however, they provide concrete evidence for that postwar mood of abiding fear of Persian revanchism memorialized dramatically in Aeschylus' *Persae*. It was a mood that Greek politicians could exploit against their enemies, justifiably or not.

Even though the Eurymedon put an end to any serious Athenian fears that the Persians could still threaten their homes, the Persians would remain the official national enemy in the prayers of the ecclesia (Ar. *Thesm.* 337, 365; Isoc. 4.157); for enmity to Persia was the linchpin of Athens' imperial ideology even in the period of peace after the Eurymedon and again after Cimon's death in 449 (e.g., Plut. *Per.* 12.1–3). Attention to Persia's attitude, if not fear of Persian power, then revived at Athens with the outbreak of the Peloponnesian War. In the second year of the war several Greek envoys from enemy states in the Peloponnese fell into Athenian hands while on a mission to seek money for their cause from the Great King. The Athenians put them to death without trial immediately upon their arrival before the assembly and denied burial to their corpses (Thuc. 2.67). It was surely in this context that Herodotus heard the official version of the suspicious Spartan mission to Xerxes, which he tells in the story of Sperthias and Bulis, whose sons the Athenians had executed on this occasion long afterward (7.134ff). The Medism of Themistocles and Pausanias was surely recalled as war propaganda at this time too, to find its way into Thucydides' work.

Fear of Persia and the power of the Persian stereotype once more played a part in politics and political persecution in the war, as it had in the era of Pausanias and Themistocles, and was deployed after 420 to blacken Alcibiades. Besides his reputation for wanton behavior and outrageous expenditures, his "effeminate purple robes, which he would trail through the agora"[7] associated him with the Persian tastes cultivated by Athens' gilded youth, and marked him in the popular mind as luxurious, effeminate, and "tyrannical."[8]

In fact most of the literary evidence which we have on the elaboration and manipulation of the barbarian stereotype comes from the period of the Peloponnesian War and afterward, when the Persians had once more taken control of Asiatic Greece and were manipulating the alliance systems of the Greeks of Europe.[9] The abundant cartoon images of comedy[10] show that one of the principal goals of putting barbarians on stage lay in disarming and denying the very real power of the Persians. Likewise in political rhetoric: as late as 367 an Arcadian ambassador to Susa (who had gone away from court unsatisfied) saw fit to inform the Arcadians on his return that the Great King had swarms of bakers, chefs, wine stewards, and butlers, but no men fit to stand up to Greeks. Even the King's great reputation for wealth was a mere smokescreen: "Why, even his famous golden plane-tree isn't big enough to shade a grasshopper!" (Xen. *Hell.* 7.1.38 *fin.*).

At Athens the *Persae* had been the point of departure for images of this nature. For at least a generation afterward, the imperial Athenians were satisfied with a picture of the Persians as an emasculated people whose image was mere tinsel; they believed that they understood the war against Xerxes in its universal significance as it had been expressed by Simonides,[11] Aeschylus, and other poets in the decade after Salamis.

In this milieu, descriptive accounts of the Persians and the peoples of their empire, *Persika* and *Barbarika Nomima*, would not begin to circulate until well into the second half of the fifth century, when the Persians had been ruling the greatest and wealthiest portions of the known world for more than a century. Even then only a handful of prose writers—all of them Asiatic Greeks—turned their attention to Persia. But their works too were full of parodistic inventions which, in passing for factual accounts, only reinforced the power of the existing stereotype. The laggard appearance and slender quality of descriptive prose literature on the Persians is striking testimony not only to the abiding distance between European Greeks and Persians enforced by Athens in the Aegean, but also to an incuriosity, fed by the stereotype in the two generations after Salamis, toward the Persians' real nature and the course of events that had brought them to world empire.

We know of only three fifth-century authors apart from Herodotus to whom *Persica* are attributed, Dionysius of Miletus (*FGrH* 687), Charon of Lampsacus (*FGrH* 262, cf. 687b), and Hellanicus of Mytilene (*FGrH* 4, cf. 687a).[12] Next to nothing is known about Dionysius; his very existence has been denied.[13] Hellanicus, Charon, and Herodotus all spent time in Athens, and they gave their works to an Athenian, and generally European Greek, audience. In Xanthus (*FGrH* 765) the Hellenized Lydian aristocracy of Sardis also produced a national historian for Greek consumption. We have enough, but only just enough, of these authors to hazard some assessment of their works and Herodotus' relation to them.

Hellanicus retailed a fable of barbarian gender-confusion in recalling how the Persian Queen Atossa was raised by her father Ariaspes[14] as a male, in order to inherit the throne of Persia.

Hellanicus credits her with establishing the character of Persian rule as it was visible to Greeks:

> She concealed her female nature and was the first monarch to wear the tiara and trousers; she also established the service of eunuchs and the issuing of judgments in writing. She subdued many peoples and was warlike and manly to the utmost in all of her accomplishments.[15]

Hellanicus' Atossa and the Queen of Aeschylus' *Persae* obviously were connected in Greek tradition, and were reflected in the less sensational notice of Herodotus that by the time of Darius' death Atossa held supreme power at court (7.3 *fin.*). But if Hellanicus wrote before him,[16] Herodotus was too clearsighted to repeat Hellanicus' fantasies, even though he did share Hellanicus' and other Greeks' fascination with the harem politics of the Persian court. Herodotus' reportage on this topic can be stereotypically revolting (e.g., 9.108–13) but nevertheless remains within the realm of possibility.

Dionysius is said to have been a predecessor of Herodotus (T 2) who wrote an *Events after Darius* in five books (T 1). The title indicates that he dealt with the Persian Wars; but his work, if it in fact existed, evidently began in the mythical past, as it allegedly named Danaus rather than Cadmus as the mediary who introduced the art of writing into Greece (F 1). It also included an account of the Magian brothers who stole the throne from Smerdis the brother of Cambyses, which evidently struck the scholiast on Herodotus 3.61 as similar to his account (F 2). Possibly Herodotus was in Dionysius' debt to an unknown but surely not great extent; it is more likely that both reflected independently a common source for their accounts of the Magi, which existed in the propaganda account of Bisitun concerning the false Bardiya, circulated by Darius in the provinces.[17]

Six short fragments of Charon's *Persika* in two books (T 1) survive, totaling fewer than 300 words. Chronologically they begin with the dream of the Median king Astyages, which foretells the conquests of Cyrus (F 2; cf. Hdt. 1.107–8) and end with Themistocles' arrival at the court of Artaxerxes. The character of the fragments suggests that Charon was subject to the same constraints that mark Herodotus' work: he appears fairly well informed about the activities of the Persians in Asia Minor and the Aegean from the conquest of Cyrus onward, but about the native history of the Iranian peoples he could glean only fantastical scraps.

Three of Charon's six fragments appear to show that Herodotus knew him;[18] if so, they provide an insight to Herodotus' use of his predecessors and the distinctions he made between the categories of evidence they provided. Astyages' dream in Charon is the second of the two that Herodotus gives to him in his own work (1.108.2). A passage of Tertullian happens to provide strong testimony that it was the only one that Charon knew.[19] Herodotus, then, supplemented Charon with further information from another source which described Astyages' other dream. But in doing so he scrupulously reproduced Charon's own account of Astyages' dream, because for Herodotus dreams were divine in provenance and beyond alteration as testimony to the deity's intention.[20]

On the other hand, Herodotus did correct material from Charon—and therefore presumably from other sources of like nature—which did not concern the divine, as in his accounts of the flight of Pactyes when the Lydian and Ionian revolt against Cyrus collapsed,[21] and the expedition of the Athenians against Sardis in 499.[22] This methodological distinction is a consequence of his goal of demonstrating a theodicy in history, because the integrity of this demonstration depended upon his accurate transcription of received material about the working of deity upon human destiny, whereas accounts of human events could safely be subjected to empirical scrutiny and alteration.

Herodotus may also have used his contemporary Hellanicus in his discussion of the ancestry of Persians and Medes from Perseus and Medea,[23] but otherwise ignored him.[24] Too little of Hellanicus' *Persika*, another brief work of perhaps no more than two books, survives to provide conclusions. Strabo (11.6.2–3 C507f) condemns Hellanicus together with Ctesias and Herodotus as credulous lovers of the fabulous whose fictions about the early history of the Scythians, Medes, Persians and Syrians were even less plausible than the hero tales of the poets. Strabo's judgment is justified at least for Hellanicus' nonsense about the transvestite Atossa.

Although Herodotus apparently did not know the *Lydiaka* of another contemporary, Xanthus,[25] he is nevertheless of particular interest in the present connection, in that he, a Hellenized Lydian aristocrat who may have been of royal ancestry,[26] not only adopted the Greek stereotype of Asiatic barbarism in presenting the history of his nation's monarchs, but even advanced it, attributing to them penchants for human butchery, cannibalism, and probably incest as well. Xanthus is a sensational author, like his spiritual successor Ctesias.[27] Both found a large audience because they ratified existing prejudices, sensationalizing according to fixed notions of an atrocious and unnatural barbarian ethos. Xanthus' attention to barbarian women in particular is fixed upon the perverse. He wrote, for example, that when an Amazon bears a boy child she plucks out his eyes with her own hands (F 22). In his treatise on the Magi he states that they have sex with their mothers, daughters, and sisters, and have their women in common by mutual agreement (F 31).[28]

Even the history of clitoridectomy, or alternatively labiectomy, among Asiatic peoples begins with Xanthus. He related that the Lydian king Adramyttes was the first to castrate (*eunoukhisai*) women in order to use them as eunuchs instead of males.[29] This assertion was memorable to a prurient posterity. Athenaeus repeated it as did the Byzantine Suda, whose author recalled it imperfectly from memory when he wrote his entry on Xanthus: "In the second book of his work he relates how Gyges [*sic*] the Lydian king was the first to castrate women, in order to maintain their youth for his pleasure" (F 4b).[30]

Xanthus, finally, is the source for the peculiar and revolting tale of the Lydian king Cambles, who was so afflicted with a mania for food and drink that he prepared his own wife for the table and ate her. Awaking in the morning, he discovered her hand still thrust into his mouth; whereupon he slew himself.[31] Nicolaus of Damascus repeated the story with moralizing embellishments.[32] Nicolaus also contributes the episode of the Mermnad Sadyattes' incestuous union with his sister, which began with her rape—again probably a story from Xanthus, as it is altogether characteristic of his violent and salacious royal portraits.[33]

Incest and cannibalism in the thought-categories of the Greeks, together with the murder of kin, came to be taboos that marked off the contemporary Greek world, not only from barbarism, but from Greek "antiquity," that is, the domain of myth and tragedy.[34] These atrocious practices had belonged also to the ancient houses of Thebes, Mycenae, and Athens. They distinguished as well the type of the tyrant, barbarian and Greek; this is quintessentially the type who opposes hubris to *nomos*. Antiquity and tyranny were in this way identified by the Greek mind, as "hot spots" of barbarism in their own world that transcended the mere distinction of Greek and foreigner.[35]

Enter Herodotus

Herodotus summed up and surpassed his contemporaries and recent predecessors, although the wellsprings of the barbarian stereotypes are naturally alive beneath his narrative.[36] Since Herodotus inquired about the world almost entirely among his Greek contemporaries, he inevitably reflected their outlook; in Herodotus also, then, the barbarian is atrocious and perverse, given to human butchery, cannibalism, incest, the feminization of men, and the masculine empowerment of women.[37]

Herodotus wove all of this into his intricate system of the world with a peculiar genius. He found his starting point for the history and eventual downfall of the Mermnads in the naked beauty of the wife of the Lydian king Candaules, the last of the Heraclids, whose unbalanced attraction for her induced him to shame her unforgivably and drove her to procure his murder (1.8.1). Of the Medes and Persians, he tells stories of Thyestian feasts, of Oedipal intended infanticide,[38] of mutilations and flayings, of sisters taken as wives. In this vein he ends as he began, with the story of the mutilation of Masistes' wife (9.108–13): as a narrative of the atrocious consequences of a barbarian king's *eros* carried out by the hand of a virago, it mirrors the story of Candaules and his queen as it closes the ring on the whole of the Histories.[39]

Such were his materials: but only in these materials was Herodotus a prisoner of the stereotypes elaborated by his inferiors. For with the exception of Aeschylus, Herodotus was the only great artist of his age who gave profound attention and meaning to the generic distinctions between Greeks and barbarians. His work as a whole is a grand meditation on the nature of he world of humans and gods in its inexhaustible variety. From this meditation arises, however, not the strict and linear opposition between barbarian and Hellene canonized by Aeschylus and caricatured by the comedians, but a taxonomy of human behavior that threatens to span the received distance between the two human poles of barbarism and Hellenism, or even to erase it: close beneath the surface of his narrative is his conviction that Hellenism—the condition of being Greek through and through—is a hard-won, fragile prize, and easily lost.[40]

Herodotus' mission was descriptive in method but not in essence. His goal was like that of his inspired predecessors, Homer and Hesiod: Homer and Hesiod had taught their age, through the divinity singing within them, how the divine will had shaped the human world. Like them, Herodotus would compose a theogony and anthropogony for his own age. But Homer and Hesiod had lived 400 years before him (2.53.2), when poets had possessed truth by an inspiration now extinct and irrecoverable. In Herodotus' age the poetic psyche had long since lost touch with divinity.

Herodotus' sources would therefore be of necessity empirical, not inspirational. For Herodotus was neither a seer nor a poet: his revelation had therefore to depend on testimonies about the gods and the divine will that existed outside himself, experiential testimonies discoverable by inquiry. Herodotus would rely on direct investigation with the eye and ear, *opsis* and *akoê*, instead of psychic inspiration from deity: when mundane facts in particular were at issue, Herodotus did not hesitate to reject the authority of the poets in favor of his own researches.[41]

In his empirical rationalism, if not in his orthodox piety, Herodotus often has been called the last of the pre-Socratics; his work altogether rejects the mythmaking elements of traditional Ionian poetic culture, a rejection that went as deep as a personal revolt against the backward-looking intellectual traditions of his own family. His close kinsman, Panyassis son of Polyarchus,[42] had revived the epic form but found no imitators.[43] He wrote an *Ionica*, about the Ionian heroes Neleus and Codrus and their foundation of the Ionian cities, as well as a *Heraclea* in fourteen books, which celebrated the ancient Lydian Heraclids' descent from the union of Heracles and Omphale.[44] But Herodotus took a significantly hostile attitude against Panyassis and old Ionian tradition.[45] He rejected Panyassis' genealogy of the Lydian Heraclids—in the Histories they are not descended from Queen Omphale but from a mere slave-girl (1.7.4)[46]—as well as the whole genre of tales epitomized by the story, which Panyassis also had told in the *Heraclea* , that the pharaoh Busiris once intended to slay Heracles as a human sacrifice.[47] In words consciously meant to bring to mind his predecessor Hecataeus' contempt for the whole tribe of mythographical poets, Herodotus goes out of his way to reject the legend of Busiris specifically as one of the many thoughtless and foolish myths told by the Greeks (2.45.1; cf. Hecataeus *FGrH* 1 F 1a).[48]

Herodotus' acquaintance with his kinsman and his poetry must have contributed to his conviction that inspiration had gone out of the poets since Homer, especially as Panyassis himself had evidently practiced some form of soothsaying.[49] Herodotus' faith in his own outlook and method was victorious over the results of inspiration, as he showed once and for all in accepting the testimony of Egyptian priests, whom he claimed to have interviewed, over the testimony of the *Iliad* on the fate of Helen (2.112ff). Stesichorus in his *Palinode* had asserted that Helen never was at Troy, and Hecataeus (FF 307–9) puts both Helen and Menelaus in Egypt. So we observe Herodotus in Egypt weighing two Greek stories in the balance of a "native" source in touch with "Egyptian" tradition (even though his "Egyptian" version appears to be simply what his Greek-speaking dragoman told Herodotus when the priests replied to his own leading questions, since similar tales were already known to the Greeks).

Herodotus' ultimate reason for rejecting Homer is typically Herodotean in its mixture of reason and religion: certainly Helen had never been at Troy, he concludes, for the Trojans would have handed her over rather than see their city destroyed; nevertheless the gods saw to the utter destruction of Troy to manifest to the world that they punish great wrongdoings greatly (2.120.5).

But Herodotus could not depend only on human memories and his own opinion of them; in the end these alone could not suffice to provide his work with a firm authority on the divine intention he saw at work in history. His self-defined task consisted in discovering, and exploring as thoroughly as his information permitted, the nexus in history between human purposes and the divine intention. His "problem", then, was to find a source of truth about the divine intention within his own world and the mundane human memory in his present, merely human, age (3.122.2). This was not simply a problem of method but the spiritual requirement of a *dévot*.

Prophets, not poets, were inspired in his era, and it was to prophecy that Herodotus turned for empirical testimonies to the divine intention.[50] Herodotus believed that the divine will is sig-naled to humankind in portents, dreams, and especially oracles—in which he placed a profound faith, which he defended polemi-cally as a fundamental ground of his work,[51] and around which he organized his narrative histories of the Lydian Mermnads and Xerxes' war.[52] The prophet Bacis had spoken with a voice of divine prevision in recent times (8.87). But Delphi stood above all other mantic authorities.[53]

Herodotus' naïve and intense faith must have formed his essen-tial outlook from the very beginning of his researches, and provided the unflagging direction of his lifelong study of theodicy in events. In this sense we might say that his intellectual biography begins at 1.20 *init.*: *Delphôn oida egô houtô akousas genesthai*, "I heard it from Delphians so I *know* that these things happened in this way."[54]

If, therefore, we need to identify a "moment" at which the nature of his design and its validating truth came to him, that moment arrived at Delphi, where he sojourned in the engaged and curious spirit of the pilgrim experiencing the sources of his faith. It was at this "moment" that Herodotus was freed from the epic past and its categories of explanation, not only because the generations within human memory had witnessed tremendous events that could stand comparison with the epic past of the heroic age, but because the gods themselves had manifestly fought for the Greeks and had left the proof of their concern, and their action, in the oracular record of those times. Herodotus was therefore able to explain these great new events according to contemporary revelations of the divine intention, discoverable by his own investigations at Delphi and elsewhere. These epiphanies in themselves not only confirmed the greatness of modern events by their testimony to the gods' intimate concern. They were a record of the role of the gods in those events.[55]

Herodotus *knew* what he learned at Delphi was true. Of the stories told by other men, which were unhallowed by Delphian provenance, he twice remarks that it is his job to record them, but not necessarily to believe them (2.123.1, 7.152.3; cf. 2.130.2, 4.173 and 195.2, 6.137.1, 7.152.3). Had Herodotus confined himself to imposing on events the causative schemata of human and divine *tisis* in the controlling ideas he inherited from his archaic predecessors, the schemata of crime and retaliation, and of the retribution that hubris brings, he could have written his account by collecting and orchestrating traditions of the works and glories of Greeks and barbarians, and in particular why they went to war with one another (*proem.*), very much as he actually did. But his work would have lacked the force of *testimonial proof* about the role of the divine in events and their causes, and therefore the truth of the oracular testimonies from which he demonstrated the role of the divine.[56]

Viewed in this way, on its own terms, his work provides a prosaic account—prose is the uninspired medium—of the formation and life of this world of gods and humans from their earliest attested beginnings in Egyptian cult, tradition, and records, down to the recent collective memory of who and what put Greeks and barbarians, Europe and Asia, into the collision and conflict that set this world into its present mold. According to these methods and purposes, Herodotus composed a theodicy of the events within human memory, delivered in the lucid and intimate voice of the storyteller. He *explained* the shape of this world from the first Asiatic who worked injustices against Greeks (1.3.1) and the discovery of the gods by the Egyptians. Because Egypt is the source of the gods and their oracles,[57] the largely "ahistorical" Egyptian logos is the Unmoved Mover of the Histories, which serves the transcendental goal of the work by providing not only the origins of divinity but humanity's means of communication with the divine. Access to the divine will through oracles and their testimonies is the Egyptian discovery that makes possible an understanding of the ultimate causes of specific events—and in this sense, therefore, makes possible the Histories themselves.[58]

Accordingly, Herodotus' explanation of the historical conflict between barbarians and Greeks begins at the earliest remembered starting place—the usurpation of Gyges—where by means of recorded oracular responses Herodotus could expose the causal nexus between human purposes and the divine intention. This sacred history enjoys its fullest articulation precisely in those episodes—the rise and fall of the Mermnads of Sardis and the war against Xerxes—for which Herodotus possessed a functionally complete record of the divine will preserved in oracular responses.[59] The particular effect of these great episodes, furthermore, teaches his audiences how the oracles, from Delphi in particular, were confirmed and their previsionary truth witnessed in the decisions and fate of humans who acted in the often murky light of these synaptic contacts with deity.[60]

The historical process itself exists in this nexus and is demonstrable as oracular history. Within this process occur the most important diagnostic differences between barbarians and Greeks. It is these in turn which explain the state of the world down to the defeat of Xerxes, the greatest of them being the congenital inability of Asiatic barbarians to understand the divine will. Heraclitus had said that "the god who possesses the oracle at Delphi neither speaks nor conceals, but gives a sign" (22 B 93 DK). Herodotus' Asiatic barbarians, like Heraclitus' possessors of barbarian souls and the Elders of the *Persae*, cannot read the signs.

At the outset of his work Herodotus speaks of a single human genus, *anthrôpos*, whose members both Greek and barbarian have done great and marvelous things worthy of remembrance and celebration in his work. Also, they have gone to war with each other, and he intends in particular to explain the reason why (*proem.*). He then plunges straight into an exploration of that enmity, telling first what "the Persians familiar with the stories" say about the ancient chain of crimes and retributions, abductions of women to and from the continents of Asia and Europe, beginning with the translation of Io from Greece to Egypt and ending with the rape of Helen and the consequent capture of Troy, "in which the Persians find the cause of their enmity against the Hellenes" (1.1.1–5.1).

Herodotus then opposes his own chain of *aitiai:* "I myself shall not go so far as to argue whether these things happened this way or that way, but point out the man who first did wrong against the Hellenes as I go onward in my story, telling alike of small cities and great," for greatness forever passes with time and human happiness never abides (1.5.3–4). He then names Croesus of Lydia "as the first barbarian known to have reduced some of the Greeks to the bringing of tribute and who attracted others as friends" (1.6.2). In this Lydian logos, which is the first arc of the great ring that units Croesus at the beginning with Xerxes at the end, Herodotus presents Croesus apodictically, as the very exemplar of the barbarian who fails to understand Hellenic wisdom and Hellenic divinity.[61] Herodotus' Croesus is very much engaged with the Greek gods and the Greek mind: he patronizes Delphi and populates his court with Greek *sophistai*. But even while Croesus lives and breathes in this Greek atmosphere, Herodotus tells his story (1.6ff) in a way that sharply distinguishes him as un-Greek. Herodotus' beginning thus anticipates the conclusion underlying the whole work: that the real causes of the enmity between the Greeks and the barbarians of Asia do not lie in the consequences of specific crimes and retributions but flow out of the underlying, "organic" differences between Greeks and barbarians.

This conclusion was full of relevance for his contemporaries. Herodotus exhibited his work during the first years of the Peloponnesian War.[62] He lived in a world now dominated not by the threat from Persia but by the empire of Athens and the conflict between the great powers of Greece. Herodotus subtly redefined the nature and extent of Asianic barbarism in order to explain to the Greeks of his day not only the deep and permanent causes of the enmity between Asiatic barbarians and Greeks, but also the thematically parallel rivalry within Greece itself between the very different peoples of Dorian Sparta and Ionian Athens.[63]

This chapter examines ambiguous and subtle treatment of the Athenians of Herodotus' own day as Greeks in some respects and Asianic barbarians in others. In the end, Herodotus' Athenians—those Athenians who were the first, and only, Greeks to demand tribute from other Greeks—appear to be a *tertium quid* between Greek and Asianic barbarian categories of humanity, just as their empire spans the territory between Europe and Asia.

It is true that Herodotus first draws the line dividing Hellenism and barbarism between the figures of Solon the Athenian *sophistês* and Croesus the Lydian *nêpios*, as he is called by Apollo (1.85.2).[64] Yet Solon himself, in the environment of Greece instead of Asia, is not altogether untouched by an implicit barbarism. He is himself a kind of *tertium quid* who is comparatively Hellenic in Asia (indeed, at Croesus' court he is Herodotus' alter ego), but comparatively barbarian in Greece. Herodotus closes his Histories, moreover, not with Xerxes' retreat from Greece and the mutilation of Masistes' wife, but with Athens' advance to Asia and the barbaric crucifixion of the Persian Artaüctes by the Athenian admiral Xanthippus, father of Pericles.[65] His work, like Aeschylus' *Persae*, respects the future in being finished but unconcluded; it remains open to the unwritten chapter of a future that includes the struggle for the liberation of Persia's former Greek subjects from Ionian Athens in his own day.

Pelasgians and Tyrants

Who is a Greek? Near the climax of his drama, in the winter after Salamis, Herodotus' Athenians declare that they will never abandon the Hellenes, for "the Greek race is of the same blood and the same speech, with common shrines of the gods and common sacrifices, and compatible ways of life" (8.144). It is simple and seemingly unambiguous: racial descent, language, religion, and ways of life together make a Greek.[66]

Yet this is not Herodotus' definition. Had it been, he would have spoken in his own voice.[67] It belongs to an Athenian who is speaking on a specific occasion in history, for a specific purpose created by that occasion, comparable in tendency to the liar Aristagoras' appeal to the Spartan king Cleomenes to "rescue from slavery Ionians of the same blood" (5.49ff). This Athenian orator's definition was created by the war itself and by the ongoing conflict between Greeks and barbarians. On the occasion of Xerxes' invasion, the Athenians had saved Greece (7.138.2–139), and at that moment they were altogether Greek. But by Herodotus' day, Athens' course of empire, spanning Europe and Asia, had made a cruel irony of this Athenian's promise never to abandon the Hellenes.[68]

For these reasons alone we must hesitate to conclude that Herodotus meant this definition to reflect the facts of Hellenism as he saw them. Moreover, Herodotus' work as a whole *breaks down* the definition of "Hellene" created by the war. One stroke in the demolition of that definition, for example, is the deliberate placement of the encomium on the Athenians' salvation of Greece, which comes directly after a reference to their recent sacriligious murder of envoys from other Greek states on a mission to the Great King (7.137.3); the contrast is a telling one, and this episode will receive scrutiny later.

The closer we look at Herodotus' Athenians, the less absolutely Hellenic they appear.[69] Herodotus argues near the very beginning of his work that most of the people who later became Hellenes were Pelasgians, and that these Pelasgians were barbarians and spoke a barbarian language. From these Pelasgians Herodotus derives the descent of the Ionians, as well as that of all the other Greeks of the present day who are not Dorians (1.56.3–58):

> In the reign of King Deucalion the Dorian people inhabited the land of Phthiotis, and in the time of Dorus son of Hellen the territory beneath Ossa and Olympus known as Histiaeotis. When this people was expelled by the Cadmeians from Histiaeotis they settled on Pindus at a place named Makednon. From there they moved again into Dryopis, and from there they arrived in the Peloponnese and were called Dorians.
>
> I cannot say for certain what language the Pelasgians used to speak, but if we judge from those Pelasgians who still live above the Tyrsenoi

in the city of Kreston,[70] who once were neighbors of the people now called Dorians, at the time when they lived in what is now Thessaly, and by the Pelasgians of Plakia and Skylake on the Hellespont, who once lived with Athenians, and by whatever other settlements that were really Pelasgian but changed their name—if, then, one must judge from these, the Pelasgians spoke a barbarian tongue.

If the whole Pelasgian nation did so, the Attic people, being Pelasgian, with their changing over (*hama têi metabolêi*) to Greeks learned a new language.[71] For certainly neither the Krestoniates [= Cortoniates?] nor the Plakinans speak their neighbors' language, but share a language in common; thereby they show [living as they do in widely separated places] that they have taken care to preserve the tongue which they brought with them to these places.

However, it is evident to me, at any rate, that the Greek nation has always used the same language. Although it was weak when it was split off (*aposkhisthen*) from the Pelasgian [at the time, Herodotus must mean, when Pelasgians and the later Dorians lived side by side in Thessaly], it progressed from small beginnings to burgeon into a multitude of peoples as ⟨Pelasgians and?⟩ many other barbarian peoples joined it. Before then, as I see it, the Pelasgian race enjoyed no great increase at all while it was a barbarian people.[72]

So much for the "common blood" of the Greeks. In these paragraphs Herodotus carries out a programmatic redefinition of human origins, according to which nearly everybody—all of humanity except the Dorians (and among the Dorians purest in descent must be the Spartans, who expelled the Minyans from their midst)—are by origin barbarians.[73]

In his day, Herodotus' arguments for identifying Homer's Hellenic Pelasgians as barbarians were not altogether new, but they breasted a strong current of contrary tradition and ancient testimony.[74] Hecataeus had said before him that the Peloponnese was inhabited by barbarians before it was settled by Hellenes. Strabo (whose family was in part of non-Greek origin)[75] cited Hecataeus' testimony (7.7.1 C321 = *FGrH* 1 F 119) and went on to argue from myth that the whole of Greece had been settled by foreign peoples in the beginning, Phrygians brought by Pelops, Egyptians by Danaus, and so on to include Pelasgians in Attica and elsewhere (cf. Strabo 5.2.4 C220f).

But we cannot tell from Strabo's gloss what consequences, if any, Hecataeus himself had seen in these barbarian origins. Herodotus, however, seized upon the lead given by his predecessor to draw fundamental distinctions between Dorians and Ionians; and to do so, he willfully went against the grain of the Ionians' and Athenians' own self-identification as Achaean Ur-Hellenes. He even implies that the Ionians are kin to the Lydians through their relationship with those Lydians, now called Tyrsenoi, who settled either among the Umbrians or in Thrace (Hdt. 1.94.6; cf. Thuc. 4.109.4, 6.88.6).[76]

The translation provided here of the passage under discussion tries to render Herodotus' meaning more clearly than the text itself. Herodotus' Greek is muddy because the argument itself is awkward. He raises difficult questions of process that he nowhere attempts to resolve: if only the original sept of the Dorians carried the Greek language into Greece how did the Pelasgians—and in particular the Athenians, whom he has foremost in mind in this passage—acquire it and when? By what manner of contacts? Before or after they "changed over into Hellenes"? So far from addressing such questions, Herodotus betrays every sign of having neglected to work through the implications of his own ideas, a neglect which implies that he deployed this distinction between Dorians and Ionians, aboriginal Greeks versus aboriginal barbarians, without serious examination for a programmatic and polemical purpose.

For once Herodotus had driven this point home for his purposes, he left it aside, inoperative in the prehistory of the Hellenes. For example, his Pelasgians of Thesprotia unaccountably speak Greek, not the original Pelasgian language, at the time when the oracle at Dodona was founded (2.52ff). Five generations before the Return of the Heraclids and the coming of the Dorians,[77] moreover, his Melampus teaches *Greeks* the rites of the Egyptian Dionysus (Osiris), having learned them from Cadmus and the Phoenicians who had occupied Boeotia during their search for Europa (2.49.2f; cf. 4.147.4)—and these Greeks turn out to be (Pelasgian) Argives (9.34.1).

Herodotus also traces the origin of the Thesmophoria to the Danaids who, he says, taught the rites to the Pelasgian women before the coming of the Dorians; and these too, of course, are the women of the Pelasgian Argives, among whom the Danaids arrived from Egypt. Herodotus relates that the Thesmophoria survived in the Peloponnese after the Dorians drove out the other Pelasgian peoples only among the Pelasgian Arcadians (*Arkades Pelasgoi* 1.146.1), who alone remained in their ancient home (2.171). Thus Herodotus' Pelasgians, among Dorians as well as others, possess the Thesmophoria, which was to become the most widespread of Greek cults,[78] at a time when they still spoke "Pelasgian."

Finally, he appears to accept elsewhere as fact Hecataeus' version (6.137 = *FGrH* 1 F 127) of the origin of the Pelasgians of Lemnos, in which the Athenians *expel* the Pelasgians of Attica, who then occupy Lemnos.[79] It is a story that agrees with the Athenians' own myth of autochthony and implicitly contradicts his own case for the Athenians' descent from Pelasgians; and to this story he adds another one, concerning the sons of Pelasgian fathers from Athenian mothers, which stresses the incompatible *differences* between Pelasgians and Athenians, in their inability even to coexist.

But none of these inconcinnities in the Histories really matter in themselves. Rather they serve as proof that Herodotus, like other Greeks, instinctively imagined the non-Dorian inhabitants of "ancient" Greece—Achaeans, Argives, Danaans, Ionians, Pelasgians, Cadmeans, Lapiths, and all the rest of the races of myth and epic—to be essentially "Greek" and ancestral to themselves, as Aeschylus imagined the Pelasgian Argives in the *Supplices*, which he presented perhaps in 463.[80]

Herodotus himself testified to the universality of the received opinion in noting that once all Hellas was called Pelasgia (perhaps with the *Supplices* in mind: 2.56.1; cf. Aesch. *Suppl.* 234ff, 252–53, 910ff), that *Arkades Pelasgoi* were among the settlers who peopled Ionia (1.146.1) and, indeed, that the Greeks identified the Ionians generically as Aegalian Pelasgians (7.94.1). Much later (and for a non-Athenian patron) Euripides exploited the canonical realtionship in Homer and the poets between Pelasgians, Achaeans, and contemporary Greeks in the *Archelaus*, written between 408 and 406 at the Macedonian court. The *Archelaus* celebrates the noble and Hellenic ancestry of the Macedonian king Archelaus, whose ancestor, Alexander I, had claimed Hellenic descent after the Persian War on the basis that the royal Macedonian house, the Argeads, were a branch of the ancient Temenid house of Argos, descendants of Danaus (Hdt. 5.22.2; cf. 8.137–39; cf. Apollodorus 2.1.4–4.5). A fragment of the play describes how Egyptian Danaus, coming to Argos, decreed that all Pelasgians would henceforth be known as Danaioi, that is, those Danaans whom the poet of the *Iliad* identified with Argives and Achaeans (fr. 228.7 Nauck; cf. Eur. *Or.* 857): although Danaus and his descendants remained "Egyptian," their subjects were the heroic ancestors of the Achaean and Ionian peoples.

In this conflict of racial definitions the Athenian orators and Euripides himself denied any Pelasgian element in their ancestry, and even distanced themselves from other Ionians, as Herodotus himself recognizes in other contexts (1.143.2–3, 6.137), while at the same time their imperial ideology continued to stress the foundation of the Ionian cities from Athens and, in the pomp of the Panathenaea, demanded that all their subjects play the role of colonists, and give due homage to Athens and Athena Polias.[81]

The first step in the Athenians' redefinition of their origins to distinguish themselves from the Ionians of the diaspora was Clisthenes' tribal reform. The differences, not the similarities, between Athenians and Ionians emerged in the Athenian propaganda themes of the Peloponnesian War, which opposed the Athenians' authochthony, and therefore their noble birth (*eugeneia*), to the vile origins of other Greeks from the barbarians Pelops, Cadmus, Aegyptus, Danaus, and so on,[82] including the now-barbarian Pelasgians (cf. Thuc. 4.109.4), who in the *Supplices* a generation earlier had been autochthonous and Hellenic.

Thucydides' views are particularly important as an index of the shifting ground of Athenian self-identity because here, as elsewhere, Thucydides reacted against Herodotus. Thucydides was probably a Philaid and therefore traced his own ancestry to the autochthonous Salaminian hero Aeacus (*Vit. Marc.* 2–4), who had given his name to one of the new Clisthenic tribes. Thucydides predictably insists on the aboriginal autochthony of the Athenians and notes that the security of Attica drew to Athens the strongest men from Greece and augmented the power of the early city. By this reconstruction, which is necessary to his main argument concerning Athens' early importance, he is able to have his autochthonous cake and eat it too—albeit with a nonautochthonous icing.

He goes on to contrast the stability of Attica with the invasions and migrations taking place elsewhere in Greece, including the Peloponnese which later became Dorian. The first Hellenes, so-called, are not the Dorians—and he implicitly overlooks them by confining his discussion of Hellenic origins to the period before the Trojan War—but Hellen and his sons, who held sway in Phthiotis, and the followers of Phthiotic Achilles to Troy. This was still at a time, he says, when the distinction between Hellene and barbarian did not yet exist, since Homer does not use the word: it was only city by city as each understood the other's speech and finally all of them together that the peoples of Greece were called Hellenes (1.2.1–3.4).

Thucydides' Ur-Hellenization of Attica foreshadows the polemic of the Funeral Oration, by its association of barbarism not with race, empire, or tyranny, but with a violent and insecure way of life epitomized in the bearing of arms. In Thucydides' Archaeology, Hellenism arrives in Greece with the conditions that would also define contemporary Athens: security of fortifications, surplus wealth, and revenue-producing thalassocracy (1.5.1– 10.2). He shifts the terms of the debate on who is really Greek from descent to history and culture, and declares that it was the Athenians who led the way to Hellenism, being the first to lay aside their swords and develop a more elegant (*trypherôteron*, 6.3) way of life—he even dares use a word, *trypheron*, which carries Asianic associations of softness, effeminacy, and wantonness, in direct contrast to the simplicity and rigor of the Dorian style of life.[83] Seen in this light, Thucydides' Archaeology is—and was meant to be taken as—a full and dismissive refutation of his predecessor's attack on the Hellenism of the Athenians.

The Athenians of Thucydides' wartime generation made a public

boast of their pure descent *ab origine* especially against the enemy
Dorians, whom they affected to consider an immigrant motley in
part of barbarian origin (e.g., Plato *Menexenus* 237b). In Euripides'
wartime *Ion*, Creusa bears Ion to the god Apollo, and then goes
on to bear his inferior half-brothers Dorus and Achaeus to a mortal
(1589–94; cf. Plato *Euthydemus* 302c).[84] Euripides' fragmentary
Erechtheus tells how Eumolpus led an army of Thracians into Attica
to help the Eleusinians against Athens. Earlier these Thracians
might have reminded Athenians of the Persian invader; but at this
date—early in the war[85]—when the Spartans were invading Attica
yearly through Eleusis, invasions that recalled the Spartan king
Cleomenes' destruction of the sacred precinct there when he invaded Attica to put down the infant democracy (Hdt. 6.75.3; cf.
5.74.2), the invading barbarians stood for the Dorian enemy.[86]

It was in this wartime environment of hostile propaganda between
Athens and Sparta that Herodotus went out of his way in the
passage cited earlier to color the Dorians, with the Spartans at
their head, as the only truly Hellenic people, and to impute barbarian origins, distant but indelible, to all the non-Dorian peoples.
He used an argument that singled out Athens, the founder of the
Ionian cities. Herodotus' imputation was offensive to the sentiments nurtured by the orators—did he ever read *this* passage at
Athens?[87] But it also makes out all of the ancestors and heroes of
ancestral tradition, Trojan and Achaean alike, to be non-Hellenic.
His view of Greek origins, which pervades his work, was rooted
in his fundamental assumptions about human nature and the
specific differences between Hellenes and barbarians. These assumptions, in turn, were firmly bound up with the circumstances
of his own birth, his society, and his times.

In barbarizing all the Greeks but his own Dorians, Herodotus
betrays his insecurities. The Herodotus visible in this prejudice is
not the phil-Athenian Herodotus alleged by later tradition and
scholarship,[88] but a contradictory soul who nursed complicated
sentiments toward his mixed racial and cultural heritage, toward
the traditionalist stance on that heritage which his elder kinsman
Panyassis had taken, and toward Athens. Imperial Athens was the

polis tyrannos of the Greek world, but had also founded the city whose citizenship he claimed, calling himself "Herodotus of Thurii."[89] The Herodotus visible here is the son of the Carian-named Lyxes, who resented Ionians and Milesians (1.143–47), the very peoples whose ancestry and foundations the phil-Ionian Panyassis had celebrated in his *Ionica*.

Herodotus was born in half-Carian Halicarnassus,[90] a town pretending like himself to a Dorian status that was denied by the other Dorian cities of the Pentapolis, and whose athletes were barred from the Triopian Games (1.144) of the Pentapolis. Earlier Panyassis had named one of the two sons of Heracles by Lydian Omphale as Hyllus in the *Heraclea*. In the Dorian tradition of the Return of the Heraclids to the Peloponnese, another Hyllus, the eldest son of Heracles, was the direct ancestor of the Heraclid kings of the Dorian peoples.[91] By this act of homonymy, Panyassis associated the leading families of native origin in "Dorian" Halicarnassus and the other communities identified as Dorian in Asia Minor with the kings of the Dorians in the Peloponnesian homeland.[92] In the same poem he derives the origin of the Lycians from a native Tremiles (cf. 2.173.1–3 *contra*) and his bride Ogygiê (or Praxidice), whose four sons are the native heroes Xanthus, Tloös, Pinarus, and Cragus.[93] Thus Panyassis apparently rejected Homer's Lycian genealogy where it touched upon Ionian royalty and by this means avoided inserting a native element in the descent of the Ionian kings, whereas he sought to associate the Lydian and other native aristocracies with the Dorian settlers in Asia Minor. If so, Panyassis accepted—and celebrated—the fact of his own and other leading families' mixed descent in the Dorian communities, attested in the preservation of native names in the family line— while maintaining that Ionian royalty, at any rate, was altogether Neleid in descent.[94]

All of this Herodotus denies. In a long passage (1.143–47) very revealing of his sensitivities, he scoffs at the Asiatic Ionians' and Milesians' claim to purity of descent, while conspicuously providing a motive for the Halicarnassians' exclusion from the Dorian community in Asia that implicitly denies any racial difference between Halicarnassus and the Dorian Pentapolis (he attributes his city's exclusion to a Halicarnassian athlete's refusal long before to dedicate his prize tripod to the god, according to custom: 1.144). Centuries later, Plutarch, admittedly in *parti pris*, was to ridicule Herodotus' Halicarnassian *campanilismo* and the Dorian pretensions of the Halicarnassians, commenting snidely that Herodotus' real attachment was to the Halicarnassians, who took their harems with them when they marched against Greece. In respect of his racial sensitivities, at least, Plutarch understood Herodotus well.[95]

Halicarnassus, moreover, was ruled by people whose origins were uncomfortably like his own, a Hellenized Carian dynasty. But it is this dynasty that Herodotus celebrates in the person of Artemisia, the female tyrant of Halicarnassus and the grandmother of Panyassis' murderer. In his heroization of Artemisia's courage and counsel in the barbarian host, Herodotus carries out an astonishing inversion of the un-Hellenic and unnatural signifiers otherwise universally carried by barbarian women of power (7.99, 8.68—69, 87–88, 93, 101, 103, 107).[96]

We may well ask, then, who in Halicarnassus was a Greek and who was a barbarian for Herodotus? We may ask, too, whether for Herodotus the distinctions he grew up with in his native city were not at least as much an immediate matter of culture as they were ancestrally racial—a matter, that is to say, of how one went about being Greek and displaying one's Hellenism to other Halicarnassians.

Herodotus' Croesus tried, but failed, to be Greek. Herodotus the mestizo succeeded. The Histories are an *apodexis (proem.)*: an exhibition, a display, a demonstration.[97] A demonstration of what? Among other things, surely, of Herodotus' Hellenism.[98] At his most polemical—where he betrays the most passionate sensitivity— Herodotus insists on three facts about his own origins and about the definitive distinctions between barbarians and Greeks. First, Halicarnassus was an original member of the Dorian community in Asia; second, the only true Greeks are Dorians; third and most important, oracles work for Greeks but not for barbarians, who cannot understand them. These facts are interconnected in his definition of himself as it appears in the exhibition of his work to the Greek world. Do not the Histories, after all, furnish exhaustive proof of his own, Hellenic and virtually mantic, understanding of oracles, and of the world and its processes? Seen in this light, the Histories are the exhaustive demonstration of their author's genuine Hellenism.

The racial distinction between Dorian and Ionian held decisive meanings for Herodotus' wartime audiences.[99] And we find in Herodotus, despite his formal and delicate silence about many of his real opinions, skeins of associations about the Hellenism or barbarism of the respective combatants that form a subtextual commentary on the nature of the present conflict and an implicit prophecy concerning its fated outcome.

Herodotus' associations between lions, camels, city walls, and dreams, in Asia and Greece respectively, carry in particular a heavy freight of portentous implications that connect the Lydian and Athenian poles of his Histories. Long ago at Sardis, he relates, when the concubine of the Lydian king Meles gave birth to a lion-cub, the king consulted the mantic priests of Carian Telmessus. They told him that he would make Sardis impregnable if he carried the lion-cub round the city walls. Meles did so, except in one place where it appeared far too steep for any besieger to scale. This was the place where the Persians long afterward would enter Sardis, after their camels had panicked the Lydians' chargers and routed their cavalry, putting an end to the empire of Croesus (1.80 and 84).

Herodotus thus explains the fall of of the greatest city and proudest citadel of its time by reference to a barbarian monarch's failure to carry out the will of the god, because he thought he knew its walls better than the god. There was a relevant message in this story for Herodotus' audiences. At this time Sparta—a city without walls—was at war with Athens, whose walls were by far the greatest in the Greek world. Elsewhere Herodotus compares Athens' Long Walls to the walls of Agbatana, which the first king of the Medes had his people build when he reestablished tyranny in upper Asia (1.97.5).

As we know from Thucydides, Pericles had placed his whole confidence in the Long Walls to exhaust Sparta in the current war.

Herodotus tells a story about Pericles' Alcmaeonid mother Agariste which puts Meles and Pericles, Athens and barbarian Asia, into portentous communication *via* walls, dreams, and lions: when Agariste was pregnant, he relates, she dreamed that she was giving birth to a lion; and a few days later she bore Pericles (6.131.2).[100] Dreams come often to barbarian monarchs in the Histories, but they visit Greeks only in the context of tyranny.[101] Agariste's select circle of Greek dreamers comprises only the Pisistratids Hipparchus (5.55–56) and Hippias (6.107.2), together with the daughter of the Samian tyrant Polycrates (3.124); all of their visions, moreover, portended only defeat or death.

By definition Herodotus' Athenians are Greeks descended from barbarians. They also hold other Greeks in subjection to tribute, as only the barbarians of Asia had done before them. They rule their empire from a fortified city that reminds Herodotus of the citadel of the Medes. Pericles, whose position at the beginning of the war Thucydides could describe as verging on monarchy, and whose faction the comedians were calling "the new Pisistratids" and the like,[102] began the present war trusting to Athens' walls to preserve a free hand for the empire in the future.[103] Pericles is carried by Herodotus, through the telling of his Alcmaeonid mother's dream, into the select company of Athenian tyrants and King Meles of Sardis, whose city fell because he did not heed the deity.

Lions born of women are not normal lions; it is this kind of "paranormal" or "unnatural" lion that puts Sardis and Athens together in a category labeled "Asianic," "tyrannical," "walled against a superior enemy." On the other hand, "normal" and "natural" lions are "European" and "Dorian" lions, which defeat what "unnatural" and "Asiatic-in-Europe" lions stand for in the Histories. Near the end of the Histories, European lions attack the camels of Xerxes, though they harm no other animal in his pack train (7.125). In Asia the camels of the Persians had defeated the power of the Lydians; the camel is an animal peculiar to Asia. Xerxes, who is also peculiar to Asia, is soon to face Leonidas, whose very name means "lionly." Leonidas' Dorian warriors will defeat the best of the Persians and fight against them, in the end, tooth-and-nail (7.225.3)—that is to say, with the natural weapons of the

lion, the animal whose stone image—the *lithinos leôn epi Leônidêi*—
will crown their tomb (7.225).

Afterward, at Plataea, the Spartans would gain what Herodotus
acclaimed to be the most splendid victory ever known (9.64.1).
This judgment implicitly devalues Salamis and the seapower of
Athens.[104] For Herodotus, thalassocracy belongs to the Asiatic and
Ionian world, and its consequences—well understood and frankly
acknowledged in his day by the Athenians themselves (cf. Thuc.
2.53.2, 3.37.2)—are tyrannical.

Herodotus thus seems to pose implicitly prophetic questions
about the comparatively "Hellenic" or "barbaric" nature of contemporary Athenians and their leaders, and about the real strength of
their walls in circumstances having to do with obeying or disobeying the divine will. These questions were directly relevant to
the Pericleans' war policy and Athens' recent fortunes in this war.
For the Athenians' walls had not protected them from a plague,
which carried away perhaps a third of the citizen population.[105] This
plague had broken out, as Herodotus must have known, in the summer when the Athenians had sacrilegiously murdered envoys of the
Spartans, who bore an immunity defended by the gods (7.137.3; cf.
Thuc. 2.67.4). At the beginning of this war, too, the Athenians had
occupied a precinct called the Pelargicum, which lay under a curse
forbidding its habitation; moreover, Delphian Apollo had warned
the Athenians that "the Pelargicum unoccupied is better."

It is Thucydides who reports this oracle (2.17.1); but surely
Herodotus, collector of oracles, knew it, as did his Athenian audience. Surely he knew also that other oracle, conspicuously published by the Spartans at the outbreak of the war itself, in which
the god Apollo promised the Spartans victory if they fought with all
their might, and promised that he would be with them in this war
whether summoned or not (Thuc. 1.118.3). Whoever knew these
oracles and the sacrilegious violence meted out to envoys protected
by Apollo's brother Hermes could well conclude that the plague of
Athens had come borne on the arrows of Far-Shooting Apollo.

These associations do not exist unambiguously at the surface of
a work whose author, after all, was the citizen of a city founded

by Athens and whom the Athenians are said to have publicly rewarded.[106] At the level of a recitative performance, dreams, lions, camels, and walls exist peripherally and anecdotally, here and gone in a moment. But then, taken in isolation, a very great deal carried by Herodotus' river of narrative is peripheral and anecdotal. If dreams, lions, camels, and walls do possess these sorts of meanings within the Histories, they do so because the widely separated stories in which they occur appealed to a mind that chose them according to a precisely formed, if overtly unexpressed, conception of the world and of the leading powers of Europe and Asia.

The meanings of these subliminal associations contradict the valuation that Athens bears on the surface of the Histories. Though Herodotus tells the story of the progressive Hellenization of the Athenians, from their Pelasgian origins through their liberation from tyranny to their declaration after Salamis that they would never abandon their fellow Hellenes, and ends ostensibly at the point when the Athenians had liberated the other Greeks by their courage and exertions, his narrative extends in meditative power into the present war as a kind of prophecy.[107]

Herodotus knew the oracles after all, including one in the possession of the Spartans concerning a fated conjuncture of peoples, which remained to be fulfilled: that they and the other Dorians must be driven out of the Peloponnese by Medes and Athenians together (8.141.1).[108] This oracle, very likely another one of those circulating during the war years, proves that Herodotus was not the only Dorian who associated imperial Athens with that other great enemy of the liberties of the Greeks, and who accordingly drew the line between Hellenism and barbarism not between Greeks and barbarians but between Dorians and everyone else.

Pisistratus, Lycurgus, Solon

Meanwhile we have located the strategy Herodotus pursued in placing his essay on Hellenic origins at the head of his digression on the earlier histories of Athens and Sparta early in book 1 (59ff): this essay on origins refers their differences to an original and ineradicable racial antithesis, and this antithesis in turn controls his swiftly framed and highly selective accounts of these peoples' antithetical character and antithetical histories.

The principal fact of Athens' earlier history was the tyranny. At the time when Croesus' fall impended, says Herodotus, the Athenians were held down and divided among themselves by the tyrant Pisistratus. This tyranny evolved out of a great portent that had once appeared to Pisistratus' father Hippocrates at Olympia, when the cauldrons he had filled with sacrificial meats boiled over with no fire beneath them. The Spartan seer Chilon, whom Herodotus remembers elsewhere as the wisest Spartan who ever lived (7.235.2), was passing by. He warned Hippocrates never to have sons, and to disown any that he might already have. But Hippocrates disobeyed this unambiguous and virtually oracular warning.[109] Afterward, Pisistratus was born to him.

This episode recapitulates the motifs marking the just-told stories of Solon and Croesus and Croesus and Delphi, which anticipate Croesus' fall and the enslavement of the Lydians by Cyrus. The wise Athenian Solon advises the barbarian Croesus, but to no avail. Soon Croesus and his people are enslaved by a foreigner. Likewise, the Spartan Chilon advises Hippocrates, but to no avail. Soon Hippocrates' countrymen are politically enslaved by his son, also a foreigner.[110] The parallels extend even to the boiling cauldrons (*lebêtes*) which indicated the divine will to Chilon. Only minutes before in Herodotus' recitation,[111] Croesus had boiled the meat of a tortoise and a lamb in a cauldron (*lebêti*) to discover which oracles really possessed the divine will (1.47–48)—which he then fails to understand. The conclusion is hardly to be avoided that Herodotus consciously associated the great Athenian tyrant and the first of his great barbarian tyrants by narrative and verbal parallels that his audience could not fail to notice. Chilon is to Hippocrates as Solon had been to Croesus.

But unlike the *nêpios* Croesus, Pisistratus was Athenian and so presumably clever. Regarding Pisistratus' first attempts at the tyranny, Herodotus selects two stratagems. In the first of these Pisistratus wounded himself and his mules and drove into the agora as if fleeing an ambush of enemies in order to deceive the Athenians into granting him a bodyguard: with this troop he seized the Acropolis, the ancient seat of Athens' kings. Although soon driven out by his enemies, he returned to power helped by a marriage alliance with his former rival, Megacles the son of Alcmaeon (1.59.3). Pisistratus was welcomed by the Athenians when he arrived in the city riding in a chariot together with a tall and beautiful woman dressed up as the goddess Athena, and preceded by criers calling on the citizens to "receive Pisistratus gladly, whom Athena, honoring him above all men, herself conducts to her own acropolis" (1.59–60).

This was Pisistratus' second ruse. Herodotus comments that "they devised a trick which in my view was by far the most ridiculous, at all events, since the time long past when the Greek nation became distinguished from the barbarian on account of its greater shrewdness and relative freedom from naïve gullibility, inasmuch as the people of Athens had even then the foremost reputation for cleverness (*sophiên*)" (1.60.3). By including in this judgment a reminder of his recently stated theory of Greek evolution from barbarian origins, he forcefully implies that the Athenians were incompletely Hellenized even at this time, since they could fall for the tricks of a tyrant and under the sway of tyrants, as is natural among barbarians.

Herodotus goes on to tell how Pisistratus fell out with Megacles and lost his tyranny because he did not want to have children by Megacles' daughter, who was tainted with the Alcmaeonid family curse.[112] But finally Pisistratus planted his tyranny firmly with mercenaries and money after returning from exile to face those Athenians who took up arms to support "the best cause," as he comments, at Pallene. "By divine arrangement" (1.62.4) he encountered a seer who uttered a prophecy in dark hexameters. Pisistratus immediately seized its meaning as portending victory and led his followers against the Athenians at this moment, when they were resting after the morning meal, and scattered them in retreat. Then, says Herodotus, he thought of a brilliant move (*boulên . . . sophôtatên . . . epitekhnatai*, 1.63.2) to keep his enemies from regrouping, by sending his sons forward on horseback to give unmolested passage home to the fugitives. A divinity took a hand in his victory—but so did Pisistratus' intelligence.

Since for Herodotus everything occurs with the arrangement
or concurrence of deity, the importance of Pisistratus' encounter
with the seer lies no less in Pisistratus' immediate grasp of prophecy, followed by his brilliant and decisive course of action, than
in the revelation of the divine will itself. The other brilliant Athenian in the Histories who seizes the meaning of a battle prophecy,
and then employs a ruse contained in a message in the course of
taking brilliant and decisive action, is Themistocles, the author of
Athens' navy and empire, the builder of the Piraeus and the walls
of Athens, and finally a Medizing grandee endowed by the Great
King. Pisistratus is the first pleonectic leader of Athens, but by no
means the last: like answers to like across the generations of
Athenian history and the span of Herodotus' work.

Herodotus' antithetical perceptions of Athens and Sparta are sus-
tained by the antithesis of *sôphrosynê* and *sophiê,* self-mastery and
intelligence, the virtues that canonically defined the respective
characters of Sparta and Athens in the Greek mind. He tells a
story that the Peloponnesians invented about the Scythian sage
Anacharsis: he was sent to pursue learning in Greece, and came
back saying that all the Greeks busily pursued every species of
sophia except the Lacedaemonians, who alone practiced sophrosyne in making arguments and understanding them (4.77.1). Herodotus disbelieves the story but tells it anyway because it makes
his point.

The view Herodotus presents was not peculiar to himself; it
was widely shared. In Thucydides, for example, sophrosyne is
what the ephor Stheneladas said the Spartans would be practicing
if they went to war against Athens (*ên sôphronômen*, 1.86.2). In
the Greek political vocabulary sophrosyne is the buzzword for
Spartiate virtue, and unlike sophia—a slippery word whose cognates connote cunning, unscrupulous cleverness—sophrosyne
stays put: it always stands for "safe thinking," balance, moderation,
prudence, self-control.[113] Sophrosyne is a word that does not appear in the great Funeral Oration, exhaustive of Athens' virtues,
which Thucydides provides to Pericles (2.35–46). But sophia does,
famously: *philosophoumen aneu malakias* (40.1), "we cultivate our

minds with no loss of manhood," says Pericles in the midst of an extended contrast between the Spartans and his Athens, the city that is intellect itself in action and "the education (*paideusin*) of all Greece" (41.1). Thucydides praises Pericles' foresight (*pronoia*, 2.65.6), strength of character, and power of judgment (*dynatos ôn tôi te axiômati kai têi gnomêi*, 2.65.8) by which "he controlled the mob freely, by constitutional means" (*kateikhe to plêthos eleutherôs*); whereas his Cleon is "in all respects the most violent (*biaiotatos*) of the citizens and also the most influential with the demos" (3.36.6). Nonetheless Thucydides' Pericles and Thucydides' Cleon agree on one point: both call Athens' empire a tyranny (2.53.2, 3.37.2).[114]

In the Histories, tyranny is created by intelligence. Herodotus' successful tyrants—Greek and barbarian alike—gain power less by violence than by employing their wits. Herodotus introduces Deioces as "a wise man who arose among the Medes . . . and, his lust for tyranny aroused, did the following" (*anêr en tois Mêdoisi egeneto sophos . . . erastheis tyrannidos epoiee toiade*, 1.96.1–2). Among Greek tyrants Pisistratus is the wiliest. Three times he tricked the brilliant Athenians, and even when they were once again free and under a democracy, they succumbed to the wiles of Aristagoras the tyrant of Miletus. "For evidently," muses Herodotus, "it is easier to fool many men than one, since he was unable to fool Cleomenes the Lacedaemonian who was one man alone, but managed it with thirty thousand Athenians" (5.97.2). In Herodotus' work, susceptibility to the kind of sophia that empowers tyrants is common to many barbarians, but among Greeks only to Athenians and to Ionian Milesians—those very Milesians whose boast of pure descent from Athens Herodotus ridicules (1.146.2), and whose tyrant calls on Athenian help to bring disaster down on all Ionia (5.97 *fin*.). Herodotus grew up looking at Athens from the other side of the Aegean; and from that perspective he summed up Athens' history in its leaders of pleonectic and tyrannical brilliance, from Pisistratus to Pericles.

Herodotus' equally selective account of Sparta's emergence (1.65–68) also proceeds from oracles, although in other respects it stands in high contrast to his description of Athens and her tyranny. Herodotus relates that the Spartans at the time of Croesus' reign had escaped from great evils, and had now gained the upper hand over the Tegeans in war, against whom alone of their enemies in the reigns of Leon and Hegesicles (*c.* 590–550) they had won no success. For if the Athenians had been divided among themselves by a tyrant, the Spartans had begun their history *kakonomôtatoi*, as the worst-lawed people of nearly all the Greeks and *aprosmêktoi*, shunning both one another and strangers. But in the reign of their third Agiad king, Leobotes,[115] his uncle, the regent Lycurgus, "altered all of the usages (*nomima*) and made sure they were not transgressed; then he established the Spartans' present military usages, including the sworn companies, the bands of thirty, and the common messes; and, in addition to these, the ephors and gerontes. Changing thus, they became well lawed (*eunomêthêsan* 1.66 *init.*), and on Lycurgus' death they erected a shrine and [still] give him great reverence." Indeed, Herodotus continues, the Pythia had preferred to judge Lycurgus to be a god rather than a man, and some (but not the Spartans themselves) say that he received the Spartiate order from the priestess herself (1.65.2–66.1).

Thereafter the Spartans flourished and, no longer content with peace, they procured a war oracle from Delphi that appeared to promise them the plain of Tegea. But the response was deceiving and they were defeated. Again they applied to the god and were told to find the bones of Orestes, which were buried in Tegea at a place where "two winds blow by strong necessity, strike beats against strike, and grief lies upon grief. "By luck and intelligence" (*Kai syntykhiêi . . . kai sophiêi*, 1.68.1), says Herodotus, a Spartan named Lichas recognized its meaning in the discovery by a Tegean blacksmith of giant bones buried near his forge.[116] Lichas brought them home to Sparta and "from this time onward, whenever they make trial of each other, the Lacedaemonians are far better in war; and they had already subdued much of the Peloponnese" (1.68.6).

In this account Herodotus emphasizes the Spartans' debt to Delphian Apollo for their way of life and their hegemony in the Peloponnese (which in fact rested largely on their strong relations with Tegea).[117] In the Histories the only oracle that any Greeks misinterpret is the one that leads the Spartans to attack Tegea in the first place (1.71.1).[118] Unlike Croesus, however, who deceives himself by reading his own ambitions into an ambiguous response, as if it were a Rorschach inkblot (1.53.3), the Spartans are purposely misled by the god, who gives them an apparently straightforward response; and from their misinterpretation of this response arises a sequel that teaches them the limits of their power and guarantees their hegemony within those limits.[119]

Herodotus meanwhile ignores the central event in early Spartan history, the Messenian Wars. He proceeds from the reforms of Lycurgus directly to the Spartan domination of Tegea, events which by his own reckoning were separated by the reigns of eleven Agiad kings (Leobotes to Leon: 7.204), or by modern reckoning some 300 years—the whole period during which the Spartans achieved the conquest of Messenia and the enslavement of her population of fellow Dorian Greeks.[120] Here his only concessions to these facts, upon which Spartan hegemony and the Spartan way of life rested, is his cryptic reference to the Spartans' escape from great evils (1.65.1), and his notice in passing that by the time they had overawed the Tegeans they had also subdued the better part of the Peloponnese.

In this foreshortened view of the Spartans, which ignores their own literal enslavement of fellow Greeks, we locate an element of Herodotus' attitude in common with his social contemporaries, and also another element in his program. Programmatically he could not present the Spartans as comparable to the Athenians, who had prospered by politically "enslaving" fellow Greeks of their own kind. For the rest, he appears to have viewed Sparta with much the same regard as other aristocratic Laconophiles whose views are more accessible to us, especially Xenophon, who in his *Constitution of the Lacedaemonians* does not so much as mention the existence of the helots. Since the helots are slaves—actual slaves and not simply political slaves like Athens' subjects—they are outside Sparta's eunomia and socially invisible. Herodotus shared the aristocratic Greek prejudices favorable to a way of life that made warriors of its men, in contrast to the maritime, artisanal, banausic, and antihoplite image of Athens, which was especially reinforced about the time Herodotus began exhibiting his work by the humiliation of Athens' hoplites at Delium in 424. For him, as for other Greeks whose ethos was grounded in the martial virtues, the Spartans were *uniquely* well lawed: Herodotus refers in these terms to no other Greeks.[121]

A significant index to his interest in Lycurgan eunomia is his considerable display of knowledge about Spartan institutions, whereas in contrast he says almost nothing about those of Athens. His informational bias may in part be accounted for by his ambition to display his knowledge to his audiences, who must have been far more familiar with the open democracy of Athens and its imitations in the cities of her empire than with the secretive ways of the Spartans. Still, the Athenians lived under the laws of Solon, surely of interest if these laws had helped to make Athens great.

However, Herodotus puts Athens' point of departure toward greatness long after Solon, with the fall of the Pisistratids and their acquisition of *isonomiê* (5.78). His one brief mention of Solon's lawgiving is only meant to explain why he arrived at Croesus' court as one among all of the other *sophistai* of Greece who were attracted to Sardis—as they were to Athens in Herodotus' day— at the height of her wealth: after binding the Athenians by oath not to transgress his laws for ten years, Solon had exiled himself to prevent them from forcing him to change any of his laws in the meantime. Herodotus mentions a single one of these laws only, in another connection. It is the law, actually invented by the pharaoh Amasis, that prescribed the death penalty for any Egyptian without visible means of support, a law which Herodotus says Solon adopted for the Athenians (2.177.2). As for Solon's poems, Herodotus says only that in them Solon praised Philocyprus, the father of Aristocyprus the king of Soli who fell in the revolt against the Persians, *tyrannôn malista*, "above all tyrants" (5.113.2).[122]

Herodotus is said to have spent an important period of his life at Athens; he knew Solon's laws and Solon's poetry, including without question the portions we possess in Plutarch's *Life* and the Aristotelian *Constitution of the Athenians*.[123] Undoubtedly he could have included the *seisachtheia* in his work had he wished to do so. But in the facts that Herodotus chooses to impart concerning

Solon, we see Solon as someone who praises a tyrant, adopts a law devised by a tyrant, and enjoys the hospitality of the tyrants Croesus and Philocyprus. Although Solon is not a tyrant himself, tyrants attract him, and the laws he made for the Athenians did not prevent the rise of a tyrant in the next generation, who, indeed, went on using those laws (1.59.6; cf. Thuc. 6.54.6). It was not Solon at Athens, but godlike Lycurgus at Sparta, who had erected an unfailing hedge against revolution and tyranny.

Solon was one of the canonical Sages, who were called *sophoi* principally for their statesmanship.[124] Herodotus calls Solon not a *sophos* but a *sophistês*, together with Melampus and Pythagoras (2.49.1 and 4.95.2). All three "sophists" employed sophia for the uses of power; possibly Herodotus was not content to award them the title *sophos* because he saw them as invidious ancestors of the new sophists and their arts, which they employed for the uses of power.[125] Melampus had bartered the rites of Dionysus for shares of the kingship at Argos; Pythagoras founded the politically powerful brotherhoods named after him, and his slave Salmoxis became a god among his own people by employing what he had learned from his master. Croesus' own interest in power, therefore, was one reason why he entertained all the *sophistai* of Greece. It is also the reason why Solon's counsel, which holds his power as nought, is irrelevant to Croesus.

In Solon Herodotus provides a full-dress portrait of an Athenian *sophistês* trying to educate an Asiatic barbarian. But Croesus pays no heed until disaster arrives in the form of Cyrus. If this is how Herodotus saw Solon then we have an answer to why there is no Solon at Athens and no *seisachtheia* in the Histories: because it did no good. Solon was irrelevant not only to Croesus but to the Athenians, who like Croesus were interested only in power, as Herodotus could know by reading Solon himself. So the Solon whom Herodotus shows trying to drum into Croesus' head the wisdom of valuing a life like Tellus', or a death like Cleobis' and Biton's, is also the Solon shown fleeing the Athenians, who were eager to coerce him to repeal his statutes. For the Athenians, like Croesus, would pay no heed until disaster arrived in the form of Pisistratus.

There is much of Herodotus himself reflected in his Solon; like him Herodotus was a *planêtes* who wandered the world for love of *sophiê* (1.30.2). Perhaps this kinship with Solon accounts for some of the pathos, the sense of the irrelevance and futility of Solon's wisdom, with which Herodotus observes Solon's impotence to stay the course of tyranny, whether at Ionian Athens or at the court of Croesus. Indeed, Herodotus' own experience of lawgivers may well have colored his view of Solon and the character of his laws more directly. For faction and violence were to shake Herodotus' adoptive city of Thurii not long after its foundation, despite its undoubtedly excellent statutes. These had been commissioned by the Athenians from the best of the *sophistai*, Protagoras of Abdera.[126]

Just as Spartans and Athenians are different, Solon too is a different kind of lawgiver from Lycurgus. We can now see that Herodotus conceived Solon and Lycurgus antithetically. Lycurgus was a divine man who remained in Sparta to see that his divinely approved mandates were carried out, instead of absenting himself, like Solon, to see and learn the rest of the world (1.29.2–30.2), while depending on the gods to enforce his self-inspired laws. As for Solon's laws themselves, Herodotus mentions only one, which is one borrowed from a barbarian, and which on its face encouraged a banausic way of life. Those of Lycurgus, brought from Dorian Crete, did just the opposite.[127]

Heraclids and Dorians

Herodotus' view of Lycurgan Sparta is also decisively influenced by the origins of its Heraclid kings, who are not Dorians but Achaeans (5.72 *fin.*) originally descended from Egyptian Perseus, whose descendants came to be counted among the Greeks (2.91.2–6, 98; 6.53–54). Sparta's kings were also of Phoenician descent, since the mother of Eurysthenes and Procles (the twins from which the two houses of Spartan kings were respectively descended) was herself descended from Cadmus (4.147.2).[128] Elsewhere Herodotus says that Perseus was also held to be the ancestor of the Persian kings (7.61.3, 150–51). This linkage of ancestries may explain why he evidently finds meaning in apparently random similarities of practice shared by Spartan and Persian royalty (6.58.2–59; cf. 7.3.3–4). It would be typical of him to prefer a genealogical canon that, beneath the surface of his narrative, binds ancestral ties between the houses of the barbarian tyrants of Asia and the Heraclids of the Dorian Peloponnese, ties that influence the history of Perseus' descendants.

Once again Herodotus addresses polemically an issue of origins which, like the original barbarism of the Pelasgian ancestors of the Athenians, he might have passed over. But here, as there, he is concerned to name who is originally Hellenic and who is not because this is a distinction fundamental to his explanation of history. What follows at Sparta from the barbarian origins of the Heraclids is the most problematic feature of Spartiate society, a feature exemplified by the renegade Demaratus and the rogue Cleomenes: bad kings are the greatest cause of troubles in the Sparta of the *Histories*, and most of what Herodotus says about the institutions of the Spartans has to do with the kings, and especially with their position vis-à-vis the Spartiate community. He is interested, that is to say, in how this genuinely Hellenic people controlled their racially barbarian kings.[129]

This is a distinctly Dorian problem, not confined to Sparta, but solved only by the Spartans, who never suffered tyranny, whereas in Dorian Argos a Heraclid king, Pheidon of Argos, had become the first tyrant in Greece.[130] Even before Lycurgus, at the dawn of their history, the Spartans had already expelled a microbe of tyranny from their body, when they drove the non-Dorian Minyans from Lacedaemon. This happened in the childhood of their very first pair of kings, Eurysthenes and Procles, and Herodotus tells the story at length in the significant context of his history of Cyrene and Barca, two cities that came to be dominated by barbarous tyrants (4.145–58; cf. 6.52).[131]

The Minyans who came to Lacedaemon were descendants of the Argonauts, who had been the shipmates of the Tyndaridae; on the strength of this ancient connection the Spartans had given the Minyans land allotments and Spartan brides. But the Spartans turned against them when they also demanded a share in the kingship and made other impious demands, and they were led out of Lacedaemon by Theras, the maternal uncle of Eurysthenes and Procles. Theras was a descendant of Polynices of Thebes, and through him and his Phoenician ancestor Cadmus, he was the kinsman of the then-Phoenician inhabitants of Thera.

Here Theras and his Minyans settled. The sequel is a tale of degeneration into barbarism. The Theraeans, suffering a drought, sent out a colony to found Cyrene, and the descendants of the founder, Battus, founded Barca in turn. The royalty of both cities then descended into crime, atrocity, and tyranny, especially in the persons of Arcesileos III and his mother Pheretime, who in Herodotus are ethically barbarian and Greek in name only (4.160–67, 200–202, 205).

The kings, however, remained as a barbarian element in Sparta after the departure of the Minyans. For Herodotus, the paramount genius of Lycurgus' laws, and the respect in which they differed antithetically from the laws of Solon, which preceded the tyranny at Athens, lay in their effect on the power of the Spartan kings. Lycurgus had instituted the ephors and the gerontes (1.65.5); together these magistrates contained the power and oversaw the lives of the kings, whose power presumably had been paramount before them.

Herodotus was very much aware that the ephors in particular possessed the chief executive function and had the power of judgment over the kings themselves (3.148.2; 5.39.2–41.2; 6.57.5, 63.2 and 65.4, 82.1; 9.7–11). Moreover the rights and privileges that the kings did possess derived from the whole community of the Spartiates (6.56.1), and could be altered or limited by the Spartans, as when they forbade both kings to campaign together (5.75.2). This ordinance impinged upon the right of the kings to make war at will (6.56.1), as did also the Spartans' right to bring their kings to trial for misdeeds committed in war (6.72).

Herodotus' piecemeal but consistent picture of Lycurgan Sparta, especially his enumeration of the kings' rights and privileges (6.56–58), shows how the Spartan kings were preserved and nourished by the community not as untrammeled monarchs but as living icons, so to speak—numinous sources of communal *mana*, divine force, comparable in essential respects to the sacred images of the Tyndaridae, who accompanied Spartan armies into battle (5.75.2), and those of the Aeacidae, who led the Aeginetans against the Persians at Salamis (8.64.2, 83.2, 84.2).[132] It was the kings who, among their other religious privileges, managed the state's relationship with Delphi at home (6.57.2–4), and on campaign carried out and ratified the interpretations of all ritual sacrifices. For the rest, the Lycurgan community was always on its guard against the kings: they are to fear the displeasure of the Spartiates (6.74.1) and the judgments of the ephors (6.82).[133]

The Spartan king who went furthest against these restraints was the king on whom Herodotus concentrates his greatest attention: Cleomenes. Cleomenes' paternity itself was tainted by his father's bigamy: although insisted upon by the ephors and gerontes to assure the survival of the Eurypontid house, it was—Herodotus adds–*altogether un-Spartiate* (*oudamôs Spartiêtika*, 5.40 *fin.*).[134] Never in his right mind from the beginning (5.42.1), Cleomenes died insane by self-mutilation as a real (6.74) and symbolic traitor to Sparta: for whenever he encountered a Spartiate in his path he would strike him in the face with his royal scepter (6.75.1).

In his insanity Cleomenes keeps ominous company: he is the only madman in the Histories besides the Persian Cambyses (3.29.1) and a brother of the Samian tyrant Maeandrius (3.145.1).[135] Herodotus lingers over the gruesome scene of Cleomenes' suicide—he slashed his flesh to ribbons from shins to belly with a knife—and its cause: the Greeks at large believed that he was punished for corrupting the Pythia to falsely confirm the bastardy of his enemy King Demaratus. This is the view to which in the end Herodotus also inclines (5.84 *fin.*); nonetheless he provides the alternative indictments in full, which relate Cleomenes' other great impieties. The Athenians, he says, think that he was punished for cutting down the sacred grove at Eleusis (cf. 5.74–76), the Argives because he impiously murdered the Argive fugitives of a battle and burned the sacred precinct where the survivors had taken refuge (6.75.2–3). The Spartans themselves deny that Cleomenes perished by the hand of divinity, but from his undue association with barbarians: by consorting with hard-drinking Scythians he learned their taste for unmixed wine and destroyed his sanity with drink (6.84). The full picture shows a barbarian Cleomenes, a "throwback" or reversion to original type. Besides Cleomenes only Persians purposely destroy sacred precincts in the *Histories*, and abuse of wine is a stereotyped behavior of barbarians.[136]

Under Cleomenes, finally, the whole Lacedaemonian community had been in danger of abandoning its historic course by an unprecedented sponsorship of tyranny at Athens. They were prevented by the Corinthians, a fellow Dorian people who had not long before liberated themselves from the tyranny of the non-Dorian Cypselids, who claimed descent from the invulnerable Lapith Caeneus.[137] On the occasion of Cleomenes' projected restoration of the Pisistratids, a Corinthian speaker sets out to educate the Spartans in tyranny by an account of the Cypselids' atrocious regime. He begins with the following words (5.92α):

> Why, the sky shall lie below the earth and the earth above the sky, and people shall live in the sea and fish where people had lived, when you, Lacedaemonians, try to destroy equality of rights in the cities and fasten them with tyrannies—the most unjust and murderous regime known to man. But if you really think tyrannizing the cities is a good idea, first put a tyrant over yourselves before you decide to put tyrants over the others. As it is you have never experienced a tyranny and take the most strenuous precautions that tyrants should never arise at Sparta: yet you abuse your allies. If you knew tyranny as we ourselves do, you would show yourselves better judges of it than you do at the moment.

To find the Spartans supporting tyrants was contrary even to nature herself in Herodotus' mind. He saw that under the tutelage of Lycurgus the Dorian Spartans had achieved a way of life that obviated tyranny by entrammeling their Heraclid kings within ironbound limits. Moreover, the Spartans afterward had opposed tyrants at Athens and elsewhere within their sphere.[138] And where Dorian peoples had fallen under tyrants, as at Corinth, Argos, and Sicyon, the tyrants themselves were not Dorian. In the Dorian world of the Histories—the world of real Greeks—tyranny is always an alien phenomenon.[139]

The Alcmaeonids and Athens

Herodotus praised the Alcmaeonids as the liberators of Athens from her tyrants and the authors of the free state that, at a stroke, was able to cow the allies of the Spartans, defeat the army of the Boeotian cities, conquer Chalcis, and hold its own against the naval power of Aegina (5.74ff). This is the Athens that defeats the Persians at Marathon; and in that context he defends the reputation of the Alcmaeonids as *misotyrannoi* incapable of the collaboration with the national enemy of which they had been accused at that time (6.115, 121, 122–24).

All of this forms the basis for the view that Herodotus favored the Alcmaeonid house and what it stood for in Athenian history against its rivals and detractors at Athens. Against this view, however, stands Herodotus' own presentation of the Alcmaeonids, and of Athens' internal history.[140]

Clisthenes was the son of Megacles, a rival of Pisistratus and then his ally for a time; Megacles was the son of Alcmaeon, Croesus' other Athenian guest in the Histories and a man who had been far more useful to the Lydian monarch than Solon. Alcmaeon had, unbidden, given every help to Croesus' envoys to Delphi. Croesus invited him to Sardis and told him that his reward would be all the gold he could carry. Herodotus' Alcmaeon now becomes the very caricature of avarice and cunning (6.125).

> Faced with such a gift, Alcmaeon had his means ready. He donned an enormous gown, draped a deep belly into it and, putting on the biggest boots he could find, entered the strongroom to which he was led. Falling upon a heap of gold-dust he first packed as much of the gold around his legs that the boots could hold; then, filling the belly of the gown with gold just as full, he plastered his hair with gold-dust, packed more into his mouth, and staggered out of the strongroom barely able to drag his boots and looking like anything but a human being; for his cheeks were puffed to bursting and he bulged out everywhere. Seeing him Croesus fell to laughing, and gave him all

that he carried and as much more. That is how his house got its great wealth, and how Alcmaeon could keep chariot-teams and win at Olympia.

In the single sentence that describes Alcmaeon stuffing himself in Croesus' strongroom, the words for gold and gold-dust occur four times. Herodotus disposes of Alcmaeon with Aristophanic brutality; no aristocrat of ancient lineage and wealth, his Alcmaeon is a figure from the comic stage with his buskins, his bloated belly, and his distended cheeks—a buffoon on the make in the world of Asiatic barbarism and "anything but a human being."

Alcmaeon's son Megacles in turn wooed Agariste, daughter of Clisthenes, the tyrant of Sicyon. Herodotus notes elsewhere that the god of Delphi had called Clisthenes a *leustêra* (5.67.2), no prince wielding a warrior's weapons but a craven "stone-thrower".[141] Among the princes of Thessaly and Molossia in the famous contest for Agariste's hand (6.126ff) were a number of *louche* characters; these included an exquisite voluptuary, the brother of the greatest misanthrope in Greece, the son of the notorious tyrant Pheidon of Argos, and from Athens the Philaid Hippoclides, whose hereditary connection with the Corinthian tyrant Cypselus approved him to his host as much as his manliness (6.128.2). As Herodotus tells the story, however, it puts the Alcmaeonids' chief rivals, the Philaids, in the more antityrannical, if hardly less dignified, posture. For it would seem that Hippoclides had no taste for marriage into the house of a tyrant since, when he was favored by Clisthenes, he purposely spoiled his chances by dancing on his head and showing his bum and his privates (though Herodotus refrains from pointing this out in so many words) to his host and the suitors assembled at a banquet. When the scandalized tyrant exclaimed that he had just lost his bride, the Philaid airily replied, "Hippoclides couldn't care less" (*ou phrontis Hippokleidêi*, 6.129 *fin.*). Hippoclides had "just been along for the ride" and left Agariste to Megacles the Alcmaeonid, who was glad to have her.

"So much for the contest of the suitors," Herodotus concludes, "and so in this way too the Alcmaeonids got a loud reputation all over Greece. From their union came that Clisthenes, named for his Sicyonian grandfather, who established the tribes and the democracy for the Athenians. He had two sons, Megacles and Hippocrates, and Hippocrates in turn another Megacles and another Agariste, named for Clisthenes' Agariste, who married Xanthippus the son of Ariphron; and being pregnant, she saw a vision in her sleep, seeming to give birth to a lion; and after a few days she gave birth to Pericles the son of Xanthippus" (6.131).

Of such antecedents were Athens' liberators: for it was the descendants of Alcmaeon, opines Herodotus, far more than Harmodius or Aristogeiton who liberated Athens—at least if it is true, Herodotus adds, that they bribed the Pythia to bring in the Spartans (5.63.1, 6.123.2). So the Alcmaeonids carried through the liberation itself by false and unholy means.[142] As we have just seen, the other person in the Histories who corrupts the Pythia is Cleomenes (6.66.2), who thereby earns his ghastly end, and the other persons who deal falsely in oracles are the Pisistratids at Susa, who thereby excite Xerxes' interest in marching on Greece (7.6.3–5). We may add Croesus, too, who thought he had paid the god of Delphi to tell him what he wanted to hear (1.53–55). The descendants of Alcmaeon were *misotyrannoi*, then, alone by virtue of their enmity to the Pisistratids (6.121 and 123) and not because they were necessarily above tyranny themselves (5.66.1).[143]

Herodotus viewed Clisthenes' tribal revolution at Athens in a decidedly negative light. He introduces Clisthenes briefly, as the man "who established the tribes and the democracy for the Athenians." The tribes and the democracy go together in Herodotus' mind in a way that points to the tyrannical aims and method behind the reform. Herodotus believed that Clisthenes was inspired by his grandfather the tyrant, who had put his own supporters into power by creating a new, non-Dorian tribe to lord it over the old Dorian tribes at Sicyon, to which he gave new and humiliating names, and transferred the honors given to the Sicyonian ancestral hero Adrastus to his enemy, the Theban hero Melanippus (5.67–69). He concluded that Clisthenes the Athenian despised the Ionians (5.69.1; cf. 1.143.3) and therefore suppressed the old Ionian tribes in order to install his own supporters in power.

Herodotus' insight into Clisthenes' reform is far more sophisticated than it appears, and it betrays his Halicarnassian concern with the reform's effects on the racial character of Athens' citizen population. The new tribes emphasized Athenian autochthony and individuality at the expense of the city's old Ionian identity; their eponymous heroes were Erechtheus, Aegeus, Pandion, Leon, Acamas, Oeneus, Cecrops, Hippothöon, Ajax, and Antiochus, heroes of Attic and Salaminian origin, as Herodotus says (5.66.2). The new tribes were also a means of introducing among the body of old Athenians who had belonged to the original Ionian tribes, and who therefore must have claimed Ionian identity, large numbers of inhabitants descended from Solonian metics and others whose ancestry was impure or unattested, and whom the faction of Isagoras, Clisthenes' traditionalist opponent for power, had tried to purge (Arist. *AP* 13.5, 21.1–4). Their membership in the community had been promoted by the Pisistratids and now by Clisthenes, just as the Sicyonian Clisthenes had promoted the non-Dorians to full citizenship by a tribal reform.

Herodotus regarded the reform itself as the fruit of a stratagem to which Clisthenes resorted to avoid defeat in the struggle between the personal factions of the Alcmaeonids and Isagoras (5.72.1). In this struggle, says Herodotus, Clisthenes *ton dêmon proseterizetai*, "draws the people at large into his *hetairêiê*, his private faction" (5.66.2, cf. 69.2). This is a conscious paradox. Everyone knew what a *hetaireia* was—a small and *personal* association of individuals aiming at political power.[144] *Hetaireiai* were the building blocks of exclusive regimes. It is revealing that the only other appearance of the verb *proseterizomai* in the Histories is found in the mouth of the Persian Otanes, when he is organizing the narrow coup by which Darius captures the throne (3.70.2). Herodotus knew (and probably shared) the doctrine that tyrants typically arise as leaders of the people, and that the people themselves are typically as violent as any tyrant (3.81.1–2, 82.4). Herodotus implies, then, that Clisthenes the Alcmaeonid was a man who aimed for a personal tyranny but had to settle for elevating the demos to the tyranny.

It is likely that Herodotus' message came through very clearly to his wartime audiences, who hated imperial Athens. Even within Athens, some of the upper classes resented, even hated, the democracy. The Old Oligarch, whose antidemocratic pamphlet should be placed in the 420s, the age of Cleon's ascendancy, would have recognized in Herodotus' Clisthenes a tyrannical man who had enthroned the most tyrannical element at Athens, which in turn had gone on the tyrannize other Greeks.[145]

It is true that Clisthenes and the Athenians were acting against Cleomenes' attempts to install first Isagoras, then Hippias, as the actual tyrant at Athens. *Faute de mieux*, Clisthenes did free the Athenians; at the end Herodotus sings a paean to liberty and *isêgoriê* (5.78).[146] Nevertheless the regime that Clisthenes established is one conceivable to Persian barbarians (4.80–82), but inconceivable to the well-lawed Spartiates.

Democracies and tyrannies alike, moreover, are wont to destroy the best men: in the Histories the tyrant Periander sends metaphorical advice to the tyrant Thrasybulus to "destroy the tallest grain" (5.92ζ2–3). Herodotus' history of the Athenian democracy, from its inception to his own day, is enclosed within mirror-imaged acts of injustice against noble victims. Herodotus ends his story of the new democracy's victorious resistance to Cleomenes and Isagoras with the first executions without trial carried out by the Athenian demos, including among their victims the excellent Timesitheus of Delphi, of whose great deeds of hand and courage, Herodotus approvingly remarks, he could tell a great deal (5.72.4). Then, of the Athens of his own day, he conspicuously recalls the recent executions by the demos of two distinguished Spartiates and a leading Corinthian (7.133–37).[147]

This was no ordinary atrocity. Herodotus chooses to recall it at the very fulcrum-point of his work—at the outset of his story of the Hellenic resistance to Xerxes and of the unflinching heroism of the Athenians, who by their steadfast resolve even in the face of terrifying oracles from Delphi saved Hellas in those days (7.139). The identities of the slaughtered envoys embraced the issues of that war and those of the present war with peculiar depth and clarity. These issues had everything to do with what the Athenians had been then, and what they were now.

The Spartiate victims were sons of Bulis and Sperthias, descendants of Agamemnon's herald Talthybius and thereby hereditary heralds of the Spartans. Herodotus believed that these men died in their fathers' place to expiate the wrath of Talthybius aroused by the Spartans' sacrilegious murder of a herald sent to them by Darius before the Marathon campaign. Afterward the fathers of Sperthias and Bulis had volunteered to die at the hands of the Persians in pious expiation for the Persian herald's murder, and the Spartans had sent them to Susa for execution. There they fought off the palace guards' attempt to force them into prostration before the Great King—a scene that Herodotus may have inserted to bring to mind the dignity and defiance their sons must have shown in the face of the Athenian assembly. However, Xerxes magnanimously refused to order their deaths, wanting neither to imitate the Spartans' violation of the universal rule of mankind (*pantôn anthrôpôn nomima*, 7.136.2), nor to release the Spartans from their blood guilt. It was in the death of their sons long afterward at Athens, says Herodotus, that the wrath of Talthybius was finally slaked.

Herodotus tells this story ostensibly as an instance of the marvelous (*theiotatom*) fulfillment of the divine wrath (137.1), and this is certainly a genuine motive. But this story also tells how the Spartans were freed from this dangerous pollution in the nick of time, almost at the beginning of the present war, and by their mortal enemy. So at the very moment when the epic conflict against Xerxes is about to begin in Herodotus' narrative, his audiences are once more meant to recall Apollo's promise to Sparta at the outset of the present war to be at their side whether bidden or unbidden, and the dreadful onset of plague at Athens in the summer of the envoys' execution.

Moreover, the whole story exemplifies the peculiar virtue of Lycurgan Spartiates in implicit contrast to the hubris of the Athenians. For in violation of the universal rule of mankind the Athenians' perform an act that Xerxes had refused to perform in accordance with that rule (for the mission of Bulis and Sperthias had been precisely to give their lives to Xerxes). Herodotus shows the Athenians doing unjustly in this war what the Persians could have done justly in the days after that other war, and thereby the Athenians performance is more than unholy; it is worse than Persian.

Moreover, the Athenians who executed Bulis and Sperthias even *compounded* their original crime, again in contrast to the Spartans; for they too had executed a herald from Darius in company with the Spartans (7.133.1). Herodotus remarks that he does not know what befell the Athenians for their own deed, except that their land and city were ravaged by the Persians, but he does not believe that the murder of Darius' herald was the cause (7.133.2). Here again Herodotus introduces an element of prophecy in the way that he frames these issues of expiation and retribution. In the Histories, Herodotus expiates the Spartans' crime in the context of the present war, while he awaits a final retribution upon Athens, which may arrive in the present war, together with Athens' present crimes against universal human law.

This is a way of looking at Athens that many contemporary Greeks would have found congenial—including the Spartan ephor Stheneladas. When war against Athens was being considered at Sparta in 432, Stheneladas told the Lacedaemonians that "if in those days the Athenians proved themselves good men against the Mede, but are bad men to us now, they deserve double punishment because they used to be good and have become bad. But then and now we remain the same Spartiates" (Thuc. 1.86.1–2).

Appendix

PELASGIANS, LELEGES, CAUCONES

In the climate of the Peloponnesian War and the Athenians' propaganda of autochthony, the original Greek view that the Pelasgians—the Pelasgians of the *Iliad*—were an ancestral species of Hellene came under attack.[148] This view, however, was wholly consistent with the facts of the post-Mycenaean settlements of the diaspora that followed the destruction of the Late Helladic IIIc palace centers in Greece, and reflected the later Greeks' racial memory of their Mycenaean predecessors. Thus the Arcado-Cypriot-speaking Arcadians of the central Peloponnesian highlands, which had never been successfully penetrated by Dorian speakers,

163

recognized themselves and were recognized by the other Greek peoples as the most ancient inhabitants of Greece, even by Athenians who themselves claimed autochthony.[149] Pausanias (8.1.14) cites the archaic genealogical poet Asius of Samos on Pelasgus, the first inhabitant of Arcadia, as the progenitor of humankind:

> Godly Pelasgus in the deep-wooded mountains
> Donated black earth, that the race of mortals might be.

Like Prometheus with his gift of fire, Pelasgus was made out to be an inventor of culture, who gave human beings the first tokens separating them from the beasts: huts and sheepskin cloaks, and acorns instead of the grasses upon which the animals graze (Paus. 8.1.5). Acorns (which require sophisticated preparation including leaching before they can be safely eaten by humans) uniquely persisted in the Arcadian diet into historical times (cf. Hdt. 1.66.2: *balanêphagoi*).

Herodotus himself testified to the universality of the received opinion in noting that once all Hellas was called Pelasgia (perhaps with the *Supplices* of Aeschylus in mind: 2.56.1; cf. *Suppl.* 234ff., 252–53, 910ff), that *Arkades Pelasgoi* were among the settlers who peopled Ionia (1.146.1) and, indeed, that the Greeks identified the Ionians generically as Aegalian Pelasgians (7.94.1). In fact the racial politics of the *Supplices*, if we may so call them, are the earliest illustration of the anti-Dorian theme used at Athens against Sparta, which becomes prominent during the Peloponnesian War. In the *Supplices*, the pre-Dorian Pelasgian Argives are assimilated to the Athenians, almost certainly in consequence of the alliance with Argos at the end of the 460s, following the Spartans' expulsion of the Athenian army under Cimon which had marched to Ithome to help them against the insurgent Messenians (Thuc. 1.102.4).

In taking issue with these beliefs and their racial implications for Greek origins, Herodotus contradicted not only Athenian beliefs about the nobility of their origins but the general body of Greek tradition ratified by the magisterial authority of the *Iliad*.[150] The Achaean Catalogue describes the homeland of Achilles in the following verses (*Il.* 2.681–85, trans. Lattimore):

> Now all those who dwelt about Pelasgian Argos,
> those who lived by Alos and Alope and Trachis,
> those who held Phthia and Hellas the land of fair women,
> who were called Myrmidons and Hellenes and Achaians,
> of all these and their fifty ships the lord was Achilleus.

However, the poet of the *Iliad* also counts Pelasgians among the
Trojans (2.840–43, trans. Lattimore):

> Hippothoos led the tribes of spear-fighting Pelasgians,
> they who dwelt where the soil is rich about Larissa;
> Hippothoos and Pylaeus, scion of Ares, led these,
> sons alike of Pelasgian Lethos, son of Teutamos.

There are strong reasons to believe that early strata of the
Iliad migrated from Aeolian Thessaly to Asia Minor.[151] The Troad
became Aeolian during historical times, including Larissa, the
home of the Trojan Hippothoos, originally the name of a community in the Thessalian Pelasgiotis. As a result, the Pelasgians of
Thessaly and those of the Troad were regarded by the early Greeks
as kindred peoples, who became associated in turn with the Trojans. The Aeolians of Lesbos claimed the Pelasgian hero Pylaeus,
for whom a peak on the island was named. In the *Iliad* Pylaeus fights
on the Trojan side as the commander of the Aeolians' ancestors and
the founder of their settlements.[152] As was stated in chapter 1,
families among the local aristocracies of the Troad, such as the
Aeneadae of Scepsis, derived their line from Trojan Anchises and
Aphrodite.[153] The founder of Aeneia in the Chalcidice and Aenus
in Thrace was likewise considered to be Aeneas,[154] who was des-
tined to carry on the line of Dardanus, "dearest to Zeus of all his
sons born to mortal women" (*Il.* 20.302–5).

Even the Athenians claimed Trojan heroes for themselves, Erichthonius and Teucrus,[155] almost surely in order to support their
claim to Sigeum in the Troad against the Mytileneans, who doubtless wielded the name of Pylaeus on their own behalf during the
sixth-century war between them for the town.[156] Such genealogical
arguments could not have borne the weight of belief—they could
hardly have been invented—had the belief then existed that the

Trojans were barbarians. The *Iliad* itself reflects no such belief, even while this poem and the *Odyssey* recognize that different peoples spoke different, non-Greek, languages. Epic does not isolate speech as an index of cultural difference.

In the context of the epic cycle as a whole, the idea that the war against Troy had been fought by Greeks against barbarians is no less unnatural than the idea that, because the Thebans were of Cadmus' line, the Theban wars had been fought by Greeks against Phoenicians.[157] Even later, a legend about the Samian sage Pythagoras taught that, in an earlier life, he had been the Dardanian Euphorbus.[158] This ancient parity of Achaeans and Trojans in the Ionian mind is expressed in the legend that the king of Delos, the island holy to Ionian Apollo and Artemis, was a friend to both sides during the Trojan War.[159]

Moreover, the Caucones and Leleges, who in the *Iliad* dwell near Troy and are closely associated with the Trojans and with the Pelasgians, were also regarded as kindred on the authority of Homer, and so remained in the local cults of the Peloponnese,[160] long after they had become generally associated with the non-Greek Carians.[161] Hesiod, or an early interpolator, identified Telephus, the Homeric king of Mysia who was wounded and healed by Achilles' spear, as Arcasides, the "Descendant of Arcas," the eponym of the Arcadians. The authenticity of this identification is confirmed by the worship at Arcadian Tegea of his mother Auge, who bore Telephus to Heracles.[162]

Six

Herodotus' Typology of Barbarism

> In those days there was still a statue of solid gold
> twelve cubits tall in the sacred precinct. Darius son
> of Hystaspes had designs on this statue but dared
> not take it; but Xerxes took it and killed the priest
> who forbade him, besides.
> —Herodotus, on the great image at Babylon which
> Cyrus had honored when he entered Babylon as
> the servant of Marduk

The fundamental categories of Herodotean history are set out at the beginning of the Histories, where Herodotus announces the intention of his whole work by opposing his own knowledge of the causes of the events to which it is dedicated against those of the barbarian Persian *logioi*: the Histories progress toward the war of Xerxes and the Greeks' triumph over Asiatic barbarism from its author's early declaration that Croesus was the first barbarian whom he *knows* made friends of some Greeks and worked injustices against others (1.5.3).[1]

With this evocation Herodotus begins his history of Lydia and the five generations of great Lydian tyrants, which is also the beginning of his history of the *anthrôpêiê geneê*, the contemporary history of the "human generation" (3.122.2) in contrast to the other history of the heroic age, known from the poets but inaccessible to *opsis* and *akoê*, the eyes and ears of Herodotus.[2] His point of departure is the Greek world at the dawn of the conflict with

Asianic barbarism in the reign of Gyges who, as noted before, is the first real barbarian named by a Greek.

The Lydian logos also contains Herodotus' Greek anthropogony, in which some of the Greeks evolve as a people from Pelasgians— a people of Tyrsenian and therefore of Lydian stock[3]—and begin to display the distinctive social development that sets them apart from barbarians. An implication of this evolution is the barbarians' continuing potential to become Greek: what happened once could happen again. There is no *a priori* reason in Herodotus why, for example, Croesus should not heed Solon's wisdom and become to that extent Greek instead of a barbarian tyrant, and then the barbarian slave of another barbarian.

This choice exists for everybody in the zone of Greece and Asia.[4] That is one reason why Herodotus places his anthropogony in the Lydian climate of tyranny. The apparently digressive architecture of the Lydilan overture in fact articulates the world according to the opposed Herodotean categories of tyranny and eunomia. Tyrants dominate in both Lydia and the Greek world in this age, and Herodotus' barbarian Asia exists not in itself, but in its relations with the Greeks at a time when most of them were linked to Asia by tyranny and were still incompletely Hellenic.

Herodotus places Croesus in this world by providing a history of his dynasty and of Croesus' own rule which, in one way or another, draws in the great contemporaries of the dynasty in its flower, the tyrants Thrasybulus of Miletus, Periander of Corinth, and Pisistratus of Athens, together with Lycurgus, the creator of eunomia at Sparta, and Solon, who did not create eunomia at Athens. The Eurasiatic world of the Histories is a single whole from the beginning.

Yet Herodotus also delineates Croesus and his ancestors in contrast and separation from the Greek world and its gods, in particular by examining the Mermnads' transactions with Delphi and with the wise men of the Greeks. In Croesus' confrontation with Solon, and Croesus' eventual fate, we see how the barbarian mind operates—or rather fails to operate—when it encounters Greek wisdom and Greek gods.[5] From this beginning Herodotus will examine the typology of the contemporary Asianic barbarian exemplified in full variety by the barbarian tyrants of Asia. His extended depictions of their careers, characters, and societies form the spine of the Histories. The tyrants of Asia fail to become Greek and so meet their barbarian fates in ways which, beneath their variety, are specified by each victim's culture on the one hand, and on the other by the nature of the land in which that fate works itself out.

Croesus the Barbarian

King Croesus had once been Greek, until he was transformed and transvaluated by Herodotus' vision. Before Herodotus, Bacchylides had sung of Croesus as a Hellenic hero-king translated in death to the Far North as Achilles had been.[6] This Croesus, *damasippou Lydias arkhagetan* (3.23–24 Snell), "stallion-breaking Lydia's High Leader," forebore to endure the slavery of the conquered but mounted the pyre in self-imposed immolation: *ho gar prophanês thnatoisin ekhthistos phonôn* (3.51–52 Snell), "for bitterest death to mortals is death foreseen." Yet then, for his myriad gifts of piety, Apollo bore Croesus and his daughters off to an everlasting dwelling in the land of the Hyperboreans.

Bacchylides' Croesus thus personified the moral that money can buy immortality in the bosom of deity. It was a moral doubtlessly welcome to that other wealthy tyrant, Hieron of Syracuse, to whom this ode was addressed on the victory of his mares at the Olympiad of 468.[7] Like other tyrants before him—notably Cypselus of Corinth, who founded the tyranny of the Dorian metropolis of colonial Syracuse—Hieron was pleased to be ranked with the opulent and absolutist royalty of the foreign Mermnads of Lydia;[8] but he preferred to be styled *arkhagetas* through his alter ego of the poem, as if he really were a Heraclid of Corinth or, indeed, of Lacedaemon. For at home the kings of Sparta were properly titled *arkhagetai*.[9] In endowing the Lydian tyrant with the title of ancestral Dorian kingship, Bacchylides also endowed Hieron with a heroic and patriotic identity, by creating a hero who combined Lydian monar-

chy and magnificence with the title and virtues of the Lacedaemonian Heraclids—a hero, moreover, whose nature and fate flattered
the grandeur and pretensions of his patron.

The occasion of the poem was highly relevant to its theme and
its association of Croesus and Hieron with Sparta. The Olympiad
of 468 marked the third quadrennial remembrance of Thermopylae. The pass and its defenders had fallen on the last day of the
festival of 480. The self-sacrifice of Bacchylides' Croesus emulates
and commemorates the perfect heroism of Leonidas, who resolved
with his comrades that it was sweetest to die, *thanein glykiston*
(Bacchyl. 3.47–48), rather than to endure conquest by the Persian
king. Their resolve had epitomized the whole Hellenic resistance
to barbarism, whose credentials Hieron was eager to share. For in
that summer of 480 Hieron's brother Gelon and Theron of Acragas
also had won a famous and decisive victory over the Carthaginian
barbarians led by their king (Hdt. 7.165). It was a victory that the
Sicilians compared to Salamis.

The Greeks who had resisted Xerxes under the leadership of
Dorian Sparta and Ionian Athens called themselves "The Hellenes,"
as if the Medizers and the Greeks in Xerxes' imperial armada were
less than Hellenes, tainted by barbarism. Gelon had conspicuously
been one of those who refused to aid the Hellenes in 480. At
Salamis the only help from Magna Graecia had arrived in a volun-
teer trireme from Croton, the Gelonids' mainland rival (Hdt. 8.47).
Like the Medizer Alexander I of Macedon, a shameless *arriviste*
who had set a golden image of himself next to the statue dedicated
at Delphi from the first fruits of Salamis (5.22.1; 8.121.2), Hieron
competed at the Olympia to publicize his own Hellenism and his
credentials of hostility to the barbarian.

As late as 468 Croesus could still do duty as a Leonidas figure
because he was still counted as a symbol of resistance to the
Mede—he had, after all, fought Cyrus to a standstill at Pteria
together with the Ionians (1.76.3–4)—and did so, moreover, as
a citizen of Delphi. In return for Croesus' gifts to Pythian Apollo
and to themselves, the Delphians had extended to him and to all
Lydians membership in their own community, an act of grace

unheard of then or afterward. It is not surprising, then, that this connection was remembered at Delphi more than a century afterward (1.54 *fin.*). Croesus himself, evidently, had even revived his dynasty's collateral connection with the ancient, virtually Greek Heraclids of Lydia, which the phil-Ionian Panyassis was still celebrating perhaps as late as the 460s.[10] A generation before Bacchylides had written his ode for Hieron, Myson showed how Croesus was remembered at Athens at the time of the Ionian Revolt.[11] He painted Croesus on the pyre as a godlike Ionian man, garlanded in the laurel that signified heroism and victory over fate. Traces of this outlook survive even in the *Histories*, where, before their defeat, the brave and civilized Lydians appear "Hellenic," vis-à-vis the Persians in their still-savage state.[12]

Yet a generation after Panyassis and Bacchylides, Croesus and his dynasty were to become archetypical barbarians. In the midst of the Archidamian War, Herodotus presented, in Plutarch's apt summation, a Croesus *amathê, alazona, geloion,* an ignorant and pretentious buffoon (*Mor.* 858D = *De mal. Her.* 18). The transformation of Croesus' image in Herodotus accompanied and expressed an all-pervasive celebration of Hellenism as the superior culture, antinomial in all respects to barbarism.[13] The influence of this outlook even among Hellenized Asiatics is clearly visible in Xanthus' scurrilous and "revisionist" history of the Lydian kings. Among Lydians of high station like Xanthus the beginnings of his viewpoint must have arisen immediately with their defeat. Herodotus characterizes the moral effect of their sudden impotence in his programmatic tale of Croesus' servile advice to Cyrus, to make the Lydian warriors (1.79.3) into soft men, wearers of slippers, musicians, shopkeepers, so that they would not revolt again and be destroyed altogether (1.155.4).

Herodotus put on view a Croesus who had neither the understanding nor the spirit to be Hellenic in his confrontations with Greek wisdom, with Greek gods, and with his death. Far from mounting the pyre in heroic self-immolation, Herodotus' Croesus is taken alive and spiritless (1.85.3) to be burned to death by Cyrus.[14] Solon had told Croesus the stories of the men whom he knew had been most fortunate in life and blessed in their deaths.

These were Tellus of Athens, who had sons and grandsons alive when he died gloriously in battle for his city and earned a public burial, and next the Argive brothers Cleobis and Biton, victors in the games who yoked themselves like oxen to bring their mother, a priestess of Hera, to her shrine at festival time. They were lauded by all the Argives for so greatly honoring their mother and the goddess whom she served, and their mother then asked Hera to grant to her sons humankind's greatest benefit. A little later they died in their sleep within the temple, "and the god," said Solon, "showed through these men that it is better to die than to live" (1.31.3).

The best lives, long or short, are only those that end in civic glory. Croesus, however, remains uncomprehending and unmoved by Solon's definition of the good life and the good death. For (1.34–45) he will deprive his son and heir of both a good life and a good death. The story is worth more than a glance. After Solon's departure, a vision came to Croesus in a dream warning him that his son would die from the wound of an iron spearhead. To otherwise occupy his son, who until then had been the Lydians' commander in war, Croesus married him off, sent him on no more expeditions, and even hid all the weapons in the palace. But then the people begged Croesus to send his son with hunters to kill a great boar which was destroying their crops. Croesus granted them all but the son for whom he feared.

His son, however, remonstrated that he was now debarred from what was for them best and noblest, the achievement of fame in war and the hunt, and would be ashamed to show himself in the agora: what kind of man would the citizens (sic: *poliêtêisi,* 1.37.3) or his newly wedded wife think he was? And when Croesus revealed to him what the dream portended, the young man disputed his father's understanding of it, arguing that only a boar with hands or an iron spearpoint could kill him. So Croesus let his son go on the hunt, in the care of suppliant who had come for refuge and purification by Croesus after accidentally killing his brother. On the hunt the suppliant's spear missed the boar but struck and killed Croesus' son. Only then did Croesus see that the god had foretold what must be (1.45.2).

In this way Croesus deprived his son, who showed all the signs of "wanting to be Greek," of a life and death in pursuit of civic glory (1.37.2–3). Instead he condemned him to a woman's life and then, relenting, to a most unworthy and ignominous end (1.44).[15] Herodotus' audiences heard his son persuade Croesus against the plainest prophecy of a dream by the most transparent arguments from nature and probability as taught by the new rhetoric of the sophists (1.38–40; cf. Ar. *Clouds* of 423 B.C.). Then Croesus puts him into the hands of a man proved by his destiny to be an unwilling murderer. Finally he takes no account of the verdict of the god, which had been given to his ancestor Gyges and thereafter ignored by the Lydian kings, which was congruent with the plain meaning of his own dream, and with it implied an alternative history to the end of Croesus and his realm. Long ago Delphi had set a limit to the dynasty in Croesus' generation (1.13.2), and therefore this oracle concerned his son as well: Croesus' only remaining choice for himself and his son, had he faced it—as Herodotus' Solon had unconsciously foreseen in the matter of his diatribe—was whether or not to live and die well, that is, to "become Greek."

The Croesus of Myson's portrait and Bacchylides' ode had done the better thing without instruction by Solon, preferring to choose the most hateful of deaths over a life in slavery. Herodotus' Croesus does the worse thing by wanting to live badly after hearing Solon's sermon on dying well. Ironically, it is Croesus' remembrance of Solon on the pyre that convinces Cyrus to spare Croesus for enslavement. Croesus himself—still unchanged by Solon's wisdom—prays to Delphian Apollo for salvation and is granted a miracle by the god. Thereafter Croesus is the most solicitous and loyal slave imaginable. About this Croesus one could say what Herodotus' Scyths would say about his Asianic Ionians: they were the basest and most unmanly considered as free men, but as slaves the most serviceable and loyal (4.142).

Herodotus' Sardis is an up-to-date Greek polis, containing an agora full of citizens vying for their own reputations and putting others' down, homes full of wives eager to bask in their husbands' distinction, and progressive young sparks who bandy the sophists' tricks against their fathers' inarticulate piety and safe conservatism. This Sardis is a little Aristophanic caricature of contemporary Athens. Croesus and the Lydians are barbarians not because they are antithetically un-Greek but because they are, so to speak, Greek moral and mental defectives. Even though they seek out Greek wisdom and Greek oracles, they fail to understand these very things, and thereby suffer the consequences. Herodotus' Croesus misuses Hellenic wisdom and misreads the new Delphic responses that he procured at so much trouble and expense, while forgetting the original response that was the key to them all. It was in his Lydian character to do so, just as the former Lydian king Meles had neglected to carry his concubine's lion around the walls of Sardis where they were thought impregnable.

King Candaules, too, the last of Meles' line, had cited the Heraclitean maxim that the ears are less trustworthy than the eyes (Hdt. 1.8.2; cf. Heraclitus 22 F 101a DK) in order to perpetrate a new and unrighteous kind of discovery. Heraclitus' other dictum about eyes and ears ("bad witnesses for men who have barbarian souls") once again provides the relevant gloss. Herodotus, the son of Lyxes, presents to the Greek world a compendium of his discoveries made with eyes and ears. His very first stories tell us what "the barbarians familiar with the stories" say about the reasons, long ago in the age of heroes, why they and the Greeks have gone to war with one another. His whole work, as I commented earlier, takes its point of departure from these stories, which are barbarian *akoê*, so that the work itself is an exhaustive test of barbarian *akoê*. Likewise, Herodotus' very first story about people who exist after the heroic age, in the time of human beings, examines barbarian *opsis*. King Candaules is so smitten by his wife's unparalleled beauty he demands that his guardsmen Gyges should see for himself by viewing her naked. Gyges responds with horror and warns his master off with a Greek maxim: "Men have long since discovered the right principles, which everyone must learn; and one of these is, " '*look only at your own*' " (1.8.4).[16]

But the despot Candaules forces the sight of his wife upon Gyges. His servant must obey. There is no way for others to stop a tyrant from going wrong, whether he is Aeschylus' Xerxes, or Thrasymachus' tyrant in the *Republic,* or any of Herodotus' gallery of hubristic despots. Inevitably, then, the queen sees Gyges spying upon her and, outraged, offers Gyges the choice of death for seeing what was forbidden to him, or herself and Candaules' kingdom (1.9.2).

There was more than one version of the Gyges story in circulation, including the fanciful one known to Plato (*Rep.* 239d–360b) in which Gyges was a shepherd who seduced the queen and slew the king with the aid of a magic ring that could render him invisible.[17] Herodotus' version is notable for containing all of the signature elements of Lydian barbarism, which is highly "evolved" (in the French colonial sense of the native *évolué*) in that it attempts Hellenism but fails to operate Hellenically. Candaules can recite the Greek maxim that the eyes are more trustworthy than the ears. But *his* eyes are untrustworthy because they are the eyes of a barbarian: his relations with his wife are deranged by the very act of looking at her; he becomes "crazy about her." Because he is a tyrant he cannot be stopped from doing something crazy by his slave's Greek appeal to *nomos;* his ears are stopped up as well.

As for Candaules' queen, she is a characteristically barbarian virago like Hellanicus' Atossa—a woman who in essential ways is functionally male and threatens the order maintained by the authority and relations of males. But she does so in an altogether Lydian way. Herodotus elsewhere explains that the Lydians' way of life is very similar to the Greek, *except* that the girls prostitute themselves to earn their dowries and give themselves away in marriage (1.93.4, 94 *init.*). These are customs antithetical to Hellenic practice, which insisted on the virginity of brides given to husbands chosen by the males who controlled them. The queen's proposal is characteristically Lydian, thus, in that she arranges her own marriage to Gyges and furnishes her own dowry.[18]

Finally, in the course of their defeat and enslavement, the whole character of the Lydians undergoes a collapse into Asiatic barbarism analogous to the distinctions in Herodotus between "Dorian" and "Ionian." This collapse is engineered by Croesus himself. For the Lydians had been the bravest of warriors in Asia (as the Spartans were in Europe) and, though accustomed to fight on horseback, they resisted Cyrus on foot with their spears to the end (1.80.5) and afterward revolted from Persian rule (1.154). Croesus feared that Cyrus would destroy the Lydians if they resisted him any longer and preferred them to become, like himself, spiritually emasculated slaves rather than brave men preferring destruction to submission. So Croesus counseled Cyrus to make them into merchants, musicians, and fashionable dandies, thereby turning them into "women instead of men" (1.155). Herodotus pointedly followed his tale of the Lydians' defeat beneath the walls of Sardis with the comparandum of the battle of the Three Hundred Champions (1.82), a victory of Sparta's steadfast and self-sacrificing hoplites that brings Sparta to its acme at the very moment of Lydia's fall. This marks the end of "Greek" Lydia in the Histories, ethically and structurally.

Cyrus

In the work of Herodotus and in fact the Lydians were *les anciens évolués,* the barbarians long since closest to Greeks in their culture and mutual relations. Their successors on the Greeks' Asiatic horizon were the Medes and their kindred Iranian successors, the Persians. These peoples were not materially distinct in their language, religion or ways of life, and to the Greeks they were a single kind of barbarian people whose history was a continuum under Median and then Persian kings. Herodotus accordingly begins his story of Cyrus with the story of the founder of the Median kingdom, Deioces, whom tradition made the inventor of the characteristic institutions of Iranian rulership (1.95–100).

As told by Herodotus, it is a story that explains the creation of the Iranian empire in terms of the generic nature of Asianic barbarism on the one hand, and native Iranian conceptions on the other. Deioces was altogether unlike the Lydian Candaules, who was a foolish man in love with his wife, who had forced his subject Gyges into unrighteousness, and who thereby lost his kingship. On the contrary, Deioces was a cunning man who fell in love (*erasthesis*), not with his wife, but with tyranny.[19] Deioces already had a reputation for righteousness, Herodotus relates, and with tyranny as his goal he began to give upright justice to all who repaired to him, knowing that "justice is the enemy of injustice" (1.96.2).

Deioces soon became the single source of justice in the great lawlessness into which the whole of Media had fallen at this time. But once he had made himself indispensable he abruptly retired, claiming the press of his own affairs. Again at a loss for good order, the Medes gathered among themselves and discussed what to do. "I would suppose," says Herodotus, "that it was the friends of Deioces who spoke up the most, saying, 'There is no way that we can live on our land in these conditions, so let us make this man king. In this way our land will become well lawed (*eunomēsetai*) and we can get on with our own work and not be undone by lawlessness (*hyp' anomiēs*).'" And so they persuaded themselves to be ruled by a king. Deioces had the Medes give him guards and build him a palace within seven walls, behind which he disappeared. But he upheld justice with an iron hand nevertheless, reviewing others' written judgments sent to him and sending out his own, overseeing the whole land with spies, and punishing malefactors according to their deserts (1.95.2–100.2).

Herodotus observes careful verbal distinctions. *Anomiē*, "having no law," is a word that occurs only here in the whole of his work, just as *kakonomiē*, "having bad laws," is a condition peculiar only to the Spartans in their early days before Lycurgus, when they were "the worst-lawed of almost all the Greeks and had nothing to do either with each other or strangers" (1.65.2). Each group, then, Greek and barbarian, becomes well lawed in its own way. But the Spartiates had never been without *nomos* of a kind, albeit a bad *nomos* of unsociable autarky antithetical to polis-life (cf. Arist. *Pol.* 1252a–1253a).

Among the Medes, however, there is no *nomos* at all to begin with and every man's hand is against another's. The Medes, like the Persians, are hubrists by nature (1.89.2, cf. 100.2), lawless within themselves. Therefore they cannot abide liberty and—in antithetical contrast to Lycurgan Sparta, whose institutions obviated tyranny not merely because they disciplined the Heraclid kingship, but because they trained the Spartans to possess law within themselves—they must have an absolute ruler, a despot, armed with all devices for securing obedience to his mandates: force, fear, and religious awe (1.98–100). "And this," concludes Herodotus, "is how Deioces brought together (*synestrepse*) the Median nation (1.101 *init.*).

There are yet other points to notice in this story. The first concerns its native elements. As an Asiatic Greek Herodotus had a working knowledge of the Persian monarchy's institutional arrangements, including some authentic acquaintance of the ideology of Persian kingship in which the King is champion of "justice," which "is the enemy of injustice," that is, the Lie. This ideology was openly and regularly enunciated by the Persian Kings in their public documents, to judge from Darius' Letter and the widely disseminated text of the Bisitun Inscription.[20]

The second, and more remarkable, point concerns the Medes' consensual and "democratic" decision to make a tyrant of Deioces, freely agreed to by a free people in assembly—an assembly beguiled, thinks Herodotus, by a demagogue's faction, which is a significant detail belonging to the Greek oligarch's description of mob democracy. The Medes were free, and for the time being behaved like Greeks *because* they were free. At this crossroads in their history they had the choice, at any rate in theory, of making Deioces their lawgiver instead of their tyrant. But they did not. The Medes chose a tyrant to discipline their hubris from above, instead of agreeing to a social contract that made them all policemen of each others' hubris.[21]

The reason lies in the story about the rise of another tyrant—Pisistratus—which Herodotus' audiences heard just before this one. In that story, the Athenians at large accepted Pisistratus when he had seized the Acropolis with his publicly approved guard of clubmen: he was then brought down not by the Athenians, but by a combination of his enemies' personal factions (*stasiôtas* 1.59.3ff), and was raised again by alliance with one of those factions. Pisistratus then gained his final primacy leading Athenians "who found tyranny pleasanter than liberty" (1.62.1), against men who were relieved to be sent about their own affairs unharmed (1.63 *fin.*).

These Athenians, then, like the Medes who elected Deioces ruler in order to get on with their own affairs untroubled by lawlessness, were unwilling to police one another's hubris and maintain communal justice by their own exertions and sacrifices. They were *apragmones* who opted out of the social contract: let Deioces—or Pisistratus—do it. So they became slaves by choice. Later on it will not be an altogether purblind Xerxes, but a Xerxes who has only this kind of human material at his disposal, who will tell the Spartan Demaratus that "fifty thousand men, even if they were free and not under the rule of one man, could not withstand my great host. But if they are beneath the rule of one man, according to our way, in fear of him they might surpass themselves or would advance impelled by the whip. But if they were let go free they would do neither" (7.103.3). The slave is the ultimate *apragmôn*.

The final point in the story of Deioces regards the tricks of the Asianic tyrant, the generic techniques by which he gains and holds power. Deioces had the Medes install him with guards within a palace into which he disappeared from his subjects, to whom he communicated his commands by royal messengers: "In these ways Deioces surrounded himself with awe; so that unseen by his peers, who had grown up with him and were of no lesser family or courage, they would not nurse resentment and plot against him, but not seeing him would believe that his nature was different from theirs" (1.99.2).

The most effective means by which a tyrant preserves an irrational suspension of disbelief concerning his nature include the manipulation of religious symbols and religious belief. Pisistratus in Athena's chariot, Deioces behind the seven shining walls of Agbatana, and Salmoxis in his underground chamber on the way to becoming the god of the Getae are recognizably brethren, as are the peoples who are taken in: the Medes, the supposedly clever Athenians who should have known better, and the Getae, who alone of men have abolished the distinction between men and gods and hold the belief—antithetical to the Greek view that death itself gives human life and effort its meaning—that they are immortal (*athanatizontes,* 4.93–94, 5.4.1).[22]

But in the end, this is what separates the Athenians, who are on the way to becoming Greek, from the barbarian Getae and the Medes: who and what is a god? The fact that Deioces is able to disappear behind a curtain of hieratic ceremonial is a particular fact about the Asianic environment of Iranian monarchy. A particular fact about the Greek environment is that disappearance of the Asianic kind is a feat impossible or nearly so in the narrow confines of a polis: Pisistratus in Athena's chariot was merely silly in the eyes of Herodotus. In his eyes, the Athenians and all other Greeks understood and observed the fundamental distinction between humanity and deity, whereas Asiatic barbarians—deficient in knowledge about the divine—confused this distinction. For Herodotus, this fact is a fundamental reason why tyranny was permanent among Asiatic barbarians but not among Greeks, who could never be persuaded that any human being was superior in any sense approaching true godhead itself.[23]

Herodotus' tale of the origins of the Iranian monarchy is therefore controlled by his conception of its character, which he based upon the two givens of oriental monarchy from that day to this one: (1) that the ruler is the law in his person and unlimited in his discretion (3.31), and (2) that the king devises his person to be sancrosanct and hieratically separated from his subjects.[24] Accordingly, he accepted, for example, the story that Cyrus was suckled by a bitch in a rationalized form that fits the second of these givens and is therefore generically true, part of "the true story" (*ton . . . eonta logon,* 1.95.1): he opined that Cyrus' parents put about the story so that his survival should "be reckoned the more an act of god" (*hina theioterôs dokeêi,* 1.122.3) to the Persians.[25]

In respecting these givens, the story of Deioces is also generically true: its "historicity," its character of being "the true story," lies in its power to explain the character of Medo-Persian kingship according to principles operating universally among orientals. Herodotus is able to present this truth in categories relevant to Greek experience because most Greeks were once barbarians. Greek experience therefore contains all experience, both "Greek" and "barbarian"; the range and explanatory power of Greek experience is accordingly universal, whereas the experiences of other peoples are peculiar to themselves.

In this way Herodotus presents, from Deioces onward, a full portrait of Iranian despotism *sui generis* in a generically accurate model which, although it contains all of the peculiar marks native to Iranian barbarism, is accessible in its fundamentals to Greeks because their experience includes tyrannical magnificence and pretension to royalty,[26] as well as the Thyestian feasts, Oedipal exposures, familial vendettas, perversions, and usurpations of tyrannical houses, both recent and in the "barbarian" histories of the ancient ruling houses of Thebes, Mycenae, and Athens.

In the Histories the potential direction of development of Asianic peoples is out of their peculiar barbarisms into Hellenism, even though this development has up until the present occurred in relative fullness only among those Pelasgians and other barbarians who changed into Hellenes. The Medes, while they were free, gathered themselves into a Hellenic citizens' assembly, and the Seven who overthrew the Magi, while free, could argue constitutional theory like Greeks (3.80ff).[27] During their episodes of freedom—which Herodotus treats as the turning points in the history of barbarian Asia—these barbarians were functionally Greek as long as they were free. But they revert to the condition of society defined by the hubris of the monarch and the *apragmosynê* of the subject, namely, to slavery.

Barbarian failure is an essential historical theme of the Histories; Herodotus' Asiatic monarchs are a gallery of barbarians who fail to become Greek. Instead they become "evolved" Asianic barbarians. In his portrait of Croesus, Herodotus introduced his audience to a highly "evolved" Asianic barbarism already in full—if futile—touch with Hellenic wisdom and Hellenic divinity. His Persians, on the other hand, enter history as primitives who inhabit a hard country, dress in skins, and drink water instead of wine.[28] They are innocent of the world's good and pleasant things, as well as of Greeks and of "evolved" Asianic barbarism—until Cyrus conquers Lydia and encounters Croesus (1.71.4). Herodotus' portraits of

Persia's kings are accordingly "evolutionary" in character. He brings his audiences from their first look at the pristine savage Cyrus, who puts Croesus on the pyre, all the way to the highly "evolved" Xerxes, conversing easily with Greeks, beheading the corpse of Leonidas, and dining off gold plate.[29]

Why, wonders Herodotus, did Cyrus put Croesus and fourteen Lydian boys on the pyre? As fit first fruits of victory? Fulfillment of a vow? Or as an experiment to test the efficacy of Croesus' god? Herodotus does not commit himself explicitly to any of these possibilities, but he does proceed with his story as if Cyrus indeed had intended to test Croesus' god: for, when Croesus in tears supplicates Apollo to save him if the god had ever been pleased by his gifts, Cyrus witnesses a resounding affirmation of Apollo's power in the cloudburst that falls out of a clear sky and quenches the pyre, and he immediately concludes that Croesus is favored by the divinity and noble in his character (1.87.2; cf. *Il.* 1.36–42).[30]

Thus the very first acquaintance of Persians with a god of the Greeks occurs in this epiphany of Apollo's power over the elements. However, Croesus—notwithstanding his miraculous salvation, and still immune to the meaning of Apollo's oracle concerning the result of his crossing of the Halys—declares immediately to Cyrus that the whole blame for his disaster lies with the god, and begs to be allowed to send his chains to Delphi together with the question—outrageous to Greek piety—whether it is the custom of the god of the Hellenes, whom he has honored above all, to double-cross his benefactors (1.87.2–3, 90.2–4).

Cyrus is typically barbaric in setting out to burn Croesus alive; it is characteristic of barbarians to burn or butcher the human body and use it in other atrocious ways.[31] But he is strikingly atypical in his sober reflection, as he hears the words of Solon from Croesus' lips, that he is burning a fellow human being who had once been as fortunate as he, and therefore he fears divine retribution (1.86.6). This is a conversion unique in Herodotus; on no other occasion is an Asiatic barbarian moved to moderation and sobriety by the words of a Greek. Only in Cyrus does Herodotus present one who, at the outset, is susceptible to Hellenic wisdom, and who witnesses the reality and power of Hellenic divinity. It is as if this is another moment in history in which Iranians could have become "Greek."

Instead, the Persians become "Lydian." Cyrus and the Persians will gain neither the benefit of Solon's wisdom nor any belief in Apollo (cf. 1.131) because, instead of believing the evidence of the sudden and irrefutable[32] miracle they have all just witnessed, they are instead convinced by the impious and uncomprehending complaints of Croesus—whose prayer has just been answered—that Apollo is not to be depended upon. Cyrus is a good sort of barbarian but a barbarian nonetheless, with barbarian eyes and ears. He will suffer his own disaster through heeding the pseudo-Solonian counsel of the "failed Greek" Croesus.

In his final campaign Cyrus turns against the savage Massagetae, a nomad people of the steppe who live and dress as the Scyths do; they do not sow and harvest but live from their beasts and the fish of the river Araxes; they drink milk and—like the Persians themselves before their conquest of Lydia—are ignorant of wine (1.216). At the time when Cyrus marched against them, the Massagetae were ruled by a woman. Cyrus first intended to conquer her as a man conquers a woman—by marriage, which he proposes *dolôi*, "guilefully" (1.205.1). Spurned, he proceeds to attempt by arms the conquest he had already resolved upon, fortified by his belief that in his birth there was something more than human and, like Croesus in his fatal misreading of the Halys oracle, by his hitherto unbroken success in war.

When Cyrus prepares bridges to cross the Araxes into the land of the Massagetae—bridges are always highways to ill fate for barbarian monarchs[33]—this woman, Tomyris, echoing Gyges' futile advice to Candaules, warns him to be content with what is already his and leave the Massagetae to what is theirs. But knowing that Cyrus desires anything rather than peace, she allows him choose his field of battle on either side of the river. The Persians in counsel with Cyrus declare for fighting on their own side; but Croesus now enters sententiously mouthing a Greek *pathei mathos* proverb, *ta de moi pathêmata eonta akharita mathêmata gegone* (1.207.1), "experience has taught me the hard way." He counsels Cyrus, pseudo-Solonically, to remember that all men are mortal and that the fortune of mortals is a wheel (1.207.2).[34]

"Desist and be satisfied" is the advice naturally implied by these maxims. But Croesus cites them to the contrary. Here we are, back in the *Persae*. Rescued from the pyre by Apollo, Croesus had blamed the "god of the Hellenes" for his fall and opined that such things occur by the agency of *daimoni kou*, "some divinity." The god himself, through the Pythia, had then set Croesus straight concerning his own part in his fall, as the Ghost of the *Persae* had set the Elders straight concerning Xerxes; but even so Croesus learns nothing in the end concerning either gods or battles (1.87.4ff).

So, forgetting that he was once advised by the Lydian sage Sandanis not to cross a river to fight savages who, like the Massagetae, had been ignorant of wine and of all the other attractions of civilization (1.71),[35] Croesus advises Cyrus to cross the river and set a guileful trap baited with the gifts abused by Asiatic luxury: rich foods and unmixed wine. And so Cyrus crosses the river to meet his end. Tomyris posthumously slakes his thirst for blood by severing his head and putting it into a wineskin filled with human blood (1.204–14). In Herodotus' biography, Cyrus sane drinks water, deluded he drinks wine, and dead of insatiable hubris he drinks blood.

"There are many stories told about the death of Cyrus," Herodotus remarks in conclusion, "I tell the one that to me is most convincing" (*ho pithanôtatos,* 1.214 *fin.*). We do not have these other stories with which to compare it;[36] but even so it is possible to see that Herodotus adopted it and gave it this shape not by virtue of any obvious internal consistency or inherent plausibility, but because just those elements that we discard immediately, as "critical historians," are the givens that perfectly fit Herodotus' own total conception of Cyrus' character and career.

Cyrus' death at the hands of thorough savages introduces that iron law of nature versus culture which Cyrus himself will enunciate to end the whole work: "Soft lands produce soft men; for both splendid fruits and strong warriors cannot spring from the same

land" (9.122.3). In the Histories the savage is stronger than civilization and will always defeat it.[37] Thus Cimmerians and Scyths
invade civilized Asia and rule there for twenty-eight years; the
Lydians then defeat the Ionians, whose very name is a byword for
luxury; next the rude and hungry Persians defeat Medes, Lydians,
and Ionians in their turn; finally the Massagetae, Aethiopians,
Scyths, and Hellenes in succession defeat the ever more wealthy
and luxurious Persians. In each case the less "evolved" people
defeats the more "evolved."

This pattern of the past once more implies a Herodotean prophecy about the future: hard-living Spartans will defeat Asianically
luxurious Athenians. It is a prophecy foreshadowed by Cyrus'
question to the Greeks around him upon the first encounter between Spartans and Persians near the beginning of the Histories.
Cyrus inquires who the Spartans are and how many (*kosoi plêthos*);
hearing the answer, he condemns the Spartans as men never to
be feared, who set aside a place in the middle of their cities
where they gather to cheat each other on oath. This dismissal,
says Herodotus, he cast into the teeth of all the Greeks, who have
established agoras to buy and sell, for the Persians themselves, he
explains, assiduously avoid agoras and have none of their own
(1.153.1). But Cyrus gets the Spartans wrong by assuming that
they are like the Lydians and Ionians whom he has just conquered,
and his error thereby anticipates the fate of the Persians in the
Histories. For the Spartans were in fact the one Greek people
whose citizens did not buy and sell in the agora;[38] nor did they
have, in its other sense, any *plêthos,* any "mob."

In the end the Spartans, whose former king Demaratus tries in
vain to educate Xerxes about his people and their number, will
defeat the best of Xerxes' Persians at Thermopylae and Plataea.
They prevail, as Herodotus implies here at the beginning, because
their virtues alone among Greek peoples answer to the Persians'
original virtues among Asiatics: against Xerxes, the Spartans will
show themselves superior to the Persians in just those ways comparable to the superiority of Cyrus' Persians to those agora-frequent-
ing Greeks of Ionia whom Cyrus conquered together with their
Lydian cousins, the inventors of marketing and money, institutions

uniquely foreign to the Spartans but central to the Ionians' way of life and to the material culture of imperial Athens.

Cambyses and Persian Religion

Herodotus' Persian portraits depict the effects that the Persian Kings' conquests cumulatively produce upon their nature. Cyrus is not the same man at the end as he was in the beginning. The young Cyrus had been ignorant of wine and of guile. But at the end he is full of the guile and luxuries of Asiatic civilization, heedless of human limitation, and deluded in his conviction of his special place in the care of the gods and his understanding of signs from the gods. At the beginning Cyrus heard Croesus tell him, against the evidence of his own senses—his *opsis* and *akoê*—that Apollo is not to be relied upon. At the end, he dreams that a winged Darius overshadows Asia and Europe. And to Darius' father Hystaspes Cyrus declares, "Your son has been caught plotting against me and my rule. I will tell you how I know it for certain (*tauta atrekeios oida*, 1.209.4): the gods care for me and show me everything that is to be." But Cyrus was wrong, says Herodotus; the *daimôn* simply showed that Cyrus himself was about to die and that his kingship would pass to Darius. Cyrus remains typically barbaric in his inability to "see" the divine intention, which to Medo-Persian kings commonly arrives in dreams.

Cyrus is "spoiled" by the civilization of the evolved Asiatic barbarian, represented in the person of Croesus, by whom it penetrates inwardly to the center of Cyrus' court and outwardly to the trans-Caspian steppe at the farthest reach of Cyrus' Asiatic dominions. Cyrus is spoiled in a "Lydian" way, a way generically true of the way an Iranian would be spoiled by Asia, the continent of Croesus and of wine. His son Cambyses conquers Egypt and, likewise, he is spoiled by Egypt in the way an Iranian would be spoiled by Egypt, the country of the gods.[39] But Cambyses differs from Cyrus. Cambyses had Cyrus the King for a father, but does not have it in him to be a Persian King, whereas Cyrus himself had a cowherd for a father, but had it in him to be a Persian King (1.114).

What Persian things, then, did Cambyses learn from his father? Herodotus tells us that Persians bring up their boys only to ride, to shoot, and to tell the truth (3.136.2); and they judge a man by his courage in battle and the number of his sons (3.136.1). As for the Persian Kings themselves, their peculiar virtue from Deioces onward lies in giving justice: in the Histories not only the story of Deioces, but others, including those of Otanes the son of Sisamnes (5.25) and Sandoces (7.194.1–2), examine the theme of Persian justice.[40]

As for Cambyses, in the Histories he will fail the Persian ideals of manhood and kingship in every respect: in horsemanship, in archery, in the telling of truth, in war, in fatherhood, and in the giving of justice. Cambyses' failure is a failure of Persian education, and Cambyses' failure is therefore also the failure of Cyrus. So, like father like son: in Cambyses' cruel test of the conquered Psammenitus' soul and his pity for him on hearing Psammenitus' words he recapitulates his father's test of Croesus and his repentance—indeed Croesus is present at Cambysees' side to hasten recognition of the parallel between father and son at the beginning of their respective careers in the Histories (3.15). But Cambyses soon goes on to burn the corpse of another pharaoh, Amasis, as Cyrus had set out to burn the living body of Croesus (3.16). In this Cambyses is worse than his father, because he violates the law both of the Persians and the Egyptians. The Persians believe fire is a god, and neither pollute fire with a corpse nor allow fire to touch the meat of sacrifices (1.132.1); as for the Egyptians, they consider fire a beast and they do not give corpses to beasts for devouring (3.16.2–4).

So Cambyses begins as his father had ended. But Cambyses in Egypt will be brought down not by a human enemy but by the gods; and instead of paying with his life Cambyses will pay with his mind. So extreme is his madness that it is as if, because Egypt itself is the antithesis of other human societies, Cambyses in Egypt is the antithesis of sanity itself.[41]

The madness characteristic of tyrants is paranoia,[42] the first symptoms of which had appeared in the Persian line when Cyrus believed that Darius was plotting against him in consequence of his dream, just as Cyrus himself had been taken from his parents by the Median king Astyages as a consequence of his dreams (1.107–8). Cambyses, too, will have his brother Smerdis put to death in consequence of a dream, which he likewise wrongly interprets to believe that Smerdis is plotting to kill him and rule in his stead. For Cambyses had sent Smerdis away to Persia when he showed himself the better man—he was the only Persian able to draw the Aethiopian bow even a little way. The dream appeared to Cambyses to confirm his fear and—like the dream that was to come to Xerxes (7.12ff)—bade him do what he already wished to do. In the dream life of Iranian monarchs history repeats itself in a characteristically Iranian way.

Cambyses will come to his senses only when he leaves Egypt for his own continent of Asia, just as Xerxes will enjoy a final, sane meditation on his own mortality and the evanescence of power in his own continent of Asia, before he crosses the Hellespont to be hailed as Zeus in his deluded march to disaster in Europe (7.45–57).[43] In Syria Cambyses is told that his two Magian palace stewards, one of whom was named Smerdis, had risen against him. The true meaning of his dream comes to him and he realizes that he had his brother killed for nothing (3.63–64). Then, leaping onto his charger in haste to return to Susa, Cambyses wounds himself in the thigh at the very spot where he had stabbed the Egyptians' god, the Apis-bull. Now the oracle of Buto in Egypt had long ago prophesied to him that he would die in Agbatana. Cambyses had assumed he would die in old age at Median Agbatana, but recognizes the outcome now, when he is told that this place where he wounded himself is named Agbatana, and he cries, "Here is where Cambyses the son of Cyrus is fated to die."

Cyrus in Asia had crossed a river to make war on savages, whereas Cambyses in Egypt sends his army across a desert to make war on Zeus. His madness is not merely the paranoia of tyrants but takes the extreme form of making war upon the gods. He orders his soldiers to burn the shrine of Zeus Ammon and to enslave the god's servants. Instead, they disappear beneath a sandstorm

(3.26)—just as a storm at sea, sent by heaven to aid the Hellenes, will afterward overcome the fleet of Xerxes (8.13 *fin.*). In the Histories it is only in Greece, besides Egypt, that the gods themselves fight the Persians.

. Cambyses himself marches with the rest of his army against the Aethiopians, as Cyrus had done against the Massagetae, to conquer them by guile, by luxuries, and by wine (3.20.1). Like the Massagetae the Aethiopians are savages—a simple, milk-drinking, unconquerable people at an extreme of the Persians' empire (3.25.1–2).

But unlike the Massagetae and the other savages of Asia and Scythia, however, or for that matter Cambyses and the Persians themselves, they are not the worse for wine (3.22.3f; cf. 3.34.2, 1.132.3–4, 212.2). The long-lived Aethiopians possess natural virtues and ways that are antithetical to—and stronger than—Asianic barbarism. The Aethiopian sees through Cambyses' spies, and warns them not to march against his land unless they can draw the Aethiopian bow, which is far stronger than the Persian bow. Then he examines Cambyses' gifts: a purple-dyed cloak and myrrh, artifices of beautification unknown to the Aethiopians, who are the world's tallest and most naturally beautiful people, whereas the deceitful Persians adorn themselves artificially with articles and vestments adopted from other peoples of their empire (3.20–22; cf. 1.135). Finally the Aethiopian king discovers that the Persians eat bread from grain grown in the soil, and remarks that they eat dung (*kopron*) for food.

The king of the Aethiopians, then, is a paragon of natural perfection, who understands the truth and sees things in their natural reality. It is against this king that Cambyses will march, unprepared and unprovisioned, heedless of the warning of the Aethiopian bow and maddened by his envoys' report, until his soldiers are reduced to cannibalism (3.25). Only now does he turn back, to arrive in Memphis while the whole populace is celebrating the epiphany of the god Apis in the form of a bull. Convinced in his madness that the Memphites are celebrating his disaster, he puts his informants concerning Apis to death as liars. Then, when the bull itself is brought to him, he again makes war on a god. To test its godhead with the sword, he stabs it and laughs at a god "of blood and flesh that is wounded by the blade" (3.29.2).[44]

Cambyses has no more respect for the laws of the Persians than for the gods of the Egyptians. For he had married two of his sisters, contrary to Persian custom, and then murdered one of them, together with his unborn child (3.30f).[45] And, like Astyages the Mede, Cambyses also murdered the son of his highest servant and butchered the body. This man. Prexaspes, had told the truth to Cambyses when he said, in response to Cambyses' own request, that the Persians thought he was too fond of wine. Cambyses responded in fury, saying "Now the Persians say that I've gone out of my mind and am crazy from wine." As the proof of his sanity Cambyses announced that he would show his skill with the Persian bow: he then shot an arrow straight into the heart of Prexaspes' son and had the body cut apart to expose the wound.

Even before this, Cambyses had twelve other Persians of the highest nobility buried alive for no cause worth mentioning (3.35.5). And when Croesus warned him that he was thereby courting revolt, Cambyses ordered him executed. But Cambyses' servants hid him instead, knowing that their master would soon want him back. So it turned out; but he nonetheless put them to death for disobedience (3.36).

In a story very much like this one, Xerxes gives a golden crown to the Phoenician captain who brings him through a storm safely to Asia after Salamis, but at the cost of putting overboard the Persian nobles who had sailed with him; for this Xerxes then has the captain beheaded (8.118–19). It is another of those significant stories that Herodotus disbelieves but repeats. Both stories test a principle of Persian justice that Herodotus admires but which his Persian monarchs breach because tyrants need not obey their own laws:[46] that no Persian, not even the Great King, may put to death or irremediably punish a servant for a single offense, but only after weighing the culprit's services against his offenses (1.137.1).

In the cases of Prexaspes and the Phoenician captain, Herodotus' audiences are meant to consider the injustice of the King's decision in return for benefits conferred according to the Persians' own standards. In Prexaspes' case, moreover, Iranian history again repeats itself in a characteristically Iranian way, since Cambyses punished Prexaspes for telling the truth by butchering his son, just as Astyages had punished Harpagus for telling the truth by butchering his son (1.117–19): afterward Prexaspes would play a principal part in raising up Darius, much as Harpagus had raised up Cyrus against Astyages.

So much for Cambyses and Persian justice. As for the Persian education to the horse, the bow, and the truth, Cambyses confused the bow and the truth in a way most unjust, in making murder the proof of truth, he who could not bend the Aethiopian's bow. Even his horsemanship is condemned by his death wound, which he inflicted on himself while mounting. As for sons, Cambyses was no man at all, since he left none (3.34.5).

In his very attempt to "penetrate" Egypt, to control Egypt *in toto*, spiritually as well as physically, Cambyses breaks down along the fault-lines of his Persian upbringing, because Egypt, though physically garrisoned by the Persians, is spiritually invulnerable and defeats its conqueror on the plane of the divine. To Herodotus, Egypt, like his Scythia, is a land impenetrable to others and essentially unconquerable;[47] neither Persians nor Greeks can "enter" either environment.[48] In Scythia and Egypt the Greeks exist by sufferance at the margins only as traders. Egypt itself is the very antithesis of Greece in its lack of rain and abundance of irrigation (2.13.3, cf. 35–36). The nomads of Scythia are unconquerable both physically (4.46.2–3) and spiritually.[49] To penetrate Scythia Greeks must themselves become Scyths (Callippidae 4.17.1; Geloni 4.108.2).

To the Egyptians, the Greeks and all other foreigners are polluted as eaters of unclean food and are called barbarians (*barbaroi*, 2.158.5). It is to the Greeks in their markets that the Egyptians sell the heads of sacrificed bulls, which are loaded with imprecations according to custom, and for this reason no Egyptian will eat the head of any creature (2.39). Nor will any Egyptian kiss a Greek on the mouth, nor use Greek utensils, nor even eat the meat of a sacrificially pure bull butchered with a Greek knife (2.41.1–3).

Herodotus even illuminates the famous Athenian disaster in Egypt in terms of the Egyptian gods' hostility to foreigners in their land. After associating the Egyptians' religious abomination of Greeks with bulls, he goes on to relate that the bones of all the bulls that die in Egypt are collected and interred on the island of Prosopitis (2.41.4–6). Now, after their disaster in Egypt "Prosopitis" must have held associations for Athenians not unlike those of "Stalingrad" for the Germans after Hitler's war. For it was at Prosopitis that a great Athenian armada besieging Memphis had been destroyed, and few out of many had escaped alive (Thuc. 2.110.1).[50] It is as if the peculiar divinity of Prosopitis—the place where an anti-Greek miasma is concentrated from every corner of the country—confers on the disaster its ultimate explanation.

Later, when the gods fight the Persians in Greece, Herodotus will also tell how the Persians were repelled by divine force alone at Delphi (Hdt. 7.36–39) and at Plataea, where to Herodotus' wonder few Persian dead were found within the grove of Eleusinian Demeter and none in the shrine itself, even though it had been the scene of the heaviest Persian slaughter: Herodotus surmises that the goddess herself denied welcome to the Persians, who had burned her shrine at Eleusis (9.65.2). In the Histories the gods protect their own against barbarian invaders in Egypt and in Greece alike.

Whereas in the *Persae* the Persians' god is all too human, in the Histories the Persians' gods are not human at all, much less animal. That is why Cambyses could make war on Zeus Ammon and stab the Apis-bull, mocking it as a vulnerable "god" of flesh and blood. Cambyses' gods were the forces of nature—the heavens, sun, moon and earth, fire, water, and wind (1.131). The Persians' deities are the most ancient elements of creation, as described in the opening verses of Hesiod's *Theogony* and also, presumably, in the *theogoniên* that the Magi chant over the animal sacrifices of Persians (1.132.3). The Persians therefore enjoy no individual communications from divinity, except in the venues of Egyptian and Greek gods, as at Buto (3.64.4) or the cave of Amphiaraus (8.135)—and little good it does them.

From our point of view, and that of Greek thinkers in the tradition of Xenophanes (21 B 11, 14–16, 23–26 DK) and Plato, aniconic conceptions of deity like those of the Persians are advances over the violent, anthropomorphic gods of Homer and Hesiod.[51] For his own part, however, Herodotus is unshakable in his belief that the individual gods exist in human form, as first the Egyptians and afterward Homer and Hesiod depicted them. The gods of most Greeks are not merely the elements of nature but those beings who, among their other attributes, are more powerful than the forces of nature, which they possess and of which they dispose.

Since the gods are persons who possess wills and speak to mortals, as Apollo speaks at Delphi, humans can speak to them, to implore them or give thanks for benefits. It is just this ground of communication between gods and mortals, founded in their likeness and crystallized in oracular shrines and the mantic gifts of individual prophets, and in ordinary human prayer and dedications, which is the fundamental basis of Greek religiosity: *do ut des.*[52]

But the Persians' gods have no voice or form; therefore the dream is the characteristic medium of divine communication among the Medes and Persians. The gods themselves, as persons, are never seen in the dreams dreamed in the Histories. In Cambyses' dream a messenger from Persia had told him that Smerdis sat upon his throne, with his head touching heaven (3.36.2). Cyrus' dream was of Darius winged (1.209.1) and Astyages dreamed twice of his daughter (1.107.1, 108.1). Xerxes dreamed that he saw a tall and handsome man standing before him (7.12.1, as did Hipparchus at 5.56.1). Certainly the divine power was driving him into his fatal course, as Zeus had sent Dream to Agamemnon (*Iliad* 2.1ff), but Xerxes recognizes a man, not a god, in the figure who stands over him. Thus dreams, into which intrude no gods imagined as persons, or even any symbols of divinity, are ambiguous in their provenance even to the wise Persian Artabanus (7.16). Xerxes himself believes that, if Artabanus dreams his dream in his master's place, this fact will prove the dream to be from a god (7.15), and so Artabanus too concludes, upon dreaming, that "some divine impulse is at work" (7.18.3: *daimoniê tis ginetai hormê*). But Herodotus does not step out of the story's Persian frame. Artabanus' conclusion remains an ambiguous inference and, in any case, the dream forces Xerxes to do what he had wanted to do in the first place, for all of the reasons characteristic of Persian monarchs and Persian imperialism (7.8).

Herodotus' sense of the profound otherness of Persian religion extends systematically throughout his description of its details (1.131–32), which begins with the statement that the Persians have no holy images, shrines, or altars and regard those who do as fools because, as he would suppose, their own gods are the elements (1.131.1). In consequence, the whole manner of their communion with their gods, of prayer and sacrifice, is antithetical to the Greek way.[53] They may offer sacrifice anywhere, using no altar or fire, pouring no libations and playing no flute (132.1). Greeks speak to their gods directly, but Persians may offer sacrifice only through the mediation of a Magus. Finally no personal petition is lawful for a Persian, but only a prayer for the welfare of the whole Persian nation and the King: in this especially, the Persian ritual as seen through Herodotus' eyes marks off the insuperable distance between the Persians and their elemental gods, a distance abolished by the Greeks' possession of individuated deities whom they may petition directly and individually.

Greek sacrificial and dedicatory rites initiate a personal gift-exchange between an individual and a god, a relationship impossible for Persians. On those occasions when Persians must communicate with Greek gods they employ Greek rituals together with their own, presided over by Magi, and they usually are not successful. Xerxes' hecatombs to Athena Ilias and libations to the heroes at Troy are followed by a panic that sweeps through his army in the night (7.43.2). Again, when the great gale strikes Xerxes' fleet the Magi howl enchantments against it and sacrifice to Thetis and the Nereids: by these means, comments Herodotus, "they brought it to an end on the fourth day—unless it stopped of its own will" (*hê allôs kôs autos ethelôn ekopase*, 7.191.2).

Among Greeks, festival life was public, concerned with the favor of the gods for the citizens as a body or in their moieties— tribes, *gênê*, phratries, *teletai*. Among Persians, celebrations were individual and private: one's own birthday was the year's highest feast, for which the celebrant himself provided the meat (1.133.1). Herodotus does tell about a public festival of the Persians, the Magophonia (3.79.3), which is the national holiday commemorating the slaying of the Magi who usurped Cambyses' throne. But this too is quite the opposite of a religious feast, since all Magi must stay indoors and out of sight on that day; and, as no sacrifice among the Persians can take place without a Magus attending, it would follow that no sacrifices can be performed on this day.

The practices of the Magi are anathema to Greek religious sentiment in exposing the bodies of their dead to the carrion beasts (1.140.1). Moreover, says Herodotus, "Magi are far different from other men and especially from the priests in Egypt," whom Herodotus admires as much as the Magi repel him. "For the latter it is a pollution to kill any living thing except those which they sacrifice; but the Magi kill with their own hands all except dogs and men, and they compete strenuously in this, killing alike ants, and snakes, and all the beasts that crawl and fly" (1.140.2).[54]

In Herodotus' mind Cambyses' insane assault upon the Apis-bull was Magian orthodoxy.

Darius

Cambyses was the first Persian King to leave Asia and thereby he lost his moorings altogether. He rejected the ways of the Egyptians and violated the ways of his own people too, not only in his incestuous sister-marriages but in every respect, failing as a Persian in truth, horsemanship, archery, fatherhood, war, and justice. The total otherness of Persian religion "explains" the madness of Cambyses in Egypt and his warfare on her gods; but for Herodotus the whole character of Cambyses' madness lies even more generally in his denying the customs of others and insisting upon his own (3.38.1–3).

Darius is unlike Cambyses in three ways that bring on a new

stage in the evolution of Herodotus' Persians. First of all, Darius' career is free of commerce with divinity beyond the elemental stroke of lightning and thunderclap at his inauguration (3.86.2). Darius dreams no dreams, is vouchsafed no portents, and receives no oracles. Second, Darius accepts the customs of others and does not insist upon his own. Herodotus relates that once he brought together the Greeks at his court with some Callatii, a people of farthest India, to have them discover to their mutual horror that the one people burned their parents' bodies, whereas the other ate them. In this way, says Herodotus, Darius showed the truth of Pindar's dictum that custom is lord of all (3.38.3–5).[55] Finally, Darius' sanity survives his sojourn beyond Asia into savage Scythia. He does not fight the gods of the Scyths; in fact, he cannot find the Scyths themselves until they decide to find him; so he sensibly calls it quits and goes home.

In a word, Herodotus' Darius is Cambyses' antithesis. Whereas Cambyses was insane in a Persian way Darius is sane in a way that is not Persian. He is by far the least hubristic Persian King in Herodotus and cynically tolerant—worldly to a fault, in failing to differentiate between cremation and cannibalism. But Herodotus' Darius is also no Cyrus. Before he was spoiled by Lydian Asia, Cyrus had made a reproach to the Greeks of fraud and faithlessness in their agoras, whereas on his entrance into history Darius makes no difference between truth and falsehood. Fully "evolved" in his mature tyrannical sophia, he is a *polytropos* full of instant resolve and Odyssean resource, ready to betray his comrades before they betray him (3.71.4–5), a schemer who has no use for Persian truth but weighs his words by the single scale of advantage (3.72.4–5). It is his argument for monarchy that will prevail in the debate to come on the future of Persia, and the monarchy will fall to him, ratified perhaps by the heavens but more surely by a trick (3.80–87).

Herodotus insists that this Persian "Debate on Constitutions" really occurred, against those Greeks who scoff at the story (3.80.1); and he points to Mardonius' institution of democracies in Ionia after the great revolt as a specific proof of Otanes' advocacy of

democracy for the Persians on that occasion (6.43.3). Like the
Ionian burlesque of mythical *aitiai* at the beginning of the work,
which Herodotus nevertheless attributes to the Persians' *logioi*, the
debate is through and through a product of the contemporary
Greek imagination.[56]

The reason why Herodotus believes this debate really occurred
among Persians has to do once again with the potential of Asianic
barbarians to become Greek and vice versa. The Persians are free
men (3.80.1, 83) and without a government in the five days
between the slaying of the Magi and the vote of the Seven for a
monarchy. The Seven themselves had fought the Magi with their
spears versus the Magis' bows, with Greek weapons versus the
Persian weapon (cf. Aesch. *Pers.* 239–40) *as tyrannicides*. Like the
Medes before Deioces, they are at a crossroads in their history,
where they are compelled by circumstances to behave as free men.
The question is, then, how do free men behave? Like Greeks, of
course, since the only free men in the world *are* Greeks: the
assembly that chose Deioces and the Debate on politics won by
Darius are not willfully solipsistic inventions, but Herodotean
calques upon the only possible cultural model, which is provided
by the Greeks with the exception of the Spartans.

The Persians belong to that category of barbarians—the barbarians of Asia—which includes the formerly Pelasgian Ionians of Asia
and Attica. Accordingly, the Persian debate analyzes the possible
Persian governments in Ionian-Athenian terms which do not apply
to the Lycurgan system. The regimes considered by Darius and
his allies are not, in Herodotus' view, generically foreign to Asianic
barbarians, because all collapse into tyranny, the "Asianic" mode
of government which all Greeks except the Spartans either suffer
or, as Pelasgians by ancestry, are congenitally liable to suffer.

With the advent of Darius, Herodotus imagines the "evolved"
Persians of Darius' and his own day as more "Ionian" than the
Medes of Deioces' day, who were unable to envision any choice
beyond that between anarchy and monarchy. Like Ionians they
have become capable of sophistical argumentation and of considering alternatives to monarchy. In this ability to conceive alternative
forms of rule, the Persians are distinguished from other barbarians,

especially the Scyths and Egyptians. The Scyths are antithetically non-Hellenic in their way of life and emphatically reject Hellenic ways (4.76–79); the Egyptians are altogether *sui generis* (2.35.2– 36). The kings of the Scyths are necessary to a way of life inconceivable without them.[57] The Egyptians are ruled by kings throughout their immemorial history; they cannot conceive of life without a monarch (2.99.2–100.1, 147.2).

The benchmark of possible Persian evolution toward Hellenism is the house of Otanes, who proposed democracy for the Persians. His house will remain the only free house in Persia vis-à-vis the Great King, subject not to his mandates but only to the laws of Persia: his only despot, therefore, is *nomos*—which is how Demaratus will describe the Spartans to Xerxes (7.104.4). Otanes and his house become free in the Greek sense, moreover, for a Greek reason: he was the only competitor for power who gave up the contest for tyranny in return for a guarantee of freedom. This is the social contract of the Greek polis.

It was Otanes' choice, not Mardonius' democracies, which proved to Herodotus that free government lay within the Persians' purview, and therefore within the theoretical scope of their historical development. If all Persians would give up the contest for tyranny, all Persians would be free like Otanes.

Darius is "evolved" in still another way essential to Herodotus' taxonomic association of Persia with Lydia, Ionia, and Attica. He was the first Persian monarch to put his subjects under tribute in silver and gold. The Persians, says Herodotus, therefore dubbed him the *kapêlos*, the "bazaari," because *ekapêleue panta ta prêgmata,* "he put a price on everything" (3.89.3).

This is the Greek perception of Darius. Cyrus and Cambyses before him had imposed no tributes but accepted gifts. The distance between Darius and his predecessors is accordingly the distance between the heroic world of gift-exchange and the commercial world of the market-stalls. This is precisely the distance between the character of the pristine Cyrus and those Persians who contemn the Greeks for cheating one another in their agoras, which the Persians do not establish among themselves (1.153.2–3), and the character of the Lydians, who invented coined money and *kapêlia,* and whose monarch Croesus was the first barbarian known to have subjected Greeks to tribute (1.6.2, 94.1; cf. 155.4).

Darius in his character of bazaari also marks the change in the Persians' character toward "evolved" or "Lydian-like" Asianic barbarism in their relation to their possessions. Just as Croesus in his day had bought responses from Delphi and used his wealth to attract the most talented Greeks to his court, the Persians now also treat their empire as a bazaar that provides them with whatever desirable things they choose. The Persians, says Herodotus, have adopted the dress of the Medes and the cuirass of the Egyptians; and from the Greeks they have learned to enjoy sex with boys (1.135). Darius tries Egyptian doctors but is cured by a Greek (3.129–30). His queen Atossa wants Darius to conquer Greece in order to browse through it as a slave market: she desires to be served by the women of Laconia, Argos, Attica, and Corinth (3.134.5). Darius himself is a fan of the famous Crotoniate wrestler Milo (3.137.5), and in his wars enlists the expertise of Greeks wholesale: the fateful bridges of the Persians are to be constructed by Greeks and, from Darius onward, the Persians will exist in the Histories almost exclusively in their relations, collaborative or hostile, with Greeks.[58]

Darius' remade Persian empire, finally, works just like the Athenian system, with its Piraeus-bazaar to which all the world's good things are brought,[59] its fixed tributes, judicial supervision,[60] and imposed democracies.[61] Darius himself possesses some striking resemblances to Themistocles, the architect of the Athenian empire. Darius is the one Persian in the Histories who knows the right thing to do and does it swiftly, who prevails in debate at a crisis in his nation's history, and who recognizes good counsel and the limits of possibility.[62] Like Themistocles, Darius is also devious, avaricious, and forcible in his demands.[63]

Xerxes

In Europe Persians first meet Greeks at the court of Amyntas and Alexander I of Macedon (5.18–21). Banqueted according to Greek custom, these Persians begin by demanding to enjoy the royal women at the dinner couches as if they were in Persia, but end by falling under the daggers of Macedonian youths disguised as women. At this first encounter, then, Greek "women" slay Persian men, anticipating the theme of reversals of the natural order in the march of Asia to Europe epitomized by Xerxes' despairing cry at Salamis that his men have turned to women and his women to men.

In the Histories Xerxes arrives in Greece as he had done in the *Persae,* as the epiphany of a false god. As soon as Xerxes steps upon the continent of Europe from the Hellespont bridge one of the locals hails him with a question: "O Zeus, why do you want to overthrow Greece in the guise of a Persian named Xerxes instead of Zeus, bringing the whole world with you? Surely you could manage it without all this bother?" (7.56.2). A Greek would have met this blasphemy with a sign of aversion; but Xerxes passes on with a sacrilegious silence that gives consent. He ignores likewise an obvious (*eusymblêton*) portent—a mare that gives birth to a hare—which foretells the destruction of his pomp and host (7.57.1). He is blind to it, just as he had been blind to the portent at Sardis that foretold how his men would become women, and his women men: a mule had foaled a colt with male and female genitals and the male organ lay below the female (7.57.2; cf. 8.88.3).

In his character Xerxes is altogether a slave to his impulses (7.39.2) and to his avarice: the great golden Ba'al of Babylon, which Cyrus had not touched and Darius coveted but did not dare to take, Xerxes would remove and for good measure kill the priest who forbade him (1.183.3). Xerxes is godless, cynical, and violent like his father, but matched with Themistocles in this war he has none of his father's Themistoclean cleverness.

Xerxes is opaque to his Greek warner Demaratus' wise advice. The only Greeks he does heed are the fraudulent oracle-monger Onomacritus (7.6.4), the nameless Greek who hails him as Zeus, and the messenger from Themistocles who lures him to disaster at Salamis. The only Greek god who piques his interest is Zeus Laphystius, "Zeus the Devourer," a deity whose ancient associations with Phrixus and Helle join Europe with Asia, and who is congenial to barbarism in the atrocity of his cult, which is centered upon human sacrifice (7.197).[64] Apollo of Delphi, whose words will show the way of victory to the Hellenes, Xerxes intends only to rob (8.35). In sum, Xerxes is purblind and sacrilegious in the environment of Greece to that extreme epitomized by the immense hubris of his armada itself.

So Xerxes passes on to his wholly deserved and divinely appointed doom. It was the Athenians, opines Herodotus programmatically, who *after the gods* routed Xerxes (7.139.5).[65] The design of the entire war narrative that follows this declaration confirms to his audiences his belief that, if it was the Athenians who at last steeled themselves and led the other Hellenes to face the Persians at sea, despite the general fear and the terrifying oracles which they themselves received from Delphi (7.138.2, 139.6), it was the gods who intended the victory. This war narrative is the most finished and finely balanced illustration of the Histories' oracular theology: informed on the plane of divine action by oracular testimonies to the divine will, and on the plane of human action by the combatants' fear (repetitively noted by the leitmotif verb *katarrôdeô*), it shows how gods and humans together destroyed Xerxes' host.

On land the story opens with the Hellenes' manifesto to the Greeks living round Thermopylae, which states the theme of Herodotus' reconstitution of this military catastrophe as a decisive spiritual triumph over barbarism. The Hellenes declare that Xerxes is not a god but a man—a man whose fall, moreover, would be as great as his eminence (7.203.2). Apollo had warned the Spartans early on that Xerxes would come with the power of Zeus to destroy a great city unless Lacedaemon mourned a Heraclid (7.220.4). The wife of Leonidas had discovered Demaratus' secret message concerning the plan of Xerxes, whereupon the Spartans had procured this response from Delphi (7.239); and it is the Heraclid Leonidas who marches to meet Xerxes at Thermopylae. There the panicky (*katarrôdeontes*) Peloponnesians at first seek to retreat (7.207). Yet when combat is joined it is Xerxes himself who three times breaks his posture of enthroned, hieratic stillness in fright *(deisanta)* for his army (7.212.1). Xerxes' field marshal Hydarnes is also struck with deep alarm *(katarrôdêsas)* lest he face Spartiates on the mountain path around the pass (7.218.2). In the final encounter again it is the Persians who quail; they must be driven with whips against Leonidas' Three Hundred, who fight to the end, tooth-and-nail, with the weapons of the lion that will crown their tomb (7.223.3, 225.2–3). By their ultimate human valor Leonidas and his warriors fulfill the god's mandate for the salvation of Sparta at Thermopylae. It is here that Herodotus first lifts the weight of fear from Hellenes, to let it fall heavily upon Persians.

Quite the opposite is the case at Artemisium. For at sea the story has opened on the eve of the battle with the Delphians' petition to Apollo, *katarrôdêkotes* for themselves and for Hellas. His counsel to the Hellenes, bidding them pray to the winds as their great allies (7.178.1), indicates that any success will be achieved less by active human valor than by the gods' agency alone. And so it is: the tally of enemy ships sunk by the gales is far greater than the number sunk at Artemisium by the Hellenes aboard the ships who, unlike the defenders of Thermopylae, remain in fear and think always of retreat *(katarrôdêsantes . . . metormizonto es Khalkida,* 7.183.1; *katarrôdêsantes drêsmon ebouleuon,* 8.4.1; *drêsmon dê ebouleuon,* 8.18). For as Herodotus himself declares, "all of this destruction was wrought by the god so that the Persian navy might be made equal with the Hellenes', and not be greater by far" (8.18.2).

At Salamis, however, the roles of the Hellenes in the first two encounters are reversed. Here it is the Athenians in their ships who steel themselves, like Leonidas at Thermopylae, to obey the god's mandate and do battle *(meta to khrêstêrion . . . tôi theôi peithomenous,* 7.144.3; cf. 8.41.2), whereas the Peloponnesians would take flight *(es tas veas esepipton . . . hôs apotheusamenoi,* 8.56; *arrôdeon . . . deimainontes hôs peri têi Peloponnêsôi,* 8.74.1); but they are held unwillingly at "divine Salamis" (7.141 *fin.;* cf. 143.1), in the grip of the gods' will and the ruse of Themistocles, whose messenger tells Xerxes that the Hellenes are ready to flee in panic *(drêsmon bouleuontai katarrôdêkotes,* 8.75.2). Then, after a ghostly procession of Eleusinian *mystai* divinely signifies the care of the Mother and Daughter for the Hellenes and the place of Xerxes' ruin (8.65), the Hellenes sail into battle led by the divine Aeacidae brought from Aegina, and by the apparition of a woman shouting from on high the galvanic question: "Fools! How long will you go on backing water?" (8.83.2–84.2). They drive on against the enemy, and the defeated Xerxes, fearing (*deisas*) for the bridges to Asia and for his own skin, now in his turn thinks of flight (*drêsmon ebouleue*, 8.97.1; cf. 103, *houtô katarrôdêkee*).

In this way Herodotus crushes Xerxes in the coils of his symmetrical thematic account. Its design perfectly expresses his faith that the history of the Great King's expulsion from the forbidden continent of Europe is not discoverable in the mere military facts, but in the moral and spiritual dimension of a struggle whose outcome preserved the order that the gods themselves had set for the world.

A Map of Herodotus' World

Herodotus says that the Persians consider the whole of Asia to be their own, together with its barbarian peoples, and regard Europe and the Greeks to be entirely separate (1.4.4, 9.116.3).[66] Notwithstanding their enmity to the Greeks over the war of Troy, and Xerxes' ambition to conquer Greece in revenge, the Persians of Herodotus' own day "know their place," the continent of Asia. His work is the story of the Persians' confinement to their continent in consequence of their successive experiences in Egypt, Scythia, and Greece. The Persians are able to coexist neither with the land, nor with the people, nor with the gods of the world beyond Asia. Cambyses defeated the people of Egypt and won their land; but he was destroyed by his inability to coexist with the gods of Egypt. Darius in Scythia was defeated not by the gods of Scythia, but by the land itself together with its people, whose single *sophiê* is their invincibility on their own soil. Finally in Greece the Persians are turned back by the land, the people, and the gods all together: Xerxes' defeat will sum up the others.

History in the Histories is made in a zone between two impenetrable extremes. South of this zone is Egypt, whose climate, river, and customs are altogether different from everyone else's (2.35.2–4, etc.), where foreigners are unclean, where the gods drive Cambyses mad, and where the gods destroy the Athenians at Prosopitis. North is Scythia, where Darius cannot go, where winter is so cold you make mud with fire instead of water and the whole climate is topsy-turvy, because the summer is wet but the winter is dry (4.28.1–3), whose people carry their houses with them and herd instead of till (4.46.2–3), and where Greeks can go only when they become Scyths.

The median zone of climate and human character, on the other hand, is shared by a "discontinuous continuum," so to speak, of individual but related peoples: Dorians, Ionians, Lydians, Persians. Lydia, where Herodotus begins, occupies the central position in this zone, lying geographically between Europe and inner Asia (*hê anô Asiê,* 1.95.2, etc.) and culturally between Greece and Persia. The Persians are to Lydians as the Lydians are to Ionians, and the Ionian Greeks are to Lydians as Dorian Greeks are to Ionians. The Lydians gave to the Ionians coins, *kapêlia,* and *paignia,* all ignoble or unserious things. Although once the manliest and bravest people in Asia, they are progressively reduced in character, as Herodotus' Lydian history proceeds, to chaffering mountebanks, musicians, and gamesters. The Persians in turn become "Lydian" in their imperial methods, their habits, and their Hellenizing approach to Greeks.

Next, the Histories' story of the Persians' conquest of Ionia and their failure in Europe becomes a drama not merely of power, but of cultural suspense. The Persians debate about their own future in Greek terms; they collaborate with Greeks and devise Greek political constitutions for some Greeks; they champion the cause of Troy to the Greeks and even claim Greek descent. In Herodotus the two nations are mutually related, "permeable" to one another, whereas Scythia and Egypt are impermeable to both peoples. The relations between Greeks and Persians are therefore at the center of the narrative, as are the gestures by which they approach one another and then mutually recede, according to the verdicts of

Thermopylae and Salamis, toward a separation culminating in
Pausanias' refusal to behave like a Persian instead of a Spartan by
impaling the head of his enemy, slain on the field of Plataea
(9.78–79). But of course it is not a clean separation: the Heraclid
Pausanias, notoriously, will go on to behave very much like a
Persian rather than a Spartan.[67] Greece and Asia are permeable to
one another, but only on the terms of cultural transvaluation.

Insofar as we can ask of Herodotus the question of nature versus
culture in the origins of the distinctions between Pelasgian Greeks
and Asiatic barbarians, it would seem that his answer is something
like "both at once."[68] His intellectual outlook straddled the climatic
determinism of the Ionians, for whom salubrious Asia was the
continent of plenty and of susceptibility to luxury and despotism,
and the idea of the natural identity of all men then coming into
being among the sophists and visible in Sophocles and Thucydides.[69] Pelasgian barbarians do become Greeks over the course of
several hundred years. Indeed, Pelasgians' actions foreshadow their
transformation into Achaeans and Ionians. They are notably inclined to atrocities—the Lemnians, notorious for their crimes, are
Pelasgians from Attica—but, on the other hand, they receive the
gods and benefit from them in ways that other barbarian peoples
cannot. For example, the Scyths reject as madness the rites of
Dionysus, by which Melampus cured the madness of the women
of Pelasgian Argos (9.34.1). And Croesus the Lydian—the most
"Hellenic" barbarian in the Histories—could not comprehend
Apollo, let alone Solon.

Herodotus constructs an Asianic barbarism on the basis of
variable but related "behavioral syndromes" which present fundamental topics of contrast with the Greek character. Within these
topics some distinctions appear to be cultural, or "learned," and
others are apparently natural, or "innate." The frame of this contrast
is built from a variety of rubrics: liberty, knowledge of the gods,
knowledge of the world, relations between men and women, the
use of wine and the world's other good things, as well as cannibalism and butchery—that is, the use of the human body as if it
were the body of an animal, a category that encompasses the

dismemberment or maltreatment of the body alive or dead. It includes such barbarian practices as leaving the dead exposed as carrion as the Magi do (1.140.2), and such atrocious barbarian punishments as crucifixion, impalement, mutilation, bisection, castration, flaying alive, and the taking of heads, which in particular is abhorrent to Hellenes (9.78–79).[70]

Four categories of beings do such things. They are (1) the pre-Hellenic barbarians of old Greece (e.g., Thyestes, Creon, and Achilles);[71] (2) the gods long ago (e.g., the punishments of Marsyas, Prometheus, and Ixion); (3) the contemporary barbarians of Asia, including Croesus, who tore an enemy to death on a carding comb (1.92.4); (4) among contemporary Greeks only the tyrants Periander of Corinth (3.48.2) and Polycrates of Samos (3.45.4)—and, finally, the Athenian admiral Xanthippus, the father of Pericles and the crucifer of the Persian Artaüctes. This is the last deed of any Greek in the *Histories* (9.120.4)—as Herodotus meant it to be.[72]

Are Herodotus' Athenians barbarians? Yes and no; they are a *tertium quid* in terms of Hartog's law of the excluded middle.[73] They exhibit the characteristics of Asianic barbarism—luxury, atrocity, tributary empire—as well as Hellenism—*sophia* and victory over barbarism. Hellenic Athens saved Hellas. But all things come round again. The moment when Athens arrives in Asia and to empire is commemorated by a crucifixion whose long shadow Herodotus casts over Athens' prophesied but unwritten future.[74]

Seven

Xenophon: The Satrap of Scillus

When Xenophon was in exile and living at Scillus near Olympia, where he had been settled in residence by the Lacedaemonians, Megabyzus [the administrator of the temple of Artemis in Ephesus] arrived to see the Olympian games and returned to him the votive deposit [of booty which Xenophon had tithed to the goddess upon his departure from Asia with Agesilaus]. Xenophon took it and bought a precinct for the goddess where the god [Apollo of Delphi] had ordained. A River Selinus happened to flow through it, and in Ephesus too a River Selinus runs by the temple of Artemis. And in each river are both fish and mussels, but in the precinct at Scillus there is the hunting of all kinds of wild game. He built both an altar and a temple with the votive money, and thereafter without fail sacrificed a tithe of the crops in their season, and all the citizens and the men and women of the neighborhood would share the feast. The goddess provided the banqueters with barley groats and bread, with wine and treats and nibbles, and with joints of the animals sacrificed from the sacred flock as well as game. For Xenophon's sons and any of the citizens and other men who wanted went hunting together during the festival, and took game both from the sacred precinct itself and from Mt. Pholoë: boars, gazelles, and stags. This land is on the road from Lacedaemon to Olympia, some two miles from the shrine of Zeus at Olympia. The precinct of this goddess has both meadow and thickly wooded hills, good for raising swine, goats and cattle, and horses too, so that even the yoke-animals of the guests who gather at the festival are feasted. Around the temple is planted an orchard of all kinds of seasonal fruit trees. The temple is a miniature of the one at Ephesus and the image of the goddess is like that in Ephesus, though in cypress not gold. Beside the temple stands an inscribed tablet:

> THIS PRECINCT IS SACRED TO ARTEMIS.
> THE POSSESSOR AND HARVESTER MUST
> SACRIFICE THE TITHE EVERY YEAR, AND
> FROM THE REST MAINTAIN THE SHRINE.
> IF HE DOES NOT THE GODDESS
> WILL TAKE NOTICE.

(Xen. *Anab.* 5.3.7–13)

Thus was Xenophon established by the gift of the Spartans and King Agesilaus as a magnate in Elis, country of magnates,[1] only a brief canter from the sacred temenos of Olympian Zeus himself. Here, in the bosom of the divinities of Olympus and Ephesus, of Greece and Asia, Xenophon presided over an estate he would fondly recall as if it were the *paradeisos* of an Iranian nobleman.[2] Here, in retirement after a career of active military command spanning many of the fourteen years between Cunaxa and the King's Peace (401–386 B.C.), he would embark on the oeuvre that preoccupied him virtually to the end of his long life. The vision of himself and of his world that it contains brings together as brethren peoples whom Herodotus had sundered at birth: Dorian Spartans and the noblest of the Persians. The task of this final chapter is to search for the inspiration, the purposes, and the hopes which that oeuvre embodied for its author and the times that he addressed.

Xenophon was one of those very many thousands of Greeks in this age who made service in arms their profession. At times in their careers a great proportion of these men served the Persian satraps and emperor.[3] Xenophon would find among the Persians what he had lost among his fellow Athenians: a cause, and a man, to believe in. Less than two years after the fall of the Thirty and the restoration of the democracy at Athens in 401, he left Athens for good, as he probably thought, a young man profoundly disillusioned by his political heroes, to find—and lose—his future in the service of the Persian prince Cyrus. Exiled while still abroad by the Athenians, he served the Spartans and Agesilaus in Asia and Europe before retiring to Scillus. Then, some thirty years after his departure from Athens he found himself restored to citizenship at the unwelcome and shocking price to his fortune and to his sentiments of Sparta's disaster at Leuctra (371). He lost his estate to the Eleans and thereafter lived at Corinth, keeping a cool distance from the public life of his Athenian compatriots. He died in his seventies at Corinth, or perhaps restored to Scillus,[4] some years after composing the life and achievements of the only world conqueror in history, Cyrus the Great.[5]

The *Cyropaedia* is unique among the works of Greeks on barbarians in presenting a Persian not simply as the practical equivalent of a perfect Greek gentleman, the very image of *kalokagathia*, but as a commander of genius—indeed as a world-historical giant whom a Greek audience could only envy and admire, and whose nature and achievements they could never hope to emulate.

Xenophon's personal outlook on the best of the Persians and their monarchy was formed far less by the patriotic antibarbarism of those demagogic politicians and rhetorical performers whom he despised, but by his intense, and in a particular sense erotic, experiences and hopes in following the younger Cyrus.[6] These hopes were contained, and perhaps also made legitimate to Xenophon as a Hellene, by the remarkable and revolutionary association of the Spartan liberators of Greece with Cyrus, who pursued his brother's throne at the head of a Greek mercenary army raised with material assistance from the Spartans. For Xenophon, a friend of Sparta was not an enemy of Greece. It was open to Xenophon to admire, even to adore, Cyrus, and he succumbed. His powerful encomium of the prince (*Anab.* 1.9) is surpassed only by his great portrait of the prince's ancestor and double, the perfect monarch of the *Cyropaedia*. It is a work that reveals Xenophon's long preoccupation, into old age, with what might have been: for with the younger Cyrus' victory at hand, Xenophon's hopes were abruptly snuffed out with the prince's death (*Anab.* 1.10.16–18; 2.1.2–3).

Führerprinzip

As a polished illustration of Xenophon's philosophy of society, and as a work addressed to the crisis of his time, the *Cyropaedia* ennobles the most irrepressible feature of the Greek character, which was the will to power. It is visible at its extreme, especially in the fourth century, in the adoration and pursuit of monarchy. In the archaic period, Delphi and the poets had gilded with royal titulatures the tyrants who had arisen in the little cities of Greece. In the succeeding age of constitutions and sophists, monarchies survived or reappeared in Greece, as in the Syracuse of the Dionysii and the Thessaly of Jason and his successors, in Macedon and in Cyprus. They were envied by many.

Immense on the horizons of the Greeks, finally, was the world empire of Persia. In the age that saw the wreck of Athens' empire and the failed atrocities of Spartan rule, the Persian monarchy drew the attention of thinkers,[7] some of whom observed power relationships with all the greater passion because—like Xenophon himself and his first model Thucydides, and later Polybius—their own ambitions for power and distinction had been thwarted by exile and directed into self-absorption. Xenophon's mentor Socrates had withdrawn from a life in politics among men who were not good enough for him, he who was the wisest man in Greece (Plato *Apol.* 21a: and it is not Plato alone who speaks for Socrates in the *Republic* but also the wise Socrates himself, creating for the space of that sunny afternoon in the Piraeus a microcosm of his ideal polity among his interlocutors, with himself as its philosopher-monarch).

If in old age Xenophon had read the *Laws*, he would have recognized himself in Plato's description of the seekers of the best, who are not to be found in Greece alone (951b–c):

Among the mass are always some men, though not many, of superhuman excellence. Association with such men, who spring up in misgoverned communities as well as in those enjoying good laws, is a privilege of the highest value. It is always a good thing if members of well-governed states, if they are incorruptible, should travel by land and by sea in search of such men, in order to confirm those good customs of his own community and correcting those which are defective.

The reductionist political ethics of some of these thinkers, their doctrines that justice is the interest of the strongest or, more defensibly, the best, and their connoisseurship of monarchies as effective governments that rewarded excellence, were in themselves intellectual responses to the profoundly disheartening and disturbing history of the generation which, for Thucydides and the political stance he represented at Athens, had begun with the eclipse and death of Pericles. Under Pericles, for the last time in Athenian history, the best men could feel assured that, although the regime was a democracy in form, its characteristic vices were reined in by the commanding mind and prestige of a single noble director: under Pericles Athens "was in form a democracy, but was operatively a rule by its most distinguished man" (Thuc. 2.65.9; cf., 2.6–13, 1.127.3 and 139.4).[8]

But after Pericles, the democracy, in the view of the *rentiers* who practiced or pretended to the aristocratic ethic of *kalokagathia*, would mature into a monster battening upon them. After the loss of the empire, with its scope for distinction and above all for profit, the last motives for tolerating the democracy disappeared.[9] As Thucydides' Phrynichus observed, it was the *kaloi k'agathoi* themselves who under the democracy had led the city into evil ways for their individual profit (Thuc. 8.48.6); and Thucydides in his own voice judged the short-lived moderate oligarchy of the Five Thousand the best government of Athens in his time (8.97.2)—a judgment that necessarily reflects the views of his Athenian friends and informants after 404, since he himself was in exile at the time (cf. 5.26.5).

After the war the demonstrated inability of any major Greek state to achieve a stable hegemony contributed further to the general appreciation of monarchy's virtue of concentrating in a single direction the power, will, and resources of the state. Xenophon closed the books on his own times in a despairing mood in the last years before his death (*c.* 354?), reflecting that after Mantinea "there was even more *akrisia* and *tarakhê*," confusion and upheaval, than before among the contending and ill-directed cities of Greece (*Hell.* 7.5.27).[10] It was only to be expected, then, that the stability of the Persian empire in its rule over so many mutually foreign peoples, which contrasted so remarkably with the anarchy and misrule in Greece, would objectively recommend a study of its founder and of the institutions which he created to assure its longevity after him (*Cyrop.* 1.1.1–6).

Xenophon's analysis of the *imperium absconditum* of Cyrus (cf. Hdt. 1.99) in the last book of the *Cyropaedia* is acute and reflects a close and sympathetic observation of the psychology and methods of Persian rule. Yet the image of Cyrus himself that emerges appears to us altogether Greek, a familiar pastiche of the *kalos k'agathos* examined in the *Memorabilia*, of Xenophon's Greek *arkhikos anthrôpos*, his *megalognômon*, his *theios kai agathos kai epistêmôn arkhôn* (*Oecon.* 13.5, 21.4–8; cf. 4.16ff on the younger Cyrus). In the *Cyropaedia*, then, as elsewhere in his works, Xenophon is familiar to us as one of those numerous politically disaffected admirers of their own exclusive fitness to rule, who are most visible in our sources congregating around the figure of Socrates. Is his Cyrus only what many have in any case supposed it to be, a portrait of his Hellenic *Übermensch* projected on a world stage?

If we did not have the *Anabasis*, with its portrait of the younger Cyrus (1, esp. 9), we could not suppose that the character of Xenophon's elder Cyrus had any grounding in an authentic imaginative reality. We should also take account of the fact that the best of Xenophon's contemporary Persians, the younger Cyrus and Pharnabazus, appear in the works of Xenophon's reportorial manner, the *Anabasis* and *Hellenica*, to be remarkably "international" in their manners and even in their acquisition of Greek.

Moreover, the *Cyropaedia* is largely informed by Xenophon's fantasy of a lost future Persia under the younger Cyrus, who was familiar with Greeks and valued their qualities highly, had he lived to rule instead of Xenophon's *bête noir* Artaxerxes II (*reg.* 405–358; cf. *Cyrop.* 8.8; *Ages.* 2.7). As such, this work deserves examination as a document that reflects the appreciation of a very large and prominent category of Greeks for a monarchy that rewarded the initiative, loyalty, and excellence of its servants. This was the category of political exiles and mercenary soldiers, many of whom had served Persian magnates, whose lives and careers were largely divorced from their cities, and whose outlook furnished the real elements of experience and opinion that nurtured the cosmopolitan tendencies of the age.[11]

The later fifth and fourth century saw the emergence of a cadre of Persian rulers and Greek *condottieri* in the West who came to resemble one another. Later societies such as the kingdom of Pontus in the West, and the Hellenizing Arsacids in the East, were not altogether the products of the Macedonian conquest, but of a symbiosis already potentially present in the person and ambitions of the younger Cyrus, which to Xenophon promised a condominium of Persian rule and Greek method that represented to him the ideal world polity.[12] For in Xenophon's view, humanity was not divided into Greek or barbarian, but only into naturally servile *andrapodôdeis* and their natural rulers.

A City of Slaves

At a young age, but already mature in the practice of arms and in his politics and prejudices, Xenophon chose service under the Persian prince Cyrus. He was not driven by poverty, for he served at his own expense (*Anab.* 3.1.4), as a nobleman would serve his prince. But he was *persona non grata* at Athens, having almost certainly served the Thirty in the cavalry;[13] he could not hope for a normal political career now.[14] The timing of his departure is significant: Xenophon left Athens less than two years after the restoration of the democracy in the autumn of 403,[15] not long before the leaders of the rump of the oligarchy at Eleusis were caught contemplating an armed coup and slain at a parley with the democrats (*Hell.* 2.4.43; Arist. *AP* 40.3).[16] Given Xenophon's connections and military experience, he was a man the oligarchs could use: he may well have been privy to their plans and decided to avoid danger by leaving the city.

The conduct of the Thirty orphaned Xenophon ideologically. His condemnation of its crimes and betrayal of its own professed intentions, which he put into the mouth of Theramenes (*Hell.* 2.3.35ff: written many years afterward), is a measure of Xenophon's bitterness. For the positive program of the regime, which was first of all to create a polity of the citizen-warriors, who embodied the values of *kalokagathia*, and afterward to cleanse the city of its commercial and foreign element, was perfectly congruent with Xenophon's ideal Athens, as it was later to emerge in the *Memorabilia.*[17]

The "Three Thousand" Athenians who retained their arms in 404 were almost certainly the surviving levy of genuine citizen-hoplites and cavalry, minus the regime's numerous political enemies.[18] The beneficiaries at large of the oligarchy were meant to be the trustworthy majority of propertied men whose self-respect lay in their will and fitness to defend the city in battle. These men blamed the democracy and the demagogues for losing the war, and their politics consisted of saving what was left of their property from the mass of poorer Athenians, who had been made desperate by defeat and privation. The oligarchic property owners feared that the democracy might now pursue radical and confiscatory policies. Talk of radical redistribution remained in the air under the restored democracy, to be parodied by Aristophanes in the *Ecclesiazusae* (in 392) and the *Plutus* (388).[19] The Thirty's first move had been to eliminate the racketeers who had used threats of prosecution to blackmail the wealthy under the democracy (Xen. *Hell.* 2.3.12; Arist. *AP* 35.2), and it is noteworthy that most of the Three Thousand remained loyal to the Thirty, if not enthusiastic in their defense against fellow Athenians of their own kind, until their decisive collapse at Munychia.

After their defeat, which had amounted to a refusal to engage the exiles, (*Hell.* 2.18–22), the Three Thousand remained in defense of the city under new generals, who were elected from each tribe to make peace and carry on the government; that is to say, they tried to constitute themselves as a polity recognizably similar to the one that had emerged out of the crisis of 411, praised by Thucydides as the best government Athens had enjoyed in his time (8.97.2). But when the Three Thousand realized that they had lost the support of the Spartans, they surrendered themselves to their arbitration (*Hell.* 2.24–27, 31–32, 37; Arist. *AP* 38 with Rhodes 1981 *ad loc.*).

The Thirty were finally abandoned by their natural constituency because their methods had not brought about the aims that had attracted the mass of their supporters, including Xenophon, but ended instead in provoking a resurgence of the demos. Not many years later (396), the restored democracy joined the coalition against Sparta that brought the Spartans under Agesilaus home from a campaign in Asia which, Xenophon thought, had bidden fair to drive the Persians out of Asia Minor. If Xenophon's alienation from Athens was not complete when he departed the city for Asia and was subsequently condemned by the demos, any surviving belief in his native city must have disappeared with Athens' connivance at the destruction of Agesilaus' prospects of victory and Greek liberation in Asia.

Home of the Free

In the *Oeconomicus* Socrates goes around Athens looking for someone truly *kalos k'agathos* but, after searching high and low, nowhere can he discover even in one person that elusive combination of virtues—until he discovers Ischomachus, the landed gentleman and alter ego of Xenophon, who is the author's principal mouthpiece in the *Oeconomicus* (6.12–18). This vignette epitomizes Xenophon's distance from the Athens of his day, where no *kaloi k'agathoi* were to be found in the public spaces. We can compare this scene to the picture drawn by Diogenes Laertius of the Cynic Diogenes searching the streets of Athens with a lantern for a "human being," *anthrôpos.* The Cynic view, as old as Heraclitus, held that the real division was not between barbarian and Greek, but between the *spoudaios* and the *phaulos,* the "worthy" and the "base."

Xenophon regarded most Athenians as *andrapodôdês,* "human

livestock." His Ischomachus is a citizen of the highest census and a member of the cavalry (11.17–20), but it is clear that he avoids public life like the plague and comes to the city only on private business. Indeed, when Socrates encounters him he is waiting in the stoa of Zeus the Liberator to meet, not fellow Athenians, but "some friends from abroad" (7.2 with 11.22–24; cf. 2.5–6 and *Symp.* 4.30–32). Ischomachus' *apragmosynê* could hardly go further; in fact he has retreated to a smaller but perfect polity of his own, which he associates in his imagination with the empire of Persia, living as a little satrap occupying his *paradeisos*-principality in the Attic countryside. Of such men Aristotle was to comment that "the man who has no need of social relationships because he is sufficient for himself is no part of a city: he is either a beast or a god" (*Pol.* 1253a25–29). Ischomachus might have replied that in an Athens populated by beasts he chooses to be a god.

While on his estate the autarkic Ischomachus is occupied by the management of his slaves, whom he trains in obedience by a Pavlovian *thêriôdês paideia* of rewards and punishments, and in honesty by applying the statutes of Dracon, of Solon, and especially those of the Great King (13.9, 14.4ff); for it is the Persian code alone which not only punishes the wrongdoer but benefits the just (14.7). In his private kingdom, Ischomachus acts the part of the Great King as lawgiver and judge, possessing the power to amplify not only the fortunes but the human worth of his most serviceable, ambitious, and loyal slaves. "Those who convince me they are honest not only for the sake of their own advantage but to win my regard," Ischomachus lectures Socrates, "I treat as free men, *hôsper eleutherois*; not only do I enrich them but I rank them as *kalous te kai agathous*" (14.9).[20] The fortunate slaves of Ischomachus live under a Persian regime, which teaches and rewards justice; they may therefore be raised up and ennobled by their lord while remaining under his total authority, just as if he were the Great King and they the King's benefactors.

No similar paedia exists among the nominally free Athenians. For Herodotus the natural slave had been the barbarian *apragmôn*; for Xenophon he is the Athenian *ekklesiazôn*. In the *Memorabilia* Xenophon's Socrates asks an interlocutor, Euthydemus, "You know that some people are called slavelike, *andrapodôdeis*?" Euthydemus knows very well that Socrates refers to the bronzesmiths, builders, cobblers, and other banausics who make up the demos and dominate the assembly (*Mem.* 4.2.22 with 3.7.6; cf. 4.2.27–39, *Symp.* 4.32). These are the *aphronestatoi* and *asthenestatoi*, the worthless fools who are ignorant of the good, the beautiful, and the just (*Mem.* 3.7.5, 4.2.22).[21] In the fourth-century Athens of Xenophon we may as well be in the sixth-century Ephesus of Heraclitus, surrounded by barbarian minds.

Worse yet, however, are those who know the good but abjure it, the hoplites and cavalry of Athens. These very citizens, who accounted themselves preeminent in *kalokagathia*, are in fact the least amenable to collective discipline and cooperation (*Mem.* 3.5.9), and so far from keeping themselves fit for combat scorn those who do (3.3.15), with the result that in their military conduct the Athenians absolutely neglect those virtues of self-discipline and good order, *sôphronein te kai eutaktein kai peitharkhein* (3.3.21), most necessary to success in warfare and in healthy community life (3.3.16–17).[22] The Athenians even glory in disobeying their commanders and magistrates (3.3.16), a civic psychology that Xenophon elucidates elsewhere with the remark that in most Greek states—Sparta of course excepted—the most powerful men do not even wish it thought that they fear the magistrates, regarding obedience as *aneleutheron*, "servile" (*Const. Lac.* 8.2).

This was not the Persian way in the age of Cyrus the Great. During the great durbar at Babylon held to define and display his style as Great King, Xenophon's Cyrus pointedly dismisses from his service a certain boorish Persian who thought he would *eleutherôteros an phainesthai*, "display more freedom of character," if he were to take his own time obeying Cyrus' directions (*Cyrop.* 8.3.21). Elsewhere in this last book of the *Cyropaedia*, in which Cyrus establishes the future relations between himself and his associates in conquest, it is made clear that his satraps are not his slaves: they obey his ordinances willingly and imitate his establishment in their own provinces because their interest is identical with that of Cyrus and the imperial people, the Persians, at large (*Cyrop.* esp. 8.4.10–12).

Xenophon voices their sentiments through Cyrus' own most distinguished and excellent companion Chrysantas (8.1.3–4, trans. Miller, condensed and revised):

> By what other means have we secured the good things we now have than by obeying our commander? Therefore if obedience is the greatest good, as it appears, in securing good things, then you may be sure that this very principle of obedience is the greatest good in founding the permanence of our good things. So, then, since you yourselves are worthy to command those under you, in the same way let us obey those whom we ought properly to obey. And we must distinguish ourselves from slaves, in that slaves serve their masters against their will, but we must willingly perform what appears most worthy. You will find, too, that even when a city [*polis*] is governed without monarchy, the one most ready to obey its magistrates is the least compelled to submit to its enemies.

Here, as elsewhere in the *Cyropaedia*, Xenophon's historical imagination intersects with his own experience, and the shadow-image of the younger Cyrus hovers behind his portrait of the great conqueror Cyrus. The young prince inspired loyal service and attachment to his person by a character and methods precisely similar to those that Xenophon attributed to his idealized ancestor (*Anab.* 1.1–2.9). The model presentation of the prince of the *Anabasis* includes the spectacle of his richly dressed retinue of the younger Cyrus' noble Persian companions wallowing through the mud in their court robes at his command, to free the mired commissariat-wagons. The occasion moves Xenophon to exclaim in recollection, "Now there was a bit of discipline (*eutaxia*) to see!" (1.5.8).

No scene is more revealing of the rapport and respect between Greeks of Xenophon's soldierly and traditional outlook and the Persian nobility than his account—which is full of the detail characteristic of eyewitness reportage—in the *Hellenica* (4.1.29–40) of the meeting between Agesilaus and the satrap Pharnabazus in late 395, after the Spartan king's army had ravaged his satrapy of Pontic Phrygia and and encamped in the *paradeisos* of his palace near Dascyleium.[23]

A truce and a parley was arranged between these adversaries by a Cyzicene Greek who had been an *ek palaiou xenos* of Pharnabazus and had recently become a *xenos* also of Agesilaus. When the satrap arrived at the meeting place he saw that Agesilaus and his staff awaited him sitting on the bare grass. Pharnabazus appeared in costly robes and his servants spread the carpets "on which," Xenophon observes archly, "the Persian recline delicately (*malakôs*)" in effeminate comfort. But Pharnabazus was abashed by the simplicity of the Spartans and propped himself on the grass just as he was, offering his right hand to Agesilaus. The Persian spoke first as the older man. In level tones he rebuked the Spartans for spoiling the lands and possessions of a former friend and ally, and making a fugitive of him, who had never betrayed them, but had fought at their side from horseback against their enemies in the war against the Athenians. "If I should understand, then, what is right in the sight of gods and of men, *ta hosia kai ta dikaia*, you may show me how these acts are those of men who know how to repay benefits they have received."

The Spartans fell silent before him in shame. Eventually Agesilaus spoke, observing that in Greece, too, friends of different cities at war with one another for their fatherlands even to the death, and that the Spartans as enemies of the Persian King necessarily would regard anything of his as legitimately hostile. Agesilaus then proposed that Pharnabazus revolt against his ruler and be free, rich, and in the enjoyment of his own possessions without having to kowtow to a master, *mêdena proskynounta mêde despotên ekhonta*. Pharnabazus replied frankly that if the King were to demote him beneath a new commander,[24] he would ally himself with Agesilaus; but as long as he held the King's command he would make war to the best of his ability, "so strong, it seems, is *philotimia*," that love of distinction which is at the heart of *kalokagathia*. Agesilaus thereupon hailed him as the "best of men," *ô lôiste*, and hoped that such a man could become his friend, while undertaking for the future to evacuate his satrapy and leave his possessions in peace.

Of course, much in their meeting was policy. Here Agesilaus

was putting the best face on failure. Agesilaus' whole strategy and his address to Pharnabazus was aimed at inducing him, by force or persuasion, to change sides, especially as the Spartans' first impulse to send Agesilaus to Asia had followed upon their discovery that the Phoenicians were preparing the fleet that Pharnabazus was soon to command with the purpose of forcing the Spartans to retire from Asia (*Hell.* 3.4.1 with Philochorus *FGrH* 328 F 144–45). In any case Agesilaus' troops had stripped the country bare after a whole season's raiding and foraging. Agesilaus himself was planning a campaign in a new direction, and it is likely that he was already anticipating his early recall in view of the coalition forming against the Spartans in Greece. Pharnabazus, for his part, was secure in the tenure of his hereditary satrapy, and was looking forward to joining his Athenian admiral Conon at sea in the spring.

Nonetheless we gain from this encounter an ineradicable impression not merely of mutual respect and understanding between Greek and Persian at the highest levels of their respective societies, but of a shared rapport based on similar codes, in which ingratitude is the worst of offenses,[25] and *philotimia* the highest of virtues. Agesilaus' talk of Pharnabazus' kowtowing to a master is only word-play, at the level of the Athenian Xenophon and the Spartan Chirisophus ragging each other in the *Anabasis* (4.4.16ff) about their respective national customs of thievery.

No Persian scene could be further from the hermetically servile atmosphere of Aeschylus' *Persae*. For Xenophon wrote from experience: he recognized that Persians gained self-respect and a sense of honor in properly rewarded service to the monarch, and in the *Cyropaedia* he would present the whole machinery and impetus of Persian rule as a nexus of gratitude for favors in recompense for benefactions between the monarch and his followers. A reciprocity of personal service and personal reward, and not a servile submission to a despot, is the cement that holds the whole imperial system together. The political ethics of Pharnabazus, whose family had been distinguished as satraps of Dascyleium with an unbroken record of loyalty since the 470s, during an era that included a number of dangerous revolts against royal authority in the West, are just those which in the *Cyropaedia* Xenophon would put into the mouth of his fictional Persian Chrysantas.[26]

That Xenophon should look down on the ordinary Athenian as *andrapodôdês* is part of the ancient outlook of men of his class, present from the beginning in their political wisdom literature. Homer created Thersites for Odysseus to thrash, and Theognis the aristocratic poet of archaic Megara wrote as if the peasants who had gained power in his city were beasts rather than men.[27] This attitude was reinforced in this age by other contemporary reactionaries, including Antiphon, who directly compared the division between high and low in Greek society to that between barbarian and Greek.[28] That Xenophon should regard Persians of his own status to be as noble and essentially as free in their choice of loyalties as himself and his Spartan hero Agesilaus, completed the formation of a new outlook toward the imperial people that stood Aeschylus and the ideology descending from the *Persae* on its head. This outlook belonged to the future, for Xenophon anticipated in remarkable ways Alexander's own evident regard for the Persian nobility and military populations; and like Alexander's outlook, Xenophon's was not the product of academic indoctrination but the fruit of personal discovery by a man who was a professional warrior through and through.

Xenophon's Prince

Why did Xenophon follow the younger Cyrus? He was presented to the prince by his Theban friend Proxenus, who commanded a force of hoplites in Cyrus' service and expected great rewards.[29] Proxenus had described Cyrus to Xenophon in terms reflective of the outlook of such men as these, who had given up on their prospects at home, as "greater for me than my own fatherland" (*Anab.* 3.1.4–8).

Xenophon sidestepped his mentor Socrates' advice to seek the judgment of Apollo, for he had already made up his mind to the adventure. He eagerly accompanied Proxenus to Sardis on his friend's promise to make him the friend of Cyrus. In the afterlight of events Xenophon doubtless remembered these words of Proxenus, *kreittô heautôi nomizôn tês patridos*, because if at the time they had not already expressed the choice of this disaffected Athenian aristocrat, they assuredly did when he wrote them.

Whatever sanguine expectations Proxenus' enthusiasm encouraged in Xenophon at the beginning could only have grown with his experience of Cyrus' character and aims. Xenophon never speaks of his own ambitions, but his testimony on those of his associates and the corresponding generosity and virtue of Cyrus is ample and circumstantial. It was disingenuous to inform his audience that he accompanied Cyrus' army simply as a private gentleman at his own expense, *oute stratêgos oute lokhagos oute stratiôtês* (*Anab.* 3.1.4), in the belief that Cyrus was bound merely against the klephts of Pisidia (cf. *Anab.* 1.1.11), and in the assurance of Cyrus' promise that he would see to his passage home after the campaign. He explains to his contemporary readers of the *Anabasis* that, when it became evident the army was to contest the throne for its leader, he pressed on nevertheless with the other Greeks accompanying Cyrus, only because he was ashamed to play the coward in the sight of all of them and of Cyrus (*Anab.* 3.1.8–10).

Against this confession of virtuous naïvete are the facts. Cyrus marched from Sardis with more than 7,000 hoplites. But he had only 800 light infantry—the troops most needed against agile brigands in steep country (*Anab.* 1.2.3, 6; cf. *Mem.* 3.5.26–27). Cyrus' enemy Tissaphernes calculated the purpose of this army immediately and rode to warn the King (*Anab.* 1.2.3–5). But even if Xenophon and the rest of the Greeks had few suspicions as yet (which is most unlikely) they could not have remained blind to Cyrus' purpose after he was met on the march with large reinforcements that brought the total force of hoplites to nearly 11,000 but made up the light infantry to only just more than 2,000 (*Anab.* 1.2.9).

This was a force absurdly unbalanced for its announced purpose; armies of this scale and composition were meant for decisive encounters in the line and not for chasing mountaineers. But surely this had been clear already to the men of long experience in the army at Sardis, if not to Xenophon himself directly; and he himself must have realized what was in the wind at this time, if not even before he left Athens. For quite apart from Cyrus' open announcement of royal prerogative (Hell. 2.1.8–9) and his fixed designs on his brother's throne, which caused an open and violent rivalry between Cyrus and Tissaphernes well known to Greek observers at the time (Anab. 1.1.3–8, 6.6, 9.9; Plut. Artox. 3.3ff), there was little prospect of glory or great prizes to attract the cavalryman Xenophon in the dismounted scut work of policing the broken countryside of Pisidia.[30]

Cyrus had advertised both his royal ambitions and his generosity from the beginning (Plut. Artox. 6.2; cf. Xen. Anab. 6.4.8). The treasure that Lysander brought home to Sparta (Xen. Hell. 2.3.8) and tithed to Delphi (Plut. Lys. 28.1) must have impressed the wealth and largesse of Cyrus upon the Greeks' imagination much as had the dedications of Croesus long before. If Xenophon had not arrived in Sardis already ambitious for a highly rewarded career in Cyrus' service his horizons must have opened, at the latest, when Cyrus intimated to his Greek officers before the decisive battle with Artaxerxes that undreamed-of rewards would be theirs with his possession of world empire. Xenophon says that when the officers who heard these promises spread them throughout the army, many Greeks sought out their rewards from Cyrus in person, "and Cyrus sent every one of them off with their expectations filled to the brim," ho de empimplas hapantôn tên gnômên apepempe (Anab. 1.7.2–8). We should assume that, like the elder Cyrus of Xenophon's imagination, the young prince promised them "lands and cities, women and slaves" (Cyrop. 7.1.43; cf. 45).

It can be taken as certain that Xenophon attended this meeting of commanders and captains. Not only does his account appear to reflect firsthand witness, but by this time he was serving in arms, most likely seconding Proxenus in command of his hoplites.[31] At Cunaxa he was mounted like the commanders themselves for the battle, where he gave the watchword to Cyrus himself (Anab. 1.8.15–17).

What was Xenophon's visualization of the relationship between Cyrus and his Greeks, and what did Xenophon himself hope to gain? Undoubtedly Xenophon sought a generous material reward, as high as any of the Greeks who served him for pay should receive; but his chief ambition was a place in Cyrus' personal estimation. For Xenophon had volunteered himself not as a mercenary but freely and unconditionally, wishing, as he said, to become Cyrus' *friend*. And Cyrus was a man who

> honored the brave in war especially, making them rulers over the conquered territories and honoring them with other gifts too, so that the cowards were ranked as their slaves. And as for anyone who wanted to make himself conspicuous for righteousness (*dikaiosyne*) Cyrus considered it essential that he should live more richly than the corrupt. Thus everything was administered justly for him, and in particular he had the use of an army that was a real army. For the generals and officers who sailed to enter his service knew that there was more to be made from the loyal fulfillment of his commands than just their monthly pay, inasmuch as he never let an order well carried out go unrewarded.
>
> Whenever he would see an intelligent and just administrator (*oikonomos*) with his responsibilities well in hand and earning revenues from the land he would never decrease the man's scope but add to his rule. As for the friends he made, whom he knew were devoted to him and considered good comrades (*synergoi*)[32] in the pursuit of his aims, it is universally agreed that no one ever served them more beneficially and vigorously in return. And when he was on the march and visible to the multitude of the army he would call his friends to him and hold earnest conversation with them, to show whom he honored. Thus I myself from what I have heard conclude that no man, Greek or barbarian, has ever been more widely loved. (*Anab.* 1.914–28, trans. Brownson, condensed and revised)

From this text arises the compelling image of the young prince and his comrade of the hour, Xenophon, riding past the dusty files with their heads together, Xenophon bursting with pride, only an arm's length from the next Great King. Perhaps that evening he would dine with the invited company in Cyrus' pavilion; another time he might receive a joint from his table, accompanied by a fond message (cf. *Anab.* 1.9.25; *Cyrop.* 8.3.7; *Ages.* 5.1). Surely Xenophon loved Cyrus. And why not? Cyrus may have been beautiful and was physically still ephebic:[33] he must have possessed in some measure that uncanny power of unmarked youth combined with maturity of carriage and high military prowess which the magnetic genius of the young Alexander would personify.

Xenophon adopts the posture of the philosophical lover vis-à-vis his heroes, in which love is directed not to the corporeal man himself in carnal desire but to his virtues, his *kalokagathia* (*Symp.* 8, *passim*); such love is never unreciprocated admiration from afar but is inseparable from a personal relationship, *philia* (ibid. 8.13). This is Xenophon's definition of the erotic relationship, which is distinguished in particular by the fusion in his mind, everywhere visible in his works, between the functional and the emotive connotations of *philia, to ôphelimon* and *to philon* (e.g., *Mem.* 2.7.8–10), of service to and affection for one's friends.[34]

Scholarship no longer underestimates the importance of homoerotic emotions and rituals in the social bonding customs of Greek males.[35] When these were extended to and came to be shared by Persian males, we encounter the historical moment when the alliances of convenience hitherto visible between Persians and Greeks could open into relations of intimacy, family alliances, and even cultural fusion between Persians and Greeks of high station. When Pharnabazus rode away from his meeting with Agesilaus just recounted (*Hell.* 4.1.39–40), Pharnabazus'

> son by Parapita, who was still at the age of beauty, remained behind and ran up saying, "I make you my *xenos*, Agesilaus."
>
> "I accept for my part," said Agesilaus.
>
> "Remember, then," the boy answered and immediately gave his javelin—a lovely weapon—to Agesilaus, who took it and gave in return the gorgeous cheekpieces adorning the horse of his staff officer Idaeus. Then the boy bounded into the saddle and rode after his father.
>
> When afterward, during his father's absence, [the boy's] brother [Ariobarzanes][36] deprived him of his rule and made him an exile, Agesilaus showed him every courtesy; in particular he did everything to see that the son of Eualces the Athenian should be admitted to the

men's sprint at the Olympia for his sake, as he was the biggest of the boys; for the Persian had fallen in love with him.

The Pharnacids of Dascyleium may well have been unique as a satrapal dynasty in the intimacy of their association with Greeks, and probably in the degree of their Hellenization as well.[37] But in the fourth century other Persians of high station cultivated individual relations with Greeks, some of them erotic. In the days of his alliance with the Persian Spithridates, Agesilaus fell in love with his son, although according to Xenophon Agesilaus succeeded in controlling his passion short of a kiss (*Ages.* 5.4–5; cf. *Hell.* 4.1.28).

It is true that Agesilaus' passion for his son did not prevent Spithridates from decamping when he was outraged by Agesilaus' chief of staff (*Hell.* 4.1.26f): liaisons of this nature could end badly, as did the homoerotic relationship between the Thessalian Meno and the satrap Ariaeus of Ionia, who betrayed Meno in the course of transferring his loyalties to the victor after Cunaxa (*Anab.* 2.1.5. 5.31ff, 6.28–29). Meno enjoyed the hereditary *xenia* of the Persian King, a diplomatic *entrée* to Susa that must have gone back to the Aleuads' alliance with Xerxes (Plato *Meno* 78b–d):[38] he was worth wooing by a Persian of high station. Had Cyrus won the empire, Meno might well have risen high in Persia in association with Ariaeus. The luck of battle and the predicament of Ariaeus after Cunaxa determined the fate of this relationship; Ariaeus did not intervene to prevent Meno from dying a miserable death in Persian captivity (*Anab.* 2.6.29). Whatever their outcome, however, the importance of such relationships for us lies in their testimony to the personal rapport that Persians and Greeks of high station could achieve in this age—testimony that gives weight to the erotic element that we sense behind Xenophon's enduring attachment to the person and memory of the younger Cyrus in the *Anabasis* and in the imaginative passion of his recreation in the *Cyropaedia*.

Arnaldo Momigliano observed that in the encounters of Greeks with foreign peoples the major cultural accommodations were made by the barbarians.[39] It was the Persians, on the whole, who troubled to learn Greek and not the Greeks Persian.[40] Admission of Persian aristocrats to Greek society was strictly on terms of Hellenization, as in the case of Pharnabazus' exiled son, as well as that of an earlier notable exile at Athens, Zopyrus II, a son of the hereditary satrap of Syrophoenicia and the descendant of one of the Seven, Megabyzus I. This Zopyrus was to die leading a force of Athenians against Caunus in Lycia during the first years of the Peloponnesian War.[41] He appears to have spent some years at Athens (41–42), where he set aside his Persian name in favor of the Greek translation *Zôpyros,* "Living Fire."[42] Changing one's name—especially when it is a great name in one's native society—is a significant concession by an immigrant to the ways of his new home.

In consequence of their accommodation to the Greeks, observers such as Xenophon still would know Persians at a cultural remove; those Persians with whom Greeks dealt were largely, if not almost always, ones who could present themselves in the Hellenic idiom. To achieve their ends, Persians, both "good" and "bad," had to deal with Greeks directly. Xenophon represents such personages as Tissaphernes, Pharnabazus, Ariaeus, and the younger Cyrus speaking to Greeks in Greek; we may trust him in this, for he does not eliminate the presence of interpreters as an inconvenience to his narrative, but includes them when they are present (cf. *Hell.* 7.1.37). The adventitious "Hellenism" of these individual Persians in turn colored Xenophon's perceptions of the native character of the Achaemenid nobility. It was easy for him to imagine that his favorite Persians were generically similar to Greeks.[43]

This perspective helps us to understand the presentation of the most exemplary Persians in the *Cyropaedia* after Cyrus himself, the invented characters Aglaïtidas, Chrysantas, Panthea, and Pheraulus. They bear Hellenic names and stand preeminently beside Cyrus as portraits of virtue. But to Xenophon's mind they represent authentic Persian characters, because some contemporary Persians really did, in the eyes of Greeks who dealt with them in Asia Minor, resemble Greeks and cultivate Greek expertise. Xenophon's inspiration for the *Cyropaedia* as a whole, as well as his inspiration for these characters and their conspicuously Greek nomenclature, reflected his experience of the "best" Persians, Cyrus and Pharnaba-zus—both of whom had acquired a Greek patina as well as a gratifying appreciation of Greek abilities in warfare.

The Cyropaedia *as History*

Modern critics are inclined to treat the *Cyropaedia* as an ancestor of the novel.[44] In the intention of its author, however, the *Cyropaedia* was not a didactic romance set in a stagelit Persia that never was, a mere vehicle for Xenophon's up-to-date expertise on virtue, warfare, and rule.[45] To be sure, the work is thoroughly Hellenic in its unyielding cultural solipsism, but it is nonetheless a thorough-going attempt to explain to Greeks on Greek principles—which Xenophon and his audience regarded as universal—the unique phenomenon of world conquest represented by a figure who must have struck the Greeks as no less astonishing than Alexander is to us, and about whom much less was securely known than the little enough we know about Alexander.

In its assumptions, the *Cyropaedia* is comparable to Polybius' historical analysis of the stability and imperial achievement of the Roman *res publica* in terms of the Greek theory of constitutions, which Polybius had inherited from Plato and Aristotle.[46] It was impossible for Polybius to regard the Roman achievement as a phenomenon *sui generis*; the only solution possible for a man of his culture lay in reasoning that the Romans had succeeded where the Greeks had failed because they had created and maintained a constitutionally balanced and directed polity according to universal principles.[47]

In the *Cyropaedia* variations of the phrase "even now," *eti kai nun*, concerning Persian ways and customs appear some twenty-four times, and of these instances more than half (thirteen) occur within 8.1.–6; they testify to the author's attention to perceived continuities into his own day of the institutions and style of rule established by Cyrus. For Xenophon was in great measure trying to reconstruct the Persians' *patrios politeia* in the age of their degener-ation: his effort is paralleled by the contemporary attempts of other savants and political ideologues to work their way back to a lost ideal politeia in the laws of Solon and Clisthenes at Athens, and in the case of Xenophon himself, to those of Lycurgus at Sparta.[48] Cyrus' achievements on the one hand, and his knowledge of the contemporary Persian state on the other, were Xenophon's only givens. From these givens he worked his way back, according to universal principles, to a pristine Persian polity of the kind that would necessarily have produced a Cyrus, whom he then set in motion on the world stage.

The pristine Persia ruled over by the father of Cyrus bears some resemblances to the Sparta of Xenophon's *Lacedaemonian Constitution*.[49] But the correct inference is not that Xenophon created an imaginary Persian utopia as an anachronistic calque upon a Sparta of the ideologues' imagination, which could carry no power of conviction. He was, rather, compelled to reason that the Persians of Cyrus' generation were virtuous and invincible because their institutions brought them up to be virtuous and invincible; if so, then the Persian pattern must have generically resembled the Spartan way of life because it produced a similar human type. His Persian politeia is based on inferential argument from *eikos* and *physis*, from probability and nature, that derives means from ends, and causes from their effects.[50]

We recognize that the ethos and *epistêmê* promulgated in the *Cyropaedia* is purely Hellenic and fourth century, but to Xenophon it was natural and therefore timeless and universal. This assumption appears nowhere more clearly than in his description of Cyrus' formation of his corps of *hoplomakhoi*, which is the closest descriptive approach to a contemporary hoplite phalanx that he was able to achieve while retaining the characteristic Persian arms of target and saber.[51] Cyrus is able quickly to train a first-class corps recruited from the Persian political class of "inferiors" because hand-to-hand combat is *pantas anthrôpous physei epistamenous*; it is instinctive to human beings and therefore a thing depending more on resolution than art, *prothymias mallon ê tekhnês ergon* (*Cyrop.* 2.3.9).

The theoretical assumption upon which the *Cyropaedia* proceeds—that there is only one right way to do human things—leads Xenophon to create what appear to us to be profound anachronisms and inaccuracies. Cyrus' army of footmen is again an exam-

ple: it is trained, tented, and rewarded according to the best professional principles of Xenophon's own day and, in particular,
according to the methods that the Spartans had developed to use
large numbers of *perioeci*, former helot *neodamôdeis*, and mercenaries in their service.[52]

A closely similar theoretical assumption had been made by
Xenophon's exemplar Thucydides, who applied a canon of causal
identity *kata to anthrôpinon* (Thuc. 1.22.4; cf. 3.82.2 with 82–84)
not only to his own times but to the distant past (1.2–21), with
the result that his picture of the early growth of Greece and of
the Trojan War redraws the evidence of myth according to contemporary principles of finance, organization, and supply based on
Athenian naval expertise and imperial experience (1.2–11). These
principles, and humankind's constant desire for possessions and
rule, are observed throughout the Archaeology. Thucydides' reconstruction, drawn in conscious mistrust of Homer (9.3 *fin.*)—indeed, from a positive desire to refute the testimony of the poets—
is rigorously faithful to the abiding and universal patterns that he
perceives in the history of contemporary wars and empire.[53]

Xenophon's own primary canon is the Socratic premise that
rule is an *epistêmê*, an objective science whose aim is to secure
the willing obedience of the ruled. Since Cyrus won willing obedience from a vast congeries of unrelated peoples, the conclusion
follows that he was a supremely *epistamenos* ruler (*Cyrop.* 1.1.3).
This *a priori* conclusion is reinforced in Xenophon's mind by the
unanimity of the tradition about Cyrus' character and descent.
Cyrus' lineage was divine (7.2.24), and as for his person "even
now it is said and sung by the barbarians that he was the most
beautiful of men, and in spirit the most generous, the most devoted
to learning, and the most ambitious, so that he endured every
labor and every danger for the sake of winning praise" (*Cyrop.*
1.2.1); moreover his subjects revered him as they would a father
(e.g., 8.8.1). Finally, he was the instrument of destiny. When night
had fallen at the beginning of the Persians' march against Croesus
and the Lydians, "it is said that a light from heaven showed forth
upon Cyrus and the army, so that all were awed by the divine
sign (*to theion*) and were filled with courage against the enemy."[54]

Xenophon concludes his description of the ideal ruler and commander in the *Oeconomicus* by enumerating the sources of his powers as "learning and natural genius—but above all that divine gift for charismatic leadership," *paideia . . . physis . . . kai to megiston dê . . . theion, to ethelontôn arkhein* (21.11). Once granted his demonstration that the real Cyrus had been an ideal ruler, then Xenophon can with no felt trespass of historical truth recreate Cyrus as the exemplar of his own image of the ideal ruler in terms of his nature, training, and divine genius, within a genre of invented history that is no less "historical" in its assumptions and method than Thucydides' picture of the Trojan War or, *mutatis mutandis*, the methodological assumptions of modern historians when they press into areas lacking documentation. Xenophon states his program in these words (*Cyrop.* 1.1.6):

> Because we consider this man so worthy of the highest admiration, we have examined (*eskepsametha*) what kind of man he was by birth, the character of his natural gifts, and what kind of education formed him, that he was so great a ruler of men. Whatever we have found out (*eputhometha*), then, and whatever we think we have sensed (*êisthêsthai dokoumen*) in him, we shall try to tell in detail.

I have tried to catch in the translation the note of diffidence I hear in the Greek. The verbs of thought are *skopoumai, punthanomai, aisthanesthai,* and *dokeô.* They honestly define Xenophon's method and his results: observation, discovery, intuition, and hypothesis, fully elaborated in a panoramically imagined solution to the biographical and historical problem of the foundation of Persia's universal empire presented by the career and accomplishments of Cyrus, as they were then known to the Greeks. This work he presented to an audience educated, as Thucydides had been, to retroject current models of experience to explain past phenomena.

Pothos: *The Motivation of the* Cyropaedia

The *Cyropaedia* is the maturest work of a mind haunted by the lost possibilities of the unachieved reign of Cyrus II and repelled by the degenerate spectacle of his killer's rule (*Cyrop.* 8.8 *passim,* esp. 12–13). Xenophon promulgated the *Cyropaedia* as a program for a possible Persian future which, he believed, had been within an ace of coming into being under the younger Cyrus—an empire revivified by the infusion of a Greek *epistêmê* that was no more than the codification and practice of natural principles of justice, state-craft, and war common to the Greeks and the early Persians when they had been animated and led by the genius of the elder Cyrus.[55]

Seen from outside the author's internal vision, the *Cyropaedia* appears as an extended power fantasy in which the mind of Xeno-phon wins the empire of Cyrus.[56] This view is correct in the methodological sense that I have just discussed, in the biographer's inevitable association with his subject,[57] and also in that the assump-tions of the *Cyropaedia* identify an authorial self-regard thwarted in its highest ambitions and cheated of its deserts. Xenophon's vision of his relationship with the younger Cyrus, had he lived to become Great King, is the emotive engine that drives the *Cyropae-dia*. The man whose service Xenophon entered freely and nobly, accepting no pay and relying conspicuously upon the degree of Cyrus' eventual regard of him for the shape of his own future, was "the man who of all Persians born since the elder Cyrus was the most kingly and worthy to rule," *basilikôtatos te kai arkhein axiôtatos* (*Anab.* 1.9.1).

In his person and propaganda the younger Cyrus had, in fact, claimed to embody the native Persian values of the first Cyrus. This is the point of his jibe that his brother Artaxerxes he could keep his seat neither on his horse in a hunt nor on his throne in a crisis (Plut. *Artox.* 6.3)—an altogether oriental image of the monarch as master of the hunt (cf. Hdt. 1.36ff). On the other hand, the younger Cyrus projected to the Greeks around him an impressive Hellenism. According to Xenophon's picture of him, he spoke Greek fluently and communicated directly with his Greek officers. In his native *noblesse* he displayed in the highest degree the rectitude, loyalty, and active beneficence to one's friends that were the foundation stones of Hellenic *kalokagathia*; he conspicu-ously preferred the Greeks in his service to his unsteady native levies; and he let the Greeks know how much he depended on them to gain the throne and to lend him their courage and expertise afterward. He himself spoke with that contempt of barbarians typical of Greeks. All in all, he was able to project himself perfectly in the Greek idiom. Even his mistresses were Greek. To one of them, who was clever, he gave the name Aspasia; and like Pericles' Aspasia she became famous in her own time.[58]

In a Persia ruled by such a second Cyrus, Xenophon could imagine himself a dynast with lands and revenues, the traditional and expected rewards of conspicuous servants of the King such as Gongylus, Demaratus, and Themistocles.[59] When Cyrus was killed, Xenophon was left to imagine the shape of what might have been in the vivid and abiding afterlight of the hopes and experiences of his youth, predicated upon the friendship of a Hellenizing Great King who united the virtues of both conquering peoples. The result was his *magnum opus*, in which for the first time the Persians entered the Greek imagination provided with an epic and heroic past, a past that dwarfed the mere conquest of Troy,[60] a past presented in the achievements of a monarch imbued with a Socratic moral *epistêmê* and armed with the genius of current Greek military science. Seen as an emotional landscape, therefore, the *Cyropaedia* is an elegiac fantasy of what might have been, had the younger Cyrus become Great King, and had elected to keep near him such Hellenic experts and complete men, such *pepaideumenoi*, as Xenophon himself and Proxenus, his boyhood friend and pupil of Gorgias of Leontini (*Anab.* 2.6.17ff).

The work is suffused with *pothos* for a lost future and lost associates: Xenophon's offering to Apollo, which lay in the Treasury of the Athenians at Delphi, bore Proxenus' name together with his own (*Anab.* 5.3.5). The virtues of the elder Cyrus in the *Cyropaedia* are the virtues of the younger Cyrus in fruition: the vignettes we glimpse through Xenophon's eyes of the young prince show us a personality of the charm, generosity, and personal genius for friendship that also illuminates Xenophon's imagined conqueror.

The Cyropaedia *and Hellas*

The elegiac impulse is very strong in Xenophon's work. He memorialized the great friends and great men in his life for his public and his posterity. In the course of his lifetime Xenophon's loyalties journeyed from Socrates, to Cyrus, to Agesilaus. He was a man who needed to live in the ambit of a personal hero; and when they were all gone he found his great solace and pleasure in recalling them intimately to himself. It is an impulse plainest in the Socratic works (cf. *Mem.* 4.8.11, *Apol.* 34), and it is there as well in the vivid attraction of his portraits of the younger Cyrus and Agesilaus. But Xenophon never wrote a word without an argument in mind: thus the Socratic works and the *Anabasis* are essays in defense of his mentor and of his own conduct, respectively; and his *Lacedaemonian Constitution* and his *Agesilaus*, portraying him as "the last of the Spartiates," as it were, are meant to defend the person and principles of the man whose influence had been paramount at Sparta, even though Xenophon well knew that his policies had brought about its decline.[61]

Understanding the argument of the *Cyropaedia* depends likewise upon determining when and why was it written, and in solving the enigma of the angry postscript deploring the utter perversion of the virtues and institutions of Persia, which Xenophon had delineated so appreciatively in the body of the work.[62] Compositionally the *Cyropaedia* ends with the death of Cyrus and was completed before the betrayal of the leaders of the Satraps' Revolt indignantly referred to in the postscript, an event that probably occurred in 362.[63] This terminus, and the finish which distinguishes the *Cyropaedia* alone of his longer works, puts its completion within the period between Leuctra and Mantinea (371–362).

Its energy and urbanity, further, suggest leisure and optimism. But in the years after Leuctra, Xenophon was no longer resident at Scillus; he is said to have established his family at Corinth, and then must have occupied some time at Athens after his recall in order to secure an estate for his sons, who became citizens of the highest census and were enrolled in the cavalry.[64] So leisure and optimism could not have arrived again for Xenophon after Leuctra before 368 at the earliest, when he was not only once more secure in his own affairs, but Spartan fortunes also were seemingly on the rise again: the "Tearless Victory" over the Arcadians in that year, and the weakness of the new state of Messene, revived hope that the Spartans could regain their old primacy in Greece (*Hell.* 7.1.29–32, Diod. 15.72.3).[65]

The *Cyropaedia*, then, must belong to Xenophon's years in Corinth between 368 and 362, and the work needs to be understood in light of this period of Greek history, which possesses a specific character of its own. These were years of watchful waiting for the Spartans to recover their old position in Greece. Sparta's power and eminence had been continuous and unbroken almost from the beginning of historical memory among the European Greeks. Contemporary opinion by no means recognized what only became clear to most Greeks after Mantinea, that Sparta was finished for good.[66] Xenophon devoted almost a quarter of the *Hellenica* to the period between Leuctra and Mantinea (6.4.22 *ad fin.*), as much space as he devoted to the fall of Athens and the restoration of the democracy (1–2).[67] Surely Xenophon, a prejudiced but not a blind observer, was recording events at the time, or remembering them afterward, in a manner reflecting his contemporary hopes, and those of his Peloponnesian friends and informants, of witnessing Sparta's recovery. A comparandum is Diodorus' treatment, which must preserve the attitude of his contemporary source, Ephorus. Here not Leuctra but Mantinea was the defeat in which the Spartans lost everything for good, *tois holois esphalêsan kai tên hêgemonian anelpistôs anebalon* (15.33.2–3).[68]

Ephorus' own master Isocrates also betrays in his remarks at the time the hope of a Spartan resurgence in spite of his normally firm anti-Laconism, which he put aside following the alliance in 369 between Athens and Sparta. The contrast in mood between Isocrates' *Letter* 20 to Dionysius I of Syracuse and his *Archidamus* is striking. Isocrates wrote to Dionysius, presumably to canvass his ambition to lead Isocrates' then-quixotic crusade against Persia, not long after the shocking winter of 370–69, when the Thebans had invaded Lacedaemon itself and wrested Messenia from the Spartans, while detaching from them most of their traditional allies, the Arcadians first of all. Under the impact of these unprecedented reversals, Isocrates at this time portrays the Spartans, without much exaggeration, as grateful even to be still living in their own homeland (*Ep.* 1.8).

Then a few years later follows the *Archidamus*, a fiercely optimistic, never-say-die harangue put into the mouth of King Agesilaus' son: it was composed in the atmosphere of Sparta's apparent revivification following the event of her alliance with Athens, the Tearless Victory of 368, and Thebes' consequent diplomatic humiliation in the following year.[69] Assembled at Thebes to hear what the Thebans had brought home from their shameful diplomacy at Susa, the envoys of the Greek states—led by the Mantineans and their Arcadian allies, who were now moving back into the Spartan orbit—refused to follow the Thebans into the hegemonial peace they had secured from Persia, which recognized the independence of Messenia and ordered the Athenian navy into the stocks (Xen. *Hell.* 7.1.33–40).

Xenophon correctly interpreted this rebuff as a collective Greek refusal to recognize the primacy of Thebes as the formal arbiter of Greece, which was the goal to which her Persian diplomacy had been directed.[70] This judgment is also reflected in Diodorus' summation of the state of Greece after Leuctra: neither the Athenians nor the Argives were in a position to claim the hegemony, and *the Thebans were not worthy of the first rank (tôn proteiôn axious mê einai*, 15.60.2). The Greeks were unready to digest the new facts of power and a certain lack of realism prevailed among them, especially as a consequence of the new Spartan-Athenian axis against Persia's friend in Greece—a combination that reproduced the diplomatic landscape of the war against Xerxes, and which nourished rhetorical indulgence in moving recollections of those grand ancient days.[71]

The appeal of comparisons to the Hellenic alliance of the Persian wars was all the more powerful in the context of Thebes' destruction of Plataea and Thespiae in 374—cities that had been living shrines to heroism and sacrifice in the sacred cause. The anti-Boeotian party within the Athenian democracy had achieved a moral ascendancy from the moment of these cities' destruction; it began moving immediately toward *rapprochement* with the Spartans, who themselves invaded Boeotia with the specific goal of restoring Plataea and Thespiae and dissolving the Theban federation (*Hell.* 6.2.1–3 and 3.1–4.3). Xenophon even records a *mot* of the Spartan envoys who made the alliance at Athens after Leuctra. One of them exclaimed in grandiose reminiscence to the ecclesia that, if the two powers agree upon alliance, "the hope will now appear, as we used to say, of tithing the Thebans" (*Hell.* 7.5.35). The reference, of course, was to the famous oath of the Hellenes on the eve of the invasion of Xerxes, when they vowed to make war on Medizers and tithe the spoils to Delphi (Hdt. 7.132.2).

The Thebans themselves did not scruple to boast of their ancestral loyalty to the Persians before Artaxerxes II, in the presence of envoys from other leading Greek states. At court in 368,

> Pelopidas gained great advantage with the Persians. For he was able to argue that not only had they alone of the Greeks fought with the Great King at Plataea and had never afterward made war against the King, but that the Lacedaemonians for this very reason had made war on them, namely that they had refused to campaign against him with Agesilaus and had prevented him from sacrificing to Artemis at Aulis, the very place where Agamemnon sacrificed and thence set sail for the conquest of Troy. (Xen. *Hell.* 7.1.34)

This was the mood of the years when the *Cyropaedia* was composed, the years when Sparta and Athens were joined together as equal leaders by land and sea for the first time since Xerxes. Athens at this time had brought her naval league to a height of power and stability, and seemed to be on the verge of creating a new Aegean empire during the campaigns waged by Timotheus (366–362). Timotheus began by expelling a Persian garrison from Samos and replacing it with a cleruchy to hold the island for Athens. Thereafter he was said to have taken no less than twenty-four places in the north Aegean, including Sestus, Torone, Pydna, Methone, and Potidaea, where he again planted a cleruchy.

It is true that Athens' Aegean resurgence, as well as Thebes' adventures in Thessaly in these years, go unnoticed in the *Hellenica*, in which Xenophon's vision remains fixed even more firmly than before upon the Peloponnese and the fortunes of Sparta.[72] But the *Agesilaus* testifies that Xenophon was indeed watching affairs in the East as well. The principal effects of the alliance between Sparta and Athens were occurring in this theater; meanwhile Artaxerxes' grip on the western satrapies appeared to be disintegrating, as in the days of Cyrus more than thirty years before. First Agesilaus and the Athenian admiral Timotheus together rescued the rebel satrap Ariobarzanes of Dascyleium from his enemies; two years before, in 368, Ariobarzanes had supported Sparta's claim to Messenia against his sovereign and had backed the Spartans with funds to hire mercenaries.[73]

With the Athenians once more in command of the Aegean, the Spartans too were at the center of a new Peloponnesian coalition that included Elis, the Achaeans, the Mantineans, and other Arcadians, following the Tearless Victory and the subsequent fracture of the Arcadian federation. These were the powers that forced the Thebans to defend their position once again at Mantinea. Even in defeat after Mantinea the Athenian alliance remained alive, and both powers decided to recoup once again by playing the Eastern card in concert. Agesilaus was sent out to the Egyptian ruler Tachos with an official staff of 30 Spartiates and a personal command of 1,000 hoplites to take charge of an invasion of Persian Phoenicia. The Athenian Chabrias commanded the fleet and the whole campaign was conceived in coordination with the satraps in revolt, including Ariobarzanes, Sparta's best friend in the East.

It seems evident that Agesilaus and his associates at Sparta saw an opportunity to regain in the East what they had lost in Greece.[74] A successful war against Artaxerxes' generals in alliance with the rebel satraps would insulate Greece decisively against Persian interference in support of Thebes' hegemony. Ariobarzanes or another Persian might even be used as a stalking horse in Asia against Artaxerxes, as Agesilaus once hoped to use Pharnabazus. Best of all, Ariobarzanes or another ambitious Persian magnate might furnish the wealth and influence to enforce Sparta's claim to Messenia, with all that implied for the restoration of her traditional position in Greece.

Agesilaus had seen it happen before. He had been nearly forty years old when the unstinted wealth of the younger Cyrus enabled Sparta finally to defeat Athens; he was approaching fifty when he saw Athens' walls and navy called into existence again and his own victories in Asia nullified by the gold of Pharnabazus: Xenophon, surely reflecting this view, was to blame the outbreak of the Corinthian War on Persian gold (*Hell.* 3.4.9). These decisive experiences of Agesilaus' life taught him that Persian alliances and Persian wealth were everything in this new age, and it is impossible to imagine that this lesson did not guide his estimation of the possibilities when he sailed to Egypt as a still-vigorous octagenarian after Mantinea.

Xenophon, who was not much more than a decade younger than Agesilaus, must have nursed similar hopes founded on similar experiences.[75] The years when he was writing the *Cyropaedia* were years full of apparently reborn promise for the prospects that had disappeared, seemingly for ever, at Cunaxa. Surely he wrote with the careers of his sons in mind, both of whom had passed through the Spartiate *agôgê*; he himself was in his sixties, aging but probably still vigorous.

But everything fell apart soon after Xenophon reached the end of the work. The satraps were betrayed and the Egyptian Tachos himself was overthrown in the midst of his attempt to wrest Phoenicia from the Persians. Agesilaus could only succeed in installing his successor for a prize of 230 silver talents. The aged king, whose career had personified for Xenophon the war against Artaxerxes' kingdom and the hopes of Sparta's resurrection, died that winter (361–60) on the voyage home.[76] Nothing remained thereafter of Xenophon's hopes: now, on top of Mantinea and the death in that campaign of his eldest son Gryllus, had come the loss of his dearest friend Agesilaus, together with the finish of a grand expectation of Artaxerxes' eclipse or overthrow and a new Greek adventure in Asia.

This Xenophon of exhausted hopes and many griefs, whose imagination in the previous years had created the *Cyropaedia* in the bright hope of a new return of Greece to Asia, now appended to the recently finished work a bitter reflection on the terminal decay of the Persian character, exemplified by the treachery of the rebel satraps against their own comrades and fathers (*Cyrop.* 8.8.4)—a treachery that had ended the second great hope of overthrowing Artaxerxes II, and which had finished Agesilaus' last and greatest opportunity. It was this Xenophon, too, who ended his *Hellenica* after Mantinea careless of the future and despairing of his own times (*Hell.* 7.5.26–27).[77]

Xenophon, then, presented his portrait of Cyrus the conqueror as a contribution to the ongoing debate on the nature of the Persians at a moment when this debate had taken on urgency from the Spartan-Athenian alliance and Sparta's own connections with Ariobarzanes and the Satraps' Revolt. It was a moment, too, when for the first time in more than thirty years Xenophon could sojourn freely at Athens and, presumably, cultivate acquaintance with the circles around Isocrates and Plato. As is well known, the form of the *Cyropaedia* draws upon antecedents from these directions. Xenophon must have had in mind the dialogue of the Socratic Antisthenes entitled the *Kyros ê peri basileias*;[78] the scanty remaining fragments indicate that it was a theoretical and homiletic treatise of no great originality, an impression that corresponds with Xenophon's own waspish portraits of Antisthenes in his *Symposium* and *Memorabilia* (*Symp.* 4.34ff; *Mem.* 2.55ff). One of Xenophon's subsidiary motives in composing so long and so rich a treatise on Cyrus may well have been to show up Antisthenes and, for that matter, Isocrates as well. Isocrates' epideictic *Busiris* (composed *c.* 385 or earlier), which defended its subject as the founder of the Egyptians' institutions and the author of their national virtues, may have served Xenophon as a rhetorical and thematic exemplar.[79]

But Xenophon's main purpose was neither agonistic nor epideictic. His emphasis in the beginning on the pristine virtues and institutions of the Persians, which had formed Cyrus and his conquering people, and the architecture of Cyrus' *ars imperii*, which he dissects at the end, shows Xenophon explaining to his Greek audience the apparently obnoxious features of Persian rule as necessary consequences of a universal monarchy over servile Asiatic peoples. It is notably the "Assyrians" (that is, the Babylonians) who contribute the central rite of *proskynesis* to the court protocol instituted by Cyrus. Xenophon remains true to his conception of monarchy as the manipulation of slaves.

Xenophon spoke to slaveholders, as Aeschylus had done. The contribution of the *Cyropaedia* lies in its implied scenario of the possession of the native peoples of Asia under a Greek *epimeleia*, to use the word employed by Isocrates in his public address to

Philip urging him to take on Persia (5.154) following the Macedonian peace with Athens in 346. But it was not a part of Xenophon's
vision to anticipate anyone but a Persian upon the throne of the
Achaemenids. Xenophon imagined his early ambitions realized by
other Greeks in collaboration with a new Cyrus to be found in
some such figure as Ariobarzanes, and the consequent institutional-
ization of Hellenic *epistêmê* in the government of the Empire. But
this dream crashed too: hence the disillusioned postscript, once
again blaming Artaxerxes II, the hated corrupter of the Persians
and the villain at the center of Xenophon's imagination, for dashing
his hopes—hopes that Alexander would soon fulfill beyond Xenophon's or the world's imagining.

Xenophon erred only in living too soon.

Appendixes

PREJUDICE AGAINST METICS AT ATHENS

It is an attractive, though unprovable, possibility that the reign of
terror carried on by the Thirty against the metics (Xen. *Hell.* 2.3.21,
40) had been not merely a device to get money and to destroy
the mercantile element that had nourished Athens' prosperity and
the strength of the old naval democracy. This purgation of Athens
of her foreign residents might also have been a *Rassenhygiene* meant
to appeal to nativist ideologues like Xenophon. A *xenêlasia* of this
kind would rid the city of a large group of non-Greek Asiatics
largely if not altogether of servile origin, who in Xenophon's view
were polluting the hoplite muster (*Vect.* 2.1.4). Among the well-
to-do they sometimes even gained citizenship by irregular means
and then married Athenians' daughters. As the comic poet Anaxan-
drides (fr. 4 Edmonds: 352?) wrote,

> Slaves have no city anywhere, my friend.
> Chance gives men first this status, and then that.
> Many who have no liberty today
> Tomorrow become Sunians; the next
> They're in the agora. So Fortune shifts
> The helm for each.

Pericles' citizenship law of 451/0 had to be reenacted in 403/
2, and in 346/5 a thorough purge of the rolls was undertaken by
means of investigation in the demes.[80]

If the danger of Athens' deracination was not confined to mixed
unions among the city's poor, but was being felt by the class to
which Xenophon and the Thirty belonged, then we have a major
reason why metics were regarded by those who thought of themselves as true Athenians to be barbarizing the city population, with
predictable political consequences.[81] Plato was to remark in the
Republic (563b) that the most extreme phase of democratic license,
a ready soil for despotism, arrives when "the slaves of both sexes
are no less free than those who bought them."[82]

THE HELLENIC ATTACHMENTS OF THE PHARNACIDS

The Pharnacid dynasty of satraps had long been in touch with
Greeks by Xenophon's day, and its members took the lead in
forging close personal links with Greeks, and later with Macedonians. Pharnabazus' teenage son by Parapita spoke Greek, as did
Pharnabazus himself. In his manhood this boy was to pass without
difficulty into the elevated society of those Greeks who bred their
boys up for the games and professed the name and values of
kalokagathia.

Ariobarzanes too cultivated Hellenism: in 368 the Athenians
granted him the citizenship for his efforts on their behalf and that
of the Spartans against Thebes after Leuctra.[83] In the fourth century
the Athenian citizenship was not bestowed lightly on non-Greeks,[84]
and this must have been meant in part as a compliment to Ariobarzanes' Hellenism. At about the same time the Athenians similarly
honored the Hellenizing king Strato of Tyre, but in his case only
with the *proxenia*.[85]

Ariobarzanes' other half-brother Artabazus succeeded to his
father's satrapy about 360 and wed the sister of the Rhodian
professional generals Memnon and Mentor.[86] Afterward, the career
of this other Hellenizing son of Pharnabazus was founded on the
closest association with Greeks and Macedonians. When Artabazus
rebelled in the 350s he received the support of the Theban general
Pammenes, who was dispatched to his aid by the Theban state

with 5,000 troops. Then, suspecting that Pammenes would betray him, he fled to the court of Philip of Macedon with his Rhodian wife and brothers-in-law.

Later he was restored to favor at Susa through the offices of Mentor, who had meanwhile distinguished himself in the service of Artaxerxes III. Artabazus is said to have sired eleven sons and ten daughters by his Rhodian wife, and after Alexander's conquest his family served the Macedonians. One of his sons, named Cophen, entered the Horse Companions in 324; two of his daughters were wed to Alexander's officers Eumenes and Nearchus. After Alexander's death, another son fought under his kinsman-by-marriage Eumenes, the founder of the Pergamene kingdom.[87]

The Pharnacids of Dascyleium had come to associate with the Greeks and their culture so intimately in great part because of their long tenure of five generations, spanning nearly eighty years, in the rule of the Greeks of the Aeolis and Propontis.[88] Their capital was itself a largely Greek town less than fifty miles (eighty kilometers) from Cyzicus, a short day's canter. Sardis too was the domicile of many Greeks; but its satraps were often Iranians from the interior sent down from Susa. Some of them, like the younger Cyrus, learned Greek; but others remained thoroughly Iranian in language and outlook. By contrast, Eumenes' Pharnacid brother-in-law was present at the creation of the Pergamene monarchy; and his cousin Mithridates, whose original seat had been the Greek port of Cius in the Propontis, founded the Greco-Persian kingdom of Pontus.

Conclusion

We have now reached the end of a long road, along which we have seen how some Greek authors manipulated, or departed from, the common view of the Asiatic to send messages about Greek as well as barbarian human nature. From the age of the Ionians' cultural flowering onward, contradictions and complexities arose. First the Ionians defined Asiatic foreigners as a kind of kindred, and then as the antithesis of what it meant to be Greek, while nevertheless keeping them within the Greek family in their mythographers' universal prehistory and ethnography.

This mythological groundwork provided the Greeks with yet other ways of thought that emphasized simultaneously their differences from, but also their similarities to, the contemporary Asiatic foreigner. In the end, aristocratic prejudice masquerading as political philosophy viewed "base" or "ignoble" Greeks as equivalent to barbarians, beginning with Heraclitus. His barbarians were all those who could not make sense of the world in his terms: so he, for one, counted almost everyone, Greek or native, as "barbarians."[1]

This is an outlook that describes a world full of "Greek barbarians"; it belongs to the mentality of an immigrant people always sensitive to the dangers of "going Asiatic." Who is "really" Greek, and what it means to be "really" Greek, appear to have remained essential issues for a people who were in close touch with, and deeply influenced by, the native societies in Asia. This is also part of the outlook of Herodotus concerning Greek and barbarian history, and the roles of Athens and Sparta in that history. Beyond the stereotype of the Asiatic barbarian, which in any case was not native to Ionia but arose in European Greece in the context of the Persian wars, definitions of "Greek" and "barbarian" concerning Asiatics were never in reality absolute, and were subject to conscious redeployment at various times. We have seen how Croesus began as a Hellene in the imagery of the archaic Ionians; but in Herodotus' hands he became the very type of the Asiatic barbarian in his infirmity of mind and moral ethos. And, in a subsequent age whose outlook was defined by a despairing outlook on the prospects for Greece, Herodotus' barbarian conqueror Cyrus became conversely a universal hero of impeccable Greek excellences *via* the pseudophilosophical *Führerprinzip* of Xenophon.

When we look at the world through Greek eyes, then, we see "barbarian Greeks" in the squares and precincts of Heraclitus' Ephesus, in the Ionia of Herodotus, and in Athens as well, in the age of Xenophon, who defined an international caste of *kaloi k'agathoi*: warriors and warrior-princes born to rule the servile mass of inferior humanity, whether nominally barbarian or nominally Greek.

It is plain from Xenophon, as I hope I have shown, that the attitudes of Alexander and the Hellenistic age were already in the process of formation during the fourth century. They form an enormous topic in themselves; here I will only say briefly that Greek thought concerning barbarians in this age took the directions pointed out by Heraclitus the Ephesian and Xenophon the exile in Persian service, not Aeschylus the European, of whose

> Famous courage the grove of Marathon might speak,
> For the long-haired Mede knows it well.[2]

This was only to be expected, after all, since the attitudes of archaic Ionians and those of the new citizens of Greek Asia alike worked themselves out in a climate of partial assimilation between Greek and native aristocracies.

As for the question of Xenophon's possible influence on Alexander, I should remark that it cannot be solved, because we do not even know whether Alexander had read Xenophon.[3] This is, in any case, a presumptuous question. Alexander inherited the rule of a largely un-Hellenized kingdom which, like Persia, had been welded out of numerous village-dwelling tribes. In its finished state under Philip II Macedon contained numerous peoples, barbarian and Greek, and Philip himself shaped the institutions of his realm consciously toward the Persian model.[4] As a child and youth at Pella, Alexander had encountered Persian ambassadors and exiles, notably Artabazus, whose Greek wife made him the brother-in-law and ally of the Rhodian mercenary generals Memnon and Mentor. Artabazus was at Philip's court from about 354 to perhaps 340 B.C., when Alexander was about sixteen. And once in Asia, Alexander was altogether capable of making up his own mind about the imperial people he had conquered. Any contribution from Xenophon in his school days would have been immaterial compared to his own needs and experience. If Alexander acted upon views about the quality and assimilability of Persians of the military class which were similar to Xenophon's, he did so because, as a warrior like Xenophon in Persian Asia, he came to know Persians at first hand in their own continent.[5]

Notes

Chapter One. Mythology and Representation: The Greek
Appropriation of the World

1. E.g., Hdt. 1. 158, Thuc. 1.2–3. The older scholarship on Greek origins, even when skeptical, reflects the Greeks' own views well: e.g., Grote 1888, vol. 1; other older works are cited by Sakellariou 1958, pp. 5–6.
2. Cf. Malkin 1987, p. 90.
3. Strabo 1.2.8 C19 is exemplary on the psychologically manipulative power of myth.
4. E.g., the *Arimaspea* of Aristeas. Fränkel 1973, pp. 241–43, discusses the poem in this vein and notes that "there is a certain affinity between the geographical legends of an Aristeas and the religious cosmology of Pherecydes," a rough contemporary of Aristeas who wrote the first Greek work in prose in the mid-sixth century.
5. *PMG* frr. 192–93; Pausanias 3.19.11–13. Lesky 1966, p. 151, puts Stesichorus in the late seventh and early sixth centuries with fair confidence. Cf. Bowra 1961, p. 77.
6. Pindar *Nem.* 1.26; cf. Lacroix 1974; Bickerman 1952.
7. On archaeological links between Sardis and the Mycenean world: Hanfmann and Mierse 1983, pp. 24–25 with nn. 24–40.
8. Apollodorus 2.127ff. The earliest version we have dates to the early fifth century: Panyassis fr. 17 Kinkel with Matthews 1974, pp.

96–99. Panyassis appears to have still regarded the relationship a compliment to the by then extinct Lydian monarchy. Later versions have Omphale putting Heracles to women's work, but this detail was undoubtedly elaborated by the playwrights after the assimilation of the Lydians to the image of the effeminate Asiatic barbarian: cf. Soph. *Trach.* 248ff, with Hall 1989, pp. 203–4; Hdt. 1.155.4 versus 1.79.3. Date of the Heraclids' fall: Kaletsch 1958, pp. 8ff, 25ff.

9. Cf. Hartog 1988, pp. 24–26, on the "hybrid" nature of the Scyths.

10. Greco-Scythian communities: Hdt. 4.17.1 and 108–9. Scythian pit-dwellings and artifacts are numerous in the excavated portions of the northern Pontic sites, especially at Olbia and its environs. Olbia: Wasowicz 1965, esp. catalogue of sites on pp. 139–51, and Kocybala 1978, pp. 247, 268–69, 278–80. Other sites: Kocybala 1978, index, s.v. "native population." On Scythian-Greek relations see now Georges 1994.

11. Poetic invention is indicated by the role in the Scythian origins legend of Hesiod's Echidna, who in the *Theogony* lives in a cave far from mortals and gods in the land of the Arimoi (*Theog.* 295–305); possibly Herodotus learned the Heracles story from the epic *Arimaspea* by the shadowy shaman-poet Aristeas of Proconneus (4.13–15). If the name of a minor settlement of Gorgippia ("Horsey Gorgon") in the Kuban commemmorates her, it is evidence that the Greeks even accepted the Scythian consort of Heracles into their local pantheon in some places. Cf. Hartog 1988, pp. 22ff.

12. Hall 1989, pp. 27–28 with n. 81, pp. 145–48 with nn. 138–48, 211.

13. Hdt. 2.39.2, 41.3.

14. Austin 1970, pp. 15ff. Egypt as a whole was closed to large-scale Greek exploration until the Persian conquest; accordingly, knowledge of the "real" as opposed to the "Homeric" Egypt begins only with Hecataeus in the early fifth century (*FGrH* 1 T 4 = Hdt. 2.143).

15. Dates in this study are B.C. unless otherwise noted. Snodgrass 1971, p. 348, notes that "definite Greek imports are not visible on Phrygian soil until the seventh century," i.e., after the fall of the Mita kingdom. Balcer 1987, p. 71, notes the late and sparse Greek settlement of the Aeolis, citing Coldstream 1977, p. 267. There appears to have been considerable stylistic influence between East Greece and Gordium, and some exchange of artifacts (DeVries 1980, esp. pp. 33–34 with nn. 1 and 2); but the traffic largely went from Phrygia to Greece, not vice versa (Young 1964, pp. 52–57; Birmingham 1961; Coldstream 1977, p. 266), and the offerings said to have been given by Midas which Herodotus saw at Delphi, if they were in fact Phrygian artifacts of the Mita period, were undoubtedly votives

offered by Greeks to a shrine of only local importance: see chapter 2.

16. Masson 1991, p. 666; the specimens from the Great Tumulus at Gordium are dated *c.* 720; another solitary find may go back to *c.* 750, although most of the Gordium texts are from the fifth and fourth centuries.

17. Midas' son's fate (his name was Lityerses) at Heracles' hands: Rose 1958, p. 200 with n. 69. For sources and discussion of the Midas legend see Roller 1983. Eusebius' dates for this Midas are 738–696 B.C. The story that he married a princess of Aeolian Cyme, whose father the king first struck coins there (Heraclides *FHG* ii 216, Pollux 9.83) is obviously anachronistic: any truth in it would point to a connection not with Cyme but with the Lydian Mermnads, who struck coinage and cultivated dynastic connections with the Greeks on their coasts. Nor can his supposed offering (a throne) at Delphi (Hdt. 1.14.2) belong to an eighth-century date.

   DeVries 1980, pp. 33–42, rests a case for cultural exchange (but not settlement) between Phrygians and Greeks in the eighth and seventh centuries on sherds of six Geometric pots found at Gordium, Phrygian fibulae and bronze bowls in Greek sanctuaries, a parallel use of alphabets, and presumed similarities in stylistic tastes and a "Homeric" way of life. But there is no evidence yet for Greek communities on the Aeolian mainland at this time. See Coldstream 1977, pp. 266–67; Young 1964, p. 52; cf. Snodgrass 1971, pp. 347–50, on the difficulties of interpreting the scanty evidence.

18. Plin. *N.H.* 34.40; see Momigliano 1975b, p. 19, who notes that the tradition of Arcadian settlement in Latium was accepted by Fabius Pictor at the end of the third century B.C. (fr. 1 Peter).

19. *FGrH* 137 F 16; Strabo 11.5.3–4 C504.

20. Lesky 1966, pp. 715–16, 728–737. Apollodorus' master Callimachus produced an enormous body of mythographical works, even a *Galatea* (frr. 378–79 Pfeiffer; cf. *11.* 18.45) which made the nymph of that name the mother of Galatus, eponym of the Galatians, a destructive Celtic people who crossed into Anatolia in his lifetime (278 B.C.) and continued their depredations until they were subdued in 230 by Attalus I and again after Magnesia by the Roman Manlius Vulso.

21. See Fränkel 1957, esp. pp. 3–5 on the poet's conscious deployment of etiologies to link the present world and the world of the Argonauts.

22. On the cult of Cybele at Cyzicus see Vermasaren 1977, pp. 28–29; Vermasaren 1987, nos. 251, 278–91, 284, 292, 294, 339, 562, 686, for the documentation. Hdt. 4.76 indicates that the cult was well established there by the mid fifth century at the latest.

23. Witt 1971, esp. pp. 95ff.
24. Cyrene: Hdt. 4. 186.2; cf. Chamoux 1953, p. 341; Athens: Plato *Laws* 657b; cf. Simms 1989.
25. Brady 1935.
26. Cf. Hdt. 7.62.1 from Hellanicus.
27. Hdt. 3.122.2; cf. Xen. *Mem.* 4. 3.13, Drews 1973, p. 11.
28. Plut. *Theseus* 15.2ff. On Herodotus' empiricism see chapter 5.
29. Strabo 2. 3.8 C104 with 1.2.2 C15 and 1.2.34 C41 (*Zênôn d' ho êmeteros*).
30. Cf. Rist 1969, pp. 256–62, on the unity of the person and the identity of the human species in Stoic thought.
31. Aly and Honigman 1931, stemma at cols. 77–78. The phenomenon must have been general from the time of Alexander's settlement of worn-out mercenaries and Macedonian troopers in his numerous "Alexandrias," but soon reached to the top of society. For example, an inscription of Delos from 279 (*IG* xi.161.B.72 = *IDélos* 1441a) identifies a dedicand to Apollo as one Tlepolemus son of Artapates, of Xanthus in Lycia. The name Artapates is Persian and had belonged to a son of the Achaemenid courtier Tiribazus, satrap of Sardis under Artaxerxes II (Olmstead 1948, p. 424 with n. 19).
32. Pindar, *Pyth.* 5, esp. line 110. Cf. Broholm 1924, cols. 158–59.
33. Cited by Bregman 1981, pp. 81, 217.
34. *FGrH* 1 T 4 = Hdt. 2.143 and *Komm.* p. 317, citing E. Meyer's calculated date of 1150 B.C. Hecataeus' pedigree, like that of the Ionian aristocracies generally, was made to go back to the Ionian migration. Menander Rhetor (third century A.D.) comments on the nobility conferred by such genealogies, which signify that one's ancestors are "from birth notable and did not begin as slaves" (*Rhet. gr.* iii p. 356.30 Spengel).
35. Bockisch 1969, pp. 118–33; see below, chapter 2.
36. Veyne 1988, p. 84; cf. Habicht 1985, esp. pp. 140ff, on the coexistence of Pausanias' skepticism and belief.
37. Veyne 1988, esp. chs. 3–7.
38. Ibid., p. 111, and Bickerman 1952.
39. Momigliano 1958, esp. pp. 3–5.
40. *Vit. Marc.* 2–4.
41. Thuc. 1.2–12. Cf. Gomme 1956, pp. 91–121, and Hunter 1982, pp. 17–49. Lateiner 1989, n. 6 on p. 232, observes that "Thucydides seems readier to accept the historicity of Minos (1.4), a figure whom Herodotus would prefer to discard as prior to retrievable history (Hdt. 3.122; but cf. 1.71, 173; 7.169–71)."
42. E.g., Polyb. 4. 77.8 on Triphylus son of Arcas; cf. 34.4.5.
43. On Pausanias' progress from skepticism in detail to faith at large in

the symbols of a mystery he does not pretend to understand, see the sensitive study of Habicht 1985, esp. pp. 140–57.

44. As such the *Theogony* is often cited in works on the origins of scientific thought. See Sambursky 1956, and especially the remarks of Fränkel 1973, pp. 96–97 and 102, n.15, comparing Hesiod to Linnaeus, the founder of systematic taxonomy. On the explanatory functions of myth see also, among an enormous literature, Horton 1967; Evans-Pritchard 1937; and Kirk 1970, esp. pp. 226–51.

45. Veyne 1988, p. 17 with n. 28.

46. Porphyry *Vit. Plot.*

47. E.g., Thucydides in the Archaeology (1.2–15): cf. Hunter 1982, pp. 17–49.

48. E.g., Pausanias 8.8.3, cited by Veyne 1988, p. 11; Also Diod. 3.62: a pre-Stoic example of allegorization.

49. Against this in particular, however, Diodorus of Sicily, for one, protests (4.8).

50. Bickerman 1952, pp. 70, 78.

51. E.g., Eusebius, who synchronized the Hellenic and Old Testament historical mythologies in his *Chronography:* cf. Veyne 1988, pp. 110–15.

Chapter Two. Asia and the Image of Tyranny

1. The Greeks' self-consciousness is archaeologically visible in the contrast between Greek and native ("Lelegian") settlement patterns in Asia Minor, where even in the interior the Greeks developed centralized polis communities focused on a fortified *asty,* whereas the natives lived scattered in villages and farmsteads. Cook 1982, p. 753, comments that "the Ionians' addiction to city life and development of its potentialities must have been an important factor in the historical evolution of ancient Greek life."

2. On the ancestry of epic see Kirk 1984, pp. 1–19, who points out that epic unquestionably developed in the offshore islands and served as a cultural beacon to the mainland. See Kirk 1962, pp. 105–25 or 1976, pp. 22–36, on the difficulties of postulating a Mycenean epic tradition proper; the possibility must be allowed that oral poetry was post-Mycenean, migrating with survivor groups from the mainland after 1000 B.C. (contemporary with Attic Protogeometric pottery). West 1988 sees the distant origins of Greek epic in Vedic poetry; Chadwick 1990 notes, with others, that dactylic hexameter accommodates Mycenean Greek and argues for its Mycenean Greek origin. Yet it seems counterintuitive to posit the transmission of stories about Mycenean rulers and heroes as simple prose

tales, given the priority of poetry to prose in the Greek literary tradition.

3. The question of whether the Homeric poems depict a society that once existed is insoluble. See Long 1970, pp. 122–23 versus Adkins 1960, chs. 2–3. The *internal coherence* of the poems' social, economic, and moral world is, however, demonstrable: cf. Adkins 1960; Finley, 1979; Rose 1975 on evidence in the *Odyssey* for social struggles in the seventh century; Strasburger 1953; Thomas 1966. Thucydides (1.2–12) and Aristotle (*Pol.* 1285a3ff) exemplify the Greeks' own recognition of the coherence of the society of the epos.

4. E.g., Momigliano 1975a, p. 15; lately, Hall 1989, pp. 13–40, on the *Iliad* and early poetic literature generally.

5. Mellink 1991, pp. 664–65, sums up:

> Archaeologically the study of Caria confronts the same problem as encountered in Lydia, that of separating Carian from Greek material. The Carians forcibly intermingled with Greek newcomers in the Bronze Age and Iron Age. . . . In the Iron Age at Iasus, the levels of Protogeometric and Geometric periods show such strong Greek traits that the native elements remain obscure. Even inland sites such as Lagina and Beçin near Mylasa show this Hellenized aspect. Native sites are the "Lelegian" protected farmsteads investigated in the Bodrum [Halicarnassus] peninsula and similar buildings near Iasus, but these are rural establishments, not the residences of the leading Carian families.

6. See *LSJ*[9] s.vv. *nastêr, nastês*.

7. Noted by Hall 1989, p. 9, n. 30. Thucydides remarks (1.3.3) that Homer did not use the term "barbaros." Cf. Dörrie 1972, p. 148, on the word's objective use here: the poet means only that the Carians did not speak Greek; the ethical treatment lies only in the description of Nastes—which in itself may have prompted the later substitution of *barbarophônoi* for *karterothumoi*.

8. On the literary tradition concerning the Carians, see Aly 1909, esp. pp. 431–32 on Homer and Archilochus. The Carians were considered non-Greek from Homer onward, but were assimilated in Greek genealogy and religion (e.g., in the worship of Zeus Carius: p. 429), as Carians and Leleges came to be assimilated into Ionian society: pp. 438–44. Cf. Cassola 1957 on the Carians' origins in the Greek mind as a mixture of Cretan and autochthonous elements. They were, on the Cretan side, pre-Greek or "Pelasgian," rather than an altogether unrelated people. By the fifth century their elites were largely Hellenized: see Hornblower 1982 and Robert 1953. On the penetration of Greek language and culture among the peasantry see my later discussion of the native Gergithes at Miletus and the Troad.

9. Pherecydes (*FGrH* 3 F 15 = Strabo 14.1.3 C632–33) includes

Ephesus as well: the Ephesians' first settlement occupied the heights above the later city. Miletus and Old Smyrna were fortified by *c.* 900: Coldstream 1977, pp. 303, 314; Nicholls 1958–59.

10. Berve 1967, 1:101–2, 2:579; treated by Robertson 1987, pp. 373–78.

11. See later discussion in this chapter.

12. Archilochus, fr. 24 D; cf. Ephorus *FGrH* F 12 with Cassola 1957.

13. Demonstrated by onomastic evidence. Note Histiaeus son of Tymnes, tyrant of Carian Termera at the end of the sixth century (Hdt. 5.37.1), and Heracleides son of Ibanollis, son of the deposed tyrant of Mylasa, who led the Carians in alliance with the Milesians during the Ionian Revolt (Hdt. 5.37.1 and 121). Their names indicate dynastic alliances with leading Ionian, probably Milesian, families, and presuppose bilingualism.

14. According to tradition, Clazomenae was founded by Ionians under a *ktistes* from Colophon (Paus. 7.3.5). Exiles from Colophon appropriated Smyrna, whose people resettled in the Aeolis (Hdt. 1.150.1). Mimnermus sings that his people set out from Pylos the city of Neleus (i.e., Nestor's Pylos in Messene) to Asia, where they took Colophon by force under their Pylian *ktistes* Andraemon (fr. 9 Bergk) and dominated the (native) inhabitants; then they took Smyrna from the Aeolians. Greek tradition put the Aeolian migration earlier than the Ionian (Pherecydes *ap.* Strabo 14.1.3 C632 *fin.* = *FGrH* 3 F 155).

A later, and apparently confused, tradition recalls that the site was originally inhabited by Leleges, who were driven out by Greeks from Ephesus (also called Smyrna in early times), who were in turn driven out by Aeolians. The Smyrnaeans then took refuge at Colophon and with Colophonians recovered their city: Strabo 14.1.4 C634–35. Strabo's authority is Mimnermus fr. 9, but Mimnermus agrees with Herodotus.

15. Bilabel 1920, pp. 209ff (inscriptions and commentary). Cf. Picard 1922, index s.v. "Héraclides lydiens (Sandonides)." On Claros' and Colophon's possible connections with a native Cilician "house of Mopsus" at Karatepe, see Parke 1985, pp. 112–19.

16. Plut. *Lysander* 2.2 is emphatic for the later fifth century. But Ephesus had been part of the Lydian kings' sphere from early in the archaic period; see n. 17.

17. Berve 1967, 1:98–100, 2:576–77.

18. Lydians: A phratry named *Tylonioi* existed at Miletus; this was the native name of the Lydian Heraclids: Huxley 1966, n. 81 on p. 202, citing L. Robert, *Gnomon* 31 (1959), p. 673. In the list of *Stephanophoroi* of Apollo of Didyma appears the Lydian royal name

Sadyattes: *Milet* 1.3, no. 122, lines 55, 108. Carians: see above, n. 5. The foundation legends and other testimonies reflecting miscegenation and cultural syncretism in Miletus and the rest of Ionia are collected by Sakellariou 1958, esp. pp. 414–37; cf. Huxley 1966, pp. 15–39.

19. Hdt. 5.122.2 and 7.43.2; Suda s.v. *Gergithes;* Strabo 13.1.19 C598; cf. Leaf 1923, p. 102.
20. Kleiner 1966, pp. 14–26.
21. One of them may have been the aristocratic *genos* of Thales the philosopher, a contemporary of these events, who claimed "Phoenician" descent from the heroes Cadmus and Agenor. His claim clearly glosses a more prosaic foreign origin, since Thales' father bore the Carian name of Examyes: Sakellariou 1958, p. 368.
22. Discussion in Berve 1967. On pre-Greek Didyma and the non-Greek eponym Branchus see Parke 1985, pp. 3–7.
23. The *Bennaioi* or *Bembinaioi, Euonymoi, Karêneioi;* the others were the *Ephesioi* (evidently the original inhabitants) and *Têioi,* settlers from Teos: Ephorus *FGrH* 70 F 126. Huxley 1966, p. 33, mistakenly suggests the tribal reform, in which the original Ionian tribes were submerged, took place under the tyrant Pythagoras, *c.* 600. It was carried out not long before the Persian conquest under an Athenian *aisymnêtês* named Aristarchus: Suda, s.v. *Aristarkhos.*
24. Sakellariou 1958, p. 67, notes that the name recurs as that of tribal divisions at Ephesus and Samos and suggests that it became attached to "un ou plusieurs éléments égéens" incorporated into the body politic in some Ionian towns.
25. Huxley 1966, p. 32, with nn. 118–25. Other assimilations of natives into civic tribes: Roebuck 1961. A "Boreis" tribe also existed at the Samian colony of Perinthus; Sakellariou 1958, pp. 73–74 and 104, concludes that the tribal name refers at both places to Thessalians, not non-Greek foreigners, on the grounds that a cult to Poseidon Enipeus, believed to be originally Thessalian, existed at Miletus. But if they were identifiably Thessalians, or for that matter any other kind of Greek, why call them by the vague collective "Northerners"?
26. Hunt 1947.
27. Comparative material and complete references for all the Ionian cities in Sakellariou 1958, pp. 361–410 and 414–34; Picard 1922, pp. 539–54. These cities' relations with the Lydian Heraclids are discussed later in this chapter.
28. Hdt. 1.147.2; Sakellariou 1958, p. 251–52.
29. Gusmani 1980–86, p. 34, s.v. *artimu-.* Pherecydes of Athens *FGrH* 3 F 155 = Strabo 14.1.3, an early testimony: Jacoby 1947a would put him between 508 and 476; Nilsson 1955, p. 481; Hanfmann

1958, p. 65 and 81, n. 4. In Pausanias' day the foundation legend of Ephesus and the Artemisium still related that Androclus "expelled from the country the Leleges and the Lydians who inhabited the citadel. But those who dwelt round the sanctuary [of Artemis] had nothing to fear; they plighted faith with the Ionians and were left in peace" (Paus. 7.2.4–5, trans. Frazer, adapted).

30. Roebuck 1955, p. 35.
31. These relations are discussed later in this chapter; see also n. 90.
32. Gusmani 1980–86, p. 39.
33. Strabo 13.4.14 C629; cf. Calder and Bean 1958.
34. Hesychius s.v. *Bakkhiadai*; cf. Hdt. 5.92β1; Will 1955, pp. 295ff; Sakellariou 1958, pp. 44–45.
35. The early Corinthian poet Eumelus (*FGrH* 451: fl. 730?), by tradition a Bacchiad, is the most probable source. His epic *Corinthiaca* told the story of the city at least as far as the kings Sisyphus (F 4) and Glaucus (F 6), respectively the grandfather and father of Bellerophontes.
36. See Prinz 1979, pp. 107–11.
37. On Delphi and Didyma see later discussion and nn. 66ff.
38. *Ap.* Strabo 14.4.3 C668 *init.* Malkin 1987, p. 19, n. 20, links Callinus' version in Strabo and Delphian Apollo, thus concluding (against Defradas 1954) that "the Pythian Apollo was already conceived of as a god of colonization" in the early seventh century. However, there is no trace of Delphian Apollo to be found in Strabo's brief notice, which cannot be securely related to Pausanias' version.
39. Strabo 14.1.27 C642f = Hesiod fr. 278 MW. Cf. Prinz 1979, pp. 16–28.
40. Sakellariou 1958, pp. 25–26 traces the belief that the Ionian cities were founded by Neleid royalty from Athens no further back than Panyassis' *Ionica,* written in the early fifth century. It became a stock theme of Athens' imperial propaganda thereafter, but undoubtedly the belief predated the empire: see Meiggs 1972, pp. 294–96. Solon, fr. 4 D = Arist. *AP* 5.2, calls Attica "the oldest land of Ionia." Also, the archaic sanctuary of Athena at Miletus lay within the area of the earliest post-Mycenean settlement, indicating that it was the principal cult of the first settlers, whereas the shrine of Apollo Delphinius, the city's other principal recipient of cult, seems not to be pre-Persian; the earliest remains so far found are later than the fifth century: Kleiner 1966, p. 17; Kleiner 1976, p. 580. The Protogeometric poetry of the Milesiad and the Halicarnassian peninsula, of the tenth or even the eleventh century, seems closely related to that of Athens: Snodgrass 1971, p. 67 with n. 45.

41. Goldman 1923; Holland 1944, pp. 91 and 94; Coldstream 1977, p. 97.
42. Later coins of Telmessus bear the head of Apollo: Head 1911, p. 698.
43. *FGrH* 90 F 16 with Xanthus 765 F 17a. On Mopsus see Hanfmann 1958, pp. 72ff, and Barnett 1953, pp. 141–43, with Parke 1985, pp. 112–19. The Mopsus of the Colophonian foundation legend may refer to a native Cilician "house of Mopsus" ruling at Karatepe at about the date of the Mycenean tholos tomb at Colophon. Meles: Hdt. 1.84.3 and Nic. Dam *FGrH* 90 F 45 (independently of Xanthus). On Nicolaus' dependence on Xanthus through a Hellenistic intermediary see von Fritz 1967 i.2, pp. 348–77.
44. Bilabel 1920, pp. 209ff. On the actual pre-Hellenic background of the shrine see above, n. 43, and Picard 1922, pp. 539ff. Picard notes (pp. 198–202) that the Heraclid Ti. Claudius Ardys served as the high temple official, the *thespiôidês,* for at least ten years and concludes that the priesthood was a life appointment (p. 211) as were the priesthoods of the Milesian Branchidae, a clan which continued to preserve a hereditary right to the office of *thespiôidês* at Didyma into the Roman imperial era (p. 212).
45. Chapter 5, Appendix "Pelasgians, Leleges, Caucones."
46. Hall 1989, p. 11 and index s.v. "Troy, Trojans."
47. Callimachus, *Epigram* 6 Pfeiffer.
48. Also a Thessalian place-name, later Crannon: Pindar *Pyth.* 10.55; an early name for Corinth as well: *Il.* 6.152; Eumelus (?) *ap.* Paus. 2.1.1. On Tlepolemus see Prinz 1979, pp. 78–94, with stemma on p. 80.
49. Teucrus' much stronger identity in myth is as the founder of Cypriote Salamis, which Nilsson 1951, pp. 64–65, would connect with Athens' interest in Cyprus after 478.
50. Apollodorus (2.103ff) names Teucrus' mother as the Trojan princess Hesione, given to Telamon by Heracles when they had sacked the city of Laomedon in the previous generation. Also in Servius *Ad Aen.* 8.157 Danielis and schol. *Il.* 20.145ff.
51. Cf. Hdt. 1.7.3; 7.74.1.
52. *Palmys* becomes naturalized to the Ionian dialect in the lyrics of the Lydianizing seventh-century poet Hipponax of Ephesus (1.15 Bergk); Gusmani 1980–86, p. 82; *galmlu-*.
53. Huxley 1957, p. 211; cf. How and Wells 1912 1:439: *c.* 1280. The Lydians themselves traced the dynasty's foundation to a native hero, Tylon (Nic. Dam. *FGrH* 90 F 45), whom the Greeks then identified with Heracles: Balcer 1984, p. 34 with n. 7.
54. The *omphalos* proper was the stone within the temple that was

believed to mark the center of the earth; but the poets used the word as a synonym for Delphi: *LSJ*⁹ s.v., III.1. Matthews 1974, p. 98, observes that the Heracles-Omphale story was so widely known in the fifth century (Pherecydes *FGrH* 3 F 82b; Hellanicus *FGrH* 4 F 112; Soph. *Trach.* 248ff) that Panyassis is far more likely to have been using the traditional story than making up a new one.

55. Schwabl 1962, pp. 19–23.
56. Archilochus, fr. 25.1 Bergk; cf. *Il.* 9.46.
57. Hanfmann and Mierse 1983, pp. 24–25, with bibliography in nn. 24–40. Ramage 1987, pp. 6–15, on the constant presence of Greek pottery at Iron Age Sardis. Mellink 1991, 648–54.
58. Ramage, esp. 75.
59. Balcer 1984, pp. 34–39, 60–69.
60. This conclusion emerges from chs. 2 and 3 of Balcer 1984, although it contradicts Balcer's own thesis that Greek encroachment on Lydian estates prompted the Lydian nobility, led by Gyges, to overthrow the Heraclids. He may be on firmer ground in blaming Phrygian encroachment (p. 34; cf. p. 73).
61. Page 1955, pp. 54–55, 226ff on Sappho. frs. 16, 96, 98, and Alcaeus D11. Lydian musical forms and instruments in archaic Lesbos: Comotti 1989, pp. 18–20.
62. Cf. Balcer 1984, pp. 50ff.
63. Communications between Sardis, inland Anatolia, and the Ionian ports: Birmingham 1961; Calder 1925. Calder and Bean 1958 provide a detailed picture of the road network in the Roman period.
64. Balcer 1984, pp. 46ff.
65. Flower 1991, p. 61 with n. 27. Self-immolation is attested in the ancient orient. See Burkert 1985b, pp. 8–10, for the evidence; he concludes that Croesus did burn himself, as reflected in Bacchylides, whose version solves the problem of Apolline theodicy raised by his fate, which was also addressed in another way by Herodotus (1.91). Burkert compares the "realism" of Herodotus' account of Croesus' salvation to the scene of the empty tomb in the Gospel of Mark, "where the forcibly displaced stone provides a dimension of realism" (p. 14). Cf. Evans 1978.
66. For a survey of opinion on the question of Delphi's early reputation abroad see Malkin 1987, pp. 18–22. Forrest 1957 (supported by Malkin, pp. 22–91) would deny the thesis of Defrades 1954, that the colonization oracles supporting the widely repeated assumption of Delphi's early rise to international prominence are fictions. But Forrest himself later (1982) notes that "Delphi before 600 was by no means an exclusively Dorian sanctuary but there is a strong Dorian flavour to it."

I am persuaded that Defrades is correct, especially concerning Ionia, where Delian Apollo spoke from Didyma and Claros, but the point is not vital. What "international" reputation Delphi may have achieved in the seventh century would have been due almost entirely to Corinth's early patronage of Delphi and to the activities of her merchants: see Coldstream 1977, pp. 178–79 and 186–87). At Smyrna the earliest Corinthian pottery dates to perhaps 730, contemporary with the earliest Sicilian foundations: Anderson 1958–59, p. 139 with n. 16. Some foreigners passing through Corinth must be presumed to have made the pilgrimage to Delphi, but there are no grounds on which to postulate a swelling traffic to the shrine from all corners of the Greek world in this period, let alone from Ionia with her native oracles of ancient prestige.

67. Ammon: Cook 1914–40 1:346ff; Parke 1967, ch. 9. Ammon was an Egyptian oracle of Amun which entered the Hellenic sphere through the patronage of the Cyrenaeans: Chamoux 1953, pp. 167, 240, 331–39. The major oracular shrines in Greek Asia Minor were Milesian Didyma (Herodotus' "Branchidae"), Telmessus in Lycia (or Caria: cf. Parke 1985, pp. 184–85), and Claros in Colophon. The first two play important roles in Herodotus' Lydian and Ionian narratives (*Branchidae:* 1.46.2, 92.2; cf. 5.36.3–4 and 6.19.3; 1.157–59; 5.36. *Telmessus:* 1.78.2–3 and 84.3). Claros is not mentioned at all by Herodotus and is much less visible in the archaic tradition: *Hom. Hymn* to Apollo 3.40; to Artemis 9.5: the latter, perfunctory hymn suggests that Claros was overshadowed by the great shrine to Artemis at nearby Ephesus (cf. Picard 1922, pp. 45ff).

   At Didyma, the first temple has been dated to the eighth or early seventh century. Temple II, begun *c.* 550–540, was the first monumental temple on the site. Like the slightly older Artemisium it was probably begun with Mermnad aid, and like the Artemisium it was built on a scale emulating the great Samian Heraeum of *c.* 570. By contrast, Delphi did not receive a comparable edifice before the late sixth century (Parke 1985, pp. 24ff with Tuchelt 1976 and Roux 1976). The earliest habitation site associated with the area of the Apollo sanctuary dates only from the last quarter of the seventh century: Lerat 1961, pp. 352–53.

68. Amandry 1939, 1944–45, and 1962. See Rolley 1969 for objects of ivory, chryselephantine, and gold of seventh-sixth century dates. But these obviously could have been imported by Corinthian or other continental Greek traders.

69. Based on an examination of the exhaustive Catalogue of Delphic Responses in Fontenrose 1978, pp. 240–429. Note *Hom. Hymm* 3 to Apollo, where the situation in the archaic period is epitomized

in the mutual exclusivity of the (originally separate) parts, to Delian and Pythian Apollo respectively: the first part is Ionian (schol. Pindar *Nem.* 2.2: Cynaethus of Chios: fl. *c.* 504–501) and the second continental in composition. Lesky 1966, pp. 86–87 assigns both parts a seventh-century date; also Wade-Gery 1952, p. 21.

70. Accordingly, Parke 1985 postulates for Milesian Didyma an oracular role in the colonization of the Black Sea, which was dominated by Miletus.

71. The single exception concerns the building of the archaic Artemisium, to which Croesus largely contributed, but inasmuch as the Mermnads were heavily involved with Delphi, as well as in Ephesian affairs and in the building of the Artemisium itself, this is an *exceptio probans regulam.*

   The story goes that Pythagoras, tyrant of Ephesus *c.* 600, claimed a response from Delphi in a time of plague and famine, and from fear for his own position, to build a temple and bury the dead: Baton of Sinope (*FGrH* 268 F 3: third century B.C. = Q82 Fontenrose), who is a good source, despite Fontenrose's disclaimer (1978, p. 76, n. 33). Cf. Hdt. 1.19.3 and 22.4 = Q98 Fontenrose, where Alyattes of Lydia built two shrines in the Milesiad in obedience to Delphi. The Artemisium at Ephesus was probably begun in his reign and finished in that of Croesus.

72. On the first Sacred War see Cadoux 1948, pp. 99–101; Forrest 1956. The first attested victors (Paus. 10.7.3) were from Cephallenia, Arcadia, and Argos (586 B.C.); Tegea (578); Phlius and Heraea (536).

73. *Il.* 2.519, 9.404-5; often considered a late passage; likewise *Od.* 8.80, 11.581; also Hesiod *Theog.* 497–500, Tyrtaeus 4.1.

74. Morgan 1990, pp. 125–34. Deposits of local Geometric pottery are copious from the early eighth century: Lerat 1961, pp. 352–53.

75. Below, n. 82. Mercenaries: Hdt. 2.152.3-4; cf. Austin 1970, p. 17, and Kienitz 1953, pp. 12 and 37–44. Psammetichus' Ionian and Carian mercenaries may have been sent to him by Gyges: Kaletsch 1958, p. 29.

76. Drews 1972 argues cogently that the essential condition for tyranny was fulfilled when mercenaries arose in the Greek world with the development of expensive, but superior, hoplite armor and tactics, and suggests (pp. 142–43 with n. 61) that Gyges invented the precursor of true coinage to pay the troops with which he carried out his usurpation. His coup may have been imitated by Pheidon of Argos in 668 (p. 143 with n. 63; for the date see Hammond 1960, pp. 33ff, followed by Psamtik I in Egypt *c.* 663, Cypselus at Corinth *c.* 655), and Theagenes at Megara *c.* 640.

77. See above, n. 43.

78. Picard 1922, p. x–xvii, 11ff, 45ff, 329ff, 419ff, 539ff; above, n. 65.
79. See Picard 1922, pp. 597–606.
80. Hdt. 7.103; How and Wells 1912, 2:270.
81. Hanfmann 1958, pp. 65 and 81, n. 4; Nilsson 1955, p. 481.
82. This attachment encouraged a strong bent toward the survival of the monarchy at Ephesus, to the extent that the Ephesian kings evolved into tyrants during the succeeding Mermnad dynasty. What remains of Ephesian history during the archaic period is in fact little more than the memory of successive Basilid rulers and their rivals for the tyranny, interrupted briefly by the government of *aisymnêtai*. The Ephesian tyrannies were sufficiently famous to attract the attention of a third-century B.C. historian, Baton of Sinope, who wrote a monograph *On the Tyrannoi of Ephesus (FGrH* 268 FF 2–3 with *Komm.)*
83. Athenaeus *Deipn.* 525c. Nic. Dam. 90 F 62 furnishes a *casus belli*. The Magnesians were said to have been incensed by the shame of the appropriation of their women by a Smyrnaean poet, Magnes, who was Gyges' lover. They retaliated by mutilating the poet on the pretense that Magnes had celebrated the Lydians' feats rather than their own in an epic poem (another instance, incidentally, of the Lydians' assimilation into legend as "part of the family"). In revenge, Gyges took Magnesia. Whatever the story's origin—which must be placed before Alyattes' destruction of Magnes' city of Smyrna *c.* 600 (Hdt. 1.16.2; cf. Strasburger 1956, pp. 139–40)—its real value lies in its assumption once again of easy and intimate personal relations between contemporary Greeks and Lydians within a common culture.
84. A necessary interference from Nic. Dam. 90 F 63.2 with 1.
85. The Cimmerians are known to have invaded Asia Minor early in Gyges' reign: Kaletsch 1958, p. 20 on Strabo 13. 1.40 C647 (cf. 13.4.8 C627); cf. Hartmann 1962; Cogan and Tadmor 1977, esp. p. 84, reconstruct the history of this period from the Assyrian documents: Gyges became a vassal of Ashurbanipal in the 660s against the Cimmerians but renounced his allegiance and allied himself with Psammetichus I; whereupon the Cimmerians (now allied with Ashurbanipal) overran Western Asia as far as Ephesus. Ardys sought Assyrian protection once more and with their help was able to turn back the enemy during the 640s.
86. Sources and bibliography: Huxley 1966, pp. 53–54 and nn. 58–81; cf. Balcer 1985, pp. 43ff.
87. Discussed later in this chapter.
88. Aelian *VH* 3.26. Probably during Sadyattes' persecution of the Basilids, a non-Basilid named Pythagoras had been able to take power

at Ephesus; he massacred many of the Basilids (Baton *FGrH* 268 F 3). But, with his family's Mermnad connection restored, Melas II promoted his family's ancient prerogatives into a tyranny.

89. Hdt. 1.26.1-2; cf. Polyaenus 6.50.

90. Aelian *VH* 3.26; Cf. Polyaenus 6.50. His name was Pasicles. On his Basilid descent and fate (he was assassinated by personal enemies) see Stroux 1934, pp. 310ff. The Basilids survived into Strabo's day, still enjoying their traditional prerogatives, including purple regalia and scepter, and the rites of Eleusinian Demeter (Strabo 14.1.3 C633); cf. Roebuck 1953, p. 35. The strength and antiquity of the Basilids' ties to the Lydian monarchy are attested by the dynastic name Melas, a form of Meles, the name of the Heraclid king remembered as the fortifier of the Sardis acropolis (Hdt. 1.84.3). His name is *Mêlês* in Herodotus and Nic. Dam. (FF 16, 45), but *Melas* in Aelian *VH* 3.26; Hipponax fr. 40 Diehl also mentions the name of a Lydian god *Malis*.

91. Strabo 14.1.21 C640.

92. For Croesus' contribution to the Artemisium see Bammer 1972, pp. 6ff; Lydian electrum coins in the foundation deposit and elsewhere in the temple: Head 1908 and S. Robinson 1951, pp. 85ff; inscribed column dedications: Tod i² 6.

93. Above, n. 90.

94. The Ephesians sent to Athens for this man, a certain Aristarchus, who instituted a tribal reform while ruling Ephesus with monarchical powers for five years before the Persian conquest (Suda s.v. *Aristarkhos*). Tribal reform is an unmistakable symptom of a social revolution that brings new groups into the community. Ephorus (*FGrH* 70 F 126) gives the Ephesian tribal names in his time: Ephesians, Teans, Bennaeans or Bembinaeans, Euonymoi and Carenians (= Carians?). The last three tribes must be foreign, since the original Ionian tribal names survived as subdivisions of the Ephesian tribe: Keil 1913. The Teans may have been refugees from the Persian conquest: see Hdt. 1.168. Aristarchus may well have been sponsored by Croesus, since the latest Mermnads cultivated close links with prominent Athenians.

95. The only other known Ionian harem connection with the Lydian court is the Milesian wife of a son of Alyattes. Any son of theirs would have been Croesus' nephew, not half-brother, and as a grandson of Alyattes not in the line of succession since Alyattes' sons took precedence.

96. Hdt. 1.92.2-3; cf. Nic. Dam. 90 F 65.2-4.

97. Hdt. 1.92.3-4. Cf. Berve 1967, 2:577.

98. Above, n. 44.

99. Polyaenus 7.2; cf. Heraclides Ponticus *FHG* ii 218 (fr. 22).
100. Mazzarino 1947, pp. 194–95 with n. 547; Talamo 1973, pp. 343–44. The hippotrophoi cultivated Lydian fashions even before Alyattes' conquest: Xenophanes fr. 3 Diehl. Cf. Bowra 1941 and Lesky 1966, pp. 208-9. On the political domination of Colophon (and also Smyrna and Aeolian Cyme), see the interpretation of Talamo 1973, who believes that the Mermnads encouraged or supported popular revolutions in those cities.
101. Smyrna was originally Aeolian but was conquered and repopulated by the Colophonians: Huxley 1966, p. 47, citing Hdt. 1.150 with 1.143.3 and Mimnermus F 12.6 Diehl.
102. Hdt. 1.16.2; cf. Pausanias 7.3.5 Huxley 1966, p. 28.
103. Heraclids at Miletus: above, n. 13. Picard 1922, p. 410, believes that the cult of Heracles at Claros and at Branchidae (Pausanias 5.13.11) was originated by the Lydian Heraclids.
104. Graham in *CAH*² iii. 3, p. 121; Burstein 1974, p. 16.
105. Strabo 13.1.22 C590. At Troy nearby the earliest datable sherds are Rhodian bird kotyles *c.* 720-700, but evidence of organized settlement does not appear until after the fall of the Phrygian kingdom: Blegen et al. pp. 247–48 with Coldstream 1968, p. 376, on Troy VIII.
106. Akurgal 1956 reported Subgeometric, Protocorinthian, and Orientalizing sherds from soundings, in his opinion indicating the beginnings of Greek settlement at Cyzicus from the end of the eighth century. But the circuit wall itself is only late archaic. (Eusebius' foundation dates are 756 and 679: the first foundation was said to have been destroyed by the Cimmerians.) Similar pottery finds at Dascyleium, a center that was Phrygian, Lydian, and Persian in turn, probably indicate the early presence of Greek mercenaries and their market.
107. Tylonids: above, n. 13.
108. Finds in Sinope do not indicate a Greek presence before 600: Boardman in *AR* 1962–63, pp. 50–51. The literary tradition names two Milesian *ktistai* who are said to have revived an early settlement after its destruction by the Cimmerians (Pseudo-Scymnus 992ff Diller). Against the archaeological indications, Drews 1976 defends the mid-eighth-century dates for Sinope and Cyzicus from the Eusebian chronographic tradition; but these dates, together with the tale of the Argonauts, probably reflect early interest and exploration of these coasts carried on in the aftermath of the post-Mycenean Aeolian diaspora eastward. Emporia did not always survive to grow into poleis.
109. The Lydian prince's name was Sadyattes, named after his grandfather

Sadyattes the king. Nicolaus (F 63.3) even names him instead of Croesus as the successor to Alyattes. The list of Milesian aesymnetae of the Molpoi also lists a Callithemis son of Sadyattes in 472/1, a Sadyattes son of Callithemis in 419/8, and a Deilochus son of Sadyattes in 363/2: Mazzarino 1947, pp. 192ff.

Alyattes' isolated war against Priene late in his reign now receives a context: the Milesians and Samians also fought a war against the Prienians in the time of Bias, but like Alyattes they were unable to take the city (Plut. *QG* 20; cf. Huxley 1966, p. 87 and n. 70). It is therefore likely that our separate sources speak of one war, waged by Lydians in alliance with those Greeks whose territories abutted, and who coveted, the lands of Priene. Priene lay between the Milesiad and the *peraia* of the Samians around Cape Mycale, which also was bounded by the territory of Magnesia-on-the-Maeander (Shipley 1987, pp. 31ff). This history apparently repeated itself at the time of the Persian conquest, when the Persians made an alliance with Miletus and then attacked Priene and Magnesia. Until the defection of his fleet from Cambyses' Egyptian campaign, Polycrates of Samos was also on good terms with the Persians.

110. Salmon 1984, pp. 84–89; decorated Corinthian pottery votives appear in large quantity after *c.* 750. From *c.* 650 onward more than 70 percent of the tiles and architectural terracottas from the site are Corinthian. Salmon comments (p. 120): "Almost every building in Delphi, if it had clay and not marble tiles, was roofed by Corinthians." Also much building stone, including that of Cypselus' treasury, came from the Corinthiad, and probably wood as well (p. 124).

111. Will 1955, p. 542, n. 2.

112. Salmon 1984, p. 219.

113. Ibid., pp. 185–87; 218; Morgan 1990, pp. 178–83. On the oracle's political *modus operandi* see Georges 1986, pp. 31–37.

114. Cf. Arist. *Pol.* 1314b–1315a: "Men are less afraid of being treated unjustly by a ruler, when they think that he is god-fearing and pays some regard to the gods; and they are less ready to conspire against him, if they feel that the gods themselves are his friends" (trans. Barker).

115. Cypselus claimed an equally ancient and heroic descent through his father's lineage from the invulnerable Thessalian hero Caeneus the Lapith (Hdt. 5.92β1; cf. *Il.* 1.263–73, 738–46).

116. Hdt. 5.67.3 = Q73 Fontenrose 1978.

117. *Ap.* Eus. *PE* 5.35 p. 235b, cited by Fontenrose 1978, p. 288.

118. Georges 1986, p. 36, where I argue that "Delphi was patronized by an exclusive clientele of states and individuals for the purpose of receiving, or advertising, divine sanction for their plans or policies.

The mantic session . . . was private [and it was thus possible] to impute anything not shameful to the Pythia with impunity."

119. Salmon 1984, p. 186 with n. 1: *c*. 655. Sealey 1976, pp. 53–54 with discussion of the evidentiary problems: *c*. 635 at the latest. The lower chronology is supported by the early evidence of Herodotus and the date of the treasury at Delphi and the temple to Apollo at Corinth attributed to Cypselus. The higher chronology is supported by the elevation to the archonship at Athens of Cypselus' grandson, also named Cypselus (he was almost certainly the father of Miltiades I) in 597: *SGHI* no. 6, commentary on p. 11.

120. Radet 1893, pp. 80–85.

121. Above, n. 74.

122. Salmon, pp. 107–8; Hanfmann and Mierse 1983, p. 28: In Level III (700-650), which shows the first evidence of a growth of material prosperity at Sardis, Corinthian wares replace Rhodian and Cycladic, to the extent that "subsequent Lydian shapes seem clearly related to Corinthian models."

123. See Hdt. 5.95, where Periander is said to have arbitrated between Athens and Mytilene concerning Athens' possession of Sigeum in the Troad (cf. 3.48.2 on his intended gift of 300 youths to Alyattes for castration). It is unlikely that Periander could have dealt with a case within the Lydian kingdom and important to Sardis' interests if he was not also trusted by Alyattes. (The chronological problems raised by Herodotus' account are done away with by Page 1955, pp. 154–55, with a correct translation of Hdt. 5.94.1–2.)

124. A view long maintained but now assessed critically; see Malkin 1987.

125. "Tyrannis" and its cognates are certainly Anatolian, but not necessarily Lydian, in origin (despite the attractive but probably misleading resemblance to "Tyrsenos," "Tyrrhenos"): Berve 1967, 1: 3ff, 2:517–18. Known Lydian words for monarch are (1) *palmys* (Hipponax fr. 1.15 Bergk; glossed by Tzetzes *Chil.* 5.546 as *basileus ho sumpas,* confirmed by its use as an epithet for Zeus: Lycophron 691), which first appears as the name of an Ascanian warrior in the *Iliad* (13.792); (2) *lailas: ho mê ek genous basileus,* i.e., "tyrant," in the late lexicographers: Gusmani 1980–86, s.vv. Cf. Berve 1967, 1:89.

126. Above, n. 100.

127. Herodotus (6.125) names Croesus but Alcmaeon was Alyattes' contemporary; in the story as Herodotus heard it Croesus had eclipsed his father's memory.

128. See Herman 1987, pp. 19–21, on the Athenian Croesus, whose tomb dates to some time before 500.

129. *ARFP*^{2} i.238 = Louvre G 197; see discussion in chapter 5.

130. Mazzarino 1947, p. 18, on the "Graeco-Lydian cultural *koinê* in Asia Minor," and pp. 180–81, 236ff, on the *habrosynê* of Ionia and Sardis, cross-fertilized by mutual imitation. Mazzarino wrote before the excavations at Sardis fully confirmed, from the Geometric pottery sequence onward, the virtual identity of material life at the top between Sardis and Ionia. Pedley 1968 summarizes conveniently: evidence of wealth does not appear before Gyges, for whom the first of the great royal tumuli was erected (pp. 43 and 63ff); the crop of sixth-century stone architectural fragments excavated "is purely Greek and speaks forcefully for the existence in the reign of Croesus of a court school of architects and sculptors active in Sardis," and the image of Cybele from the archaic temple possesses "unmistakable and pronounced" affinities with the products of the contemporary workshops of Samos (pp. 101–2). For a detailed summary see Pedley's ch. 5, "The Arts of Lydia." On Greco-Lydian music, see pp. 113ff and Plut. *De musica* 16 (= *Mor..* 1136c); cf. *OCD*[2] "Music."

131. Fr. 3D. See Bowra 1941.

132. *On Airs Waters Places* 12 and 16; cf. Arist. *Pol.* 1327b. Backhaus 1976. In this book I use "Asianic" in reference to the character or quality of Asiatic barbarism in the Greek mind, since barbarism occurred on both sides of the Aegean. "Asiatic" denotes geographic location.

133. Conspicuously in the camp at Lade: 6.11–12.

134. Powell *Lexicon* s.vv. *tyranneuô, tyrannis, tyrannos;* cf. Ferrill 1978 and Hartog 1988, pp. 200, 324–25.

135. See Lateiner 1989, table on "The Characteristics of Autocrats and Their Illustration in the *Histories* of Herodotus," pp. 172–79.

136. The Egyptians likewise established twelve kings over themselves although they were free at the time, "since they were unable to conduct their lives without a king for any duration at all" (Hdt. 2. 147.2). The best and earliest *comparandum* to the Deioces story is the group of village elders who are pictured publicly adjudicating the end of a vendetta in the *orbis parva* of Achilles' shield (*Il.* 18. 497–508).

137. See chapter 5.

138. Hornblower 1982, pp. 1–77.

139. Diesner 1959a. In Herodotus all but one of the seven uses of *megaloprepeiê* and its cognates refer to autocrats or their actions: Powell, *Lexicon* s.vv.

140. On chronological grounds: see Evans 1978. Solon was archon in 594/3 (Cadoux 1948, pp. 93–99), and Arist. *AP* (5.2) regards his reform as the outcome of his archonship, but a case has been made for putting his work in the 570s, which would provide a chronological window

for this encounter; the argument is conveniently set out in Sealey 1976, pp. 121–23, with n. 6. See now Wallace 1986 for a restatement of the older view based on the Aristotelian *AP* and detailed bibliography on the history of the question.

141. Two talents yearly instead of one hundred minas: Hdt. 3.131.2.
142. On the great Heraeum (3.60.2-3), built to rival the Artemisium at Ephesus, and the palace of Polycrates see Berve 1967, 1:585, for sources, and 2:111–12 on "der luxuriöse Hofhalt des Tyrannen" influenced by Sardis, and in turn influencing the "Musenhof" of the Pisistratid Hipparchus, which Berve thinks had as its example the Samian *tyrannis*. (Doubts concerning the extent of Polycrates' wealth and building activity have been raised: see Barron 1966, pp. 17ff, Barron 1964a, pp. 210ff; cf. Shipley 1987, pp. 81ff.)
143. Sources cited and discussed in Comotti 1989, pp. 18–20.
144. Sappho fr. 96.6f and 98b.2f LP.
145. Berve 1967, index s.v. "Königtum." On the Gelonids see n. 146. The Pisistratids claimed to belong to the ancient Neleid royalty of Athens Hdt. (5.65.3-4). The identical claim was made by some tyrants in Ionia, such as the Basilids of Ephesus, with greater color; that is why they could do without Delphi.
146. Dunbabin 1948, p. 411.
147. On the Pisistratids' self-ennoblement through the Neleids, see Nilsson 1951, p. 63.
148. Berve 1967, index s.v. "Kultbauten." Material accomplishments and patronage of the Gelonids: Dunbabin 1948, pp. 428ff with ch. 14; Berve 1967, 1:145, 151; 2:601, 606. Cypselids: Berve 1967, pp. 12, 22, 525ff. Pisistratids: Berve 1967, 1: 53–60, 66f; 2:548f, 551–53, 556f; Andrewes in *CAH*[2] iii.3, pp. 410–15.
149. Syme 1938 remains unsurpassed on Augustus' self-creation.
150. Hellanicus *FGrH* 4 F 22 = Marcellinus *Vit. Thuc.* 2–4.
151. Hdt. 6. 103; cf. Wade-Gery 1951, p. 212.
152. Boardman 1972 and 1975, p. 6, argues, from an analysis of contemporary black-figure ware depicting Heracles, that Pisistratus identified himself with the hero, and Heracles in turn with Athena and with the Eleusinian Lesser Mysteries, the legend of which recalled a relationship between Heracles and a Neleid "ancestor" of the Pisistratids.
153. Above, n. 72.
154. Young 1980, esp. pp. 13, 24–26, 38–43, 98. He rejects much of the literary evidence for the buildings attributed to the tyrants because they lack archaeological substantiation, including Cypselus' connection with the temple of Apollo at Corinth (pp. 24–26: cf. *contra* Salmon 1984, p. 219), which is surely wrong. His criteria

are too severe in an area where the evidence is scanty. Thus in discussing the Pisistratids—for whom we have the best evidence—he accepts at least fifteen of the twenty seven projects variously attributed to them, versus only two of the seventeen attributed to Polycrates of Samos.

155. The victory that secured Salamis is usually dated 651/0, the year of Pisistratus' first coup; but the evidence, Arist. *AP* 14.1 on his coup, and 17, on his polemarchy, provide no connection between the two; cf. Hdt. 1.59.4. The foundation date of the Panathenaea is supplied by Pherecydes (*FGrH* 3 F 2) and games at Eleusis were founded at about the same time (*IG* i.817). The tragic competition at the Dionysia was definitely instituted under Peisistratus, traditionally in 537 (*Marm. Par.*). On the centrality of festivals to politics, see now Connor 1987.

156. Thuc. 6.54.5-6; cf. Arist. *AP* 14.3 and 16.

Chapter Three. Tabula Rasa: The Invention of the Persians

1. *Od.* 4.187–88, 5.1; *Il.* 9.1, 20.237; *Hom. Hymn* 5.218ff; Pindar *Pyth.* 6.28ff with schol. The Memnon myth was fully elaborated in the late seventh-century (?) *Aethiopis*: the date is from Lesky 1966, p. 82. Cf. Pausanias 10.31.5: "Memnon was king of the Aethiopian people, although he came to Troy not from Aethiopia but from Susa in Persia and the river Choaspes, after conquering all the nations in between." The figure of Memnon was localized throughout the East, in the Troad (Strabo 13.1.11 C587: his tomb; cf. Pausanias 10.31.2), Ionia (Hdt. 2.106.2–5), Syria (Strabo 15.3.2 C728, citing Simonides' dithyramb, *Memnon*), Egypt (Strabo 17.1.42 C813), and Susa (Strabo 15.3.2 C728 and next note).

2. Cf. Pausanias 1.42.1. The earliest known association of Susiana (= Cissia: Hdt. 5.49.7, 52.6) with Memnon is attributed to Aeschylus by Strabo (15.3.2 C728 = fr. 94 Nauck), who says that the poet called the mother of Memnon Cissia. Possibly it occurred in the lost *Egyptians* or in the *Psychostasia,* which was evidently based on the post-Homeric *Aethiopis.*

3. Pherecydes (born 480/79 according to the Suda, fl. 456/5 according to Eusebius: TT 3 and 6; Jacoby 1947a, p. 33, would put him between 508 and 476) wrote after the Persian Wars, but the marriage connection was still in existence when Herodotus described it in the 420s. The occasion of its formation was probably the Persian expedition to Thrace in 492, when Alexander I, who contracted it, was already on the throne (accession *c.* 495: Hammond in *OCD*[2] s.v. Alexander I).

4. Cook 1985, p. 211: "To the Eastern Mediterranean world [Cyrus' conquest of Media] may have appeared nothing more than a change of dynasty; for in the eyes of Jews, Greeks, Egyptians and Arabs the ruling power long after continued to be the 'Mede' ": cf. Graf 1984, pp. 17–29, on the origin of the confusion having arisen from the early Achaemenids' own self-presentation as the continuators of the Median empire and its institutions.

5. This link is discussed later in the chapter.

6. The examination of Walser 1967 of careers of notable figures at the Persian court—political refugees, artists, technicians, doctors, and military men—reveals the breadth and nuance of relations between Greeks and Persians, but the literary sources reflect largely the formality, distance, and difficulty of direct Greek-Persian contacts at the official level. It remains to be explained why familiar contacts between Greeks and Persians are not more prominent in the sources if they in fact existed with any frequency. Cf. Mosley 1971 on Greek communication with non-Greeks through interpreters: the venues are almost exclusively political or commercial.

7. Root 1979.

8. Above, n. 4.

9. Jacoby 1913, cols. 262–63. Some recent scholarship has tended to cast doubt on the extent of Herodotus' travels: Fehling 1989; Armayor 1978a, 1980a, 1985. Against them see Dewald and Marincola 1987, pp. 27–33, and Georges 1993, where I argue that Herodotus visited the Black Sea area but gathered most, if not all, his information at Olbia and during a short voyage upriver. The problem is, as usual, insoluble: my own view is that Herodotus traveled very widely but was less adventuresome than his account implies: there is, I think, more *akoê* and less *opsis* in the Histories than older views have assumed.

10. Hdt. 1.123.3, 5.35.3, 8.98, Xen. *Hell.* 7.1.25 on the guards and posts on the roads. Escorts and *laissers-passers:* Hallock 1969 and 1985. A genre of stories about ruses to escape the guards' vigilance arose: in Herodotus messages are sent in the slit belly of a hare in a hunter's net (1.123.4), tattooed on a messenger's scalp (5.35.2), and beneath the wax of a blank writing-diptych (7.239.3).

11. Stronach 1978; Girshman 1951, pp. 114ff, on the simplicity of Medo-Persian culture in the seventh and sixth centuries.

12. Olmstead 1948, pp. 119, 162–63, 166–71; Haerinck 1973 on the Achaemenid palace at Babylon, which measured 36 by 21 m. (the Parthenon's dimensions, by comparison, are 69 by 30 m. at the top step): this palace resembled Darius' palace at Persepolis, and Haerinck prefers to attribute it to him rather than to a later monarch

(pp. 127–29). It would appear certain, in any case, that a royal residence in some form existed at Babylon from Darius onward, as a necessary headquarters when he turned Persia's attention to Western Asia and Europe.

13. An example: Schefold 1973.
14. Burn 1985, pp. 273–76; Sekunda 1985 and 1989. Cf. Xen. *Cyrop.* 8.10–14 on institutionalized satrapal imitation of the royal style.
15. Clermont-Ganneau 1921. The archaeological evidence for the Persians' self-segregation in the non-Iranian provinces is well summarized, with bibliography, in Moorey 1980: "As rulers they seem primarily to have lived in military enclaves or in military strongpoints, widely scattered, but linked by a highly efficient communications system and by the strongly centralized administration system it served and fostered. . . . The Persian contribution was generally confined to the reconstruction of existing administrative buildings or to the creation of parks and palaces in the Iranian manner, particularly in the satrapal capitals. Landscape gardening, the most ephemeral of arts, was a Persian specialty" (p. 128).
16. Hallock 1985.
17. Gnoli 1974.
18. *FGrH* 688; see Jacoby 1922, cols. 2051, 2066–68; Drews 1973, pp. 103–19; Sancisi-Weerdenburg 1987d, p. 36, notes that the "private life of a Persian monarch was screened off by a cumbersome ritual and [was] thus virtually invisible to even a highly esteemed Greek doctor." She accordingly dismisses as absurd Ctesias' claims to high access at court (*FGrH* 688 FF 15, 51), as well as the story of Democedes in Herodotus; she also argues that his material, as well as that of Herodotus (e.g., 9.108–13), concerning feuds and vengeance within the imperial harem was formed within an oriental tradition that contained this plot genre (pp. 40–42): cf. Murray 1987, pp. 113–14, who suggests that this material is derived from accounts of court life as the Persian nobility saw it. Yet indications remain that Ctesias could be reliable for contemporary matters of public knowledge: e.g., he mentions one Menostanes as *hazarapat* of the usurper Secundianus. This Menostanes is known to have been a royal kinsman of high status; he is named in four tablets from Nippur dated 424–423: Lewis 1977, p. 18 n. 94, who comments that "this is by far the best evidence we have for Ktesias' reliability for events near his own day." Cf. Lewis 1977, pp. 20–21, defending the identification of Ctesias' Artoxares the Paphlagonian (who put Darius II on the throne) with an Artahsarü in the Babylonian texts.
19. Best demonstrated by the attestations arranged chronologically by Hofstetter 1978. See also Welser 1967.

20. Argued by Wells 1907; often repeated and followed lately by Gould 1989, pp. 22–23, 113–14.

21. If the so-called Peace of Callias between Athens and Persia was a reality, then one of its terms called for the withdrawal of Persian forces to a stated distance from the coast, reported by Plut. *Cim.* as a day's ride (13.4) defined as 400 stades (19.3). Other sources in Hill 1951, Index I 6.15. Badian 1988 cogently defends the historicity of the Peace. See now Bosworth 1990 on the reinterpretation of a key testimony long thought to cast doubt on its historicity.

22. Herodotus uses *logios* only of foreigners (referring to Persians here; to Egyptians at 2.3.1 and 77.1; to Anacharsis at 4.46.1). But his Egyptians depend on written records (2.145) and Herodotus himself says he used interpreters in Egypt (2.125.6; cf. 2.154.2) and must have done so in the Pontus too (cf. 4.24), if he did not in reality depend altogether on such Greek-speaking informants as Tymnes, who told him about Anacharsis, a (mythical) personage who was known only to the Greeks and was no part of genuine Scythian lore, according to Herodotus himself (4.76.5–6). See Gould 1989, pp. 24–25. All of this appears to compel the conclusion that Herodotus' Persian *logioi* were Greeks who professed to know what the Persians themselves said. Raubitschek 1978–80 suggests that Herodotus derived these *aitiai* from a poetic source, possibly Phrynichus' *Phoenissae*. My own belief, discussed later, is that they were circulated by Xerxes' Greek agents in the context of his invasion of Greece.

23. Benveniste 1966 provides a total of some twenty loan words, and of these the majority are Persian words defined by Greek authors for their audiences, e.g. Hdt. 8.85 on *orosaggai* being the Persian term for "King's Benefactors." By contrast some forty genuine loan words from Semitic have been identified in Greek, beginning in Mycenean times (Braun 1982, pp. 25–26); almost all have to do with commerce, including the words for gold, saffron, cinnamon, various woven fabrics, and one's pledged word (*arrabôn*).

24. Xen. *Oec.* 4.20–25, a passage whose ethical content appears to confirm its truth, since for Zoroastrian worshippers of Ahura Mazda, whatever their status, it was an important religious duty to increase the good things of the world by one's own efforts. In the *Cyropaedia* (6.1.41) Xenophon also shows acquaintance with Persian dualism.

25. Xen. *Hell.* 4.1.30ff. See chapter 4.

26. Lattimore 1939.

27. Demaratus' descendants possessed great estates in the Aeolis into Xenophon's time (Xen. *Hell.* 3.1.6; *Anab.* 2.3, 7.8.17: Pergamon, Teuthrania, Halisarna). Lewis 1977, p. 54 and nn. 29–30 (followed by Cartledge 1979, p. 201), suggests that Herodotus talked to them;

if so, Herodotus' inventions may preserve the spirit of the relationship between them as recalled by Demaratus to his kinsmen. On the character of Demaratus' portrait by Herodotus see Boedecker 1987, esp. pp. 192–201.

28. On both passages How and Wells 1912 is still useful. Cf. Armayor 1978b.

29. Kent 1953, pp. 25–40.

30. E.g., *Astyagês* (Hdt. 1.73 etc.) = "Leader of the City"; two sons of Darius *Abrokomês* and *Hyperanthês* (7.224.2) = "Luxurylocks" and "Superbloom"; *Harpagos* (*bis*: 1.80.2, 6.28.2) = "Seizer"; *Dôtos* (7.72.3) = "Giver." *Zôpyros* (*bis*: 3.160.1ff; 4.431.1ff; cf. Ctesias 35ff Henry) = "Living Fire," an appellation reflecting Zoroastrian piety which must be a direct calque on the Persian: the younger Zopyrus was an exile resident in Athens for some time in the 420s. *Smerdis* (3.30.1: Bardiya, the Mardos of Aesch. *Persae* 774) is purely Greek, recalling *smerdaleos,* meaning "terrible, fearful, awful." Greek proper names include *Smerdios* (Maximus of Tyre 37.5; *Smerdiês* (Anth. Pal. 7.25 and Eustathius 1542.7); *Smerdis* (Arist. Pol. 1311b29). On the other hand, most Medo-Persian names in Herodotus are recognizably native in form, as shown by Schmitt 1976.

31. Hall 1989, pp. 18, 133–34 and n. 91.

32. It was drunk by the priests, but according to the *Avesta,* Yasnas 9.4ff, 22; 10.15, 90; 11.3, any male worshipper could use it. Its function was connected with fecundity and the bearing of sons—a matter of great moment to the Persians (Hdt. 1.136.1). It was also used by the priests for divination and access to the spirit realm: Schwartz 1985, pp. 653, 676–77, 688, 695. Schwartz would identify *haoma* as *Peganum harmala,* a plant with psychotropic and aphrodisiac qualities; see Flattery and Schwartz 1984.

33. Grant 1983, pp. 283–87, 292, remarks upon Herodotus' much stronger interest in accurate investigation of religious matters, as opposed to warfare or political life. On the theodicy of the Histories, see below, chapter 5.

34. Zaehner 1961, pp. 100–102 on Mithra. In Zoroastrian belief fire is the symbol of truth (pp. 46ff) and is identical to the Holy Spirit (pp. 76ff). In the *Avesta,* Fire is the fourth horse yoked to Mithra's chariot and is spoken of as the Force (*Xwarənah*) by which kings rule righteously and legitimately (Yasht 10.31.127). It is the element which protects Truth's creatures: conceived of as a son of Ahura Mazda, it is associated with the victories of just kings (Yasht 19.7.48–54). Water is identified with wholeness (Zaehner 1961, pp. 46ff) and venerated (76ff).

35. I am not convinced by the emendation of Corsten 1991, esp. p.

168, who imagines that an iotacizing scribe heard *Mêtera* for *Mitran*. His article is, however, otherwise illuminating on the pre-Zoroastrian origins of the Anahita cult.

36. Boyce 1982, 2:201–4, 216–21. In fairness to Herodotus one should note that Berossus (*FGrH* 680 F 11) puts the introduction of the Anahita cult in the reign of Artaxerxes II; it is in his reign that the triad of Ahura Mazda, Anahita, and Mithra appear in the surviving palace inscriptions (Kent 1953: A²Sa 4f, A²Sd 3f, A²Ha 6). Herodotus inadvertently disproves Berossus, but in his day the conspicuous worship of Anahita in the West may well have arrived recently; Herodotus himself treats it as an innovation. For the fourth century see Robert 1953 on the Amyzon inscription; Robert 1975 on Persian administration of a cult of Zeus at Sardis; Sekunda 1985 on the Artemisium.

37. Hardly anything is known concerning this personage: discussion in Picard 1922, pp. 222–28 and 163ff. The earliest Greek references to Persian interest in Ephesian Artemis date from the end of the fifth century: Thuc. 8.109; Xen. *Hell.* 1.2.6 and *Anab.* 5.3.4ff. *Magoi* at Ephesus in the mid-fourth century: Plut. *Alex.* 3.7. Cf. Barnett 1948, pp. 20ff; Jacobsthal 1951, p. 93 and plate 35 c–d: the image of a priest of Ephesus in ivory from the sixth century, which Jacobsthal interprets as a Megabyzus.

38. Below, chapter 6, section "Cambyses and Persian Religion." Contrast the dualistic philosophy that Xenophon knowledgeably attributes to Cyrus: *Cyrop.* 6.1.41. By the mid-fourth century the Persian sage had attracted the attention of the Platonic circle. Heraclides Ponticus, for one, wrote a *Zoroaster* (Diog. Laert. 5.86).

39. Cf. the appreciation of Momigliano 1958, pp. 2–3 and 8–9. Though blurred in the intervening years by the many demonstrations of complex artifice and conscious patterning on Herodotus' part, his verdict has stood the test of time remarkably well.

40. *SGHI* no. 12, found in a wall near Magnesia-on-the-Maeander, an inland city that probably did not participate in the revolt, which was led by the Ionian naval powers. This "Letter of Darius," reproduced on stone in the early second century A.D., is almost certainly authentic; see the commentary of Meiggs and Lewis, ibid. It may date from the last decade of the sixth century, when Darius was at Sardis after the Scythian expedition, in which the Ionians served loyally. The evident purpose of this reproduction lies in the document's support of the antiquity of the temple's charter in order to define its rights to the Roman authorities according to ancient precedent. Cf. Tac. *Annales* 3.60–63, on the senatorial investigation under Tiberius into sacred charters in the province of Asia: the

oldest claims were those of Hierocaesaria and Miletus, founded on references to Cyrus and Darius (62.3, 63.4).

41. The Lindian Chronicle by Timachidas, commissioned in 99 B.C. (*FGrH* 532 C para. 32; cf. D). The inscription records two dedications, by one Artaphernes (?: the name is wholly restored) of uncertain date, and by Datis (presumably the same person as Herodotus' Datis); Datis' dedication, of his own raiment, accompanied the miraculous lifting of a Persian siege in the context of the campaign of 490. Herodotus is conspicuously silent concerning the Dorians of Asia in his account of the Ionian Revolt, and they are not recorded as participants in the scanty testimony outside Herodotus; cf. Tozzi 1978, p. 144 with n. 49. Persian gifts of princely raiment, etc.: Hdt. 3.84.1, 7.116 (a precise parallel to the Lindian case); cf. Xen. *Anab.* 1.2.27, Ctes. *FGrH* 688 F 13.25.

42. Dandamayev 1975.

43. Greeks regularly carried out the Persians' Greek diplomacy: e.g., Arthmius of Zeleia (Plut. *Them.* 6.4, Dem. 9.40–44), Alexander I of Macedon (Hdt. 8.140ff), Alcibiades (Thuc. 8.45ff, 56), Apollophanes of Cyzicus (Xen. *Hell.* 4.1.29), Heracleides of Clazomenae (*SGHI* no. 70), Ctesias of Cnidus (*FGrH* 688 FF 30–32). Others in Hofstetter 1978. The Athenian envoy who interprets for Pseudartabas in the *Acharnians* (100ff) is modeled on a real type.

44. Hdt. 5.102, 105; 6.43–44 *init.*, 94, 101; 7.1, 138 *init.*; 8.68, 102.

45. Above, n. 34.

46. Cf. XPh 35–41 in Kent 1953.

47. Cf. DB iv 63, DNb 12 in Kent 1953.

48. Heraclitus 22 F 93 DK: "The god . . . neither speaks nor conceals, but gives a sign." Deceptive oracles abound in Herodotus, and he labels two of them outright *khrêsmous kibdêlous* (1.66.3, 75.2); note too the transaction between the Cymaeans and Apollo of Branchidae (1.158–59). Other examples may be garnered from the corpus of Fontenrose 1978; see esp. the fable of the villain who tries to turn the tables on Apollo (Aesop *Fab.* 36; Babrius 229 = Fontenrose L155. Plato, *Apol. Soc.* 21b, has Socrates asserting at his trial that Delphian Apollo cannot lie; but Socrates was notoriously eccentric.

49. Discussed further in chapter 6.

50. Trans. Pritchard *ANET*, p. 314. Olmstead 1948, pp. 51–56, is excellent on Cyrus' Babylonian propaganda.

51. Ezra 1:1–4; cf. DB I.11–20 in Kent 1953, echoing earlier "favor of Ahuramazda" kingship formulas of Ariaramnes and Arsames: AmH 4–9, AsH 5–14 in Kent 1953. Deutero-Isaiah, which was reedited about this time, calls Cyrus "the Lord's anointed" (Isaiah 45:1)—

Khristos in the Septuagint. Cf. Bickerman 1946 and Mallowan 1985, pp. 409ff.

52. Hdt. 3.2. Cf. Posener 1936, p. 17, with Bresciani 1985, pp. 503–9. It is nevertheless possible that Cambyses was a religious eccentric of some kind, as Herodotus' portrait of him suggests; he behaved untraditionally at Babylon, but due to insuperable evidentiary problems, the episode of the Apis-bull remains vague and without satisfactory explanation. See Oppenheim 1985, pp. 554–58.

53. Artemis: Picard 1922, pp. 439–40; Gusmani 1980–86, s.vv. +*artim*−, +*artimuli*−. The earliest written evidence is Thuc. 8.109 *fin.*: cf. above, n.37. At Sardis the great altars to Cybebe and Artimu/Artemis were modified by the Persians to serve as fire altars soon after the conquest, suggesting that the Persians offered reverence to the Lydians' native deities according to their own practice: Ramage 1968, pp. 11ff; Hanfmann 1975, pp. 53–87.

54. They identified Apollo Helios with Mithra, Artemis with Anahita, and Ahura Mazda with Zeus Nomothetes: Robert 1975.

55. On these: Walser 1967.

56. I owe this point to Raphael Sealey.

57. Courby 1931, p. 213. It is arguable that the Persians did not at first intend to burn the Acropolis in 480; see Georges 1986, pp. 27–28.

58. See chapter 2, first section.

59. Strabo 13.1.52. On the Aeneads: Momigliano 1982, p. 7.

60. Lampsacus claimed a Trojan connection in requests to the Roman Senate in 196 (Dittenberger *Syll.*[3] 591. 18ff), a tradition unlikely to have been invented simply for the occasion. On Lesbos and Cyme, see chapter 5, Appendix.

61. Ibycus: *Pap. Oxy.* 15.1790.

62. A "barrow of Memnon" existed at Troy in the second century A.D., at any rate, when it was seen by Pausanias (10.31.2).

63. Herodotus' own account of Mycale compels the conclusion that the Persians began to doubt the steadfastness of the Ionians only after the Hellenic fleet brought the war to Asia (9.99; cf. 8.85.2–3: the Samians whom the Persians disarmed at Mycale had distinguished themselves at Salamis).

64. Bacon 1961 and Hall 1989.

65. His contemporary Duris placed the crossing to Asia one thousand years after the fall of Troy (*FGrH* 76 F 41a).

66. Sekunda 1985, pp. 17–18. Troy was in the satrapy of Pontic Phrygia, whose Pharnabazid dynasty Hellenized conspicuously: see chapter 7, Appendix, "The Hellenic Attachments of the Pharnacids."

67. Burkert 1985a, pp. 130 and 248 on Zeus *herkeios, hikesios, xenios.*

68. Plut. *Alex.* 2.1; for the Epirot kings' claim to descend from Andromache and Neoptolemus (also the name of Achilles' son, with whom he was confused) see Eurip. *Troades* 704ff, *Andromache* 1ff, 1243ff; cf. Vergil *Aeneid* 3.321ff, Bosworth 1988, p. 281.

69. Pausanias 9.8.5. Parallel cases of transhumation included Orestes (Hdt. 1.67), Theseus (Plut. *Cimon* 8.4), and Tisamenus (Paus. 7.1.3).

70. *SGHI* no. 27.

71. For the date see Georges 1986, pp. 23–24.

72. Cf. *Pers.* 79–80, where schol. M reads *khrysogonou,* understanding a reference to Zeus' union with Danaë, who bore the hero Perseus. On this connection with Perseus see Delcourt 1934, pp. 242–43.

73. Here Herodotus may have used and "corrected" Hellanicus' *Persica* (*FGrH* 4 FF 59–60). Drews 1973, pp. 24ff, gives the case for antedating Hellanicus.

74. Herodotus probably knew the name "Termilae" from Hecataeus or Panyassis: Steph. Byz. s.v. *Tremilê* = Panyassis F 18 Kinzl = Hecataeus *FGrH* 1 F 10. The presence of the Neleid Lycus may reflect Athenian propaganda disseminated in connection with the coastal Lycians' temporary inclusion in their empire. They were "liberated" by Cimon in the 460s and appear on the Tribute List for the year 446.

75. Jacoby 1912, col. 2680. Hellanicus called Medea's son Polyxenus (*FGrH* 4 F 132), evidently preferring the alternative tradition that made Medea herself the eponym of the Medes.

76. Cf. Plato *Hipp. Maj.* 285d: when Hippias gives lectures at Sparta he speaks of "heroic or human genealogies, of the foundations of cities in primitive times, more generally, of the matters pertaining to antiquity."

77. See the analysis of the Spartan foundation legends (Paus. 3.1.1–5) by Calame in Bremmer 1986, pp. 153–86, with the stemma on p. 181. Thuc. 1.207.1, 3.92.4; Xen. *Hell.* 6.3.6: evidence that mythological arguments were employed, sometimes with effect, at Sparta.

78.

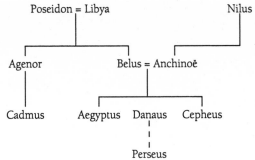

79. The title of this section is cited from Hdt. 7.140.2.
80. Freymuth 1955 would deny political significance to Phrynichus' *Fall;* but his arguments are of no consequence in the light of this passage and the fact that Themistocles was the choregus. See below, chapter 4.
81. See chapter 4, section "Aeschylus' Darius."
82. Hdt. 6.9.1–2, 13.1, exaggerated by Samian apologetic.
83. I give the total of Herodotus' individual figures; his own total is 371 (8.47 *fin.*).
84. Hdt. 7.144.1; Arist. *AP* 22.7: the fleet was voted in the archon-year 483/2.
85. On the Greek and Persian plans and warmaking power see Georges 1986, pp. 42–59.
86. The list of imperial peoples ruled by Darius in his inscriptions becomes canonical in the inscriptions of his successors; i.e., the loss of Europe was never acknowledged officially at court. Xerxes in particular preferred the formula that he ruled not "Ionians" and "petasos-wearing Ionians" (cf. DNa 28f), but "Ionians, those who dwell by the sea and those who dwell *across the sea*" (XPh 23f in Kent 1953; cf. DPe 13–15 in same). See Cameron 1955, p. 83, citing the Cyrus Cylinder's description (5.22) of Cyrus as "king of totality . . . king of the four world quarters."

Chapter Four. Aeschylus: The Human Fabric of the Persae

1. Biographical material is drawn from Lesky 1983, pp. 37–41.
2. Hdt. 5.77.6 = Simonides fr. 132 Bergk. Date: Ostwald, *CAH²* iv (1988) 308. Sealey 1976, p. 151 with n. 3, puts the date too late, between *c.* 503 and 499 B.C. An early date for the Spartan reaction is preferable, since it was the very consolidation of the new regime, with its military potential, that the Spartan king Cleomenes feared. Chronology accepted here: (1) expulsion of Pisistratids 511/10; (2) archonship of Isagoras 50<u>8</u>/7; (3) eclipse of Isagoras, election of Alcmaeon, kinsman of Clisthenes as archon for 50<u>7</u>/6; (4) abortive intervention of Cleomenes, then defeat of Boeotians and Chalcidians in spring 506.
3. The statuary group by Antenor was erected by the demos between 510 and 480: for the evidence see Taylor 1975, esp. pp. 198–209; Brunnsäker 1971. Cult: Arist. *AP* 58.1; Fornara 1970.
4. The Athenians had no reason to assist the Milesian Aristagoras in 499 by making open war on the Persians unless they had been pressed to restore the Pisistratids before that date. The election as eponymous archon in 496 of Hipparchus son of Charmus (Dion.

Hal. *RA* 5.77.6, 6.1.1), a cousin by marriage of Hippias, has been seen as an attempt to finesse Persian pressure: see Williams 1952, p. 18: "a compromise with the Persian demand."

The story (Hdt. 5.73.3) that the Athenians greatly reprehended their envoys' decision to render earth and water is almost certainly tendentious apologetic. Kuhrt 1989, pp. 91–92 postulates a close relationship broken by the Athenians when they joined the revolt. In fact, relations between Darius and Athens had already existed under the Pisistratids through the Philaid tyranny in the Chersonese, which lasted until the end of the Ionian Revolt (during which the tyrant Miltiades played a role as ambiguous as that of Histiaeus) and the Pisistratids' own possession of Sigeum. The new regime, then, merely renewed these ties. In general, see Raubitschek 1964, Schachermeyer 1973, and especially Orlin 1976 on Herodotus' tendentiousness. Also see chapter 5, section "The Alcmaeonids and Athens," on Herodotus' jaundiced view of Clisthenes and his clan.

5. Among tyrants allegedly owing their position to the Persians before Darius, Berve 1967, who is comprehensive for the evidence, names only Pytharchus of Cyzicus erroneously from Agathocles' early Hellenistic *Peri Kyzikou,* Athenagoras and Comes in Ephesus (Suda s.v. *Hippônax*) before Darius, and the statement of the Peripatetic Heraclides Ponticus, *Kyros de katalysas tên politeian monarkheisthai autous* [i.e., the Ephesians] *epoiêsen* (*FGrH* ii 217, fr. 11.5). However, there is no evidence that Athenagoras and Comes came to power through Cyrus; of all Asiatic Greek cities Ephesus was most accustomed to tyranny (Berve 1967, 1:98–100 with 2:576–78).

   As for Pytharchus, Agathocles (*FGrH* 432 F 6) wrote merely that Cyrus gave him seven "cities," all of them insignificant, and that afterward he "undertook to tyrannize his fatherland, gathering an army. But the Cyzicenes charged out against him, facing in serried ranks the danger." In other words, the Cyzicenes *overcame* this threat. Heraclides, finally, was a self-important scribbler who wrote nearly fifty treatises on ethics, physics, grammar, music, and rhetoric, as well as history (Diog. Laert. 5.86–94 Long). His isolated and programmatic testimony (he preached tyrannicide: ibid. 89 = *FHG* iv 382) cannot controvert the implied contrast between the policies of Cyrus and Darius toward the Greeks implicitly present in Herodotus.

6. The arguments of Segal 1971a, pp. 40ff, suggest a possible Croesus tragedy lying behind Croesus' portrait on the pyre by Myson and Bacchylides' Ode 3. There is also an apocryphal story, in which Solon rebukes Thespis for lying in public and then accuses Pisistratus of an Odyssean deception in faking his injuries to receive a bodyguard, as if Pisistratus were playing Odysseus in a tragedy. Solon

thus is made to object to tragedy as a schooling in tyranny (Plut. *Solon* 29.4–30.2; cf. *Od.* 4.244–64; see too Vernant in Vernant and Vidal-Naquet 1981, p. 5). The opposition between reality and *mimêsis* in this story, together with the canonical opposition between the lawgiver and the tyrant, which must have arisen after the democracy came to look back to Solon as a hero (Arist. *AP* 9, cf. Plut. *Solon* 3–7; Rhodes 1981, pp. 119, 159–63), indicates a late invention; but it can reasonably be argued that the story preserves an echo of the original uses to which the tyrant had put the new tragic theater which he patronized.

7. Lesky 1983, p. 26. Even these titles might be uncertain, since Aristoxenus (fr. 114 Wehrli) said that Heraclides Ponticus published plays of his own under Thespis' name: but the Hellenistic critics cannot have been so easily fooled.

8. Lesky 1983, p. 32.

9. Hyginus *Fabulae* 187, cf. 252; Aelian *VH* 12.42.

10. Hipparchus (who was later thought to have been the tyrant by the Athenians, not his brother Hippias, as a result of his assassination by the "Tyrannicides," Thuc. 6.55.4) was slain by a youth who had rejected his advances and whose sister's honor he insulted. The youth and his lover attacked Hipparchus during the Panathenaea festival "in a fury, the one inflamed by love and the other by insult," as Thucydides remarks (55.3). We may at least speculate that Hipparchus' mistaken identity is the residue of a tragedy on his death; if so, it may have been performed in his memory by Hippias before his own fall, if the alleged response to Delphi attached to the tale that ennobles his fate comes from the same source: Hdt. 5.56.1.

11. Vidal-Naquet 1973, p. 10; cf. Hartog 1988, p. 335 (citing Vidal-Naquet) on the barbarism of tragedy and "the 'little tragedies' incorporated in the great narrative of the *Histories*. Croesus, Candaules, Polycrates of Samos, Cleomenes of Sparta, Cyrus, Cambyses, Xerxes—are they not all tragic heroes?" Vernant and Vidal-Naquet 1981, pp. 3, 9–18; earlier recognized by Fohl 1913.

12. Lesky 1966, pp. 253–63; esp. p. 262; Podlecki 1966, pp. 77ff. See also MacLeod 1982 on the meaning of the progress of the *Oresteia* from monarchy to democracy. Bacon 1961, p. 38, notes that Aeschylus associates the Erinyes, creatures of the world of Mycenae and the old gods, with atrocious Persian punishments (lines 185–95; cf. Hdt. 3.48, 125; 7.39; 8.104–6; 9.112.

13. Hdt. 5.71; Thuc. 1.126.2–127.2; Arist. *AP* 1; Diogenes Laertius 1.109ff.

14. Podlecki 1966, pp. 98–100, believes that Aeschylus was an anti-Periclean concerning the Areopagus reforms; this can hardly be the

case, especially since Athena's argument that the mother is only the *nurse* of the father's seed is relevant to Pericles' Alcmaeonid descent from his mother's side alone. Athena's genetics absolve Pericles from the Almaeonid curse.

15. Hammond 1986, p. 289 with n. 2.

16. Hecataeus, for one, had believed that the Greeks of the heroic age were by origin barbarians (*FGrH* 1 F 119 = Strabo 7.7.1 C321, who expands on Hecataeus). He was followed by Herodotus (see chapter 5), A school of thought must have held that the ancients depicted in tragedy according to a barbarian ethos were racially barbarian. Cf. Thucydides' observation that only recently had barbarian traits died out in most of Greece (1.6, with 3.3).

17. They are (anachronistically) Persian: see n. 87.

18. Date: Lesky 1966, p. 230.

19. *Hypothesis:* below, n. 22. On the tradition connecting the two plays and attempted reconstructions of the *Phoenissae* see Marx 1928, Stoessl 1945, Freymuth 1955. Raubitschek 1978–80, p. 280, suggests that Herodotus' account of Xerxes and Artabanus (7.8–18, 44–52) was based on the *Phoenissae,* in which Artabanus may have played a part analogous to that of Darius' Ghost in the *Persae.*

20. Wade-Gery 1958, p. 177, would place the *Fall of Miletus* in 494/3; but it is attractive to place it, with Lesky 1966, pp. 230–31, in 493/2, which is both the year of Themistocles' archonship and the year of the Persians' northern Aegean armada.

21. Miletus was geographically a Carian city and drew cultural influences from Caria, as we infer from Herodotus' characterization of them as mestizos (1.146.2–3) and the onomastic indications of intermarriage with Milesians by leading Carian families: Histiaeus son of Tymnus, tyrant of Carian Termera (Hdt. 5.37.1), and Heraclides of Mylasa, son of Ibanollis (121 *fin.*), and at Miletus itself, Liatos son of Bremmius (*Milet* I 3.225 n. 122). Speculative reconstructions of the *Fall* assume that lamentations (Freymuth 1955; Manganaro 1960) and Carian dirges would have been both dramaturgically correct and poignantly familiar to his audiences, since at Athens troupes of Carian dirge musicians were hired to accompany the cortege: Plato *Laws* 800e1–3 with schol., which reads *Karikê mousê: tei thrênôdei: dokousi gar hoi Kares thrênôdoi tines kai allotrious nekrous epi misthôi thrênein,* cited from Alexiou 1974, p. 210, n. 59. In the *Persae,* Aeschylus' Elders lament in Mariandynian (line 938) and Mysian (line 1054) modes, in apparent reference to this custom at Athens.

22. *Hypothesis* from the *Peri Aiskhylou mythôn* of Glaucus of Rhegium: *ek tôn Phoinissôn Phrynikhou phêsi* [sc. Glaucus] *tous Persas parapepoiêsthai.* Michelini 1982, p. 130, n. 6, notes correctly that "the

word *parapepoiêsthai* seems to indicate a very close dependency on Phrynichus. Cf. *LSJ*⁹ s.v. *parapoieô,* esp. I.3: "parody." The *Persae,* a liturgy of the young Pericles, is dated to the 473/472 (= archonship of Menon) by Glaucon.

23. E.g., Lesky, 1966, pp. 245–46; Benardete 1956, p. 45: "sine ira et studio."

24. Compare the analogous role played by Cyrus at his last appearance, which concludes the Histories (Hdt. 9.122); cf. Lateiner 1989, pp. 48–50.

25. This Darius is discussed in this chapter.

26. Cf. Plut. *Apophth. Lacaenarum,* esp. 241F (no. 16), *ê tan ê epi tas,* "with it or on it," (i.e., the warrior's shield) for sentiments deemed ideally appropriate to the occasion, and Thuc. 2.44–45 on the bearing demanded of the women of the dead interred at the public funeral of 431.

27. Momigliano 1975b, pp. 129ff; 1975a, p. 15; Finley 1986, who might also have cited Heraclitus on "War the Father and King of All" (fr. 53 DK; cf. fr. 80).

28. E.g., Smyth 1924, pp. 69–70 and 84ff; Lattimore 1943 (a very influential article); Benardete 1956, p. 44; Broadhead 1960, pp. xvi–xix. Pompella 1974 and Levi 1977–78 go so far as to argue that Aeschylus was encouraging a policy of conciliation with Persia.

29. A bearded Athenian holds his penis erect and identifies himself, "Eurymêdon eimi," as he advances to sodomize a Persian warrior, who submits to him on the opposite side of this oenochoe (the appropriate vessel: *nunc est bibendum*). Illustrated in *AthMitt* 90 (1975) plate 25.1–2.

30. Cf. Michelini 1982, p. 105.

31. E.g., Broadhead 1960, p. 331, and Lattimore, 1958, p. 33n., who calls Aeschylus a "rampant liar." Scholars also have seen in the Psyttaleia account a desire to balance the fight at sea with laurels for the Athenian hoplites, or to magnify the role of Aristides (who commanded the hoplites on Psyttaleia) against the accomplishment of Themistocles at sea.

32. Kitto 1966, pp. 91–92, appreciates the Persians' viewpoint. Cf. Aeschylus' epitaph, attributed to his own hand: *Aesch. Vit.* 15–18; c.f. Plut. *Mor.* 604 F. Herodotus was later to treat Artemisium as the work of "a mob of poltroons repeatedly retreating or meditating retreat" (Hignett 1963, p. 190, citing Macan 1908, 2:261) and depicted Salamis in an impressionistic and anecdotal account, whereas he narrated Thermopylae and Plataea—where the Spartan commander Pausanias gained the most splendid victory ever known to him (Hdt. 9.64.1)—in painstaking detail.

33. See chapter 3.
34. Long 1986 collects the evidence comprehensively.
35. Garlan 1988, pp. 20–21, glossing *andrapodos.*
36. E.g., Rosenmeyer 1982, pp. 318–19, cf. 291–92; Broadhead 1960, pp. xviii and xxiiif, citing predecessors, concludes that Aeschylus "has treated the Persians in much the same way as he would have treated the Greeks in similar circumstances"—a rare overt statement of the assumption common to critics, which appears founded upon the structural and thematic comparisons noted between the *Persae* and the *Agamemnon* from Wilamowitz 1914, p. 45, etc., onward.

    I have found no discussion of what might be called the sociology of Aeschylus' imagined Persia, even though the play is normally considered in discussions of Greek views on Persians and other barbarians. I know of no attempt to understand the *Persae* by regarding Aeschylus' Persians functionally and ethically *qua* Persians. Delcourt 1934 breaks no new ground. Petrounias 1976, pp. 1–32, analyses the imagery, not the *Gestalt,* of the play. Jüthner 1923 remains fundamental on the antithesis between Hellene and barbarian, followed by Diller 1961; but their method is largely descriptive.
37. By ethos I mean *Gestalt,* "a persistent and coherent set of interests and tendencies" (Michelini 1982, p. 139); see Easterling 1973 and Jones 1962, pp. 30–33 and 37–38. Bacon 1961, pp. 62–63, concludes that Aeschylus' barbarians are ethnographically correct, and that their ethos is integral to their dramatic function.
38. Cf. Michelini 1982, p. 115, on lines 495–507: "As always, the *Schadenfreude* of the Greek view is the underside of the Persian tragedy: that the unnatural and monstrous army should suffer a monstrous catastrophe is a reassertion of the natural order of things, and a proof of divine concern." Cf. ibid., pp. 69–71, 127.
39. Lately Rosenmeyer 1982, pp. 291–92, realizes this but decides to blame Aeschylus instead of his own critical assumptions. Similarly Broadhead 1960, *Persae* 23, thinks "Xerxes, unsuitable as he was for the role of tragic hero, is nevertheless the mainspring of the tragedy."

    See Jones 1962, pp. 11–20, for the elimination of the "tragic hero" from the *Poetics;* further, House 1964, pp. 83–86; Adkins 1966, Stinton 1975.
40. Winnington-Ingram 1973, p. 217. But the play continues nevertheless to be interpreted as a drama of progressive enlightenment, e.g., by Paduano 1978, p. 87 ("un processo gnoseologico"), whose notes do not include Winnington-Ingram's article. (See the scathing review of Paduano by Diggle in *CR* 31 [1981] 105). The older view is well represented by Deichgräber 1941, pp. 161–63. The thesis of Ley

1982, that lines 829–381 are an actor's interpolation, makes nonsense of the play.

41. On the meaning of these expressions in the thought of Aeschylus see Dodds 1973.

42. Broadhead 1960, pp. xv (citing the *Praefatio* of Blomfield's 1818 edition of the *Persae*, p. xiv), xxiii, xxxviii with n. 1, xlvii. It should go without saying that Xerxes entered alone, in rags, and on foot; see now Taplin 1977, pp. 121ff. Avery 1964, p. 184, would clothe Xerxes at line 1038, when he assumes the directing role of exarchos, because he is troubled by the apparent contradiction between the depiction in the play of Persia's defeat as complete versus the fact of Persia's actual survival and continued power. In fact this contradiction is recognized within the play and is fundamental to its relationship with the reality outside the orchestra: see Thalmann 1980, pp. 267–82, on the crucial significance of the ruined state of Xerxes' robes.

43. Taplin 1977, p. 126, comments: "The father is stately, wise, resigned to the justice of the gods: the son is abandoned to lachrymose and indiscriminate lament, his despair is total and immediate, *without moral or theological depth*" (my emphasis).

44. This assumption informs Aristotle's discussion of dramatic diction and the critic's interpretive task, *Poet.* 1460b–1461b26: the critic cannot deny the literal meaning where it is plain. Cf. especially the dictum of Glaucon cited at 1461b1–4.

45. Broadhead 1960, p. 69, glossing line 157. Here and at p. 168, glossing line 643, he ignores the chorus's locution *Persan Sousigenê theon*. Cf. Murray 1939, pp. 79–80, who calls *theos* in line 157 "apparently one of Aeschylus' mistakes."

46. Below, n. 48.

47. See Arist. *Poet.* 1449b24–25 and 1405b21–34.

48. Broadhead 1960, p. xxxviii.

49. The *Persae* is a complete tragic sequence in "drei Akten" for Wilamowitz 1897, p. 382, and 1914. Adkins 1952, p. 51, likens it more satisfactorily to a tetralogy in miniature, in which the kommos is appended to the tragic climax of the Ghost's epiphany as the equivalent of a satyr-play. Cf. Michelini 1982, p. 74: Xerxes is "reduced almost to the status of epilogue. . . . The Dareios episode is the play's crowning event, overshadowing and displacing the ending scene with Xerxes."

50. Michelini 1982, p. 133. Cf. Dawe 1963, pp. 27–71.

51. Taplin 1977, pp. 92–98, is the latest to criticize the apparent weakness of this device as misdirection, and to advocate moving lines 529–31 to follow 851—with corresponding violence either to 529

or to 850 and with no cogent defense of this Odyssean textual migration. Cf. Dworacki 1979, p. 102, Broadhead 1960, p. xxxviif, and Dawe 1963, pp. 56–57, 92, 138, 320: the same arguments apply *pari passu* to the more radical transposition by Nikitine, Weil, etc., of 527–531 to follow 851.

Many critics have recognized that where they occur in the mss., lines 527–31/529–31 not only maintain the expectation of the momentary appearance of Xerxes after the Messenger has brought the survivors as far as Persia (508–11); they reinforce at a necessary point the theme of the Queen's concentrated interest in her son. After 301–2 and the preceding material (her dream of 181ff and her description at 169 of Xerxes' presence) as the only desideratum, it would be odd if she were to go off without further reference to her chief concern, *pace* Taplin, who believes that characterization has at most an incidental function in these lines.

52. Cf. Broadhead 1960, pp. xxxviii and 208 on line 838, and Dworacki 1979, pp. 102–3.

53. Michelini 1982, p. 134. However, she believes that the audience would not have been taken in: "When the theme of premature exit appears a second time, the warm assurances that the Queen will return are fatally weakened by the echoes [from her first exit]. The audience is not surprised to see Xerxes emerge instead." But the principle that "you can fool all of the people some of the time and some of the people all of the time" holds good for drama as well as politics. Cf. Dawe 1963, esp. p. 28, on lines 849–51. Dawe is cited in this connection by Thalmann 1980, p. 264, who provides a complete defense of the view taken here of the poet's intention.

54. Taplin 1977 missed this, and so did not see that the counterpreparation of line 838 and the Queen's (untampered-with) exit at 849–51 together fulfill the conditions of his own observation on satisfactory counterpreparation, by evoking "a scene which never in fact takes place": p. 94. See Kitto 1966, pp. 104–3.

55. Broadhead 1960, p. xxxviii.

56. *Ed. maj.* (1914) p. 171 and n. ad loc. Xerxes would demand an explanation because the Elders had encouraged his plan to invade Greece, an inference which the aggressiveness of the Elders demands, and which answers to their role as privy councillors of the realm: see Korzeniewski 1966, pp. 553–56.

57. Meiggs 1972, pp. 59–60, with attention to Plut. *Aristides* 25.1, argues that the work of assessment was only *begun* in 478–77. On the history of the period after Mycale see Meiggs 1972, pp. 23–91.

58. Hdt. 7.151: Artaxerxes succeeded to the throne in 465 and it is commonly inferred that these missions were at Susa no earlier than

464/3 or alternatively soon after the Argive-Athenian alliance of 461. Bibliography in Hofstetter 1978, pp. 97–98; see now Badian 1988.

59. Cf. Hdt. 6.115, 121.1, 123f on the accusation that the Alcmaeonids were conspiring to readmit the Pisistratids at the time of Marathon, refuted by Herodotus on the grounds of their reputation as the liberators of Athens from the Pisistratids, and implicitly by modern research on the reforms of the Alcmaeonid Clisthenes, which concludes that the reforms favored the already strong position of the clan in Athenian politics. As Herodotus comments, there were none at Athens of greater reputation or more honored than they; and they could have had no interest in admitting their old rivals with the strength of the Persians behind them. On the force of the reforms see esp. Lewis 1963; Bicknell 1972a, pp. 1–53 and 1972b; usefully summarized by Sealey 1976, pp. 161–64.

60. The treaties sworn between the Spartans and the Persian satraps of Asia Minor in 413–412, as reported by Thucydides, are definitive evidence of the abiding Persian imperial attitude toward the lost territories. The first two agreements confirm Persian claims to *all* ancestral conquests however ephemeral; and these documents are compacted both with the King and his satrap Tissaphernes (Thuc. 8.18.1 and 37.1–2). These unbounded claims were unsatisfactory to the Spartans. A revised treaty specified that only "the King's territory, *as much as is in Asia,* is the King's" (8.58.2). But only Tissaphernes and his opposite numbers at Dascyleium swore to this treaty, which therefore did not bind the King.

61. The earliest date suggested for a peace with Persia is 464/3 (lately by Badian 1987), seven years after the *Persae.*

62. Cf. Michelini 1982, p. 78, on lines 87–90; "The army itself is likened [by the chorus] to an invincible natural force, which it would be folly to oppose."

63. Cf. Alexanderson 1967, p. 10: "The chorus suddenly seems to be in a more enterprising mood and suggests the sending of a new army to Greece, although it spoke despondently before about Asia's being no more controlled by the Persians and their power destroyed." Alexanderson believes that Aeschylus is making the Elders behave inconsistently. Again, it is preferable to avoid blaming Aeschylus instead of one's assumptions. What the Elders want from Darius is *not* admonitions to stand pat but advice from their late conquering hero on how to retrieve the disaster (*kakôn akos,* 631). Broadhead 1960 wrongly denies this, because he believes that the Queen speaks for the chorus; but in fact Aeschylus contrasts the Queen and chorus in every respect; even so, Broadhead too is moved to comment that

at lines 787–89 "the Chorus speaks as if they were somewhat bored by the King's excursion into Persian history" (p. 198).

64. Winnington-Ingram 1973, p. 215.

65. Cf. ibid., p. 217.

66. In an important discussion, Michelini, pp. 33–34 interprets the disobedience of the chorus at 694–96, "where the chorus' initial role is very hard to justify dramatically, their only contribution being their refusal to speak," as a device to allow the insertion of the second actor, as the Queen, in this scene of a play which "follows the format of a single-actor play quite exactly." This is to argue that the form is Aeschylus' master and not Aeschylus—by 472 more than twenty years a tragic poet—the master of his (admittedly evolving) form. The chorus' refusal to speak springs, rather, from the ethos which the playwright has bestowed on them. Whatever one may infer about earlier tragedy from Aeschylus' manipulation in the *Persae* of the two-actor form, it is demonstrably wrong to regard the *Persae* as flawed or immature, in the tradition descending from Wilamowitz. Dramatic function and ethical definition are closely wedded in this play; misinterpretation has proceeded from a failure to appreciate the Persians' ethos as Aeschylus delineated it for an audience of cognoscenti of the differences between barbarians and Hellenes. Later I discuss the first choral ode and the Queen's absence from the closing scene.

67. Note that they had ignored these words of the Queen in the stasima that followed her exits (532ff, 852ff), which are full of hostility to Xerxes and anticipate the character of their reception of him (here is another reason why lines 529–31 should stay put: above, n.51). Cf. Dworacki 1979, pp. 105ff.

68. Indeed, it is probable that only recently had foreign slaves become common in numbers at Athens as the result of the war and the slave-razzias that must have occurred during the allies' succeeding campaigns against the King's possessions: see Miller 1985, pp. 14–21. If so, Athenian slaveholders must have studied the character of this new type, much as antebellum slaveholders in the Southern United States studied the distinctions among African slaves of various tribal origins.

69. See the first section of chapter 7.

70. Other instances in Herodotus when tyrants inhibit free speech are listed by Lateiner 1989, p. 184.

71. See chapter 6.

72. Hirsch 1985, pp. 14–38, 153–63.

73. See Clifton 1963, p. 114, on the "vein of savagery and brutality running through the description of the Persians" in the *Persae;* cf.

Petrounias 1976, p. 17: "Die Perser pflegten Menschen wie Tiere zu 'jagen.'" On Greek observation or invention of Persian cruelties see, e.g., Hdt. 1.119.3–4; 3.118.2, cf. 154.2; 4.43.6; 5.25, 33.3; 7.39.3, 194.1; 9.122; Ctes. *Persica FGrH* 688 FF 9.1 and 6 (Cyrus' and Amytis' notable cruelties); 14 = 40a.12–15 Bekker (cf. Plut. *Artox.* 16.2–4), 40b31–34, 41b21–23 and 33–34; 15 = 43a2–4 and 35, 43b6–9, 44a3–6 Bekker; Plut. *Artox.* 14.2 and 5, 16. 2–4 and 17.5 (from Ctesias), 19.4–6 (from Dinon). These examples illustrate retrospectively the assumption lying behind the ethos of the Elders in the *Persae.*

74. Aeschylus himself provides the comparandum to the Elders in the chorus of the *Choephori,* who are Electra's Asiatic bondmaidens. There is no hint of fear in these slaves' regard. In this play mistress and maids alike share a loving and intimate common interest in their desire to secure vengeance for the murder of Agamemnon. The chorus members not only serve a different dramatic function in the *Choephori*—they encourage and abet, rather than baffle, their masters' barbaric intentions—but they appear to be also the products of a different household regime.

75. On the chorus' theology see Winnington-Ingram 1973, pp. 212–14. Their theology—their belief in the unfathomable and devious malice of deity—remains unaffected whether or not one prefers to transpose the (ruined) mesode, 93–100, with some editors to follow 106.

76. Dover 1974, s.v. "Slavery," cites the significant evidence in his discussion.

77. Although the functional aim of good treatment is to affirm the master's own nobility of character (cf., e.g., Dem. 47.55–56), while securing the slave's readier submission to his condition (Plato *Laws* 777d–e), the argument necessarily recognizes the slave's humanity in attributing to him feelings of dignity and gratitude.

78. For the condition of public slaves see *SEG* xxvi 72.13–16, 30–32, where stern flogging is mandated for malfeasance—but the number of strokes is carefully specified. Most instructive on the courses of relief available to private slaves against outrageous abuse is Christensen 1984.

79. Garlan 1988, esp. ch. 3, "The Theory and Practice of Slaveholding," is an antidote to optimistic views of the slave's lot at Athens; nevertheless institutionalized "escape-hatches" into personhood existed at Athens—and were exploited as encouragements by masters—which do not exist in the *Persae.*

80. Harsh 1955. Cf. Ehrenberg 1951, ch. 7, esp. 188–91; Dover 1972, pp. 204–8, on the "dominating and resourceful" slaves of New

Comedy, foreshadowed by Aristophanes' Xanthias and Carion (who bear foreign slave names, Lycian and Carian respectively). Dover notes that this type is absent from Aristophanes' earlier plays—a warning of the danger in retrojecting later evidence.

81. See Diller 1937, pp. 145–47, and Garlan 1988, pp. 70–71, for this category of slave at Athens. Manumitted metics: Whitehead 1977, pp. 16–17, 114–16.

82. Richardson 1952, pp. 58–59 thinks wrongly that the play's several references to stasis following the defeat reflect an imagined potential for rebellion of the part of the *Persians* as epitomized by the chorus; he cites in particular line 738 (a *double-entendre*) to support his case: *logos kratei saphênês touto g' ouk eni stasis* (Queen to the Ghost), "At any rate a certain report assures this; there is no doubt/rebellion." Precisely: there is *no* room in the Elder's nature for rebellion.

83. The term and its definition are those of Patterson 1982, ch. 11. His cases are the *familia Caesaris*, the military slaves of the medieval Islamic empires, and the court eunuchs of China and Byzantium.

84. Lesky 1966, pp. 243 and 267. Aristophanes' *Frogs* (405 B.C.) assumes the audience's familiarity with the *Persae*.

85. The impassivity of the male versus the histrionic and emotive role of the female is a fixed characteristic of Greek funerary custom from Geometric times onward. See Ahlberg 1971, pp. 77–78, for the earliest visual evidence, corresponding to *Il.* 10.78 and 406, 24.711, etc. Evidence for the classical period is summarized by Alexiou 1974, pp. 5ff. and nn. p. 206, with pp. 14–16, 102ff, and 132ff; also Garland 1985, pp. 21–35 and 137–45. Alexiou demonstrates exhaustively the linear persistence of the female mourners' role and function through later antiquity and the Byzantine period to our own day in rural Greece.

86. Hellenic opinion strongly depreciated histrionic excess as socially threatening, and the ritualization of female *akosmia* was supplemented by legislative discipline from Solon onward (Plut. *Solon* 21). See Humphreys 1980, pp. 99–100.

87. As do barbarian slave women in the chorus (*dmôai gynaikes* 85) at *Choeph.* 423–24, with their breast-beating, rending of garments and cheeks, etc. (22ff), behavior which Aeschylus identifies specifically as Persian (Arian, Cissian: 443).

88. Cf. Michelini 1982, pp. 88–91, on the Queen's first speech.

89. See ibid., pp. 87ff and 92ff; Fraenkel 1950, 2:378 on *Ag.* 820, comments that "Aeschylus forcibly over-emphasizes the note of excess, because it is for him an extremely important idea: excess, *to lian, to agan,* etc., is in his opinion the very thing which imperils human happiness and peace more than anything else. It is not an

exact parallel, but a case closely resembling this in thought, when Darius, whose chief mission consists in constantly renewed rejection of impious excess, uses twice in quick succession a very similar redundance of expression, *Pers.* 794 *kteinousa . . . agan* and 827 *Zeus . . . epestin.*"

90. Oddly, Winnington-Ingram 1973 treats the attitudes to divinity of the chorus and Queen in identical terms in order to contrast the theology of Darius with the theology promulgated before—and after—his epiphany. This is not strictly correct, because the Queen does not identify a man (Darius) as a god. It is true that she also treats the deity as incalculable but her attitude produces opposite ethical consequences. Her innate sense of limit, measure, and caution about divine action stands in antipodal contrast to the Elders' heedlessness.

91. Wilamowitz-Möllendorf 1897, pp. 382–83. However, Wilamowitz was at a loss to explain the chorus's aporia in terms of Aeschylus' intentions and regarded it as a flaw in an immature work. But this is perverse, since Aeschylus had been presenting tragedies for nearly two decades, and had won his first contest in 484. Others have been disturbed by the Elders' intention here instead of interpreting it as an early signpost of their ethos. Stoessl 1945, p. 150, attributes their behavior to imitative dependence on Phrynichus' *Phoenissae;* cf. Korzeniewski 1966, pp. 554–56. Kitto 1961, p. 35, reads with Wilamowitz an "awkward moment" in which Aeschylus' art fails him: "The chorus is, in fact, in an unprofitable situation, and we are glad when the Queen arrives, to rescue them from it."

92. I cite lines 116, 142, 161, 165, 245, 372, 374, 472, 606, 703, 707, 725, 750, 767, 782, 808, 820, 828, 950, without reckoning a handful of related locutions. The disaster of the Persians itself is the direct consequence of Xerxes' *athea phronêmata* (808).

93. See Michelini 1982, pp. 77–78, on the irony of heroic language as applied by barbarians to themselves; *isotheos phôs* in is a particularly striking oxymoron (they abound: see Petrounias 1976, pp. 1–31).

94. Prickard 1879, p. 60, on lines 215–25: "As readers of dreams the Chorus are meant to be well-affected but incompetent."

95. Cf. Michelini 1982, p. 66, n. 2.

96. Cf. Goldhill 1988, esp. pp. 191–92, for the significance of the Queen's response.

97. Cf. Plato *Laws* 720c–e similarly on physicians to slaves, themselves slaves, who neither give an account of their patients' symptoms nor rationally justify their treatment, in contrast to free physicians and their free patients, whose treatment is founded on achieving an active and rationally understood collaboration in a regimen of cure.

98. Michelini 1982, p. 107, remarks that to a psychological critic, the Queen "might be revealed as unmaternal or unnatural in her lack of extended emotional reaction." The Queen is comparatively stoic not only in consonance with her "personal" ethos, her conviction that man must bear the burdens assigned by the gods, but with her "institutional" ethos as mistress of a slave household. The contrast in her mind lies between the survival of her son, which guarantees the continuity of her house, and the loss of mere slaves, albeit valuable slaves.

99. Winnington-Ingram 1973, p. 215. The Elders will not again name Zeus, even though the Ghost will identify him insistently (740, 762, 827) as the master of events and Xerxes too, upon his entrance, will invoke the name of Zeus (915). On "Zeus" in line 915: "This final naming of the name of Zeus is of course intended to remind the audience of the words of Darius; and it might also seem to be the cue for the Chorus, if they had learnt their lesson, to repeat it. But nothing comes from them except the familiar mention of a *daimon* of destruction (921)" (p. 218).

100. Note that they cry out in *barbarasaphênê* (635), a *double-entendre:* the chorus believe they chant their invocation in *barbara saphênê,* in "clear barbarian," whereas the Athenian audience knows that they speak—and think—in *barbar' asaphênê*—"unclear barbarian." Attempts, like those of Broadhead, to choose between the two readings are therefore otiose; cf. Broadhead 1960, p. 166, on lines 633–39.

101. The shade of Darius unquestionably is an exalted spirit, who knows the purpose of Zeus and has achieved place and influence with the gods below (line 691; cf. Broadhead 1960, on lines 691–93, glossing *endunasteusas*). But he is not a god in any sense understood by the Greeks, for it is only a few begrudged moments that his position in the underworld has won him in the world of the living above the tomb, *à la* the apparitions of *Odyssey* book 10. In the untidy hierarchy of the underworld, Darius' stature is comparable to no greater a personage than the Theban seer Teiresias, son of the mortal Eueres and the nymph Charicle (*Od.* 10.492ff, etc.), who alone of mortals was granted his wits to keep in the underworld, or at best to "Minos and Rhadamanthus and Aeacus and Triptolemus, judges of the dead who," says Plato's Socrates (*Apol.* 41a), "were upright in their earthly life," and whom he imagines as semidivine in status (*hêmithoi*). But these figures, unlike Darius, were hallowed by myth and lived in a nobler age.

102. See Plato *Phaedr.* 258b, where Darius is included with the lawgivers

Lycurgus and Solon. Darius is lawgiver again at *Laws* 695 c–e; note the contrast to Xerxes descending from the *Persae*. Cf. *Ep.* 7.332a.

103. See chapter 7.

104. Hdt. 5.102.1, 105; 6.44.1, 94; 7.1.1.

105. Cf. Thuc. 1.14.3, implicitly "correcting" Herodotus, in order to make his own Themistocles appear all the more foresighted.

106. Hdt. 7.5.2, 8β1f, 138.1; 8.α2, 102.3.

107. If that is the meaning of the text.

108. To imagine the Queen playing Xerxes would postulate an astonishingly quick change, given the brevity of the ode (852–906) between the Queen's second exit and Xerxes' entrance.

109. As when the Queen discovers that the Athenians "are called slaves or subjects of no mortal" (242) and thereupon exclaims (243), "Then how can they withstand the manhood of a foreign enemy?" Cf. Xerxes at Hdt. 7.103.3–5.

110. Van Gennep 1960, pp. 146–65 is the seminal theoretical treatment. See Huntington and Metcalf 1979, esp. pp. 8–11, Garland 1985 for an anthropological perspective on the ancient rites: on histrionic lamentations see pp. 29–31 and 141–42.

111. Bloch and Parry 1982, pp. 225–26: "The devalued side, the side of decomposition, is so often acted out by being associated with women while the other side—the eternal order of traditional authority which shines pure and creative against this contrasting background—is associated either with men or with the group as an undifferentiated entity."

112. The year of the Eurymedon has been argued variously between 469 and 466. Meiggs 1972, pp. 80–82, argues for 467/6; Badian 1987, p. 4, would place it "not later than 466." The case for 469 is best made by Jacoby 1947b, esp. p. 3, n. 1. The Messenger's words at *Pers.* 894ff, *Salamina te / tas nun matropolis tônd' / aitia stenagmôn,* may well reflect that ambition to control Cyprus which led to the long-prepared-for Eurymedon campaign (for which a fleet of new-model triremes was built: Plut. *Cimon* 12.2). The play therefore furnishes some encouragement to accept an early date for the Eurymedon, with the consequence that the *Persae* was first performed in an atmosphere of aggressive feelings and preparations against the Persians' positions in Cyprus and Syro-Phoenicia.

113. Herodotus was probably at Athens in the 440s: Jacoby 1913, cols. 226, 240.

114. Sparta was in fact saved by the naval victory of Salamis, where according to the traditions mined by Herodotus, the Spartans played an inglorious part. The Spartans' own claim to have possessed this response long before the events (7.239, cf. 20.1: 484 B.C.) is another

compelling indication that they circulated it very soon after Thermopylae. On the Spartans' responsibility for the failure of the Greeks'
war plan see Georges 1986, pp. 42–59. On oracles as propaganda
and the Spartans' relationship with Delphi see ibid., pp. 23–37.

115. The association hung on in Athenian popular thought, to appear
in the name of an overelaborate dish called "Zeus' Brain" (Ephippus
comicus, fr. 13 K: fourth century), which was known also as "The
King's Brain" according to Zenobius (3.41 L-S): cited by Long 1986,
p. 70. I exclude as uncontrollable the Persian evidence for the King's
nature and position in the eyes of his subjects, e.g., the Letter of
Darius (*SGHI* 12) and royal inscriptions of this period, even though
the Bisitun text (DB in Kent 1953; cf. pp. 131ff) has turned up in
a papyrus version from Elephantine (Cowley 1923, pp. 248ff) and
is reflected in Herodotus' account of Darius' accession. It was circulated as a kind of *Res gestae sacri Darii* throughout the provinces
(DB 4.90f).

In the inscriptions the King rules and accomplishes his every
work and deed by grace of the universal god Ahura Mazda (AmH
6–8, AsH 5–9, Db I 11–14, DPJ 1–5 in Kent 1953, for Darius;
Kent's XP a, b, c and note esp. XPf 27–43 for Xerxes). This is a
formula closely comparable to Aesch. *Pers.* 762–64. But we cannot
assume that in 472 the Athenians, or for that matter Aeschylus
alone, had been reliably informed about the Persians' ideology of
kingship. *Persae* 762–64 stands on its own as the application to a
particular case of the principle that everything is determined by the
divine will, and for the rest of what appears in the *Persae,* much
could have been taken from impressions gained from the spoils and
from captured Persians (cf. Hdt. 9.79–82), as well as the claim of
Xerxes' Ionian diplomatic agents at Argos and probably elsewhere
that Xerxes and the "Persidae" (= Achaemenids, Hdt. 1.125.3 *fin.*)
were descended from Perseus and thereby from Zeus (Hdt. 7.61.3
and 150.2).

Chapter Five. Herodotus' Typology of Hellenism

1. Cf. Thébert 1980, p. 100.
2. See Pritchett 1985, pp. 159–77, for the evidence on battlefield
burials from legendary into historical times. Although battlefield
burial and battlefield honors to the dead were universal among the
Greeks, Marathon is the first *archaeologically certain* instance in
Greek history of the *heroization* of the dead upon the battlefield, to
be followed by the tombs of the fallen at Thermopylae and Plataea:
for these burials only the barrows at Troy furnished a true precedent.

The 192 Athenian dead (Hdt. 6.117.1) would return to Athena's precinct as the 192 ephebic horsemen in the Panathenaic frieze of the Partheon: Boardman 1985, p. 250.

3. Herodotus (7.144.1–2) is emphatic on this point and represents the superior tradition against Thucydides (1.14.3), who was influenced by an inordinate admiration for Themistocles' foresight (cf. 1.93.7).

4. On these oracles' contemporaneity and relationship to the events of the war see chapter 4 and Georges 1986, esp. pp. 19–40.

5. Date: Badian 1988, pp. 301–2, 313–14.

6. See Evans 1988 on Pausanias; Podlecki 1975, pp. 37–42, on Themistocles.

7. Plut. *Alc.* 16.1. Cf. Connor 1971, p. 147 and n. 147, citing and translating Eupolis' *Demes,* fr. 147: "And no longer, lords Miltiades and Pericles, let swinging teenagers rule us, dragging the generalship around their ankles."

8. On Persian fads and fashions at imperial Athens see above all Miller 1985, esp. ch. 4 on costume.

9. See Ryder 1965 and Seager 1974 on Persia's role in Greek politics in this era.

10. Long 1986.

11. Bowra 1961, pp. 308ff.

12. Drews 1973, pp. 20–36, provides an excellent brief discussion concerning them as well as the poets. Jacoby's case for Herodotus' priority to Hellanicus, based on the testimonia and Hellanicus' synthetic treatment of the "Pelasgian problem," is a strong one: *FGrH* 4 *Komm.* pp. 430–44 and 328 (Philochorus) *Komm.*, p. 412. Lateiner 1989, p. 116, would include Scylax (*FGrH* 709) as a fourth author on the Persians, and names (p. 106), as authors known to Herodotus, Charon, Xanthus (based on *FGrH* 765 T 5), and Evagon of Samos (*FGrH* 535). I would agree concerning Charon and disagree concerning Xanthus (Lateiner misinterprets T 5 as testimony to Xanthus' priority: below, n. 25); concerning Evagon almost nothing is known, hence a verdict of *non liquet.*

13. By von Fritz 1967, 1.1:78; cf. Pohlenz 1937, p. 21. Cf. Drews 1973, p. 154, n. 7.

14. The other authorities unanimously give her father as Cyrus, not Ariaspes.

15. *FGrH* 4 F 7; cf. 7c: Atossa introduces the service of eunuchs from Babylonian practice.

16. Discussion in Drews 1973, pp. 23–24, 27–29.

17. Bisitun: see chapter 4, n. 115. Cf. Lehmann-Haupt 1902, p. 338, and Drews 1973, pp. 20–22, 30, 80 with notes; Balcer 1987.

18. On Charon's dates I accept Drews 1973, pp. 24–26.
19. Tertullian *De an.* 46: *Astyages Medorum regnator quod filiae Mandanae adhuc virginis vesicam in diluvionem Asia fluxisse somnion viderit, Herodotus refert; item anno post nuptias eius ex isdem locis vitem exortam toti Asiae incubasse. hoc etiam Charon Lampsacenus Herodoto prior dedit.*
20. Cf. Theognis 805–10 on the hazard awaiting those who alter the words of the god (i.e., Delphian Apollo: the warning is against forgery).
21. F 4; cf. Hdt. 1.156–60.
22. F 5; cf. Hdt. 5.99–102.
23. See chapter 3.
24. Drews 1973, pp. 23–24.
25. Ibid., pp. 91, 100ff. Later authors put Xanthus' birth in the mid-sixth century (T 1), but this date is too early since he mentions an event of the reign of Artaxerxes I (*reg.* 465–425: F 12) and wrote a monograph on the mid-fifth-century philosopher Empedocles of Acragas (F 33). Thus he was a contemporary of Herodotus. Although Ephorus is often cited for the statement that Xanthus was Herodotus' basic authority for Lydian history (*FGrH* 70 F 180 = Athenaeus 12.515d), he actually says only that Xanthus provided his starting point (*tas aphormas*): Drews 1973, p. 102. There is no point of contact between the extant fragments of Xanthus and Herodotus, and no reason therefore to presume that Herodotus knew his work.

    Xanthus' *Lydiaka* was in four books (T 1); they were probably intended to associate the Lydians with the Trojans and thereafter with the history of the Greeks of Asia, since they included reference to the fall of Troy (F 21), the existence of a Lydian town named Melampeia after the seer Melampus (F 27), whom Herodotus credits with the introduction of the cult of Dionysus into Greece (2.49; note in this connection the Lydian vintage-god Bakillis [Gr. Bakchos]: Gusmani 1980–86, p. 74), the migration of the Phrygians into the Troad led by Scamandrius from the Berecyntes and Ascania (F 14), and the foundation of Thasos (in the eighteenth Olympiad = 708/5: F 30).
26. His father's name was Candaules (T 1), indicating that the family may have claimed direct or collateral Heraclid blood.
27. Cf. chapter 3, n. 17. Still useful on the character of Xanthus' work is Pearson 1939, pp. 109–38. Lateiner 1989, p. 218, in a section titled "The Isolation of Herodotus," notes that not the Histories but "the fraudulent Ctesias and the romancer [*sic*] Xenophon met the desire for accounts of the Orient and the Persian court" in the fourth century. The "popularity of Ctesias suggests that many Greeks were

not interested in accurate history. Simplification, distortion, omission, and deformation of the record better served the interests of orators, adventurers, and patriotic historians."

28. Cf. Eur. *Andromache* 173, 243–44: Hermione accuses Andromache of barbarian incest.

29. *FGrH* 765 F 4a (from Athenaeus) with T 5.

30. The Suda's author was thinking of males, who remain epicene when castrated before puberty. The clitoris is anatomically homologous not with the male gonads but with the glans. Following severe trauma the permanent effect of this mutilation upon women is the loss of their principal organ of sexual arousal. Accordingly, the practice understood by the Suda's author—if it is not an invention—may have instead been labiectomy, an operation that reduces the entrance to the vagina by scarring. The practice of female "castration" also came to be attributed in antiquity to other Asiatic peoples: Strabo 16.2.37 C761; 3.5, 9 C767, 4.9 C771; Diod. 3.32. Both clitoridectomy and labiectomy continue to be practiced in some parts of the Middle East and Africa, according to Russell and Van de Ven 1984, pp. 194–95. I owe this reference to my colleague Arlene Eskilson.

31. *FGrH* 765 F 18 (from Athenaeus); cf. Pearson 1939, pp. 131–32, on this story and the preceding anecdote.

32. *FGrH* 90 F 22. On Xanthus' relationship to Nicolaus through a Helenistic intermediary see von Fritz 1967 1.2:348–77.

33. F 63; cf. Xenophilus *FGrH* 767 F 1. Drews, 1973, p. 102, adduces good arguments for limiting the *Lydiaka* in their original form to the Heraclids, but also recognizes a motive for Xanthus possibly including slanders against the Mermnads.

34. See Detienne 1979, p. 154.

35. Ibid., p. 144 and esp. Vernant 1982.

36. The literature on Herodotus' originality and his place in the intellectual history of his times is immense: see briefly Immerwahr 1966, pp. 1–16, and Dihle 1962.

37. On the question of possible native sources of the stereotype, however, see the suggestive article of Murray 1987, pp. 113–14, discussing the possibility that the *Palastgeschichte* of Herodotus, Xanthus, and Ctesias had a common derivation in *Persian* conceptions about their ruling circles at court, and are fundamentally accounts of court life as Persians in the provinces saw it. He points further to the existence of a unified Persian-Lydian aristocratic culture in Asia Minor as the direct source of this picture, which fused Persian and Lydian traditions into a single image of Asiatic barbarism. He

comments that in Xanthus of Lydia, "Lydian history became fully assimilated to the Persian model" (p. 114).

38. Benardete 1969, p. 24.

39. Noted by Lateiner 1989, pp. 36, 46 with n. 108, and 141–42.

40. Cf. Lloyd 1990, p. 244: "On the one hand, the work presents historical manifestations of the cosmic *polemos* to maintain order; on the other, it takes the form of an intense enquiry into which the human element in the cosmos was seen to divide and by such mechanisms as *interpretatio Graeca,* the detection of similarities, and the predilection for diffusionism attempts to bring about an accommodation between the two. The subject of the work is . . . neither war nor ethnography" but an "exploration of a major element amongst the dualities which, to Herodotus and his contemporaries, were built into the very fabric of the universe." In short, "the *Histories* are nothing less than an attempt to render comprehensible the human world in which Herodotus lived."

41. See Hunter 1982, pp. 53ff.

42. Suda s.v. *Hêrodotos,* where he is called Herodotus' *exadelphon;* alternative family stemmata are given by the ancient authorities. Panyassis is usually called Herodotus' uncle, but Matthews thinks that they were first cousins: Matthews 1974, p. 11. Panyassis is a Carian name: see *SGHI* 32.15f, from Halicarnassus.

43. Dion. Hal. *De imit.* 2; Quintilian 10.1.54. He was the last of the five canonical epic poets; the others besides Homer and Hesiod were Antimachus and Pisander: Lesky 1966, p. 107.

44. Suda s.v. *Panuasis.* Cf. Matthews 1974, pp. 26–31.

45. See Gillis 1979, pp. 1–37, with bibliography. Barron 1964b, p. 46 with n. 65, suggests that at 1.146, where he ridicules the Ionians' racial pride, Herodotus is attacking Panyassis' *Ionica,* if not Pherecydes. Probably Herodotus was rejecting both them and others.

46. Panyassis gives Heracles' son by Omphale the name Acheles or Acheletes: cf. Herodotus' Alcaeus (1.7.2: the first Heraclid king of Lydia). Hellanicus (*FGrH* 4 F 112) mentions the name of a Lydian town, *Akelê,* derived from Acelus, son of Heracles and Malis, a slave-girl belonging to Omphale. Herodotus' slave-girl is nameless and belongs to a certain Iardanus, who also appears in Nicolaus (*FGrH* 90 F 22a), almost certainly *via* Xanthus. Herodotus does not further identify Iardanus, in this way too implicitly rejecting Panyassis, who had identified him as Omphale's father in the *Heraclea.* As usual, Herodotus had alternative traditions from which to choose—or even to construct for himself—his "true" version.

47. Fr. 26K = Athenaeus 4.172D, with Matthews 1974, pp. 127–28. Cf. Huxley 1969, pp. 177–78, who notes that "Herodotus, it seems,

tactitly disagreed with his kinsman," whom he never mentions, "remarkably enough."

48. Herodotus uses *mythos* twice only, here and at 2.23.1; in both cases it signifies disbelief.

49. The Suda, s.v. *Panuasis,* calls him a *teratoskopos,* literally an "examiner of portents," and more loosely, a prophet or soothsayer. Cf. Huxley 1969, p. 188.

50. Cf. Hartog 1988, p. 289: "He had not the words to express what he was actually doing; he wanted to be a rhapsode but could only be a rhapsode in prose." Ibid., p. 315: "Where the poet invoked the Muse, claiming to be no more than her mouthpiece, Herodotus introduces *historie,* inquiry. And by the end of the nine books he has replaced the epic memories with a new type of memorial for the city. No doubt the inventory if the Persian army in Book 7 does 'resemble' the catalogue of ships in Book 2 of the *Iliad,* but the one is dictated by the Muse whereas the other is presented simply as the transcription of an inventory."

51. Note in particular Hdt. 8.77.2. Cf. Kirchberg 1965, esp. pp. 9–10, 92–94, 118–20; the roles of the oracle and that of the historian, working after the event to reconstruct the pattern, are parallel and synergistic.

52. His history of the Mermnads is precisely bracketed by the oracular material at 1.13 and 1.91; cf. von Fritz 1967, 1.1:215, 234. The account of the Hellenic resistance is similarly bounded by the oracles at 7.140–41 and 8.77 and 96. The structural function of oracles in Herodotus is elucidated in detail by Immerwahr 1966, index, s.vv. "Delphi," "oracles."

53. See Kirchberg 1965, pp. 11–29, and Schwabl 1969, pp. 258ff, on Herodotus' exalted Delphian piety.

54. Cf. Flower 1991, p. 61 with n. 27, on Herodotus' confidence in his Delphian source.

55. Others, especially Drews 1973, pp. 32ff, and Evans 1991, p. 146, point to the Persian Wars as the "Great Event" that motivated, and then shaped, Herodotus' work. There is much obvious truth in this, although I would place stress also on the influence of Athens' rise to empire over other Greeks in his own lifetime. External motivations aside, I see Herodotus' deeply religious outlook driving the whole armature of his thought concerning the historical process. I might add that my views on the Herodotean *Entwicklungsfrage* are close to those of Fornara 1971a, pp. 1–23. Views descending from Jacoby 1913 make use of modern categories that did not exist in the mind of Herodotus, and have been made obsolete by the kinds of structural analysis pioneered by Immerwahr 1966, Detienne, and Hartog

1988. The Histories obey laws of purpose only, and reveal nothing substantial concerning Herodotus' "maturation" apart from the necessary growth of a genius devoted throughout life to a single grand project.

56. Lateiner 1989, pp. 197ff, denies a significant role to Herodotus' religiosity in the Histories, but he is far more concerned with Herodotus' methods than with his aims.

57. Dodona: 2.53–57; Zeus Ammon: 2.42.3. Herodotus says nothing about Delphi, but he makes clear that Apollo is Egyptian (2.83, 144, 155–56), although at 2.155 the oracular Egyptian goddess whom he identifies with Leto is the nurse, not the mother, of Apollo and Artemis. Herodotus almost certainly accepted the canonical myth that the god himself slew the serpent Python at Delphi, which hitherto had been an oracle of Earth (earliest reference *Hom. Hymn* 3.300ff; cf. Apollodorus 1.22).

58. A final note on the *Entwicklungsfrage*: this view of the Egyptian logos also helps dispose of the dissectionist notion that Herodotus first gathered his material as a "Hecatean."

59. See n. 42 above and von Fritz 1967, 1.1: 234ff, 247–50, 294ff. On Xerxes' war, see chapter 4.

60. His method was accordingly circular, for "the ideal of a *vaticinium ex eventu* does not seem to have crossed his mind": Nock 1942, p. 476.

61. The Lydians were the foreigners most familiar to the Asiatic Greeks and most like the Greeks in their customs (1.94.1). They are the only barbarians, besides Darius and his confederates who participate in the Debate on Constitutions (3.80ff), to whom Herodotus provides sophisms. Cf. the fatal arguments from *eikos* and *physis* employed by Croesus' son against his father (1.39ff) and Croesus' impious argument from *to kathêkon* against Pythian Apollo (1.90.4ff). In thus placing a critically destructive parody of sophistical argumentation in the mouths of barbarians, his position is close to that of Heraclitus on persons with *barbarous psykhas*. Herodotus took a jaundiced view of the political results of the new rhetoric but in other respects he owed a great deal to the sophists: see esp. Dihle 1967 on Herodotus' intellectual debts to them.

62. Herodotus' treatment of the Athenians' execution of Spartan and other envoys to the Persian King in 430 seems to be a reaction to contemporary events. The arguments, and the bibliography, on the date of the Histories are recoverable *via* Jacoby 1913, col. 233; Fornara 1971b; Cobet 1977; Fornara 1981; Evans 1979 and 1989.

63. See Alty 1982 on Dorians and Ionians constituting separate and hostile *ethnê* in the Greek mind, having differing *physeis*. He com-

ments correctly that Herodotus' work is "pervaded by a systematic bias against the Ionians": p. 11 with n. 60. Cf. Neville 1979 and Murray 1979, p. 274. In Thucydides the contrast between free Dorians versus servile and mongrelized Ionians is a strong rhetorical topos in the mouths of Spartan and Dorian speakers: Thuc. 1.124.1, 5.9.1, 6.77.1, 7.5.4; cf. 3.86.2 and esp. 8.25.5, where Thucydides notices the distinction in his own persona.

64. See Edmunds 1990 on the connotation of *nêpios* in Homer of disconnection from society, from future fame and even from life itself, as well as with an inability to make cognitive connections between past and future.

65. Application of the barbarian stereotype to Greeks—and vice versa—was of course not unique to Herodotus; it pervaded contemporary Athenian drama: see Hall 1989, ch. 5.

66. Other relevant passages: 1.4, 58, 60; 7.139, 145; 8.12.

67. On Herodotus' "authorial voice" and his stance as an authority, see Dewald and Marincola 1987, esp. pp. 160–68.

68. Cf. Fornara 1971, pp. 84–86.

69. Herodotus' ambivalence to Athens has been frequently recognized since the seminal article of Strasburger 1955; cf., e.g., Fornara 1971, pp. 75–90; Schwartz 1969; Forrest 1984.

70. Kreston = Umbrian Cortona? Briquel 1984, pp. 101–68, sums up the controversy on the alternative readings. See below, n. 76.

71. At 8.44.2 Herodotus states that "when the Pelasgians possessed the country now called Greece the Athenians were Pelasgians, having the name Cranai, until in the reign of king Cecrops they got the name of Cecropidae; when the kingship passed to Erechtheus their name changed to Athenians, and when Ion son of Xuthus became their commander the Athenians were named Ionians after him." Here he does violence to Athenian tradition: see How and Wells 1912 *ad loc.*

72. On the textual and grammatical problems of this text and its interpretation see now McNeal 1985, esp. p. 21: "Herodotus gets himself into verbal difficulties," he concludes, "because ... he wants to establish an antithesis between Spartans and Athenians ... [but] he has to square this contrast with the respective traditions of these two peoples," especially those of the Athenians.

73. On the barbarism of Minyans see below, n. 118.

74. See Appendix, "Pelasgians, Leleges, Caucones." Still useful is Myres 1907: although he asserts that already "within Homeric times time *Hellên* and *Pelasgos* came ... to stand for 'civilized' and 'uncivilized' respectively" (p. 183), his own discussion of the logographers from Acusilaus to Hellanicus, and the tragedians who followed them (pp.

186–91) shows that this conclusion is by no means certain. What his discussion appears to demonstrate, rather, is the progress of change in belief concerning the Pelasgians' identity, from Hellenic to barbarian, in the course of the fifth century. The question of the Pelasgians in general, versus the Pelasgians of Attica and their identity with the Tyrsenoi, is treated with typical lucidity by Jacoby, Philochorus *FGrH* 328 FF 99–101 *Komm.*

75. See chapter 1, first section.

76. Cortona (if that is the true reading) was an Etruscan city: Neppi Modona 1977. Hellanicus (*FGrH* 4 F 4) and Thucydides (4.109.4) identified the Tyrsenoi as Pelasgians, as did also Philochorus (*FGrH* 328 FF 99–101, with Jacoby's discussion, *Suppl.* i, 407ff). Dionysius of Halicarnassus' manuscript of Herodotus apparently read *Krotôniê-tai* for *Krêstoniêtai* at 1.57.3, and he identifies Cortona as the chief town of the Pelasgians in Italy (*RA* 1.29). The arguments for this reading are set out by How and Wells 1912, ad loc. Cf. Briquel, above n. 70.

77. See How and Wells 1912, 1:438.

78. Burkert 1977, p. 242.

79. Myres 1907, pp. 197–202, distinguishes in Herodotus two groups of Pelasgians in Attica: (1) the ancient Pelasgians of Athens who became Greek even before the Ionian Revolt; (2) more recent Pelasgian immigrants, who were expelled and settled in Lemnos. This is manifestly correct, save that Herodotus never makes the distinction explicit.

80. On the problem of dating the *Supplices* see Lesky 1966, pp. 243–44. The racial politics of the *Supplices,* if we may so call them, are the earliest illustration of the anti-Dorian theme used at Athens against Sparta, which becomes prominent during the Peloponnesian War. In the *Supplices* the pre-Dorian Pelasgian Argives are assimilated to the Athenians, almost certainly anticipating or celebrating the alliance with Argos at the end of the 460s, following the Spartans' expulsion of the Athenian army under Cimon which had marched to Ithome to help them against the insurgent Messenians (Thuc. 1.102.4).

Pelasgus son of Palaechthon ("Ancient of the Earth"), king of Argos in *Suppl.* 463, is the wholly Greek aboriginal eponym of the Pelasgians and, *pace* the Argives' pro-Persian policy in 480, antibarbarian (the lustful and imperious Egyptians of the play are given an Asiatic character). Argos itself is no tyranny but—uniquely in surviving tragedy—a Greek polis where the people's will is law. Pelasgus is also master of a realm that includes the whole of European Greece as well as Dodona (cf. *Il.* 16.233; Hes. fr. 319 MW), the

Strymon watershed and the territories of the Paeonians (*Suppl.* 249–59), barbarian districts colonized by Athenians and other, mostly Ionian, Greeks who were members of Athens' imperial league.

81. Meiggs 1972, ch. 16, "Religious Sanctions," esp. pp. 292–95.

82. See Loraux 1979 and 1986, pp. 1 with n. 4 (citing Plato *Menexenus* 245d2–4), 148–49, 193–94.

83. *LSJ*⁹, s.vv. *tryphê, trypheros.*

84. The *Ion* criticizes the narrowly exclusive ideology of autochthony that this genealogy expresses: Saxonhouse 1986, esp. pp. 256–60, building upon Loraux 1979. Thereby it provides evidence for its strength and pervasiveness at Athens.

85. For the date see Lesky 1966, pp. 376–79.

86. Cf. Thuc. 5.77.1 with Dover's note in Gomme and Dover 1970; Parker 1987, pp. 194–95, citing also Hdt. 7.161.3 and Eur. *Erechtheus* fr. 50.6–13 (= 360 Nauck). Note the irony of Hdt. 9.27.

87. Podlecki 1977 argues that Herodotus never visited Athens; but I am not persuaded.

88. Jacoby 1913, cols. 237ff.

89. The oldest tradition indicates that *Thourios* was read in the *proemium; Halikarnêssios* was presumably inserted by the Alexandrian editors: see Arist. *Rhet.* 3.1409a29; Duris *FGrH* 76 F 64 = Suda s.v. *Panuasis Polyarkhou Halikarnasseus;* cf. Plut. *Mor.* 604F = *De exil.* 13. Discussion: Jacoby 1913, cols. 206f.

90. Bockisch 1969, pp. 118–33; Matthews 1974, p. 6, with collected reff., noting that the "large numbers of Karian names in the early inscriptions must indicate a strong mixture of native Karians among the Greek settlers of Halikarnassos." See too Bean and Cook 1955, p. 96, and *SGHI* 32, from Halicarnassus of mid-fifth-century date, which appears to show that, while a good deal of intermarriage was going on, the Greek and Carian communities still had their own magistrates.

91. Hdt. 6.52.1, 7.204, 8.132.2, and esp. 9.26, with Rose 1958, p. 267 and n. 44 for later sources.

92. According to schol. Ap. Rhod. 4.1149–50, p. 308 Wendel and schol. Vict. *ad Il.* 24.616 (cited by Huxley 1969, p. 181), Panyassis' *Heraclea* had Heracles name *two* sons Hyllus and, likewise, two other sons Acheles, after two rivers *in Lydia* which had healed or purified him. By elimination the other Lydian-born Hyllus—perhaps a twin—must be the ancestor of the Peloponnesian Heraclids.

93. Huxley 1969, p. 186.

94. Significantly, the names of Milesian *stephanophoroi* are almost all Greek: *Milet* i 3, no. 122.

95. Plut. *De mal. Her.* 35 = *Mor.* 868A.

96. Munson 1988 is exemplary on the ironies and contradictions in Herodotus' presentation of Artemisia. But she does not note the possibility of a simpler, though not exclusive, explanation of Herodotus' treatment of Artemisia: that she was his great-aunt. Bockisch 1969, p. 127, n. 2, cites Dittenberger *Syll.*³ i 55 N 46, an inscription *c.* 450 from Halicarnassus, naming a certain "Lyxes son of Pigres." Lyxes was the name of Herodotus' father and Pigres that of the brother of Artemisia.
97. *LSJ*⁹, s.v. *apodeixis.*
98. Cf. Nagy 1987 on Herodotus as *logios,* esp. pp. 179ff and 183ff; note, however, M. Lang's corrective on p. 204 of the same volume: Herodotus did not regard himself as a *logios* (he calls only foreigners *logioi*) but as someone of far higher authority: on this, C. Fornara on p. 139 in the same volume: "Herodotus correctly assumed that his personal experience was a part of his apodexis which would count high with the Greeks when he was in the position to vouchsafe it (see esp. ii 148)."
99. Alty 1982, esp. pp. 3–11, is a very nuanced study of anti-Dorian feeling at Athens during the Peloponnesian War, which coexisted with an "inferiority complex" vis-à-vis Dorians, as when the Athenians distinguished themselves from their defeated and Asiatic Ionian subjects. The quality of these prejudices is better expressed, I think, by the older term "racial" than such less-loaded words as "ethnic."
100. Cf. Schwartz 1969. The story was evidently well known at Athens, for Aristophanes was soon to call Alcibiades, Pericles' ward and kinsman through his Alcmaeonid mother, the "lion's whelp" (*Frogs* 1425). For the meaning of the simile to Athenians, see Aesch. *Ag.* 716–36.
101. Hartog 1988, p. 269 with n. 31.
102. Thuc. 2.65.9; Plut. *Per.* 16.1–2.
103. Thucydides leaves this in no doubt (e.g., 1.86.5: the Spartans' fear of Athens' future imperial growth; 1.144.1: Pericles' advice to the Athenians not to attempt new gains *while the war was still in progress*; 2.36.2: Pericles on the superior virtue of their forefathers, who added to their inheritance by procuring the empire in the first place; 2.62.2: Pericles on their absolute mastery of the sea with reference to even greater power at sea for the future). Among the latest of a large literature see Hornblower 1983, pp. 127–38; Fornara and Samons 1991, pp. 140–46.
104. Cf. Lewis 1977, p. 148, citing Fornara 1971, p. 50.
105. Gomme 1933 and 1959; Jones 1957, appendix on population.
106. Diyllus FGrH 73 F 3 = Plut. *Mor.* 862 A–B (*De mal. Her.* 26). Cf. Jacoby 1913, cols. 226f.

107. See later discussion on "the wrath of Talthybius," in this chapter.

108. Incidently, this is a neglected bit of evidence for a Peace of Callias.

109. An oracle of Zeus existed at Olympia (Parke, 1967, ch. 8, esp. pp. 184–86 on this episode). Chilon, one of the canonical Seven Sages, who in Herodotus is always prescient (cf. 7.235), interprets a portent that occurs within the sacred precinct of Olympian Zeus. Both in its provenance and in its function, his interpretation corresponds to an oracle from the divinity.

110. Pisistratus claimed royal Athenian descent from the Neleids of Pylos, foreigners (*epilydes:* 5.65.3) who became kings of Athens, as Herodotus points out, seemingly gratuitously: everyone knew who the Neleids were.

111. Six Oxford Classical Text pages: about twelve minutes' recitation at my own pace.

112. He used her *ou kata nomon,* in unlawful coitus that prevented conception (1.61.1). In the Histories tyrants typically practice unnatural and sterile relations with women. The tyrant Periander had coitus with the corpse of his wife (5.92ζ.3) and stripped all of the women of Corinth naked in public, as Candaules had shown his wife naked to Gyges (1.8ff); and Cambyses' incestuous unions with his sisters, wholly contrary to Persian custom, were without issue (3.31, 34.5). Pisistratus and Periander: Hartog 1988, p. 232; on childlessness among tyrants: Lateiner 1989, pp. 142–43.

113. North 1966, pp. 95, 101–8, 128, 191, 247.

114. The grounds of their agreement, and much else concerning Athens' imperial ideology, are admirably set forth in Raaflaub 1985, summed up in the idea (p. 73) that "Nur der Tyrann ist wirklich frei!" See also Strasburger 1958 on Thucydides, and the Athenians' consciousness of their double image as the savior of Greece in 480 and as the contemporary tyrant city of Greece. Diesner 1979b argues that Thucydides thought Pisistratus comparable to Pericles and valued the tyranny over the democracy after Pericles.

115. Leobotes may have reigned *c.* 870–840: Forrest 1968, p. 21.

116. Herodotus imputes wisdom (*sophiê*) to only two Spartans, Lichas and Chilon. They are wise in his truest and best sense: they understand the divine intention.

117. Forrest 1968, pp. 73ff; Cartledge 1987, pp. 11, 15.

118. An apparent exception, which proves the rule, is that given to Arciseleos of Cyrene (4.163.2); but he in fact *disobeys* the Oracle's unambiguous first admonition, to keep the peace in Cyrene; and he is in the act of disobeying its cryptic second admonition when he realizes its meaning too late. Herodotus himself is unsure whether he did so "willingly or unwillingly." Note that the Minyan-descended

and anti-Spartan Battiad (4.145–50) Arciseleos and his daughter Pheretime are models of barbarism: he burns his enemies alive (4.164), and she—a virago who would rather lead an army than spin wool like a proper female—impaled her enemies on the walls of their city, lopped off their wives' breasts, and hung them on the walls too (4.202).

119. Cf. Immerwahr 1966, pp. 201–2.: even Lycurgan eunomia leads to imperialism of an oriental kind (1.66.1); but for Herodotus "Sparta's history . . . differs from Oriental history in that her expansionist tendencies were at once checked by the divine. . . . Sparta did not fully conquer Tegea and the rest of the Peloponnesus. Thus her conquests did not develop into a true Peloponnesian empire."

120. Forrest 1968, p. 21.

121. Powell, *Lexicon,* s.vv. *eunomeomai* and cognates.

122. Cf. fr. 19 Bergk = Plut. *Solon* 26.4.

123. Benardete 1969, p. 17 with n. 16, notes that Herodotus uses the word *atê* ("doom"), which occurs frequently in the poetry of Solon, in Solon's address to Croesus (Hdt. 1.32.6) but nowhere else in his work (6.61.1 is a false reading).

124. Dicaearchus. *ap.* Dion. Laert. 1.40: *synetous kai nomothetikous deinotêta politikên kai drastêrion synesin.* The candidates vary from list to list in the later authors, but Solon, Thales, Pittacus, and Bias are always present: Grote 1888, 3:317.

125. Dewald 1983, p. 54, notes underlying similarities between savants and tricksters in Herodotus, especially in that both are clearsighted realists.

126. Guthrie 1969, p. 264 n.1.

127. Lateiner 1989, p. 133 and n. 18, would deny "Herodotus' Dorian preferences and supreme admiration for the Spartans and their system," against Macan 1908 at 7:102.2 and 209, Jacoby 1913, col. 357, Fornara 1971, pp. 49f., and Forrest 1984, pp. 6–8. But Herodotus was supremely interested in *results:* he is not enamored of the Scyths, but he awards them "the single most brilliant (*sophôtata*) invention concerning the most important of human affairs": their way of life itself renders them invincible in warfare and impossible for any enemy to catch them (4.46.2–3).

128. Herodotus disagrees with Spartan tradition concerning the ancestry of its kings. How the Spartans themselves derived the ancestry of the Heraclids Herodotus does not say. Although he implies that Spartiate tradition about their kings differed in essential respects from that of the poets (6.52.1 and 53.1), the main point—that the Spartan Heraclids called themselves Achaeans—is guaranteed by 5.72 *fin.*

129. On the "otherness" of Sparta's kings and the barbarism of Spartan royal funerals see Hartog 1988, pp. 152–56, and Cartledge 1987, pp. 333–36. Cartledge remarks upon these obsequies as being "virtually un-Greek," and notes that Herodotus uses a word, *oimôgê*, to describe the lamentations for deceased Spartan kings (6.58.3) which otherwise appears only in Persian contexts.

130. Reff. in Berve 1967, 2:518. Herodotus reveals once more the paramount value he gives to things sacred over things profane in judging Pheidon to have been the greatest hubrist of all the Greeks for usurping the Olympic games from the Eleans (6.127.3).

131. Cf. Tigerstedt 1965, pp. 28–36, on the development of the story of Sparta's origins and early history.

132. Heirs-apparent to the Spartan kingship did not undergo the *agôgê* universal for the citizen-warriors (Plut. *Ages.* 1.4), and they presided over their own messes, apart from the *syskania* of the citizen-warriors: see Cartledge 1987, pp. 23–24, 32. Cf. his comment on pp. 104–5, "The usual necessary links between successful passage through the *agôge,* membership of a mess, and full Spartan citizenship were snapped in the case of the kings. In short, properly speaking the kings were not Homoioi." On the sacred character and charisma of Spartan kings: pp. 109–10, 334ff.

133. Cf. Lewis 1977, pp. 43–49, on the constraints placed on the kingship and the comparative impotence of the Spartan kings in Herodotus' day and before, from the death of Cleomenes onward. In the fourth century, Agesilaus' unique influence was based on his personal adherence to the traditional Spartan virtues, his personal connections, and his collaboration with the other men of power in the state: Cartledge 1987, esp. chs. 6–9.

134. Cf. Benardete 1969, p. 141. Cleomenes' half-brother Leonidas, who is the purest hero of the Histories and Cleomenes' antithesis, was born of Cleomenes' father's *first* wife (5.41.3): Leonidas' birth, then, not only his end, was "altogether Spartiate."

135. See Hartog 1988, pp. 337–38, on the similarities between the Herodotean Cleomenes and Cambyses. The whip is the weapon of the master over the slave (4.3) and, in the Histories, belongs to the barbarian despot. Among Greeks only Cleomenes wields a whip in the Histories (6.81).

136. See Hartog 1988, pp. 166–68.

137. Hdt. 5.92b.2: *q.v. Il.* 1.264; Rose 1958, pp. 256–57 and 280, n. 7.

138. Thuc. 1.18.1, 19.

139. The only well-known tyranny in a Dorian polis that Herodotus does *not* mention is the one which may have violated this principle. It is that of Theagenes of Megara: Thuc. 1.126; Arist. *Pol.* 5.1305a24–

26. Herodotus' silence about the Megarian tyranny stands in contrast to his knowledge of Cylon's attempt to become tyrant at Athens (5.71.1), since according to Thucydides (ibid.) Cylon was the son-in-law of Theagenes, who supported his attempt.

140. Cf. Benardete 1969, pp. 176–79. My views owe much to Fornara 1971, pp. 40–58, who would probably disagree with them.

141. It is noteworthy that Herodotus appears to ignore a favorable Delphian tradition about Clisthenes in favor of this insult. Cf. Diod. 8.24; *FGrH* 105 F 2; Plut. *Mor.* 553A-B, *pace* Fontenrose 1978 Q73.

142. Evans 1991, p. 126, notes the story's "odor of sacrilege."

143. Cf. Herodotus on the Phocians' motive for fighting at Thermopylae. They joined the Hellenes simply because their hereditary enemies the Thessalians were on the other side (8.30), and not from any nobler motives. Herodotus asserts that had the Thessalians fought with the Hellenes the Phocians would have been the Medizers.

144. E.g., Thuc. 3.82.4–6, 8.48.3, synonymous there with *synomosia;* Lysias 12.43, 55; Isoc. 3.54; other reff. in *LSJ*⁹ svv. *hetaireia* 1.2, *hetairos* I.4.

145. In other words, the author of Ps.-Xen. *Resp. Athen.*, seems to me far more at home in the war years of the early 420s than in the middle 440s, following the Thirty Years' Peace but before the Samian Revolt: Lévy 1976, pp. 273–75. *Contra:* Bowersock 1966, who makes the best case for the 440s.

146. Which of course is not the same thing as the democracy at Athens; when the Thirty were installed in 404 their job was to frame the "ancestral laws" of Solon and *Clisthenes* (Xen. *Hell.* 2.24.2; Arist. *AP* 29.17).

147. Thucydides (2.67.4: 430 B.C.) says that they were condemned without out trial on the very day when they arrived as captives at Athens and their corpses were flung unburied into a ravine. To my mind, these passages must have taken shape in Herodotus' mind under the direct impact of this event.

148. Hesiod makes Pelasgus son of Lycaon the founder of the Arcadian people (frr. 160–65 MW [*Pelasgi Progenies*]), followed by Pherecydes (*FGrH* 3 FF 156, 159), who makes them kin to the Oenotrii of Italy; cf. Myres 1907, pp. 209ff. Acusilaus of Argos makes Pelasgus and Argos brothers, the sons of Niobe and Zeus, (*FGrH* 2 F 25a). Homer, *the* great authority, addresses Zeus as *Zeu ana, Dôdônate, Pelasgike* (*Il.* 16.233) and Hesiod or an imitator reflects the version of the Dodona legend in which Zeus himself founds the oracle— and not, as Herodotus would have it, an Egyptian priestess.

149. E.g., by Xenophon: *Hell.* 7.1.23.

150. Cf. Strabo (8.3.3 C337): "I compare the current state of places [in

the Troad] with what Homer says. One has to, the poet is so famous and familiar to us. My readers will think that I have attained my end only if nothing in this contradicts what the poet in whom everyone has such great confidence says on his part."

151. Cauer 1921–23, pp. 224–95, perhaps extreme; cf. Bethe 1927, pp. 81ff; Murray 1934, pp. 219–27; Kirk 1962, pp. 148–56 and 1984, pp. 186–87.

152. Strabo 13.3.3 C621; cf. *Il.* 2.842.

153. Strabo 13 C607. Cf. the Homeric *Hymn to Aphrodite,* probably of the sixth century, which celebrates the union of the goddess with the Trojan Anchises and makes clear that the Trojans are not barbarian Phrygians (5.77ff).

154. *OCD*² art. "Aeneas" (1).

155. Besides the autochthonous Erichthonius, considered the father or grandfather of Erechtheus, with whom he was often identified later, in the fifth-century Athenian sources (Eur. *Ion* 267–68; they appear together on a kylix of the Codrus painter *c.* 440/30), Apollodorus names another Attic Erichthonius, a son of Dardanus and father of Troes, whose brother Ilus on his death left the Trojan kingdom to him (3.146, cf. *Il.* 20.219ff on this Erichthonius). Against the seventh-century poet Callinus, who said that the Troad was settled from Crete, Strabo (13.1.48 C604) cites later authors who "say that a certain Teucrus came to the Troad from the Attic deme Troes, now called Xypeteon or Xypeteones, and deny that any Teucrians came from Crete. Moreover these authors take as a sign of the close relationship (*epiplokê*) between the Trojan and Attic peoples that Erichthonius was one of the founders among both of them." One of these authors was the fourth-century Atthidographer Phanodemus: Nilsson 1951, p. 64.

156. The evidence for the Sigean wars, whose prize was the *Akhilleitis khôra,* is summarized in Page 1955, pp. 152ff. The Mytileneans asserted a "proprietary interest" in the monuments of the Troad (ibid., p. 281 and reff.).

157. The version of the Cadmus myth that makes him Phoenician is in all probability later than the Theban epic: Vian 1963, pp. 52–59.

158. Pythag. A 8 DK; Diog. Laert. 8.4.5. Cf. *Il.* 16.806ff, 17.43ff.

159. Gallet de Santerre 1958, p. 176.

160. *Lelex:* Pausanias 2.29.4; *Caucon:* Strabo 8.343ff, cf. 337ff.

161. Aly 1909; Myres 1907.

162. Hesiod fr. 165.8 MW; Pausanias 8.4.9 and 48.7. Cf. Rose 1958, p. 275. The cult of Telephus, from an Arcadian mother and the progenitor of Sparta's kings, may have arisen early in the sixth century when Tegea entered the Spartan alliance (Hdt. 1.66ff).

Chapter Six. Herodotus' Typology of Barbarism

1. As stated earlier, "Asianic" refers to the tyranny, luxury, and barbarism that Greeks associated with Asia, leaving "Asiatic" as a purely geographical term.

2. Vidal-Naquet 1960. On Herodotus' recognition of the historical unity furnished to the sixth century by this "age of tyrants," and which is reflected in Thucydides in turn, see Immerwahr 1966, p. 94, and Barceló 1990, pp. 402–19.

3. Htd., 1.94; cf. Pley 1913, cols. 450–57.

4. See discussion later in this chapter.

5. See Stahl 1975, esp. pp. 4–8, 19–30.

6. Burnett 1985, pp. 61ff.

7. At this date Bacchylides had enjoyed the patronage of Hieron for some eight years, having journeyed to Sicily with his uncle Simonides as Hieron's guest about 476 (Aelian *VH* 4.15).

8. Cf. Pindar, *Ol.* 1.23–24 (476 B.C.), where the poet calls Hieron *basileus* of Syracuse, whose glory shines in the land founded by *Lydian* Pelops (Pelops was far more often identified with Phrygia). At *Pyth.* 1.94ff (470 B.C.: also for Hieron) the poet contrasts the excellence and abiding memory of Croesus with the infamy of Phalaris of Acrages, another Sicilian tyrant. Unlike Bacchylides, Pindar chose his *exempla* with an unimpaired sense of moral irony.

9. Plut. *Lyc.* 6.1: the "Great Rhetra," probably from the Aristotelian Constitution of Sparta. Cf. Forrest 1968, pp. 41–50.

10. Apollodorus 2.7.8 derives Croesus' ancestry from Agelaus son of Heracles and Omphale. Agelaus is recognizably a Hellenized form of Panyassis' Lydian ancestor Acheles or Acheletes (fr. 17 K), as is Herodotus' alternative, Alcaeus (1.7.2).

11. *ARFP*² i:238.

12. See later discussion in this chapter.

13. The change is also reflected in Attic vase painting when, in the mid-fifth century, painters forsake the Hellenic iconography of royalty, typified by Myson's Croesus, for the dress and the trappings of the oriental monarch. See Miller 1988, esp. pp. 80–81.

14. Cf. Segal 1971a, who notes verbal parallels that suggest that Herodotus knew Bacchylides' ode and was deliberately "correcting" it.

15. On the shame of an ignominious death: Dover 1974, p. 242.

16. Ascribed to the sage Pittacus by Raubitschek 1958.

17. See further How and Wells 1912, 1:374.

18. Another very prominent example of Herodotus' criterion of cultural determination in weighing his material occurs at 1.1–4, where he attributes the Greek stories of Io, Helen, Europa, and Medea to

Persian *logioi*. Benardete, 1969, p. 210, notices that these versions "removed the role that the gods had played in the Greek versions, and . . . denied there was any necessity in the actions of" these women. Since the Persians' gods are not persons but the elements of nature (discussed later in the section on Cambyses and Persian religion), the absence of the gods in these stories—which for us makes them immediately recognizable as products of the new sophism—may for him have been the very factor that proved their Persian provenance.

19. In the Histories the word *eros* is confined to kings and tyrants: Benardete 1969, pp. 137–38. The thought behind this diction is obvious: passion, the antithesis of sophrosyne, drives excess.

20. See chapter 4, n. 115.

21. Helm 1981 correctly, I think, identifies elements of Iranian and other Eastern legends, woven into a national folk epic, at the back of Herodotus' story. Here I stress Herodotus's *interpretatio Graeca*.

22. Cf. Hartog 1988, pp. 84–109.

23. That is, until Alexander of Macedon proved he was divine by making his land "coextensive with the heaven of Zeus" (Hdt. 7. 8γ1), and thereby doing what Xerxes, the failed god of the *Persae* and the Histories, could not.

24. Daniel Sinyavsky writes in *Soviet Civilization: A Cultural History* (1991) that for Stalin, who erected a "state church" on Lenin's foundations of the party dictatorship, the most important thing "was to imbue his power with an impenetrable mystery, a supreme irrationality." He was "a kind of hypnotist who managed to convince the people that he was their god by shrouding his cult in the mystery he knew power required." I quote from the review by Joseph Frank in the *New York Review of Books,* 27 June 1991 (vol. 38, no. 12).

25. For what is left of Greek traditions about Cyrus' birth, and also his death, see Weissbach 1924.

26. See chapter 2, "Tyranny and Barbarism."

27. Discussed later; cf. Hartog 1988, in whose metaphor the Persians "speak Greek" in this debate (p. 325).

28. "In the *Histories* wine is considered a 'civilized' drink": Hartog 1988, p. 166. Abusive susceptibility to wine, on the other hand, is characteristic of barbarians from Polephemus and the Centaurs onward (*Od.* 9.345ff; Apollodorus 2.83ff). Cf. Kirk 1970, pp. 152–62; Segal 1974. See Burkert 1985a, pp. 237–42, on the apotropaic aspects of the Athenian Anthesteria, "acknowledging and controlling" the awesome power of wine.

29. See Immerwahr 1966, pp. 176–83, on Xerxes as the summation of

the portraits of his predecessors: "Xerxes is the typical Persian in extreme form, both in magnificence and in cruelty" (p. 197).

30. Ordeal by fire to discover the truth may have existed in Avestan Persia: Boyce 1975. If so, this practice may lie behind Herodotus' account of Croesus on the pyre.

31. See later discussion and cf. Hartog 1988, pp. 142–62 and 332–34.

32. Cf. 7.188.2 on the storm of Artemisium sent by the god; Herodotus describes in almost identical language how both this storm and that one arose in fine weather out of a clear sky.

33. "Among those who, quite literally, transgress and who generation after generation repeat the transgression are, first and foremost, the Great Kings. To transgress means, through *hubris,* to step outside one's own space and enter a foreign one, and the material sign of such transgression is the construction of a bridge over a river or, worse still, over a stretch of sea": Hartog 1988, pp. 330–31f, anticipated by Immerwahr 1956, p. 250 and 1966, p. 43 and index, s. "River motif"; cf. Solmsen 1974, p. 5 with n. 10.

34. Above, n. 5.

35. Sandanis, a Lydian, is the sage who completes the canonical number of seven sages named by Herodotus in the first half of his first book: he represents Lydian "Hellenism" before the fall of Croesus and the descent of the Lydians into Asianic barbarism.

36. See, however, Drews 1974 for some stereotypical oriental patterns belonging to Herodotus' Cyrus logos.

37. See Cobet 1971, pp. 101–14; Hunter 1982, pp. 275–76.

38. Cf. Lewis 1977, p. 148: beginning with Cyrus' ignorance here of the Spartans, it is "a theme of the History that the Persians gradually discover what the Spartans are like."

39. On the place of the Egyptian logos in the Histories see the remarks in the previous chapter. As for Egyptian history proper, Herodotus had no accounts that he believed reliable which went beyond the memories of the Greeks settled in Egypt by the recent Saïte pharaohs: on these accounts see Murray in Sancisi-Weerdenburg 1987b, pp. 101–3, and Lloyd 1975–88, 1:14ff.

40. The ultimate inspiration of these and other instances in Herodotus would seem to be Persian tradition, since they reflect an essentially Iranian concern that the Kings be genuine Enemies of the Lie, as Darius and his successors declared on their inscriptions. But in the Histories, as Lateiner 1989 comments (p. 153), "admirable Persian *nomoi* are frequently conspicuous for the Kings' unpunished and unpunishable failures to observe them," as well as "the frightening caricatures of justice that the Kings perpetrate."

41. Cf. the discussion of Munson 1991 of Herodotus' unique and overdetermined treatment of Cambyses' insanity.
42. Citations in Herodotus are tabulated by Lateiner 1989, pp. 172ff, category IA4.
43. Cf. Flory 1978, pp. 146–47. *Contra* Konstan 1987 (citing Flory in this extremely perceptive article), who does not take Xerxes' reflections "as the sign that . . . he has momentarily acquired a deeper insight." Instead he sees Xerxes as a man who measures time as he measures power, by quantity (p. 64). I would nevertheless agree with Flory on Xerxes at the bridge, in part due to the parallel furnished by Cambyses.
44. This is another instance of Herodotus' choosing material appropriate to his preconceptions and his purposes, since (as is well known) both hostile and favorable traditions existed among the Egyptians concerning Cambyses: see Lloyd 1988, esp. pp. 60–62; Lloyd 1982. In particular, inscriptional evidence exists that Cambyses had the Apis-bull which died in his reign (525) given ceremonial burial: Posener 1936, pp. 30–36.
45. Sibling incest was practiced by the pharaohs and later by the Ptolemies as pharaohs, as evidently did Cambyses in reflection of a genuine policy of accommodation to his new subjects which finds no reflection in Herodotus' account. However, his brother-sister marriages were unique among Achaemenid royalty, although other forms of endogamy were common: see Herrenschmidt 1987.
46. Cf. the legal maxim that arose with the Caesars: *rex legibus solutus est.*
47. Scythia and Egypt were intimately linked in Herodotus' mind: Hartog 1988, pp. 15–19.
48. In fact the Persians' hold on Egypt was never secure and they never controlled the whole country; the Delta in particular was beyond their effective control. See Ray 1987, who concludes that the Persians relied essentially on strategically placed garrisons and a good intelligence network; they aimed to maintain Egyptian disaffection at a tolerable level, rather than to govern the country with administrative rigor for high revenues, which would have required an enormous commitment of men and treasure, and would have dangerously strengthened the satrap in charge. See also Briant 1988 and 1987a, esp. pp. 6–11, on the character of Persian rule in Egypt and the Egyptians' immutable resistance to the Persian presence and also on the virtual invisibility of Persians in Egypt, citing Michaélides 1943, p. 91: "Les Achéménides ont occupé militairement le pays et ne l'ont jamais conquis, il y ont campé."
49. Since in their religion they resemble neither Persians nor Greeks:

see Hartog 1988, pp. 61–192, on Scythian religion and Scythian sacrifice in Herodotus; esp. 112–72 on the spiritual centrality of the Scythian kings. Note 4.127: the Scyths will fight Darius only if he discovers the tombs of their forefathers. These appear equivalent to the tombs of their kings, whose burial place Herodotus knows and locates for his audience (4.71; cf. 19f, 53).

50. Holladay 1989, esp. pp. 181–82, gives the best analysis of the event and defends Thucydides' characterization of it as a great military catastrophe (1.104.4 and 110.4).

51. West 1971, esp. pp. 137–203, on Heraclitus, has tried to identify Iranian influences in the religious teachings of some of the pre-Socratics. Although I am not competent to judge, I would agree with him that Xenophanes, whose thinking he considers largely a product of Greek rationalism, pp. 227–29, owes little or nothing to Magian doctrines.

52. In one of the more remarkable documents of the Greek religious imagination, the Athenians hymned Demetrius the Besieger as a god who, unlike their city's gods who were either absent or deaf, was a present god who could hear and answer their prayers: Duris *FGrH* 76 F 13.

53. See Hartog's exhaustive analysis of the anti-Greek character of Scythian sacrifice in Herodotus: 1988, pp. 173–92. He notes (p. 182) that Herodotus does not indicate how the Persians slay their sacrificial animals. It is the cooked meat that they present for sacrifice, not the live animal itself, whose death, butchery, and roasting of entrails constitutes the act of sacrifice itself in Greece. Cf. also Burkert 1990, pp. 19–21, on Herodotus' description of Persian religion as a "reconstruction" based on "theory."

54. The practices of the Magi had evidently already repelled Heraclitus, who mentions *nuktipolois, magois, bakkhois, lênais, mustais* as practitioners of impiety (22 F 14a DK from Clement, *Protrepticon* 22); cf. Robinson 1987, pp. 85–86. The list's authenticity has been convincingly defended by Kahn 1979, p. 262, and now at length by Papatheophanes 1985. On the Zoroastrianism of Magi from the latest sixth century B.C., see Dandamayev 1975.

55. Pindar fr. 169 B = Plato *Gorgias* 484b. The first full sentence provides a subtext that associates Darius with tyrannical violence: "Custom, lord of all things mortal and immortal leads the way, justifying the most violent course by the hand of superiority." (Comparable is Herodotus' notice of Archilochus' mention of Gyges at 1.12.2, which appears superfluous and was duly excised by the indefatigable Stein. But the line that Herodotus evidently had in mind [fr. 25] runs *ou moi ta Gygeô tou polykhrysou melei,* which

indicates the direction of Herodotus' thought. Herodotus' recollection of Archilochus here is also "subtextual" and should not be athetized.)

56. Bleicken 1979, esp. p. 156. I do not accept the arguments of Brannan 1963 against him. The problem concerning the sources and the historicity in some form of this debate are insoluble by conventional means: bibliography and commentary in Lateiner 1989, pp. 167ff with nn. 12–14. I would argue that Herodotus once again simply chooses a version of events that fits his preconceptions; these were merely ratified by his belief that Mardonius established democracies in Ionia.

57. See Hartog's exhaustive structural demonstration: Hartog 1988, pp. 112–72.

58. On Herodotus' treatment of Xerxes in this connection, see Konstan 1987, esp. pp. 61–67.

59. Thuc. 2.38.2; cf. Ps.-Xen. *Resp. Ath.* 2.7, 11–13.

60. Cf. Hdt. 6.42.

61. Cf. Hdt. 6.43.

62. Darius heeds the advice of Gobryas in Scythia, 4.132ff; cf. Themistocles after the flight of Xerxes, 9.108ff.

63. E.g., the golden image at Babylon, 1.183.2; the tomb of Nitrocris, 1.187; the organization and hoarding of the imperial tribute itself.

64. Cook 1914–40, 1:416ff on Zeus Laphystius' myth; 2:899 and 3:525 on human sacrifice; Rose 1958, pp. 196ff; Henrichs 1981, esp. p. 234.

65. The following paragraphs are adapted from Georges 1986, pp. 40–42.

66. Stein's deletion of *barbara* at i 4.4 is egregious: from Herodotus' point of view the empire of Athens had succeeded the Great King's sway over Asiatic Greeks.

67. Thuc. 1.130; cf. Fornara 1971, pp. 62–74 on Pausanias and Themistocles.

68. Cf. Evans 1991, pp. 23–24.

69. E.g. Antiphon F 44 B_2 DK. See Reverdin 1962, pp. 89–91, and in general Baldry 1965, pp. 24–51.

70. Crucifixion and impalement (of the living, the dead, and of severed heads): Hdt. 1.128.2; 3.125.3, 132.2, 159.1; 4.43.1 and 6, 202.1; 4.103; 6.30.1; 7.194.1, 238.1; 9.78.3. Mutilation: 3.69.5, 118.2, 154.2ff; 4.62.4 (corpse), 202.1; 6.75.3; 7.88.2 (horse); 9.112. Bisection: 7.39.3 (corpse). Castration and the employment of eunuchs: 1.117.5; 3.4.2, 77.2, 130.4; 4.43.7; 6.32; 7.187.1; 8.104–6; note 105.1: *ergon anosiôtatôn*; flaying: 4.64.3f, 5.25.1 (corpse); 7.26.3

(Marsyas by Apollo). Beheading: 3.79.1; 4.68.3, 80.5; 103.3; 5.114.1; 7.35.3; 8.90.3, 118.4.

71. Interpretations: Segal 1971a and Vernant 1991.
72. See the penetrating article of Boedecker 1988.
73. Hartog 1988, pp. 258–59. This section in general owes much to Hartog's Part Two: "Herodotus, Rhapsode and Surveyor."
74. Cf. Lateiner 1985, p. 91: "The often sinister verb of 'crossing', *diabainein,* appears last (9.114.2) when the Greeks sail north to Abydus. . . . The *crossing* marks the radical change from a Hellenic *defensive* to and Athenian *offensive* campaign, a moment not meaningless to an audience in 430 B.C."

Chapter Seven. Xenophon: The Satrap of Scillus

1. Arist. *Pol.* 1306a12ff; cf. *OCD,*[2] art. "Elis."
2. A conscious assimilation: Hirsch 1985, n. 11 on pp. 152–53.
3. Parke 1933 remains fundamental. Cf. p. 21 in the importance of Greeks in the service of Persia, and chs. 5, 6, 11, and 21 on Greeks serving in the East. Parke's Table II gives known numbers of Greek mercenaries; Cyrus the Younger's (more than) Ten Thousand was immense for its time, but from the 370s onward armies of 6,000 to 20,000 men were common. In the year 344, the sources give a total of 42,000 Greeks serving professionally on both sides in wars in Egypt and Sicily. The surviving prosopography is no less astonishing. Parke's Index I names no less than 222 "Employers and Commanders of Mercenary Soldiers"; his Index II names 151 "Mercenary Generals and Soldiers." The great majority in both categories lived during the age of Xenophon.
4. J. K. Anderson's affectionate speculation, based on Pausanias 5.6.6: Anderson 1974, p. 196.
5. The insoluble problems of reconstructing the course of Xenophon's life and the chronology of his works are succinctly discussed by Cartledge 1987, pp. 55–57. Since any attempt to assess the relationship between his life and works is necessarily inferential (p. 57), I simply forge ahead in this chapter without going over old ground.
6. My view in this chapter denies the notion that Xenophon was a thorough hater of Persia and Persians, e.g., in Delebecque 1957, p. 199, and Higgins 1977, pp. 83–84; the latter perversely regards Xenophon's encomium of the younger Cyrus (*Anab.* 1.9) as an ironic depiction of a great villain.
7. See Lévy 1976, a valuable study of the ideological crisis attending Athens' defeat, from the Athenian intellectuals' identity crisis after the Melian massacre in 413 to the consequences of defeat after 404;

see esp. pp. 197–205 for the fourth-century idealization of Persia (and Egypt) in a climate of political despair and the failure of Sparta as a political model.

8. Cf. Diesner 1989b, who argues with some plausibility that at 7.54–58 Thucydides meant the reader to draw a contrast between the intelligence and superiority of the Pisistratid tyranny and the democracy after Pericles.

9. See Ober 1989, pp. 98ff and ch. 5, "Class: Wealth, Resentment, and Gratitude," on the financial requirements of the restored democracy, which were paid for by the wealthy.

10. I agree with Cartledge 1987, pp. 57–59, 65, that the *Resp. Lac.* and the second part of the *Hellenica* (from 2.3.9 onward) were composed at this time, together with the *Agesilaus,* which he probably wrote soon after Agesilaus' death in the winter of 360–359 (p. 55). Cartledge's views are well supported by the arguments of McLaren 1934.

11. Cf. Baldry 1965, p. 61. On the rise to prominence of mercenary armies in this period, see above, n. 3 and now the excellent discussion, with bibliography, of Cartledge 1987, pp.314–30, with emphasis on the influence of Spartans and Spartan methods in mercenary service.

12. Xenophon was close to Isocrates' idea of a Greek *epimeleia* over barbarians (*Antidosis* 209–14; *Nicocles* 12). Baldry 1965, p. 70, comments that "*epimeleia* here does not mean merely 'protection'; it implies . . . that under Greek guardianship the barbarians can be raised above the slavish level at which despotism has kept them." In the mid-third century B.C., Eratosthenes (*ap.* Strabo 1.4.9) was among those who inveighed against a division of humanity into Greeks and barbarians, putting forward instead of a distinction based on virtue and vice, while including the Persians (*Arianous*) among nations who, like the Greeks, are *houtô thaumastôs politeuomenous.* The others were Indians, Romans, and Carthaginians.

13. Cf. Delebecque 1957, pp. 61–64; Anderson 1974, pp. 47ff, who takes Xenophon's service under the Thirty for granted (p. 55); also Cartledge 1987, p. 59, citing Rhodes 1981, p. 458. Xenophon's membership in the cavalry is a fairly secure inference from the following facts. (1) He kept a string of horses in Asia at his own expense (*Anab.* 3.3.19). (2) He almost certainly did not join the exiles at Phyle but remained in Athens, where he could not refuse service; at any rate his hero of the time, Socrates, stayed in the city, and in the *Memorabilia* Xenophon portrays him as ironically pretending anxiety to obey the laws to the letter (1.2.31–38). Xenophon's disillusioned Theramenes, without irony, takes the line that

he has always worked for a hoplite democracy at Athens when accused of political complaisance by Critias (*Hell.* 2.3.45–49; cf. 30–33). Either stance, or both at once, could have served as Xenophon's defense of his own conduct. (3) Xenophon provides a minutely detailed narrative, evocative of an eyewitness account, whenever the cavalry is present during the events that led to the fall of the Thirty (*Hell.* 2.4.4–8, 24–27, 31–34).

14. Cf. Lysias 16 (*c.* 390): the defense of a member of the cavalry at his *dokimasia* for membership of the Boulê, who must above all refute the charge that he had served under the Thirty.
15. Rhodes 1981, pp. 462–64, on Arist. *AP* 39.1.
16. Delebecque 1957, pp. 83–89; see also Strauss 1986, ch. 4, for the political atmosphere.
17. See Appendix, "Prejudice against Metics at Athens." Ober 1989, pp. 197–98 with n. 10, connects citizenship with autochthony, and the ideal of the autochthony in turn with the hereditary aristocracy. Among the Thirty were men claiming old and distinguished family: see Krentz 1982, pp. 45, 51–56 for the prosopographical problems.
18. Arist. *AP* 37; *Hell.* 2.3.19–20, where the Three Thousand are those defined by the Thirty as the *beltistoi* and the *kaloi k'agathoi,* terms that Xenophon elsewhere applies to the hoplites and cavalry in their military role (e.g., *Mem.* 3.5.9): this suggests that the Three Thousand were to be understood as military effectives, not merely those of hoplite or cavalry property-census. The Thirty were supported by a garrison of 700 troops commanded by a Spartan harmost (Arist. *AP* 37.2; Xen. *Hell.* 2.3.14). With these plus the Three Thousand, the Thirty felt secure enough to work their will upon the rest. A broad view, approaching a consensus, puts citizens of hoplite status and above at Athens in the fourth century at some 6,000: see the long note of Ober 1989: n. 59, pp. 128ff. Ober, reviewing the demographic question on pp. 127–30, would, however, put their number at some 8,000. But these figures reflect demographic recovery, on the one hand, and represent the property-census rolls, not willing effectives, on the other. In the last two years of the war alone, the Athenian hoplite levy had suffered staggering losses at Arginusae and Aegospotami (where at least 2,500 Athenian officers and marines were executed, counting 14 marines for each of 180 triremes). Added to these must be a proportion of the victims of the subsequent famine at Athens and those of the Thirty, said to number at least 1,500 (Arist. *AP* 35.4).
19. Ober 1989, p. 197 with n. 10.
20. The idea that slavery is adventitious, not natural,, belonged to the times, e.g., Eur. *Ion* 854–56; cf. fr. 511; Schlafer 1936. See Vlastos

1941 on the slave as the natural beneficiary of *dirigisme*. Xenophon means that to the extent that a slave displays virtue, alacrity, and initiative under his master's command, he displays the virtues of the free and honorable warrior, and is ethically not a slave.

21. Xenophon's Socrates was also Plato's Socrates in this respect; cf. Vlastos 1941, p. 148: the slave is deficient in reason, possessing *doxa* but not *logos,* and is therefore "unconditionally subject to his intellectual superiors." "Plato uses one and the same principle to interpret (and justify) political authority and the master's right to govern the slave. . . . His conception of all government (*archê, archein*) is of a piece with his conception of the government of slaves" (p. 152). This could just as well be a statement of Xenophon's view.

22. Xenophon's disgust is illuminated by the article of Vidal-Naquet 1983 on the ideology of the Athenian hoplite, pp. 85–105.

23. Xenophon describes Agesilaus' staff as *hoi peri auton triakonta,* which implies that they were the thirty *Spartiates* sent to him from home; however, Xenophon was replaced in command of Cyrus' surviving mercenaries after they passed into Spartan service, and he is thought to then have joined Agesilaus' staff (Cartledge 1987, p. 59), if not necessarily the inner group of Spartan *homoioi*. In this period the Spartans were even using some elite *perioikoi* in high commands: ibid., p. 178.

24. That is, beneath the successor to the recently executed Tissaphernes, to whom Pharnabazus had been (restively) subordinate; see Lewis 1977, p. 150, n. 101.

25. Xen. *Cyrop*. 1.2.7; *Mem*. 2.7.9; cf. *Hell*. 7.2.1ff, on Xenophon's admiration for the fidelity of the Phliasian oligarchs to their Spartan benefactors.

26. *Cyrop*. 8.1.3–4, quoted earlier.

27. *Il*. 2.211ff; Theognis 53–58, 189–90.

28. Antiphon fr. 44. Cf. Ps.-Xen. *Resp. Ath*. 1.4, 10–12, 2.8.

29. See Herman 1987, pp. 41–50, esp. 47, on the formalities of this encounter; on the expectations and obligations of both parties to a *xenia*-relationship see esp. op. 116–30.

30. Hirsch 1985, pp. 22–23, notes that Xenophon never blames Cyrus for deceiving the Greeks, a fact that suggests he himself was never deceived.

31. Anderson 1974, p. 85.

32. It is the word that the Cyrus of the *Cyropaedia*, significantly, also uses to describe his associates. Hirsch 1985, p. 158, n. 39, notes that *synergos* is equivalent to Old Persian *hamataxšata*, by which Darius signified those who cooperated with him (DB 4.65–67 in

Kent 1953), and suggests that Xenophon may well have been familiar with the term as an honorific, or at least as an authentic usage.

33. Born *c.* 423: Plut. *Artox.* 2.3. His attributed coin portraits show him beardless and not unhandsome, with an upturned nose; Babelon 1910, pp. 52–53; Hill 1922, p. 156.

34. Cf. Halperin 1986 on Plato's essentially similar, if highly metaphysical, view of "erotic reciprocity." On the institutional blurring of the serviceable and emotive aspects of *xenia* see Herman 1987, pp. 16–31.

35. David Halperin and others have taken up where Dover 1978 left off; see, e.g., the papers and bibliography in Halperin et al. 1990.

36. For the identification and stemma see below, Appendix B "The Hellenic Attachments of the Pharnacids," and Hornblower 1982, p. 173; wrongly doubted by Sekunda 1989, pp. 180ff.

37. See Appendix B, "The Hellenic Attachments of the Pharnacids."

38. Meno was an associate of the Aleuad Aristippus of Larissa and commanded the army that Aristippus had raised on behalf of his *xenos* Cyrus (*Anab.* 1.1.10, 2.6).

39. Momigliano 1975b, esp. pp. 7ff (Romans, etc.), 90ff (Jews), 138ff (Iranians).

40. Many Greeks knew Persian, of course, and the story of Themistocles comes to mind (Plut. *Them.* 29.3); but the bilingual Greek was most often an interpreter of low status. Greeks of high station rarely seem to have bothered, whereas Persians who set out to cultivate Greek connections did, including Persians in Mardonius' retinue in 480–479 (Hdt. 8.16). See Mosley 1971.

41. Meiggs 1972, pp. 436–37.

42. Guthrie 1969, 3:397: Diog. Laert. 2.105; cf. Cic. *Tusc.* 4.37.80 and *De fato* 4.10.

43. Compare the unknown Persian who conversed in Greek on the eve of Plataea (Hdt. 9.16): the first Persian in Greek literature, we might say, who died almost a Greek. Herodotus says he heard the story himself from Thersander, a notable of Orchomenus who shared a dining couch with this Persian officer of Mardonius. Having dined and drunk together, and made a bond of fellowship at table, the Persian confided in tears to Thersander: "Do you see these Persians at our banquet and the army we left in camp by the river? Of all these you will soon see only a few left alive." As he spoke—and he spoke in Greek—he wept bitterly, while Thersander urged him to warn Mardonius of his fears. The Persian answered, "My friend, what must happen from the god none can turn aside; for none will be persuaded even by cogent speakers: many Persians know this—

we follow bound by necessity, and the bitterest pain of man is this, to know everything and control nothing."

44. Although my views differ in a number of ways from Hirsch's, I learned a great deal from his 1983 and 1985, ch. 4, and from the courageously speculative Delebecque 1957.

45. The *Cyropaedia* as protonovel: Tatum 1988.

46. See von Fritz 1954. pp. 94–95.

47. For a recent (in my view not altogether convincing) defense of Polybius 6 as grounded in contemporary Roman political practice, see Millar 1984.

48. See Lévy 1976, pp. 191–95. Cf. Waters 1976 for clarification of the issues and further bibliography.

49. Tigerstedt 1965, pp. 177–89, ascribing these similarities to a tacit reelaboration influenced by Xenophon's "mirage spartiate." Briant 1987b, pp. 7–10, argues that Xenophon's account reflects some knowledge of the actual palace cadet system for the sons of the Persian governing elite.

50. Thus for my own reasons I agree, generally speaking, with those who deny usefulness as a historical source to the *Cyropaedia*. See Sancisi-Weerdenburg 1985 and 1987c. Hirsch 1985, pp. 66–91, provides a balanced discussion inclining on the whole to find considerable historical value in the work. I would except from any general condemnation knowledge on the part of Xenophon of specific customs and rituals, to be tested on a case-by-case basis, and his usefulness on the psychology of Persian autocracy.

51. *Gerron* and *sagaris*; the latter is the Greek *kopis* or *makhaira*: 2.1.9, 16. Cf. Hirsch 1985, n. 86 on p. 179.

52. On the military practices of this time see Anderson 1970.

53. Thus Veyne 1988, p. 52: "Speculation, *eikasia,* replaces confidence in tradition. It will be based on the notion that the past resembles the present. This had been the foundation on which Thucydides, seeking to know more than tradition, had already built his brilliant but perfectly false and gratuitous reconstruction of the first days of Greece." Cf. ibid., pp. 103–4, on "historical retrodiction."

54. 4.2.15, cf. 8.7.2. A related passage is *Anab.* 3.11–13: Xenophon's dream after the assassination of the generals of the Ten Thousand. It reveals how closely he associated his imaginative Cyrus not only with the younger Cyrus, but with his own persona. Xenophon had dreamed that his father's house was enclosed by a nimbus of light from a bolt of lightning and feared that, since thunderbolts come from Zeus the King, the dream portended that he would be unable to leave the (Persian) King's territory. But he also reflected that in the midst of dangers he had beheld a great light from Zeus, and

remarks that the meaning of the dream is to be found in what happened next—which was his initiative in organizing a new army leadership and his election to one of the commands. The action of the first half of the *Anabais* proceeds from Xenophon's petition to Delphi; the action of the second half from this dream.

55. Cf. Delebecque 1957, p. 394, who remarks that "one could truly say that the *Cyropaedia* was less a history of the elder Cyrus than the dream of what Cyrus would have done on the throne had he conquered and lived to rule."

56. A common viewpoint: e.g., Picard 1980, p. 14; Reverdin 1962, p. 94.

57. See above, n. 38.

58. *Anab.* 1.2.18, 7.3ff, 9, 10.2–3; Plut. *Artox.* 26.3–27.3, *Per.* 24.7. Cf. Hirsch 1985, p. 75: Xenophon "had received a particular vision of Cyrus the Great and Old Persia from the younger Cyrus. So powerful was this impression that Xenophon could not easily disassociate the younger Cyrus from the ancestor whom he claimed to imitate and, in a sense, to reincarnate." Starr 1977 argues from material evidence, where literary testimony is lacking, that lines of syncresis in the art and material culture of the Levant in the fourth century are clues to a cultural *rapprochement* involving, among other peoples, Greeks and Persians.

59. The residue of this vision may lie behind Xenophon's desire to found a city in Pontus with the survivors of Cyrus' Greeks, where he would at once have created for himself a very powerful position vis-à-vis the satrap at Dascyleium, as Pharnabazus well knew (*Anab.* 6.4.24, 5.7, 5.30; 7.1.2), and again in his seduction by the Odrysian king Seuthes' phantom promise of strongholds on the Thracian coast, Bisanthe, Ganos, and Neonteichos (*Anab.* 7.2.25, 2.36, 5.8, 6.34).

60. Cf. Thuc. 1.8.11 on the magnitude of *his* subject compared to the Trojan War.

61. Cartledge 1987, pp. 55–57, on their authenticity. I see no reason to deny that Xenophon wrote both of these works. Nor does *Const. Lac.* 14, the condemnation of contemporary Sparta, seem to me necessarily misplaced, as it follows immediately the description of Lycurgus' *military* institutions—and it is these that Xenophon knows have notoriously failed, together with the Spartan character upon which they depended. After the Spartans had gained a free hand in Greece by the Peace of Antalcidas, whereby they renounced their ambitions (and Xenophon's) in Asia, the harmost Phoebidas violated the very oaths of the Peace. It was this crime that Xenophon, writing in retrospect, saw as the act that brought the vengeance of the gods

down on Sparta (*Hell.* 5.4.1): thus the moral corruption of the Spartans preceded and caused their downfall. What has not changed, Xenophon goes on to say (15), is the character of the Spartan kingship. As in the comparable postscript to the *Cyropaedia,* which pronounces the Persian empire rotten to the core and awaiting a conqueror, Xenophon blames society for having failed his hero.

62. See Hirsch 1985, pp. 91–97, with nn. 100–12, for a history of the controversy; he himself argues against its authorship by Xenophon, while conceding that on stylistic grounds its author must have been a contemporary of Xenophon. As discussed later, I take it as genuine and place its inclusion after the Satraps' Revolt and the failure of Agesilaus' last overseas expedition and death.

63. Date: Hornblower 1982, pp. 176–81. The moral and emotional contempt and hatred reserved for those who betrayed their allies is well brought out by Herman 1987, pp. 122–28, esp. p. 126: "A man's whole moral personality . . . was at stake" in the obligations of *xenia.* "Being left in the lurch was interpreted as an affront to honour, and if one party ignored his obligations the other was not only freed from all obligations but saw it as his own duty to punish the offender." Since, for Xenophon, Artaxerxes II was a monarch who encouraged betrayal, indeed the first of them to do so far as he knew, it follows that for him Artaxerxes II was the *fons et origo* of the perversion of Persian aristocratic values.

64. Xenophon's friends may have secured his recall to Athens as early as the summer of 369, in the atmosphere of the new alliance with Sparta. His "Athenian" works, *Hipparchus, Oeconomicus, Memorabilia,* and *Poroi* (355–354), suggest an "Athenian period" in any case. When in Attica, however, Xenophon's public demeanor may be inferred from that of his Ischomachus in the *Oeconomicus.*

65. On Messene see Grote 1888, 8:214 and 335: Messenian independence depended mainly on the Arcadians and their fortress-city of Megalopolis, which stood on the Spartans' communications with Messenia through the southern Arcadian plain; cf. Cartledge 1987, chapter 20.

66. For the period between Leuctra and Mantinea see Hamilton 1991, p. 212: contemporaries found the extent of the significance of Leuctra "difficult to gauge"; pp. 215ff and ch. 8 in general note the slow and partial recognition of the Spartans' decline after Leuctra. Even after Mantinea Xenophon could write that "many Greeks now are calling on one another to prevent them from ruling once again" (*Const. Lac.* 14.6). One is reminded of the belated recognition of the decline of Britain and France in our century.

67. Books 1–2 occupy 61 Oxford pages, 6.4.22 *ad fin.* 60 Oxford pages, almost a quarter of the whole (265 Oxford pages) in each case; the period between Leuctra and Mantinea occupies nearly a third of the events-chronicle portion: books 3–7.
68. Cf. Diod. 15.54.1, however, where he repeats this judgment with reference to Leuctra; but here Diodorus sees the earlier battle in retrospect of the later one; it may even be a careless repetition. See also Strabo 9.2.5 C402 fin.
69. I am not convinced by Harding 1973, who argues that Isocrates' *Archidamus* was composed *c.* 356 with the *On the Peace* as a pair of *antilogiai.*
70. Xenophon's political outlook remained uninfluenced by the goal of a common peace (*koinê eirenê*), which Persian diplomacy sponsored and which pan-Hellenists advocated as a solution to Greek disunity, albeit without the interference of the Persians. Martin 1944 discusses Xenophon's distance from the rhetorical pan-Hellenism of his age; what Xenophon desired was not the end of Persia but a Persian empire that offered a rich *carrière ouverte aux talents* to Greeks like himself.
71. See Loraux 1986, pp. 155ff, on the Persian Wars as a topos in the fourth century, citing Isocrates, *Philippus* 147 and *Panegyricus* 74; Ar. *Rhet.* 1396a12–14; Lysias 26 (p. 155, nn. 168–70).
72. Cf. Cartledge 1987, pp. 61ff. He describes the work as "the memoirs of an old man," limited by the parochial character of his informants. This certainly seems true of the latter part of the *Hellenica,* although I do not think that it is based altogether on memory, but rather on notes or a diary kept over a long period of time (cf. Lesky 1966, pp. 618–19). The attention paid to Jason and Alexander of Pherae in a work whose "geographical scope rarely extends beyond the Peloponnese" (Cartledge 1987, p. 61) is explained in part, at any rate, by their potential for distracting the Thebans; in particular, the Thebans invaded the Peloponnese after Leuctra only after Jason was assassinated in the midst of a mobilization whose purpose was undeclared, but which necessarily kept Epaminondas close to home. Xenophon's notorious lack of attention to Athens' resurgence at sea seems natural, given its irrelevance to Sparta's fortunes in peninsular Greece, especially in the hindsight of Mantinea, of Athens' decline at sea and the deplorable outcome of the Satraps' Revolt, and of Agesilaus' death. Finally, Xenophon may have felt it unnecessary or even inappropriate to include events treated by other writers of the time: he may be referring to these at *Hell.* 7.2.1, and we should

note that the *Hellenica* continued Thucydides, without trying to supplement what Thucydides had already related.

73. *Hell.* 7.1.27; *Aqes.* 2.26; cf. Demosthenes 15 and 23, Polyaenus 7.26.

74. So Cartledge 1987, p. 389.

75. Xenophon ignored the idea of a *koinê eirênê* (above, n. 70). He appears to have thought strictly in terms of Spartan leadership of Greece from his earliest experiences in Asia to the death of Agesilaus. It was only after Agesilaus' death that Xenophon finally turned his remaining energies to the problems faced by Athens, in the *Poroi* (dated by internal evidence to 355/4).

76. Chronology: Kienitz 1953, pp. 175–77.

77. It is in this chronological and emotional context, between Mantinea and Agesilaus' death, that I would also place ch. 14 of the *Resp. Lac.*, for reasons paralleling those that inspired *Cyrop.* 8.8.

78. Höistad 1948, pp. 73–94.

79. Münscher 1920, pp. 3–25, explores the possible relationship between Xenophon and Isocrates, who were fellow demesmen of Erchia.

80. Sealey 1987, pp. 15–16, 23–24, with nn. 32, 52.

81. Ps. -Xen. *Resp. Ath.* 1.10–12, 2.8, with Xen. *Vect.* 2.3: "Many metics are Lydians, Syrians, and other barbarians of all kinds." In this document Xenophon, near the end of his life, advocates extending metic rights at Athens in order to augment a class most useful to the city. But this represents only a concession to utility in the years after Mantinea and Agesilaus' death, especially as he must have been anxious to secure his surviving son's position at Athens. For the numbers of metics at Athens we have only Ctesicles for a late fourth-century census under Demetrius of Phalerum, who gives 10,000 metics, 21,000 citizens, and perhaps 400,000 slaves; these numbers were probably higher in the fifth century: Whitehead 1977, p. 97.

82. Whitehead 1977, pp. 19–35, is very rich on prejudice against metics in the literary sources, especially in his references from tragedy, who introduce "the metic in contexts which, to a citizen audience, suggested something unattractive, precarious, and pathetic." This impression is largely borne out by passages from the orators, cited and discussed in his ch. 5. See also pp. 109–124, on race, servile origin, and *banausia* all informing prejudice against metics.

83. *IG* ii^2 103 = Dittenberger *Syll.*^{3} 163. Cf. Xen. *Hell.* 7.1.27, Diod. 15.70.2.

84. See Osborne 1981–83, 4:139–85, 204–6.

85. *IG* ii^2 141; cf. Theopompus *FGrH* 115 F 114, Aelian *VH* 7.2, Athen. *Deipn.* 12.531A, on his reputation as a Hellenizer.

86. Stemma, based on Beloch 1923, p. 146:

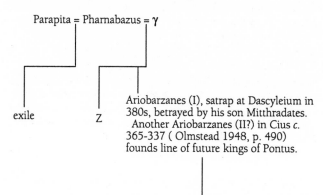

Parapita = Pharnabazus = γ

exile

Z

Ariobarzanes (I), satrap at Dascyleium in 380s, betrayed by his son Mitthradates. Another Ariobarzanes (II?) in Cius *c.* 365-337 (Olmstead 1948, p. 490) founds line of future kings of Pontus.

sister of Memnon and Mentor = Artabazus, satrap at Dascyleium in 360s

Burn 1985, pp. 381–82, is tempted to identify Artabazus with Pharnabazus' son by Parapita on the ground of his "uniquely strong Greek connections." This is possible. Artabazus named one of his sons Ariobarzanes (II?). Burn's suggestion would do away with an apparent superfluity of Persians named Ariobarzanes in this period. Objections to this solution include Xenophon's apparent suppression, for no apparent reason, of both names at *Hell.* 4.1.39–40 (he certainly knew of Ariobarzanes I: *Ages.* 2.26; *Cyrop.* 8.8.4), and the new difficulties it introduces into the history of the satrapy.

87. Intermarriage between Greeks and Persians of high station may have been more common than we know by this time, since it constituted a political relationship of importance to Greeks operating within the Persian sphere. Cf. Dionysius, tyrant of Heraclea in this period, whose wife was Amestris, daughter of the Achaemenid Oxyathres, and a niece of Darius III: Strabo 12.3.10 C544.

88. The founder, Pharnaces son of Arsames, had an Ionian scribe while directing the palace supply administration as early as 499: Lewis 1977, pp. 12–13, who is valuable on Greeks in official service to high-ranking Persians from early in the fifth century.

Conclusion

1. Cf., e.g., fr. 14 DK.
2. From the epitaph in the anonymous *Vit. Aesch.* (lines 17–18).
3. It is tempting to suppose that he must have, since Plutarch's Alexander is insatiably curious even as a child about the Persian empire,

and also a reader of books (*Alex.* 5.1–3, 23.3). Arrian reports from a vulgate source that Alexander gave a speech in which he recalled Xenophon and the Ten Thousand (*Alex. Anab.* 2.7.8). But the case rests only on the parallels to be drawn between Xenophon's *Cyropaedia* and the career of Alexander. See, e.g., Tatum 1988, p. 12 with n. 23.

4. Kienast 1973, esp. pp. 33ff.
5. Bosworth 1988, pp. 271–73, summarizes what is known about Alexander's incorporation of Iranian troops into his army, from the winter of 328–327 onward; his measures included the creation of new and elite "Companion" hipparchies composed of Iranian horse, and a phalanx of oriental hypaspists trained in Macedonian drill.

Bibliography

Abbreviations follow the conventions of *L'Année philologique*: "Index des périodiques dépouillés."

Adkins, A. 1960. *Merit and Responsibility: A Study in Greek Values*. (Oxford).
———. 1966. "Aristotle and the Best Kind of Tragedy." *CQ* 16: 78–102.
Adkins, S. 1952 . "Salamis Symphony: the *Persae* of Aeschylus." In White: 46–54.
Ahlberg, G. 1971. *Prothesis and Ekphora in Greek Geometric Art*. Goteborg.
Akurgal, E. 1956. "Recherches à Cyzique." *Anadolu* 1: 1–12.
Alexanderson, B. 1967. "Darius in the *Persians*." *Eranos* 65: 1–11.
Alexiou, M. 1974. *The Ritual Lament in Greek Tradition*. Cambridge.
Alty, J. 1982. "Dorians and Ionians." *JHS* 102: 1–14.
Aly, W. 1909. "Karer und Leleger." *Philologus* 68: 428–44.
———. 1950. "Zum neuen Strabon-text." *PP* 5:228–263.
Aly, W., and E. Honigmann. 1931. "Strabo von Amaseia" (3), *RE* ser. 2, vol. 4, cols. 76–155.
Amandry, P. 1938. "Vases, bronzes, et terres cuites de Delphes." *BCH* 62: 307–31.
———. 1939. "Rapport sur les statues chryséléphantines de Delphes." *BCH* 63: 86–119.
———. 1944–45. "Statuette d' ivoire d'un dompteur de lion." *Syria* 24: 149–74.
———. 1962. "Plaques d'or de Delphes." *MDAI(A)* 77: 35–71.

Anderson, J. 1958–59. "Old Smyrna: The Corinthian Pottery." *ABSA* 53–54: 138–51.

———. 1970. *Military Theory and Practice in the Age of Xenophon*. Berkeley.

———. 1974. *Xenophon*. Berkeley.

Armayor, O. 1978a. "Did Herodotus Ever Go to the Black Sea? *HSPh* 82: 231–42.

———. 1978b. "Herodotus' Persian Vocabulary." *AncW* 1: 147–56.

———. 1980a. "Sesostris and Herodotus' Autopsy of Thrace, Colchis, Inland Asia Minor, and the Levant." *HSPh* 84: 51–74.

———. 1980b. "Did Herodotus Ever Go to Egypt?" *JARCE* 15: 59–71.

———. 1985. *Herodotus' Autopsy of the Fayoum: Lake Moeris and the Labyrinth of Egypt*. Amsterdam.

Aujac, G. 1966. *Strabo et la science de son temps*. Paris.

Austin, M., 1970. *Greece and Egypt in the Archaic Age*. PCPhS Suppl. 2. Cambridge.

Avery, H. 1964. "Dramatic Devices in Aeschylus' *Persians*." *AJPh* 85: 173–84.

Babelon E. 1910. *Traité des monnaies*, Vol. 2. Paris.

Backhaus, W. 1976. "Der Hellenen-Barbaren-Gegensatz und die hippokratische Schrift *Peri aeron, hudaton, topon*." *Historia* 25: 170–85.

Bacon, H. 1961. *Barbarians in Greek Tragedy*. New Haven, Conn.

Badian, E. 1987. "The Peace of Callias." *JHS* 107: 1–39.

———. .1988. "Towards a Chronology of the Pentekontaetia down to the Renewal of the Peace of Callias." *EMC* 23, n.s. 7: 289–320.

Balcer, J. 1983. "The Greeks and the Persians: The Processes of Acculturation." *Historia* 32: 257–67.

———. 1984. *Sparta by the Bitter Sea: Imperial Interaction in Western Anatolia*. Brown Judaic Studies 52. Chico, Calif.

———. 1987. *Herodotus and Bisitun: Problems in Ancient Persian Historiography*. Historia Einzelschriften 49. Stuttgart.

Baldry, H. 1961. "The Idea of the Unity of Mankind." In *Grecs et barbares*. Fondation Hardt Entretiens sur l'Antiquité classique 8: 169–95. Vandoeuvres-Genève.

———. 1965. *The Unity of Mankind in Greek Thought*. Cambridge.

Bammer, A. 1972. *Die Architektur des jüngeren Artemision von Ephesos*. Wiesbaden.

Barceló, P. 1990. "Thukydides und die Tyrannis." *Historia* 39: 401–25.

Barnett, R. 1948. "Early Greek and Oriental Ivories." *JHS* 68: 1–25.

———. 1953. "Mopsos." *JHS* 73: 140–43.

Barron, J. 1964a. "The Sixth-Century Tyranny at Samos." *CQ* n.s. 14: 210–29.

———. 1964b. "Religious Propaganda of the Delian League." *JHS* 84: 35–48.

———. 1966. *The Silver Coins of Samos*. London.

Beloch, K. 1923. *Griechische Geschichte*, 2d ed. Vol. 3:2. Berlin.

Benardete, S., ed. and trans. 1956. "*The Persians* of Aeschylus." In D. Grene and R. Lattimore, eds., *Aeschylus II. Four Tragedies*. Chicago.

———. 1969. *Herodotean Inquiries*. The Hague.

Benveniste, E. 1966. "Relations lexicales entre la Perse et la Grèce ancienne." In *Atti del convegno sul tema: La Persia e il mondo greco-romano*. Problemi Attuali di Scienza e di Cultura 76: 479–85. Rome.

Berve, H. 1967. *Die Tyrannis bei den Griechen*. 2 vols. Munich.

Bethe, E. 1927. Homer, Dichtung und Sage. Vol. 3. *Die Sage vom Troischen Krieg*. Leipzig.

Bickerman, E. 1946. "The Edict of Cyrus in Ezra I." *JBL* 65: 244–75.

———. 1952. "Origines Gentium." *CPh* 47: 65–81.

Bicknell, P. 1972a. "Studies in Athenian Politics and Genealogy. *Historia* Einzelschriften 19. Wiesbaden.

———. 1974b: Athenian Politics and Genealogy: Some Pendants." *Historia* 23: 146–63.

Bilabel, F. 1920. *Die ionische Kolonization. Philologus* Suppl. 14.1. Leipzig.

Birmingham, J. 1961. "The Overland Route across Anatolia in the Eighth and Seventh Centuries B.C." *AnatStud* 11: 185–95.

Bischoff, W. 1932. *Der Warner bei Herodot*. Marburg.

Blegen, C. et al. 1951. *Troy*. Vol. 4.1. Princeton.

Bleicken, J. 1979. "Zur Entstehung der Verfassungstypologie im 5. Jhr. v. Chr. (Monarchie, Aristokratie, Demokratie)." *Historia* 28: 148–72.

Bloch, M., and J. Parry, eds. 1982. *Death and the Regeneration of Life*. Cambridgeshire.

Boardman, J. 1972. "Herakles, Peisistratos and Sons." *RA*: 57–72.

———. 1975. "Herakles, Peisistratos and Eleusis." *JHS* 95: 1–12.

———. 1985. *The Parthenon and Its Sculptures*. London.

———. 1989. "Herakles, Peisistratos and the Unconvinced." *JHS* 109: 158–59.

Bockisch, G. 1969. "Die Karer und ihre Dynasten." *Klio* 51: 116–75.

Boedecker, D. 1987. "The Two Faces of Demaratus." *Arethusa* 20: 185–201.

———. 1988. "Protesilaus and the End of Herodotus' *Histories*." *ClAnt* 7: 30–47.

Bosworth, A. 1988. *Conquest and Empire: The Reign of Alexander the Great*. Cambridge.

———. 1990. "Plutarch, Callisthenes and the Peace of Callias." *JHS* 110: 1–13.

Bowersock, G. 1966. "Pseudo-Xenophon." *HSPh* 71: 33–55.

Bowra, C. 1941. "Xenophanes, Fragment Three," *CQ* 35: 119–126.

————. 1961. *Greek Lyric Poetry.* 2d ed. Oxford.

————. 1964. *Pindar.* Oxford.

Boyce. M. 1975. "On Mithra, Lord of Fire." *AI* 1: 69–76.

————. 1982. *A History of Zoroastrianism.* 2 vols. = *Handbuch der Orientalistik. 1 Abt., Der Nahe und der Mittlere Osten* Band B, Heft 2A–B. Leiden.

Brady, T. 1935. *The Reception of the Egyptian Cults of the Greeks (330–30 b.c.).* New York.

Brannan, P. 1963. "Herodotus and History: The Constitutional Debate Preceding Darius' Accession." *Traditio* 19: 427–38.

Braun, T. 1982. "The Greeks in the Near East." *CAH* iii 1: 1–31.

Bregman, J. 1981. *Synesius of Cyrene: Philospher-Bishop.* Berkeley.

Bremmer, J., ed. 1986. *Interpretations of Greek Mythology.* Totowa, N.J.

Bresciani, E. 1985. "The Persian Occupation of Egypt." *CHI* ii: 502–28.

Briant, P. 1987a. "Pouvoir centrale et polycentrisme culturel dans l' empire achéménide. Quelques réflexions et suggestions." In Sancisi-Weerdenburg 1987a: 1–32.

————. 1987b. "Institutions perses et histoire comparitse dans l'historiographie grecque." In Sancisi-Weerdenburg 1987b: 1–10.

————. 1988. "Ethno-classe dominante et populations soumises dans l' empire achéménide: le cas de l'Égypte." In Kuhrt and Sancisi-Weerdenburg 1988: 137–73.

Briquel, D. 1984. *Les Pélasges en Italie: Récherches sur l'histoire de la légende.* BEFAR 252. Paris.

————. 1991. *L'Origine Lydienne des Etrusques: Histoire de la doctrine dans l' antiquité.* Paris.

Broadhead, H. ed. 1960. *The Persae of Aeschylus.* Cambridge.

Broholm, G. 1924. "Kyrene (2)," *RE* 12, cols. 156–69.

Brunnsåker, S. 1971. *The Tyrant-Slayers of Kritias and Nesiotes: A Critical Study of the Sources and Restorations.* 2d ed. Stockholm.

Burkert, W. 1985a. *Greek Religion.* Cambridge, Mass.

————. 1985b. "Das Ende des Kroisos." In C. Schaüblin, ed., *Catalepton: Festschrift für B. Wyss zum 80. Geburtstag.* Basel: 4–15.

————. 1990. "Herodot als Historiker Fremden Religionen." In *Hérodote et les peuples non grecs.* Fondation Hardt Entretiens sur l'étude de l'Antiquité classique, vol. 35: 1–32. Vandoeuvres-Genève.

Burn, A. 1985. "Persia and the Greeks." *CHI* ii: 292–301.

Burnett, A. 1985. *The Art of Bacchylides.* Cambridge, Mass.

Burstein, S. 1974. *Outpost of Hellenism: The Emergence of Heraclea on the Black Sea.* Berkeley and Los Angeles.

Cadoux, T. 1948. "The Athenian Archons from Kreon to Hypsichides." *JHS* 68: 70–123.

Calame, C. 1987. "Spartan Genealogies: The Mythological Representation of Spatial Organization." In Bremmer: 153–186.

Calder, W. 1925. "The Royal Road in Herodotus." *CR* 34: 7–11.

Calder, W. and G. Bean. 1958. *A Classical Map of Asia Minor*. Ankara.

Cameron, G. 1948. *The Persepolis Treasury Tablets*. Chicago.

———. 1955. "Ancient Persia." In R. C. Dentan, ed., *The Idea of History in the Ancient Near East*. New Haven, Conn.

Cartledge, P. 1979. *Sparta and Lakonia*. London.

———. 1987. *Agesilaus and the Crisis of Sparta*, London.

Cassola, F. 1957. "I Cari nella tradizione greca." *PP* 12: 192–209.

Cauer, P. 1921–23. *Grundfragen der Homerkritik,* 3d ed. 2 vols. Leipzig.

Chadwick, J. 1990. "The Descent of the Greek Epic." *JHS* 110: 174–77.

Chamoux, F. 1953. *Cyrène sous les Battiades*. Paris.

Christensen, K. 1984. "The Theseion: A Slave Refuge at Athens." *AJAH* 9: 23–32.

Clairmont, C. 1983. *Patrios Nomos: Public Burial in Athens During the Fifth and Fourth Centuries B.C.* BAR International Series 161. Oxford.

Clermont-Ganneau, C. 1921. "Le Paradeisos royal achéménide de Sidon." *Révue biblique* 30: 106–9.

Clifton, G. 1963. "The Mood of the *Persai* of Aeschylos." *G & R* 10: 111–17.

Cobet, J. 1971. *Herodots Exkurse und die Frage der Einheit seines Werkes. Historia* Einzelschriften 17. Wiesbaden.

———. 1977. "Wann wurde Herodots Darstellung der Perserkriege publiziert?" *Hermes* 105: 2–27.

Cogan, M. and H. Tadmor. 1977. "Gyges and Ashurbanipal: A Study in Literary Transmission." *Orientalia* 46: 65–85.

Coldstream, J. 1968. *Greek Geometric Pottery: A Survey of Ten Local Styles and Their Chronology*. London.

Comotti, G. 1977. *Geometric Greece*. London.

———. 1989. *Music in Greek and Roman Culture*. Baltimore.

Connor, W. 1971. *The New Politicians of Fifth-century Athens*. Princeton.

———. 1987. "Tribes, Festivals and Processions: Civic Ceremonial and Political Manipulation in Ancient Greece." *JHS* 207: 40–50.

Cook, A. 1976. "Herodotus: The Act of Inquiry as a Liberation from Myth." *Helios* 3: 23–66.

Cook, A. 1914–40. *Zeus: A Study in Ancient Religion*, 2 vols. in 3. Cambridge.

Cook, J. 1958–59. "Old Smyrna, 1948–51." *ABSA* 53–54: 1–34.

———. 1982. "East Greece." *CAH²* iii 1: 745–93.

———. 1985. "The Rise of the Achaemenids and the Establishment of Their Empire." *CHI* ii: 200–291.

Corsten, T. 1991. "Herodot I 131 und die Einfuhrung des Anahitakultes in Lydien." *IA* 26: 183–80.

Courby, F. 1931. *L'Exploration archaeologique de Délos*, vol. 12: *Les Temples d'Apollon*. Paris.

Cowley, A. 1923. *Aramaic Papyri of the Fifth Century* B.C. Chicago.

Crahay, R. 1956. *La Littérature oraculaire chez Hérodote*. Paris.

Dandamayev, M. 1975. "La Politique religieuse des Achéménides." *AI* 1: 193–200.

Dawe, R. 1963. "Inconsistency of Plot and Character in Aeschylus." *PCPhS* 189: 21–62.

Defradas, J. 1954. *Les Thèmes de la propaganda delphique*. 2d ed. Paris.

Delcourt, M. 1934. "Orient et occident chez Eschyle." In *Annuaire de l'Institute de philologie et d' histoire orientales* 2 = *Mélanges Bidez* (Brussels): 244–45.

Delebecque, E. 1957. *Essai sur la vie de Xénophon*. Paris.

Detienne, M. 1979. *Dionysos Slain*. Baltimore.

———. 1989. *Dionysos at Large*. Cambridge, Mass.

———, and J.-P. Vernant. 1978. *Cunning Intelligence in Greek Culture and Society*. Atlantic Highlands, N.J.

DeVries, K. 1980. "Greeks and Phrygians in the Early Iron Age." In Keith DeVries, ed., *Athens to Gordion: The Papers of a Memorial Symposium for Rodney K. Young*. Philadelphia: University of Pennsylvania Museum Papers 1: 33–49.

Dewald, C. 1983. "Practical Knowledge and the Historian's Role in Herodotus." In *The Greek Historians: Literature and History. Papers Presented to A. E. Raubitschek*. Palo Alto, Calif.: 47–63.

———, and J. Marincola. 1987. "A Selective Introduction to Herodotean Studies." *Arethusa* 20: 9–40.

Deichgräber, K. 1941. "Aischylos' Perser." *NAWG* 10 = n.F. 4.6: 155–202.

Diesner, H. 1959a. "Die Gestalt des Tyrannen Polycrates bei Herodot." *AAntHung* 7:211–19.

———. 1959b. "Peisistratidenexkurs und Peisistratidenbild bei Thukydides." *Historia* 8: 12–22.

Dihle, A. 1962. "Herodot und die Sophistik." *Philologus* 106: 206–20.

Diller, A. 1937. *Race Mixture among the Greeks before Alexander*. Illinois Studies in Language and Literature 20.1–2. Urbana, Ill.

Diller, H. 1961. "Die Hellenen-Barbaren Antithese im Zeitalter der Perserkriege." In *Grecs et barbares*. Fondation Hardt Entretiens sur l' Antiquité classique 8. Vandoeuvres-Genève.

Dodds E. 1973. *The Ancient Concept of Progress and Other Essays*. Oxford.

Dörrie, H. 1972. "Die Wertung der Barbaren im Urteil der Griechen." In

Antike und Universalgeschichte: Festschrift fur Hans Erich Stier zum 70. Geburtstag am 25 Mai 1972. Münster: 146–65.

Dover, K. 1972. *Aristophanic Comedy.* Berkeley and Los Angeles.

———. 1974. *Greek Popular Morality in the Age of Plato and Aristotle.* Berkeley.

———. 1978. *Greek Homosexuality.* Cambridge, Mass.

Drews, R. 1972. "The First Tyrants in Greece." *Historia* 21: 129–44.

———. 1973. *The Greek Accounts of Eastern History.* Washington, D.C.

———, 1974. "Sargon, Cyrus, and Mesopotamian Folk-History." *JNES* 33: 387–93.

———. 1976. "The Earliest Greek Settlements on the Black Sea." *JHS* 96: 18–31.

Dunbabin, T. 1948. *The Western Greeks.* Oxford.

Dworacki, N. 1979. "Atossa's Absence in the Final Sequence of the *Persae* of Aeschylus." *Arktouros: Studies presented to B. M. W. Knox.* Berlin: 101–8.

Easterling, P. 1973. "Presentation of Character in Aeschylus." *G&R* 20: 3–19.

Edmunds, S. 1990. *Homeric Nêpios.* Cambridge, Mass.

Ehrenberg, V. 1951. *The People of Aristophanes.* 2d ed. Oxford.

Euben, J. ed. 1986. *Greek Tragedy and Political Theory.* Berkeley.

Eucken, C. 1983. *Isokrates.* Berlin.

Evans, J. 1978. "What Happened to Croesus?" *CJ* 74: 34–40.

———. 1979. "Herodotus' Publication Date." *Athenaeum* 57: 145–49.

———. 1988. "The Medism of Pausanias: Two Versions." *Antichthon* 22: 1–11.

———. 1989. "Herodotus 9.73.3 and the Publication Date of the *Histories.*" *CPh* 82: 226–28.

———. 1991. *Herodotus Explorer of the Past: Three Essays.* Princeton.

Evans-Pritchard, E. 1937. *Witchcraft, Oracles, and Magic among the Azande.* Oxford.

Farnell, L. 1896–1909. *Cults of the Greek States.* 5 vols. Oxford.

Fehling, D. 1989. *Herodotus and His Sources: Citation, Invention, and Narrative Art.* Liverpool.

Ferrill, A. 1978. "Herodotus on Tyranny." *Historia* 27: 385–98.

Figuera, T. and G. Nagy, eds. 1992. *Theognis of Megara: Poetry and the Polis.* Baltimore.

Finley, M. 1979. *The World of Odysseus.* 2d ed. Harmondsworth.

———. 1986. "War and Empire." In *Ancient History: Evidence and Models.* New York: 67–87.

Flattery, D., and M. Schwartz. 1984. *Haoma and Harmaline.* University of California Publications in Near Eastern Studies 21. Berkeley.

Flory, S. 1978. "Laughter, Tears and Wisdom in Herodotus." *AJPh* 99: 145–53.

Flower, H. 1991. "Herodotus and Delphic Traditions about Croesus." In M. Flower and M. Toher, eds., *Georgica: Greek Studies in Honour of George Cawkwell. BICS* Suppl. 58: 57–77. London.

Fohl, H. 1913. *Tragische Kunst bei Herodot* (Diss. Univ. Rostock). Leipzig.

Fontenrose, J. 1978. *The Delphic Oracle: Its Responses and Operations.* Berkeley and Los Angeles.

Fornara, C. 1970. "The Cult of Harmodius and Aristogeiton." *Philologus* 114: 155–80.

———. 1971a. *Herodotus: An Interpretive Essay.* Oxford.

———. 1971b. "Evidence for the Date of Herodotus' Publication." *JHS* 91: 25–34.

———. 1981. "Herodotus' Knowledge of the Archidamian War." *Hermes* 109: 149–56.

———, and L. Samons. 1991. *Athens from Cleisthenes to Pericles.* Berkeley and Los Angeles.

Forrest, W. 1956. "The First Sacred War." *BCH* 80: 33–52.

———. 1957, "Colonisation and the Rise of Delphi." *Historia* 6: 160–75.

———. 1968, *A History of Sparta, 950–192 B.C.* London.

———. "Central Greece and Thessaly." *CAH*² iii 1: 286–320.

———. 1984. "Herodotus and Athens." *Phoenix* 38: 1–11.

Fraenkel, E. ed. 1950. *Aeschylus Agamemnon,* 2 vols. Oxford.

Fränkel, H. 1957. "Das Argonautenepos des Apollonios." *MH* 14: 1–19.

———. 1968. *Noten zu Argonautika des Apollonios.* Munich.

———. 1973. *Early Greek Poetry and Philosophy.* New York.

Freymuth, G. 1955. "Zur Mιλήτου Ἁλώσις des Phrynichos." *Philologus* 99: 51–69.

Frisch, P. 1968. *Die Träume bei Herodot.* Beiträge zur klassischen Philologie, Heft 27. Meisenheim am Glan.

Fritz, K. von. 1954. *The Theory of the Mixed Constitution in Antiquity: A Critical Analysis of Polybius' Political Ideas.* New York.

———. 1967. *Die griechische Geschictsschreibung.* Vols. 1.1 and 2. Berlin.

Gallet de Santerre, H. 1958. *Délos primitive et archaïque.* Paris.

Garlan, Y. 1988. *Slavery in Ancient Greece.* Ithaca, N.Y.

Garland, R. 1985. *The Greek Way of Death.* Ithaca, N.Y.

Georges, P. 1986. "Saving Herodotus' Phenomena: The Oracles and the Events of 480 B.C." *ClAnt* 5: 14–59.

———. 1994. "Darius in Scythia: The Formation of Herodotus' Sources and the Nature of Darius' Campaign." *AJAH* 11: in press.

Gillis, D. 1979. *Collaboration with the Persians. Historia* Einzelschriften 34. Wiesbaden.

Girshman, R. 1954. *Iran*. Harmondsworth.

Gnoli, G. 1974. "Politique réligieuse et conception de la royauté sous les Achéménides." *AI* 2: 117–92.

Goldhill, S. 1988. "Battle Narrative and Politics in Aeschylus' *Persae*." *JHS* 108: 189–93.

Goldman, H. 1923. "Excavations of the Fogg Museum at Colophon." *AJA* 27: 67–68.

Gomme, A. 1933. *Population of Athens*. Oxford.

———. 1956. *A Commentary on Thucydides*. Vol. 1. Oxford.

———. 1959. "The Population of Athens Again." *JHS* 179: 61–68.

———, and K. Dover. 1970. *A Commentary on Thucydides*. Vol. 3. Oxford.

Gould, J. 1989. *Herodotus*. New York.

Graf, D. 1984. "Medism: The Origin and Significance of the Term." *JHS* 104: 15–30.

Grant, J. 1983. "Some Thoughts on Herodotus." *Phoenix* 37: 283–98.

Grote, G. 1888 [1849]. *History of Greece*. 10 vols. London.

Gruen, E. 1992. *Culture and National Identity in Republican Rome*. Ithaca, N.Y.

Gusmani, R. 1980–86. *Lydisches Wörterbuch*. 3 fascicles. Heidelberg.

Guthrie, W. 1969. *History of Greek Philosophy*. Vol. 3. Cambridge.

Habicht, C. 1985. *Pausanias' Guide to Ancient Greece*. Berkeley and Los Angeles.

Haerinck, E. 1973. "Le Palais achéménide de Babylone." *IA* 10: 108–32.

Hall, E. 1989. *Inventing the Barbarian: Greek Self-Definition Through Tragedy*. Oxford.

Hallock, P. 1969. *The Persepolis Fortification Tablets*. Chicago.

———. 1985. "The Evidence of the Persepolis Tablets." *CHI* ii: 588–609.

Halperin, D. 1986. "Plato and Erotic Reciprocity." *CIAnt* 5: 60–80.

———, J. Winkler, and F. Zeitlin. eds. 1990. *Before Sexuality: The Construction of Erotic Experience in the Ancient Greek World*. Princeton.

Hamilton, C. 1991. *Agesilaus and the Failure of Spartan Hegemony*. Ithaca, N.Y.

Hammond, N. 1960. "An Early Inscription at Argos." *CQ* 10: 33–36.

———. 1986. *A History of Greece to 322 B.C.* 3d ed. Oxford.

Hanfmann, G. 1958. "Lydiaka." *HSPh* 63: 65–88.

———. 1975. *A Survey of Sardis and the Major Monuments outside the City Walls*. Cambridge, Mass.

———, and W. Mierse, 1983. *The Archaeological Exploration of Sardis: Sardis from Prehistoric to Roman Times*. Cambridge, Mass.

Harding, P. 1973. "The Purpose of Isokrates' *Archidamos* and *On the Peace*." *CSCA* 6: 137–49.

Harsh, P. 1955. "The Intriguing Slave in Greek Comedy." *TAPhA* 86: 135–42.

Hartmann, L. 1962. "The Date of the Kimmerian Thrust against Assurbanipal according to ABL 1391." *JNES* 21: 25–37.

Hartog, F. 1988. *The Mirror of Herodotus: The Representation of the Other in the Writing of History.* Berkeley.

Hasluck, W. 1910. *Cyzicus.* Cambridge, Mass.

Head, B. 1911. *Historia Numorum: A Manual of Greek Numismatics.* 2d ed. Oxford.

Helm, P. 1981. "Herodotus' Medikos Logos and Median History." *Iran* 19: 85–90.

Henrichs, A. 1981. "Human Sacrifice in Greek Religion." In *Le Sacrifice dans l'antiquité.* Fondation Hardt, Entretiens sur l'Antiquite classique 27: 195–235. Vandoeuvres-Genève.

Henry, A. 1983. *Honours and Privileges in Athenian Honorary Decrees.* Hildesheim.

Herman, G. 1987. *Ritualised Friendship and the Greek City.* Cambridge.

Herrenschmidt, C. 1987. "Notes sur la parenté chez les Perses au début de l'empire achéménide." In Sancisi-Weerdenburg 1987b: 53–67.

Higgins, W. 1977. *Xenophon the Athenian.* Albany.

Hignett, C. 1963. *Xerxes' Invasion of Greece.* Oxford.

Hill, G. 1922. *British Museum Catalogue of Greek Coins of Arabia, Mesopotamia, and Persia.* London.

———. 1951. *Sources for Greek History between the Persian and Peloponnesian Wars.* 2d ed. Ed. R. Meiggs and A. Andrewes. Oxford.

Hirsch, S. 1983. "1001 Iranian Nights: History and Fiction in Xenophon's *Cyropaedia.* In *The Greek Historians: Literature and History. Papers Presented to A. E. Raubitschek.* Palo Alto, Calif.: 65–85.

———. 1985. *The Friendship of the Barbarians: Xenophon and the Persian Empire.* Hanover, N.H.

Hofstetter, F. 1978. *Die Griechen in Persen: Prosopographie der Griechen im persischen Reich vor Alexander* (Diss. Univ. Bern). *Archäolog. Mitteil. aus Iran* Suppl. 5.

Höistad, R. 1948. *Cynic Hero and Cynic King: Studies in the Cynic Conception of Man."* Uppsala.

Holladay, A. 1989. "The Hellenic Disaster in Egypt." *JHS* 109: 176–82.

Holland, L. 1944. "Colophon." *Hesperia* 13: 91–171.

Hornblower, S. 1982. *Mausolus.* Oxford.

———. 1983. *The Greek World 479–323 B.C.* London.

Horton, R. 1967. "African Traditional Thought and Western Science." *Africa* 37: 50–71 and 155–87.

House, W. 1964. *Aristotle's Poetics.* London.

How, W., and J. Wells, 1912. *A Commentary on Herodotus.* 2 vols. Oxford.

Humphreys, S. 1980. "Family Tombs and Tomb Cult in Ancient Athens: Tradition or Traditionalism?" *JHS* 100: 96–126.

Hunt, D. 1947. "Feudal Survivals in Ionia." *JHS* 67: 60–70.

Hunter, V. 1982. *Past and Process in Herodotus and Thucydides.* Princeton.

Huntington, R., and P. Metcalf. 1979. *Celebrations of Death: The Anthropology of Death Ritual.* Cambridge.

Huxley, G. 1957. "Thucydides and the Date of the Trojan War: A Note." *PP* 54: 209–12.

———. 1959. "Titles of Midas." *GRBS* 2: 83–99.

———. 1966. *The Early Ionians.* New York.

———. 1969. *Greek Epic Poetry from Eumelus to Panyassis.* Cambridge, Mass.

Immerwahr, H. 1956. "Aspects of Historical Causation in Herodotus." *TAPhA* 85: 241–80.

———. 1966. *Form and Thought in Herodotus.* Cleveland.

Jacobsthal, P. 1951. "The Date of the Ephesian Foundation Deposit." *JHS* 71: 85–95.

Jacoby, F. 1912. "Hekataios von Milet." *RE* vol. 7, cols. 2667–2750.

———. 1913. "Herodotos." *RE* Suppl. 2, cols. 206–520.

———. 1922. "Ktesias von Knidos." *RE* vol. 11, cols. 2032–73.

———. 1947a. "The First Athenian Prose Writer." *Mnemosyne* 13: 13–64.

———. 1947b. "Some Remarks on Ion of Chios." *CQ* 41: 1–17.

———. 1949. *Atthis: The Local Chronicles of Ancient Athens.* Oxford.

Jeffery, L. 1956. "The Courts of Justice in Archaic Chios." *ABSA* 51: 157–67.

Jones, J. 1962. *On Aristotle and Greek Tragedy.* London.

Jüthner, J. 1923. *Hellenen und Barbaren aus der Geschichte des Nationalbewusstseins. Das Erbe der Alten* ser. 2, viii. Leipzig.

Kahn, C. 1979. *The Art and Thought of Heraclitus.* Cambridge.

Kaletsch, H. 1958. "Zur Lydische Chronologie." *Historia* 7: 1–47.

Kelly, T. 1976. *A History of Argos to 500 B.C.* Minneapolis.

Kent, R. 1953. *Old Persian: Grammar, Texts, Vocabulary.* 2d ed. New Haven, Conn.

Kienast, D. 1973. *Philipp II von Makedonien und das Reich des Achämeniden.* Abhandlung der Marburger Gesellschaft 1971. nr. 6. Munich.

Kienitz, F. 1953. *Die politische Geschichte Ägyptens vom 7. bis 4. Jhr. vor der Zeitwende.* Berlin.

Kirchberg, J. 1965. *Die Funktion der Orakel im Werke Herodots. Hypomnemata* Heft 11. Hamburg.

Kirk, G. 1962. *The Songs of Homer.* Cambridge.

———. 1976. *Homer and the Oral Tradition.* Cambridge.

————. 1970. *Myth: Its Meaning and Functions in Ancient and Other Cultures.* Berkeley and Los Angeles.

————. 1984. *The Iliad: A Commentary.* Vol. 1. Cambridge.

Kitto, H. 1961. *Greek Tragedy: A Literary Analysis.* 3d ed. London.

————. 1966. *Poiesis.* Berkeley and Los Angeles.

Kleiner, G. 1966. *Alt-Milet. Sitz-Ber. Wiss. Ges. Frankfurt* 4.1. Wiesbaden.

————. 1976. "Miletos." In *The Princeton Encyclopedia of Classical Sites.* Princeton.

Knaack, G. 1896. "Apollonius (71)." *RE,* vol. 2, cols. 126–34.

König, F. 1972. *Die Persika des Ktesias von Knidos.* Graz.

Konstan, D. 1987. "Persians, Greeks, and Empire." *Arethusa* 20: 59–73.

Korzeniewski, D. 1966. "Studien zu den Persern von Aischylos." *Helikon* 6: 548–96.

Krentz, P. 1982. *The Thirty at Athens.* Ithaca, N. Y.

Kuhrt, A. 1989. "Earth and Water." In H. Sancisi-Weerdenburg and A. Kuhrt, eds. *Achaemenid History III: Method and Theory.* Leiden: 86–99.

Kuhrt, A. and H. Sancisi-Weerdenburg, eds. 1988. *Achaemenid History III: Method and Theory.* Proceedings of the 1985 Achaemenid History Workshop. Leiden.

Lacroix, L. 1974. "Héracles héros voyageur et civilizateur." *BAB* 60: 34–59.

Lateiner, D. 1985. "Limit, Propriety, and Transgression in the *Histories* of Herodotus." In *The Greek Historians: Literature and History. Papers Presented to A. E. Raubitschek.* Palo Alto, Calif.: 87–100.

————. 1989. *The Historical Method of Herodotus.* Phoenix Suppl. 23. Toronto.

Lattimore, R. 1939. "The Wise Adviser in Herodotus." *CPh* 34: 24–35.

————. 1943. "Aeschylus on the Defeat of Xerxes." In *Classical Studies in Honor of William Abott Oldfather.* Urbana, Ill.: 82–93.

————. 1958. *The Poetry of Greek Tragedy.* New York.

Leaf, W. 1923. *Strabo on the Troad: Book XIII, Cap. I.* Cambridge.

Legon, R. 1981. *Megara: The Political History of a Greek City-State to 336 B.C.* Ithaca, N.Y.

Lerat, L. 1961. "Fouilles à Delphes, à l'est du grand sanctuare." *BCH* 85: 316–62.

Lesky, A. 1966. *A History of Greek Literature.* 2d ed. London.

————. 1983. *Greek Tragic Poetry.* 3d ed. New Haven, Conn.

Levi, M. 1977–78. "Una lettura storiografica. *I Persiani* di Eschilo." *CRDAC* 9: 67–73.

Lévy, E. 1976. *Athènes devant la défaite de 404: histoire d'une crise idéologique.* Bibliothèque des écoles françaises d'Athènes et de Rome 225. Paris.

Lewis, D. 1963. "Cleisthenes and Attica." *Historia* 12: 22–40.

———. 1977. *Sparta and Persia*. Leiden.

———. 1985. "Persians in Herodotus." In *The Greek Historians: Literature and History. Papers Presented to A.E. Raubitschek*. Palo Alto, Calif.: 101–17.

Ley, G. 1982. "*Persae* 829–831, an Interpolation?" *Eranos* 80: 169–70.

Lloyd, A. 1975–88. *Herodotus: Book 2*. 3 vols. Leiden.

———. 1982. "The Inscription of Udjahorresnet: A Collaborator's Testament." *JEA* 68: 166–80.

———. 1988. "Herodotus on Cambyses: Some Thoughts on Recent Work." In Kuhrt and Sancisi-Weedenburg 1988: 55–66.

———. 1990. "Herodotus on Egyptians and Libyans." In *Hérodote et les peuples non grecs*. Fondation Hardt Entretiens sur l'étude de l' Antiquité classique, vol. 35: 215–44. Vandoeuvres-Genève.

Long, A. 1970. "Morals and Values in Homer." *JHS* 90: 121–39.

Long, T. 1986. *Barbarians in Greek Comedy*. Carbondale, Ill.

Loraux, N. 1979. "L'Autochthonie: Une topique athénienne." *Annales (ESC)* 34: 3–26.

———. 1986. *The Invention of Athens: The Funeral Oration in the Classical City*. Cambridge, Mass.

Luccioni, J. 1947. *Les Idées politiques et sociales de Xénophon*. Paris.

———. 1953. *Xénophon et le socratisme*. Paris.

Macan, R. 1908. *Herodotus. The Seventh, Eighth and Ninth Books*. 2 vols. in 3. London.

McLaren, M. 1934. "On the Composition of Xenophon's *Hellenica*." *AJPh* 55: 121–29 and 249–62.

MacLeod, C. 1982. "Politics and the Oresteia." *JHS* 102: 124–44.

MacNeal, R. 1985. "How Did Pelasgians Become Hellenes? Hdt. 1.56–58." *ICS* 10: 11–21.

Malkin, I. 1987. *Religion and Colonization in Ancient Greece*. Leiden.

Mallowan, M. 1985. "Cyrus the Great (558–529 B.C.)." *CHI* ii: 392–420.

Manganaro, G. 1960. "La *Milêtou Halosis* Frinico e l'oracolo epicino per Argo e Mileto." *RFIC* 38: 113–23.

Marg, W., ed. 1962. *Herodot: Eine Auswahl aus der neueren Forschung*. Darmstadt.

Martin, V. 1944. "Le Traitement de l'histoire diplomatique dans la tradition litteraire du IV siécle av. J.C." *MH* 1: 13–30.

Marx, F. 1928. "Der Tragiker Phrynichos." *RhM* 77: 337–59.

Masson, O. 1991. "Anatolian Languages." *CAH*[2] iii 2: 666–76.

Matthews, V. 1974. *Panyassis of Halikarnassos: Text and Commentary*. Leiden.

Mazzarino, S. 1947. *Fra oriente e occidente*. Florence.

Meiggs, R. 1972. *The Athenian Empire*. Oxford.

Mellink, M. 1991. "The Native Kingdoms of Anatolia." in *CAH*² iii.2: 619–65.

Michaélides, G. 1943. "Quelques objets inédits d' époque perse." *ASAE* 43: 19–103.

Michelini, A. 1982. *Tradition and Dramatic Form in the Persians of Aeschylus.* Leiden.

Millar, F. 1984. "The Political Character of the Classical Roman Republic." *JRS* 74: 1–19.

Miller, M. 1985. "Perserie: The Arts of the East in Fifth-Century Athens." Diss. Harvard Univ.

———. 1988. "Midas as the Great King in Attic Fifth-Century Vase-Painting." *AK* 31: 79–88.

Momigliano, A. 1958. "The Place of Herodotus in the History of Historiography." *History* 43: 1–13.

———. 1975a. "The Fault of the Greeks." *Daedalus* 104.2: 9–19.

———. 1975b. *Alien Wisdom: The Limits of Hellenization.* Cambridge.

———. 1982. "How to Reconcile Greeks and Trojans." *Mededelingen der Koninklijke Nederlanse Akademie van Wetenschappen, Aftdeling Letterkunde* 45.9: 3–20 (= 231–48).

Moorey, P. 1980. "Cemeteries of the First Millennium B. C. at Deve Hüyük." *BAR International Series* 87: 128–42. London.

Morgan, C. 1990. *Athletes and Oracles: The Transformation of Olympia and Delphi in the Eighth Century BC.* Cambridge.

Mosley, D. 1971. "Greeks, Barbarians, Language and Contact." *AncSoc* 2: 1–6.

Münscher, K. 1920. *Xenophon in der griechisch-römischen Literatur. Philologus* Suppl. 13. Leipzig.

Munson, R. 1988. "Artemisia in Herodotus." *ClAnt* 7: 91–106.

———. 1991. "The Madness of Cambyses (Herodotus 3.16–38)." *Arethusa* 24: 43–65.

Murray, G. 1934. *The Rise of the Greek Epic.* 4th ed. Oxford.

———, trans. 1939. *The Persians of Aeschylus.* London.

Murray, O. 1979. *Early Greece and Its Eastern Neighbors.* Atlantic Highlands, N.J.

———. 1987. "Herodotus and Oral History." In Sancisi-Weerdenburg 1987b: 93–115. Leiden.

Myres, J. 1907. "A History of the Pelasgian Theory." *JHS* 27: 170–225.

Nagy, G. 1987. "Herodotus the *Logios.*" *Arethusa* 20: 175–84.

Neppi Modona, A. 1977. *Cortona etrusca e romana nella storia e nell' arte.* 2d ed. Accademia toscana di scienze e lettere "La Colombaria": Studi 45. Florence.

Neville, J. 1979. "Was There an Ionian Revolt?" *CQ* 29: 268–75.

Nicholls, R. 1958–59. "Old Smyrna: The Iron Age Fortifications and Associated Remains on the City Perimeter." *ABSA* 53–54: 36–137.

Nilsson, M. 1951. *Cults, Myths, Oracles and Politics in Ancient Greece.* Lund.

———. 1955. *Geschichte der griechische Religion.* 2d ed. Handbuch der Altertumswissenschaft, 5. Abt. 2. T. Munich.

Nock, A. 1942. "Religious Attitudes of the Ancient Greeks." *PAPhS* 85: 473–82.

North, H. 1966. *Sophrosyne: Self-knowledge and Self-restraint in Greek Literature.* Cornell Studies in Classical Philology 35. Ithaca, N.Y.

Ober, J. 1989. *Mass and Elite in Democratic Athens: Rhetoric, Ideology, and the Power of the People.* Princeton.

Olmstead, A. 1948. *History of the Persian Empire.* Chicago.

Oppenheim, L. 1985. "The Babylonian Evidence of Achaemenian Rule in Mesopotamia." *CHI* ii: 529–87.

Orlin, L. 1976. "Athens and Persia ca. 507 B.C.: A Neglected Perspective." In L. Orlin, ed. *Michigan Oriental Studies in Honor of George G. Cameron.* Ann Arbor, Mich.: 255–66.

Osborne, M. 1981–83. *Naturalization in Athens.* 4 vols. in 3. Brussels.

Ostwald, M. 1969. *Nomos and the Beginnings of Athenian Democracy.* Oxford.

Paduano, G. 1972. *Studi su Apollonio Rodio.* Rome.

———. 1978. *Sui Persiani di Eschilo: Problemi di focalizzazione dramatica.* Rome.

Page, D. 1955. *Sappho and Alcaeus.* Oxford.

Papatheophanes, M. 1985. "Heraclitus of Ephesus, the Magi, and the Achaemenids." *IA* 20: 101–61.

Parke, H. 1933. *Greek Mercenary Soldiers from the Earliest Times to the Battle of Ipsus.* Oxford.

———. 1967. *The Oracles of Zeus.* Cambridge.

———. 1985. *Oracles of Apollo in Asia Minor.* London.

Parker, R. 1987. "Myths of Early Athens." In Bremmer: 187–214.

Patterson, O. 1982. *Slavery and Social Death: A Comparative Study.* Cambridge, Mass.

Pearson, L. 1939. *Early Ionian Historians.* Oxford.

Pedley, J. 1968. *Sardis in the Age of Croesus.* Norman, Okla.

Petrounias, E. 1976. *Funktion und Thematik der Bilder bei Aischylos. Hypomnemata* 48. Göttingen.

Picard, C. 1922. *Ephèse et Claros: Recherches sur les sanctuaires et les cultes de l'Ionie du nord.* Paris.

Picard, O. 1980. *Les Grecs devant la menace perse.* Paris.

Piccirilli, L. 1973. *Gli Arbitrati interstatali greci, I: Dalle origini al 338 a.C.* Pisa.

Pley, J. 1913. "Herakleidai." *RE* vol. 8, cols. 440–57.

Podlecki, A. 1966. *The Political Background of Aeschylean Tragedy*. Ann Arbor, Mich.

———. 1968. "Simonides, 480." *Historia* 17 (1968): 257–75.

———. 1975. *The Life of Themistocles: A Critical Survey of the Literary and Archaeological Evidence*. Montreal.

———. 1977. "Herodotus in Athens?" In K. Kinzl, ed., *Greece and the Eastern Mediterranean: Studies Presented to Fritz Schachermayr*. Berlin: 246–65.

Pohlenz, M. 1937. *Herodot, der erste Geschichtschreiber des Abendlandes*. Leipzig.

Pompella, G. 1974. "L' Impegno di Eschilo nei Persiani." *Vichiana* 3: 3–23.

Posener, G. 1936. *La Premier domination perse en Egypte: Recuil d'inscriptions hieroglyphes*. Cairo.

Pickard, A., ed. 1879. *The Persae of Aeschylus*. London.

Prinz, F. 1979. *Gründungsmythen und Sagenchronologie*. Zetemata Heft 72. Munich.

Pritchett, W. 1985. *The Greek State at War. Part IV*. Berkeley and Los Angeles.

Raaflaub, K. 1985. "Athens 'Ideologie der Macht' und die Freiheit des Tyrannen." In *Studien zum Attische Seebund*, Konstanzer Althistorische Vorträge und Forschungen 8: 45–101. Konstanz.

Radermacher, L. 1938. *Mythos und Sage bei den Griechen*. Baden.

Radet, G. 1893. *La Lydie et le monde grec au temps de Mermnades (687–546)*. Paris.

Ramage, A. 1968. "City Area: Pactolus North." In G. Hanfmann, "The Tenth Campaign at Sardis." *BASO* 191: 11–13.

———. 1987. "Lydian Sardis." In E. Guralink, ed. *Sardis. Twenty-Seven Years of Discovery*. Chicago: 6–15.

Raubitschek, A. 1958. "Ein neues Pittakeion." 71: 170–72.

———. 1964. "The Treaties between Persia and Athens." *GRBS* 5: 151–59.

———. 1971–80. "The *Phoinissai* of Phrynichus." *Anadolu* 21: 279–81.

Ray, J. 1987. "Egypt: Dependence and Independence (425–343 B.C.)." In Sancisi-Weedenburg 1987a: 79–95.

Reverdin, O. 1962. "Crise spirituelle et evasion." In *Grecs et barbares*. Fondation Hardt, Entretiens sur l'Antiquité classique 8: 83–107. Vandoeuvres-Genève.

Rhodes, P. 1981. *A Commentary on the Aristotelian Athenaion Politeia*. Oxford.

Richardson, L. 1952. "The Inner Conflict of the *Persae*: Athenian Dramatist and Persian Characters." In White: 55–67.

Rist, J. 1969. *Stoic Philosophy*. Cambridge.

Robert, L. 1953. "Le Sanctuaire d'Artemis à Amyzon." *CRAI*: 403–15.

————. 1963. *Noms indigènes dans l'Asie-Mineure Grecoromaine.* Paris.

————. 1975. "Une nouvelle inscription grecque de Sardis: Règlement de l'autorité perse relatif à un culte de Zeus." *CRAI*: 306–30.

Robertson, N. 1987. "Government and Society at Miletus, 525–442 B.C." *Phoenix* 41: 356–98.

Robinson, S. 1951. "The Coins from the Ephesian Artemision Reconsidered." *JHS* 71: 156–67.

Robinson, T. ed. and trans. 1987. *Heraclitus Fragments.* Phoenix Suppl. vol. 22. Toronto.

Roebuck, C. 1955. "The Early Ionian League." *CP* 50: 26–40.

————. 1959. *Ionian Trade and Colonization.* New York.

————. 1961. "Tribal Organization in Ionia." *TAPhA* 92: 495–507.

Rolley, C. 1969. *Fouilles de Delphes: Les statuettes de bronze.* Paris.

Roller, L. 1983. "The Legend of Midas." *ClAnt* 2: 299–313.

Root, M. 1979. *The King and Kingship in Achaemenid Art: Essays on the Creation of an Iconography of Empire.* AI 91. Leiden.

Rose, H. 1958. *A Handbook of Greek Mythology.* 6th ed. London.

Rose, P. 1975. "Class Ambivalence in the *Odyssey*." *Historia* 24: 129–49.

Rosenmeyer, T. 1982. *The Art of Aeschylus.* Berkeley and Los Angeles.

Roux, G. 1976. "Delphi." In *The Princeton Encyclopedia of Classical Sites.* Princeton: 264–67.

Russell, D., and N. Van De Ven. 1984. *Crimes Against Women: Proceedings of the International Tribunal on Crimes against Women, Brussels.* Abridged ed. East Palo Alto, Calif.

Ryder, T. 1965. *Koine Eirene. General Peace and Local Independence in Ancient Greece.* Oxford.

Said, E. 1978. *Orientalism.* New York.

Sakellariou, M. 1958. *La Migration grecque en Ionie.* Collections de l'Institut français d'Athènes, Centre d'études d'Asie mineure, Ionie I. Athens.

Salmon, J. 1984. *Wealthy Corinth: A History of the City to 338 B.C.* Oxford.

Sambursky, S. 1956. *The Physical World of the Greeks.* London.

Sancisi-Weerdenburg, H. 1985. "The Death of Cyrus: Xenophon's *Cyropaedia* as a Source for Iranian History." In A. Bivar, ed. *Papers in Honour of Professor Mary Boyce.* AI 25: 459–71. Leiden.

————, ed. 1987a. *Achaemenid History I: Sources, Structures, and Synthesis.* Proceedings of the 1983 Achaemenid History Workshop. Leiden.

————, ed. 1987b. *Achaemenid History II: The Greek Sources.* Proceedings of the 1984 Achaemenid History Workshop. Leiden.

————. 1987c. "The Fifth Oriental Monarchy and Hellenocentrism: *Cyropaedia* VIII viii and its Influence." In Sancisi-Weerdenburg 1987b: 117–31.

341

———. 1987d. "Decadence in the Empire or Decadence in the Sources?" In Sancisi-Weedenburg 1987a: 33–45.

Saxonhouse, A. 1986. "Myths and the Origins of Cities: Reflections on the Autochthony Theme in Euripides' *Ion.*" In Euben: 252–73.

Schachermeyer, F. 1973. "Athen als Stadt der Grosskoenigs." *GB* 1: 211–20.

Schefold, K. 1973. "Die Residenz von Larisa am Hermos." *Proceedings of the Xth International Congress of Classical Archaeology.* (Ankara, 1978): 549–64.

Schlafer, R. 1936. "Greek Theories of Slavery from Homer to Aristotle." *HSPh* 47: 165–204.

Schmitt, R. 1976. "The Medo-Persian Names of Herodotus in the Light of the New Evidence from Persepolis." *AAHung* 24: 25–35.

Schwabl, H. 1962. "Das Bild der Fremden Welt bei den frühen Griechen." In *Grecs et barbares.* Fondation Hardt, Entretiens sur l'Antiquité classique 8: 1–23 Vandoeuvres-Genève.

———. 1969. "Herodot als Historiker und Erzähler." *Gymnasium* 76: 253–72.

Schwartz, J. 1969. "Hérodote et. Périclès." *Historia* 18: 367–70.

Schwartz, M. 1985. "The Religion of Achaemenian Iran." *CHI* ii: 664–97.

Seager, R. 1974. "The King's Peace and the Balance of Power in Greece, 386–362 B.C. *Athenaeum* n.s. 52: 36–63.

Sealey, R. 1976. *A History of the Greek City States ca. 700–338 B.C..* Berkeley and Los Angeles.

———. 1987. *The Athenian Republic.* University Park, Pa.

Secondat, C. de, Baron de Montesquieu. 1979 [1721]. *The Persian Letters* trans. C. Betts. Harmondsworth.

Segal, C. 1971a. "Croesus on the Pyre: Herodotus and Bacchylides." *WS* 84: 39–51.

———. 1971b. *The Theme of Mutilation of the Corpse in the Iliad.* Leiden.

———. 1974. "The Raw and the Cooked in Greek Literature: Structure, Values, Metaphor." *CJ* 69: 289–300.

Sekunda, N. 1985. "Achaemenid Colonization in Lydia." *REA* 87: 7–30.

———. 1989. "Persian Settlement in Hellespontine Phrygia." In Kuhrt and Sanchisi-Weerdenburg 1988: 175–97.

Servais, J. 1973. "Hérodote et la chronologie des Cypsélides." *AC* 38: 39–51.

Shipley, G. 1987. *A History of Samos, 800–188 B.C.* Oxford.

Simms, R. 1989. "Isis in Classical Athens." *CJ* 84: 216–21.

Simon, C. 1986. "The Archaic Votive Offerings and Cults of Ionia." Diss. Univ. California, Berkeley.

Smyth, H. 1924. *Aeschylean Tragedy.* Berkeley.

Snodgrass, A. 1971. *The Dark Age of Greece: An Archaeological Survey of the Eleventh to the Eighth Centuries B.C.* Edinborough.

———. 1980. *Archaic Greece: The Age of Experiment.* London.

Solmsen, F. 1974. "Two Crucial Decisions in Herodotus." *Mededelingen Nederlandse Akademie,* AFD Letterkunde 37: 139–70.

Stahl, H. 1975. "Learning through Suffering?" *YCS* 24: 1–36.

Starr, C. 1975. "Greeks and Persians in the Fourth Century B.C.: A Study in Cultural Contacts before Alexander, Part I." *IA* 11: 39–99.

———. 1977. "Greeks and Persians in the Fourth Century B.C.: A Study in Cultural Contacts before Alexander, Part II: The Meeting of Two Cultures." *IA* 12: 49–116.

Stinton T. 1975. "*Hamartia* in Aristotle and Greek Tragedy." *CQ* 25: 237–41.

Stoessl, F. 1945. "Die Phoinissen des Phrynichos und die Perser des Aischylos." *MH* 2: 148–65.

Strasburger, H. 1953. "Der soziologische Aspekt der homerischen Epen." *Gymnasium* 60: 97–114.

———. 1955. "Herodot und das perikleische Athen." *Historia* 4: 1–25.

———. 1956. "Herodots Zeitrechnung." *Historia* 5: 129–61.

———. 1958. "Thukydides und die politische Selbstdarstellung der Athener." *Hermes* 86: 17–40.

Strauss, B. 1986. *Athens after the Peloponnesian War: Class, Faction, and Policy, 403–386 B.C.* Ithaca, N.Y.

Stroud, R. 1968. *The Homicide Law of Drakon.* Berkeley and Los Angeles.

Stroux, J. 1934. "Erzälungen aus Kallimachos." *Philologus* 89: 301–19.

Stronach, D. 1978. *Pasargadae.* Oxford.

Syme, R. 1938. *The Roman Revolution.* Oxford.

Talamo, C. 1973. "Per la storia di Colofone in etá arcaica." *PP* 28: 343–75.

Taplin, O. 1977. *The Stagecraft of Aeschylus.* Oxford.

Tatum, J. 1988. *Xenophon's Imperial Fiction.* Princeton.

Taylor, M. 1975. "*The Tyrant Slayers.*" Diss. Harvard Univ.

Thalmann, W. 1980. "Xerxes' Rags: Some Problems in Aeschylus' *Persians.*" *AJPh* 101: 260–82.

Thébert, Y. 1980. "Réflexions sur l'utilisation du concept d'étranger: Évolution et fonction de l'image du barbare á Athènes à l'époque classique." *Diogène* 112: 96–115.

Thomas, C. 1966. "The Roots of Homeric Kingship." *Historia* 15: 387–407.

Tigerstedt, E. 1965. *The Legend of Sparta in Classical Antiquity.* Vol. 1. Stockholm.

Tozzi, P. 1978. *La Rivolta ionica.* Pisa.

Tuchelt, K. 1976. "Didyma." In *Princeton Encyclopedia of Classical Sites*. Princeton: 272–73.

Van Gennep, A. 1960. [1908]. *The Rites of Passage*. Chicago.

Vermasaren, M. 1977. *Cybele and Attis: The Myth and the Cult*. London.

———. 1987. *Corpus Cultus Cybele Attidisque (CCCA)*. Vol 1: Asia Minor. Leiden.

Vernant, J.-P. 1982. "From Oedipus to Periander." *Arethusa* 15: 19–38.

———. 1991. "A 'Beautiful Death' and the Disfigured Corpse in Homeric Epic." In *Mortals and Immortals. Collected Essays*. Princeton: 50–74.

Vernant, J. P. and P. Vidal-Naquet. 1981. *Myth and Tragedy in Ancient Greece*. Cambridge, Mass.

Veyne, P. 1988. *Did the Greeks Believe in Their Myths?* Chicago.

Vian, F. 1963. *Les Origines de Thèbes: Cadmus et les spartes*. Paris.

Vickers, B. 1973. *Towards Greek Tragedy: Drama, Myth, Society*. London.

Vidal-Naquet, P. 1973. *Sophocle. Tragédies*. Paris.

———. 1986a. "Divine Time and Human Time." In *The Black Hunter: Forms of Thought and Forms of Society in the Greek World*. Baltimore.

———. 1986b. "The Tradition of the Athenian Hoplite." In *The Black Hunter: Forms of Thought and Forms of Society in the Greek World*. Baltimore.

Vlastos, G. 1941. "Slavery in Plato's Thought." *PhR* 80: 289–304 = *Platonic Studies* (Princeton, 1973): 147–63.

Wade-Gery, H. 1951. "Miltiades." *JHS* 71: 212–21.

———. 1952. *The Poet of the Iliad*. Cambridge.

———. 1958. *Essays in Greek History*. Oxford.

Wallace, R. 1986. "The Date of Solon's Reforms." *AJAH* 8 [1983]: 81–95.

Walser, G. 1967. "Griechen am Hofe des Grosskönigs." In E. Walder, ed. *Festgabe Hans von Greyerz*. Bern: 189–202.

Wasowicz, A. 1965. *Olbia pontique et son territoire: L'aménagement de l'espace*. Ann. Litt. Univ. Bésançon 168. Paris.

Waters, K. 1976. "The 'Ancestral Constitution' and Fourth-Century Historiography at Athens." *AJAH* 2: 129–40.

Weissbach, F. 1924. "Kyros (no. 5)." *RE* Suppl. 4, cols. 1129–77.

Wells, J. 1907: "The Persian Friends of Herodotus." *JHS* 27: 34–47.

West, M. 1971. *Early Greek Philosophy and the Orient*. Oxford.

———. 1988. "Rise of the Greek Epic." *JHS* 108: 151–72.

White, M., ed. 1952. *Studies in Honour of Gilbert Norwood*. Phoenix Suppl. vol. 1. Toronto.

Whitehead, D. 1977. *The Ideology of the Athenian Metic*. PCPhS Suppl. vol. 4. Cambridge.

Wilamowitz-Moellendorf, U. von. 1987. "Die Perser des Aischylos." *Hermes* 32: 382–98.

————. 1914. *Aischylos. Interpretationen*. Berlin.

Will, E. 1955. *Korinthiaka: Récherches sur l'histoire de la civilisation de Corinthe des origines aux guerres médiques*. Paris.

Williams, G. 1952. "The Curse of the Alkmaionidai II. Kleisthenes and the Persian Wars." *Hermathena* 79: 3–21.

Winnington-Ingram, R. 1962. Review of Broadhead. *CR* 12: 122–25.

————. 1973. "*Zeus in the Persae*." *JHS* 93: 210–19.

Witt, R. 1971. *Isis in the Graeco-Roman World*. Ithaca, N.Y.

Young, P. 1980. "Building Projects of the Archaic Greek Tyrants." Diss. Univ. Pennsylvania.

Young, R. 1964. "The Nomadic Impact: Gordion." In *Dark Ages and Nomads c. 1000 B.C.: Studies in Iranian and Anatolian Archaeology*. Istanbul: 52–57.

Zaehner, R. 1961. *Dawn and Twilight of Zoroastrianism*. London.

Index

Demeter, Eleusinian, 192
Democracy: as akin to tyranny, 160–63; at Athens, 159–63, 211; and Persians, 196–97
Didyma, 17, 19, 25–26, 27, 28, 35, 45. *See also* Branchidae, Branchids
Dindyme (Asiatic mother goddess), 6
Diodorus of Sicily (historian), 235, 236
Diogenes (Cynic), 215
Diogenes Laertius, 215
Dionysius of Miletus (logographer), 119–20
Dionysius I and II of Syracuse (tyrants, *reg. c.* 405–367 and 367–344 B.C., respectively), 210, 235
Dionysus, 18, 205; Eater of Raw Flesh, 82
Dodecapolis (Ionian), 17–18
Dorians, 35–36, 39–40; in Herodotus, 204; hostility toward Ionians, 21; and Persians, 66–71. *See also* Ionians
Dracon (Athenian lawgiver), 216
Dreams, 120, 126, 140, 188, 193; of Agariste, 141; of Astyages, 120–21; of Hipparchus, 141; of Hippias, 141; among Medes and Persians, 193–94; of Polycrates, 141

Ecbatana, 51. *See also* Agbatana
Ecclesiazusae of Aristophanes, 214
Egypt, Egyptians, 4, 6, 198, 203, 238–39; ancestors of Dorian Heraclids, 69–71; in Herodotus, 125, 128, 186–94
Eion, 63
Elaeus, 63, 64
Elders (chorus of the *Persae*), 89–100, 111–13; mentality of, 104–6; theology of, 104–5, 108
Eleusis, 44, 155, 202, 213
Elis, 208
Emathia, 49
Emathion (eponym), 49
Ephesus, Ephesians, 16, 17, 25, 28–32, 44–45, 208; kings of, 18. *See*

also Artemisium (of Ephesus), Artimu, Basilids
Ephialtes of Athens (statesman), 80
Ephorus of Cyme (historian), 67, 235
Epimenides (seer), 79
Eretria, Eretrians, 56–57, 62, 109
Erichthonius (legendary Attic/Trojan hero), 166
Erinyes (avenging deities), 80
Etruscans, 71. *See also* Tyrsenia, Tyrsenoi
Eumenes of Cardia (*c.* 362–316 B.C.; secretary to Alexander III of Macedon; general in the wars of succession), 243
Eumenes I of Pergamum (d. 241 B.C.; son of Eumenes of Cardia and founder of the Pergamene kingdom), 243
Eumenides of Aeschylus, 79
Eupatridae (ancient nobility of Athens), 45
Euripides, 71
Europe, 201, 203–4; Persians in, 199, 203
Eurymedon, battle of (*c.* 467 B.C.), 95, 117
Evagoras of Cyprus (king of Salamis, 411–374 B.C.), 51

Fabii (patrician Roman *gens*), 5
Fall of Miletus of Phrynichus, 71–72, 81
First Sacred War (trad. *c.* 590 B.C.), 27
Five Thousand, the (short-lived timocratic government at Athens, 411–410 B.C.), 211, 215
Four Hundred, the (short-lived oligarchy at Athens, 411 B.C.), 43
Friendship in Xenophon, 225

Gelon, Gelonids (tyrant of Syracuse, 490–478 B.C., and his house), 40, 41, 170
Gergithes, 15, 16, 17
Getae (Thracian people), 179–80
Ghost, *see* Darius in the *Persae*

Index

Pisistratids (*cont'd.*)
throw, 79; and Persia, 59–61, 76–77, 109
Pisistratus (tyrant of Athens, 560–527 B.C.), 39, 41, 44–45, 144–46, 147, 157, 178
Plague at Athens, 142
Plataea, Plataeans, 205, 236, 237
Plataea, battle of (479 B.C.), 53, 192; in Herodotus, 142
Plato, 193, 228; *Apology of Socrates,* 210; Darius in, 109; *Laws,* 210–11; *Meno,* 106, 226; *Republic,* 242; on slavery, 100
Plotinus (Neoplatonic philosopher, A.D. 205–269/70), 11
Plutarch of Chaeronea (biographer and essayist, A.D. 50–after 120), 8, 139
Plutô (nymph), 71
Plutus of Aristophanes, 214
Polybius of Megalopolis (historian, *c.* 200–after 118 B.C.), 210, 228
Polycrates of Samos (tyrant, *c.* 540–*c.* 522 B.C.), 40, 44
Praxilaus of Halicarnassus, 59
Prexaspes (Persian noble), 190
Priam (Homeric king of Troy), 48; tomb of, 64; tower of, 60, 61
Priene, 15, 25, 30
Proconnesus, 30
Prometheus (titan whose liver was devoured continually by a vulture, by sentence of Zeus), 206
Prosopitis (island in the Nile near Memphis), 192, 204
Protesilaus (Homeric warrior), 63, 64
Proxenus of Thebes (friend of Xenophon, d. 403 B.C.), 221–22, 223, 233
Psammenitus (Psamtik III, Saïte pharaoh; *reg.* 526–525 B.C.), 187
Psammetichus (Psamtik I, Saïte pharaoh, *reg.* 664–610 B.C.), 27. *See also* Saïte dynasty
Pseudo-Xenophon ("Old Oligarch"), 161; on slavery, 100

Ptolemies (Macedonian dynasty of Egypt), 6
Pythagoras of Samos (pre-Socratic philosopher and mystic, *fl.* later 6th c. B.C.), 151, 166
Pythia. *See* Delphi

Queen (in the *Persae*), 82–83, 84, 90–96, 98, 100, 103–9. *See also* Atossa

Republic of Plato, 242
Rhodes, 56
Rome, Romans, 5, 65, 228

Sadyattes (Lydian king, *reg.* 624–612 B.C.), 30, 31, 122
Saïte dynasty, 4, 27
Salamis, battle of (480 B.C.), 44, 81, 82, 83, 84, 155, 170, 200, 202, 204; in Herodotus, 142
Salmoxis (Thracian god), 151, 179
Samos, Samians, 39, 40–41
Sappho of Lesbos (poet), 25, 26, 41
Sardis, 22–23, 25, 37, 62, 109, 222; Xerxes at, 20, 73
Sarpedon (Homeric hero), 19, 21
Satraps' Revolt (360s B.C.), 234, 237–40
Scepsis, 61
Scythia, Scyths, 3–4, 173, 183, 185, 196, 198, 203, 204, 205; and wine, 155
Serpent Column at Delphi, 66
Seven against Thebes of Sophocles, 79
Sicinnus (slave of Themistocles), 101
Sigeum, 21, 60
Simonides of Ceos (poet: *c.* 556–468 B.C.), 119
Sinope, 33
Slaves, slavery, at Athens, 94–98, 100–101, 241–42; in the *Persae,* 96–97, chap. 4 *passim;* Plato on, 100; Pseudo-Xenophon on, 100; Xenophon on, 98–100, 215–16, 240–41
Smerdis (alleged Persian pretender in

ANCIENT SOCIETY AND HISTORY

The series Ancient Society and History offers books, relatively brief in compass, on selected topics in the history of ancient Greece and Rome, broadly conceived, with a special emphasis on comparative and other nontraditional approaches and methods. The series, which includes both works of synthesis and works of original scholarship, is aimed at the widest possible range of specialist and nonspecialist readers.